DISARMAMENT AND SECURITY
SINCE LOCARNO
1925-1931

DISARMAMENT AND SECURITY SINCE LOCARNO
1925-1931

BEING THE POLITICAL AND TECHNICAL BACKGROUND OF THE

GENERAL DISARMAMENT CONFERENCE, 1932

by

JOHN W. WHEELER-BENNETT

New York · HOWARD FERTIG · 1973

First published in 1932

HOWARD FERTIG, INC. EDITION 1973
Published by arrangement with George Allen & Unwin Ltd.

Library of Congress Cataloging in Publication Data

Wheeler-Bennett, Sir John Wheeler, 1902–
  Disarmament and security since Locarno, 1925–1931.

  Reprint of the 1932 ed., which was originally issued as no. 7 of
Information series.
  1. Disarmament. I. Title. II. Series: Information series, no. 7.
JX1974.W47   1973   341.73   70–80605

For sale only in the United States of America and its dependencies.

PRINTED IN THE UNITED STATES OF AMERICA
BY NOBLE OFFSET PRINTERS, INC.

I DEDICATE THIS BOOK

TO MY FRIEND

CARLTON ELLIOTT FRÜCHTNICHT

PREFACE TO THE 1973 EDITION

THE climate of ideas engendered by the Treaties of Locarno signed in December 1925 had for its primary purpose the creation of a state of mind in Western Europe, and indeed in Eastern Europe also, in which the fear of aggression had been eradicated, the age long sense of insecurity lulled to tranquility and the way left open for that general reduction and limitation of armaments to which the compulsory and unilateral disarmament of Germany under the Treaty of Versailles had been expressly declared to be a preliminary.

The ratification of the Locarno Treaties and the consequent entry of Germany into membership of the League of Nations were followed by the establishment by the League of Nations of a Preparatory Disarmament Commission which should prepare the way for the summoning of a General Disarmament Conference, and by the close of 1931, when this book was originally written, sufficient progress was held to have been made to justify the opening of such a Conference in February of the following year.

The sessions of the Preparatory Commission held between 1925 and 1930 had not been without their very considerable stresses and strains which had disclosed that both the spirit of Geneva and the spirit of Locarno were far from enjoying that degree of depth and durability which had been expected of them. Nevertheless the Commission *had* met and a draft Disarmament Convention *had* been prepared, albeit with many vital issues in dispute and unresolved.

Perhaps the most important feature of the session of the Preparatory Commission was that both the United States of America and the Union of Socialist Soviet Republics were full and active participants though still non-members of the League, thus, with the advent of Germany, achieving the full representation of the Great Powers.

Parallel with the work of the Preparatory Commission under the auspices of the League, a certain progress had been achieved in the field of naval disarmament, carrying forward that which had been initiated at the Washington Conference of 1922. Anglo-American, Anglo-French, Franco-Italian, Greco-Turkish and Soviet-Turkish negotiations had resulted in bilateral agreements and pacts of limitation and a general naval conference had met in London in 1930.

In the realm of security, the euphoric optimism evoked by the Locarno Treaties reached its apogee with the signature on August 27, 1928 of the General Treaty for the Renunciation of War—also known as the Pact of Paris or the Briand-Kellogg Pact—whereby the signatories renounced war as an instrument of national policy between themselves and agreed to settle all disputes arising between them by peaceful means. Since ultimately the Pact of Paris was signed or adhered to by no less than sixty-four states,—it became the most universally accepted international instrument of modern times—and was supplemented by a host of supplementary treaties and by instruments devised for the pacific settlement of international disputes, the result was theoretically a war-less world. In effect, however, it marked the opening of an era in which more naked aggression was practised than at any other time in world history, concluding, ten years later, with the eruption of the Second World War.

For the events chronicled in the foreground of this book, concerned with disarmament, security and pacific settlement, were played against the ever more lowering background of events in Germany, where the rise of the Nazi Party was creating a growing menace to the democratic institutions of the Weimar Republic, preliminary to threatening—and ultimately destroying—the peace of the world. Alarming as these new storm signals were, they had little effect upon the councils of the statesmen in control of the destinies of Britain and France, who failed to comprehend that by consistently obstructing the rearmament claims of the German Republic they were providing powerful ammunition for the clamour and rabble-rousing exhortations of Adolf Hitler to the German people. Had Britain and France, in the years following

Locarno, made of their own free will to Stresemann and to Brüning concessions in the issues of rearmament and reparation which they later made in bewildered alarm to von Papen and to Hitler, the history of Europe might have been very different. But we were, alas, in pursuit of that terrifying policy of appeasing the wrong Germans.

JOHN WHEELER-BENNETT.

Garsington Manor,
Oxon.
June 1969.

PREFACE

READERS of this book are, I think, entitled to a word of explanation as to the reason for its being written and the form adopted. I regret, and apologize for, the fact that such an explanation necessarily includes certain autobiographical details.

In 1924 I founded the Information Service on International Affairs, an organization whose objects were clearly indicated in its title. Apart from the answering of inquiries submitted by its subscribers, the two main channels through which the organization was able to disseminate its information were its fortnightly *Bulletin of International News* and its "Information Series" issued by Messrs. George Allen & Unwin.

The first of this series, which I published in 1925, was entitled *Information on the Reduction of Armaments*, with an Introduction by Major-General Sir Neill Malcolm. A year later, in collaboration with Mr. F. E. Langermann, I published a companion volume, *Information on the Problem of Security*, to which the Right Hon. H. A. L. Fisher, Warden of New College, Oxford, wrote an Introduction. These two books traced the parallel history of their respective subjects from the Peace Conference to the signing of the Locarno Agreements in December 1925.

In the present volume I have endeavoured, with what success the reader alone can judge, to provide a joint sequel to the two books already mentioned, and to give the background of the Disarmament Conference which is to meet on February 2, 1932. On the one hand there is presented an account of the labours of the Preparatory Commission and the London Naval Conference to bring about disarmament, and, on the other, a record of the movement for the Renunciation of War and of the work of the League's Security and Arbitration Committee by means of both of which it is hoped to provide that degree of national security necessary for international disarmament.

The book itself is not an entirely original work. It should be explained that in 1930, after six years of independent existence, the Information Service was amalgamated with the Royal Institute of International Affairs, of which it became the Information Department. The Council of the Royal Institute acquired thereby the control of the *Bulletin of International News*, and I am greatly indebted to them and to their Information Committee for giving me permission to reprint articles written for the *Bulletin* both by myself and by my former colleagues in the Information Department, Mr. Hugh Latimer, Mr. Stephen Heald and Mr. Ralph Arnold. The Council of the Institute, acting on the recommendation of their Publications Committee, have further most generously allowed me to reprint in full a chapter of Mr. Latimer's book, *Naval Disarmament*, published under their auspices. To all of these bodies and to the authors themselves my grateful thanks are due.[1]

In the course of a visit to the United States at the close of 1930 I was enabled to discuss the outline and construction of the book with such experts and eminent authorities on international affairs as Dr. David Hunter Miller; Professor James Shotwell, of the Carnegie Endowment;Professor Raymond Leslie Buell, of the Foreign Policy Association, New York; and Mr. Denys P. Myers, of the World Peace Foundation, Boston. In addition, the MSS. has been read in whole or part by Professor Arnold J. Toynbee, Director of Studies of the Royal Institute of International Affairs, and by his assistant, Miss V. M. Boulter, and by Mrs. Andrew George and Mr. Hubert R. Knickerbocker. I am greatly appreciative of the criticisms and comments which I have received in this way and would wish to express my sincere thanks to all those who have assisted me in completing a none too easy task.

In compiling a book of this nature one of the chief problems which confronts the author is that of construction and arrangement. It is very difficult to present to the reader a composite picture of events, many of which were parallel happenings. In an endeavour to overcome this difficulty I have provided

[1] Where authorship of articles reprinted is not given, they are my own.

a Chronological Table synoptically arranged which will I hope give the key to the general layout of the book.

One point I wish to make quite clear. Although much of the material of this book is reprinted, *mutatis mutandis*, from articles in its *Bulletin*, the Royal Institute of International Affairs is in no way responsible for any opinions which I have expressed therein. I am fully prepared to accept the onus of statements which I have made.

Finally, I wish to acknowledge the invaluable assistance which has been rendered me by the staff of the Information Department of the Royal Institute of International Affairs, who have proved untiring in their researches on my behalf. I am especially grateful to Mr. Hugh Latimer for his work in checking and correcting the proofs.

JOHN W. WHEELER-BENNETT

A.14, ALBANY,
    PICCADILLY, LONDON

November, 1931

CONTENTS

CHRONOLOGICAL TABLE

SHOWING IN SYNOPTIC FORM THE RELATION BETWEEN DISARMAMENT, SECURITY AND ARBITRATION, AND REPARATIONS, 1925–1931

Date	DISARMAMENT		Security and Arbitration	Reparations
	Military	Naval		
1925. Oct.–Dec.			Locarno Agreements	[1924, Dawes Plan] Evacuation of First Rhineland Zone
1926 May 18–26	1st Session Preparatory Commission			
Sept. 22–27	2nd Session Preparatory Commission			
1927 March 21–April 26	3rd Session Preparatory Commission [1st Draft of Convention]			
June–August		Geneva Naval Conference		
September			Assembly Resolution Outlawing Aggression	
Nov. 30–Dec. 3	4th Session Preparatory Commission			
Dec. 1–2			1st Session, Arbitration and Security Committee	

1928			
Feb. 18		Pan-American Resolutions Renouncing War, Havana	
Feb. 20–March 7		2nd Session, Arbitration and Security Committee	
March 15–24	5th Session Preparatory Commission [Russian Proposals]		
June 27–July 4		3rd Session, Arbitration and Security Committee	
July–Sept.	Anglo-French Naval Compromise		
August 27		Kellogg-Briand Pact of Peace, Paris	
September		General Act for the Pacific Settlement of International Disputes	Geneva Agreement concerning Reparations and Rhineland Evacuation, Sept. 16
December 22			Franco-German Agreement concerning Appointment of Committee of Experts
1929			
Jan. 5		Pan-American General Conventions of Arbitration and Conciliation signed	
Feb.–June			Young Committee sat in Paris
Feb. 9		Litvinoff Protocol signed in Moscow	
April 15–May 6	6th Session Preparatory Commission [2nd Draft of Convention]		

CHRONOLOGICAL TABLE—continued

SHOWING IN SYNOPTIC FORM THE RELATION BETWEEN DISARMAMENT, SECURITY AND ARBITRATION, AND REPARATIONS, 1925–1931.

Date	Disarmament		Security and Arbitration	Reparations
	Military	Naval		
April 22 .. :		U.S. Acceptance of French Thesis		
June 7 .. : August .. :				Young Plan published 1st Hague Conference [Rhineland Evacuation Agreement]
Sept.–Dec.				Evacuation of Second Rhineland Zone
October .. :		Visit of Mr. MacDonald to U.S.		
October 7 .. :		Invitations issued to London Conference		
1930 Jan. 3–20 .. :				2nd Hague Conference [Young Plan adopted]
Jan. 21–April 22		London Naval Conference		
April 22 .. : April 28–May 9		London Naval Treaty	4th Session, Security and Arbitration Committee M. Briand's Memorandum on European Federation	
May 17 .. :				Young Plan came into operation and Evacuation of Third Zone begun

Date			
September		Convention for Financial Assistance	
Oct. 20	Graeco-Turkish Naval Pact		
Nov. 6–Dec. 9	Final Session Preparatory Commission [Draft Convention adopted]		
1931 **January 23**	General Disarmament Conference convened for Feb. 2, 1932		
March 1–2	Franco-Italian-British Conversations		
March 9	Turco-Soviet Naval Pact		
May 22	Mr. Arthur Henderson appointed President of the Disarmament Conference		
June 5–9			Anglo-German Conference at Chequers
June 21			President Hoover's Proposal for a "War-Debt Holiday"
July 5			Franco-American Agreement regarding the Hoover Plan
July 18–22			Paris and London Conferences
July 21	French Memorandum on Disarmament		
August 8–17			The Committee of Experts sat in Basle
August 18			The Wiggin Report published
September	Proposal for an Arms Truce from November 1 until after the conclusion of the Disarmament Conference adopted by the Assembly	General Convention to Improve the Means of Preventing War	

DISARMAMENT AND SECURITY SINCE LOCARNO

CHAPTER I

FROM VERSAILLES TO LOCARNO
1919-1925

THROUGHOUT history peace conferences have been the grave of reputations and the womb of future wars. The Conference of Paris has more than justified the first of these attributes and there is no presently apparent reason why it should not fulfil the second function also.

Yet before the Conference had ever met, before even the ink was dry on the Armistice Agreement of November 11, 1918, victors and vanquished had undertaken a moral obligation to disarm in accepting as a basis for negotiation President Wilson's Fourteen Points, of which the Fourth Point read as follows:

"Adequate guarantees given and taken that national armaments will be reduced to the lowest point consistent with domestic safety."

It is now a matter of established history that the Fourteen Points underwent a varied process of interpretation during the Peace Conference of Paris and that while both disarmament and security figured largely in the discussions, they did so in each case in a unilateral sense, disarmament being regarded as the portion of the vanquished, while the victors alone were free to take measures of security. The principle of international disarmament was, however, recognized and the complete dis-

NOTE.—References made in footnotes to *Armaments, Security* and *Reparations* refer respectively to *Information on the Reduction of Armaments* by J. W. Wheeler-Bennett (Allen & Unwin, 1925), *Information on the Problem of Security* by J. W. Wheeler-Bennett and F. E. Langermann (Allen & Unwin, 1927), and *Information on the Reparation Settlement* by J. W. Wheeler-Bennett and H. Latimer (Allen & Unwin, 1930).

armament of Germany and her Allies was regarded as a prelude to similar action on the part of the Allied and Associated Powers. This principle was laid down generally in the first paragraph of Article VIII of the Covenant:

"The members of the League recognize that the maintenance of peace requires the reduction of national armaments to the lowest point consistent with national safety, and the enforcement by common action of international obligations."

But the specific promise to Germany was incorporated as a preamble to the very section of the Treaty which contained the provision for her own disarmament.

"In order to render possible the initiation of a general limitation of the armaments of all nations, Germany undertakes strictly to observe the military, naval and air clauses which follow."[1]

The Allied promise was further emphasized in the official reply of the Allied and Associated Powers to the observations of the German Delegation on the conditions of peace, which was handed by M. Clemenceau to Count Brockdorff-Rantzau on June 16, 1919. Part V of the Note deals with disarmament in the following words:

I. The Allied and Associated Powers wish to make it clear that their requirements in regard to German armaments were not made solely with the object of rendering it impossible for Germany to resume her policy of military aggression. They are also the first steps towards that general reduction and limitation of armaments which they seek to bring about as one of the most fruitful preventives of war, and which it will be one of the first duties of the League of Nations to promote.

II. They must point out, however, that the colossal growth in armaments of the last few decades was forced upon the nations of Europe by Germany. As Germany increased her power, her neighbours had to follow suit unless they were to become impotent to resist German dictation or the German sword. It is therefore right, as it is necessary, that the process of limitation of armaments should begin with the nation which has been responsible for their expansion. It is not until the

---

[1] For an analysis of these clauses and an account of their execution by Germany, see *Armaments*, pp. 24–27; *Security*, pp. 31–33; and *Reparations*, pp. 20–23 and 28–39.

aggressor has led the way that the attacked can safely afford
to follow suit.

III. . . . Germany must consent unconditionally to disarm in advance
of the Allied and Associated Powers. . . .[1]

Having thus dispensed for the time with the question of
disarmament, the Conference turned to a matter of much
more pressing importance both then and hereafter, the problem
of security, the solution of which was a necessary forerunner
of any talk of Allied disarmament.

By the Treaties of Versailles, St. Germain-en-Laye, the
Trianon and Neuilly the Allies drew the lines of the new map
of Europe in accordance with their own essential need for
security and in consideration of the enormities committed by
the defeated Powers. Throughout their deliberations the Allied
statesmen were aware of four potential sources of danger by
which the structure of their work might be threatened. They
were:

(1) A "War of Revenge" waged, in perhaps twenty years' time, by
a restored Germany against France.
(2) An Austro-German *Anschluss* and the re-establishment of German
domination in Central Europe.
(3) A Hapsburg restoration in Hungary and a consequent campaign
of revision against the Succession States of the old Austro-
Hungarian Empire.
(4) The Bolshevist menace, which was most likely to fall upon Poland
and Rumania.

The Allies at the Paris Conference did their best to legislate
against these dangers. They imposed a crushing reparation
bill on Germany and set about disarming her with great
thoroughness. As a guarantee for the execution of these two
obligations, they occupied the left bank and bridge-heads of
the Rhine. By the Treaties of Versailles and St. Germain they
forbade an *Anschluss*. Over the whole of the peace settlement

---

[1] It is, however, important to note that this famous document also contained
the following passage, which, if taken in conjunction with German demands
for equality of method in disarmament, assumes an added significance: "No
deviation from the organization in armament (*la constitution de l'armament*)
laid down in the present Treaty can be permitted until Germany is admitted
to the League of Nations, which may then agree to such modifications as may
seem desirable."

they threw the guarantee contained in Articles X and XVI of the Covenant of the League of Nations, with a special protection for France in an Anglo-American Guarantee in the event of unprovoked German aggression. Having built up this superstructure of security, the Allies regarded the peace settlement as complete and rested from their labours, directing their energies to the ending of their own internal post-War problems.[1]

The edifice which they had constructed did not long remain intact. On March 19, 1920, the United States Senate refused finally to ratify the Treaty of Versailles and the Treaty of Guarantee with France. Thus at one stroke the special provision of security, which M. Clemenceau had so grudgingly accepted in place of his own more drastic plans for the protection of France, was swept away and the guarantee of the League materially weakened. Not only did the American abstention have this direct effect on the League, but the attitude of Great Britain towards that organization changed considerably in view of the fact that the other great Anglo-Saxon Power had elected to remain outside.

In Europe the effect of the change of American policy was immediate. With the League of Nations as yet unformed and untested the States were driven back upon their own resources for the protection of their integrity and the European *status quo*. France returned at once to the policy of encirclement, which had formed so prominent a feature of her Programme of Security at the Peace Conference. A Military Agreement with Belgium[2] (September 7, 1920) and a defensive alliance with Poland[3] (February 19, 1921) gave her a momentary feeling of security, but it was only momentary.

The same panic spread to Central Europe. Here the Allied Succession States were faced with the double-headed bogy of the *Anschluss* and the Hapsburg restoration. Alliances were hurriedly concluded in the latter half of 1920 between Czecho-

---

[1] For further details of the struggle for security at the Conference, see *Security*, pp. 16–39, and *Reparations*, pp. 17–27.
[2] See *Security*, pp. 40–42.　　　　　　　　　　　　[3] See *ibid.*, pp. 42–44.

slovakia and Rumania[1] (August 14, 1920), and Yugoslavia and Italy[2] (November 12, 1920), and had scarcely been completed when the first attempt of King Carl of Hungary to regain his throne came as a justification of their fears. (March-April, 1921.)

Once Carl had taken to flight the work of knitting up the Succession States was carried on by the indefatigable Dr. Benès, the Czechoslovak Foreign Minister. As a result of his efforts alliances were effected between Czechoslovakia and Rumania[3] (April 21, 1921), and between the latter country and Yugoslavia[4] (June 7, 1921). Thus, when Carl reappeared for the second and last time in October 1921, he was met by a united front, known as the Little Entente, which effectively influenced the Hungarian Government into surrendering him to the representatives of the Conference of Ambassadors.

In Eastern Europe, mistrustful of the untried protection of the League, Poland and Rumania reached out hands for their mutual protection. Scorning the Curzon Line accepted by the Peace Conference as her Eastern frontier, Poland had, as a result of her war with Soviet Russia and the Armistice Convention of Riga[5] (October 12, 1920), advanced her border beyond the Pripet marshes. Rumania, by a supplementary Treaty signed between herself and Great Britain, France, Italy and Japan[6] (October 28, 1920), had been granted the former Russian province of Bessarabia, but of the Powers only Great Britain had ratified (January 1, 1921). Both Poland and Rumania, therefore, had reason to fear a Soviet invasion, and for their own greater security they concluded a defensive alliance on March 8, 1921.

Thus Europe had made the refusal of the United States to join the League of Nations an excuse for returning to the old pre-War system of military alliances, and it became clear that at least temporarily the maintenance of the *status quo* must depend upon these bilateral treaties, specifically entered

[1] See *Security*, pp. 188–189.   [2] See *ibid.*, pp. 189–190.
[3] See *ibid.*, pp. 190–191.   [4] See *ibid.*, p. 190.
[5] This agreement was confirmed by the definitive Treaty of Riga, March 18, 1921.   [6] See *Security*, p. 74.

into for that purpose, rather than upon the more vague guarantee of the League.

It soon became evident, however, that France had not sufficiently calmed her fears by her agreements with Belgium and Poland. Her fear of future aggression from Germany caused her to pursue a policy which resulted in the complete ruling out of the discussion of land armaments by the Washington Disarmament Conference and the retention of submarines, which would otherwise have been abolished as war vessels.[1] Her anxiety to preserve the European *status quo* led her to endeavour to persuade Great Britain to enter into some reciprocal treaty of guarantee which should replace the Anglo-American Treaty of 1919. M. Briand, who opened these negotiations in December 1921, was anxious for France's allies to benefit by this Treaty and wished to secure Great Britain's guarantee for the security of the frontier of Poland and Czechoslovakia with Germany. But though the British Government was prepared to go a certain distance to meet French desires, and Mr. Lloyd George even went so far as to put forward a draft treaty at Cannes in January 1922, it was on the main condition that Great Britain's obligations should be limited to the guarantee of the eastern frontier of France and Belgium.

The fall of M. Briand and the appearance of M. Poincaré resulted in the French Government's presentation of a counter draft treaty which proved unacceptable to the British, and by the end of the year the two countries had drifted so far apart on the reparation issue that all thought of an Anglo-French Pact vanished with the invasion of the Ruhr in January, 1923.[2]

In view of the definitely cool relations existing between London and Paris over the French occupation of the Ruhr, M. Poincaré sought to cement more firmly his relations with the Little Entente. It was agreed that M. Beneš should persuade his Yugoslav and Rumanian colleagues to conclude treaties with France, and as an example a Franco-Czech Treaty of

[1] See *Security*, pp. 45–46.   [2] See *ibid.*, pp. 48–58.

Alliance and Friendship was signed on January 25, 1924.[1]
But for once the Little Entente team did not answer unanimously to the crack of the whip. A rival master had entered
the ring, and, for the time being at least, had distracted the
attention of one of the team before it could leap through the
hoop.

Italy, revivified by eighteen months of Fascismo after the
lethargic Liberalism of her post-War years, had re-entered
European politics to bid against France for the allegiance of
the smaller Powers. And not without effect. Yugoslavia, who
had refused an alliance with France, not only composed her
Fiume controversy with Italy, but concluded a Treaty of
Cordial Co-operation and Friendship with her on January 27,
1924, just two days after the signature of the Franco-Czech
Pact. Nor was this the only blow which French prestige
suffered at this period, for M. Benès brought about an Italo-
Czech Treaty on July 5, 1924, on the same lines as that concluded six months earlier with Yugoslavia.[2] With regard to
the third partner of the Little Entente, though M. Poincaré
went to the length of ratifying the Bessarabian Treaty of 1920
(April 30, 1924)[3] as a bait for a Franco-Rumanian alliance, no
answering gesture was made from Bucharest.

The recrudesence of the question of the *Anschluss* towards
the close of 1925 caused renewed anxiety in Central Europe.
In January, 1926 Yugoslavia approached France and Italy, with
a plan for a Central European Pact on the lines of Locarno,
which should embrace allied and ex-enemy States alike in
a mutual guarantee of the *status quo*. The Foreign Minister,
M. Ninchitch, visited Rome in February and was met by a

[1] See *Security*, pp. 65–67.   [2] See *ibid.*, pp. 194–195.
[3] This treaty has never become operative. Of the BIG FOUR who signed it,
Great Britain ratified in 1921, France in 1924, and Italy in 1927; the fourth
Power, Japan, has never ratified, and there is reason to believe that at the
time of the Soviet-Japanese Treaty of January 1925 some agreement was
arrived at as to Japan's non-ratification. The U.S.S.R. was not a party to the
Treaty and has never accepted it, a fact which was emphasized by M. Litvinoff
as recently as the signature of the Moscow Protocol, February 1929, and it is
of interest to note that official maps issued in Moscow still show Bessarabia
as part of Soviet territory. Rumania's possession of the province would seem
therefore to be *de facto* rather than *de jure*.
The United States refused to be a party to the original treaty.

suggestion from Signor Mussolini for the extension of Article 3 of the Italo-Yugoslav Pact of 1924 (which provided for consultation in the event of common interests of the two parties being threatened by international complications) to include a mutual undertaking for the prevention of the *Anschluss*. To this M. Ninchitch agreed, on condition that France became a party to the agreement, but this proposal proved unacceptable to Italy, and M. Ninchitch proceeded treaty-less on his way to Paris, where M. Briand was quick to take advantage of the opportunity to regain the ground lost in 1924. A Franco-Yugoslav Pact, on the lines of that already negotiated with Czechoslovakia, was drafted and initialed in March 1926, though it was not actually signed until November 11, 1927, at a time when Italo-Yugoslav relations were severely strained.[1]

The summer of 1926 saw a race between France and Italy as to which should be the first to secure an alliance with Rumania. M. Briand won, a Franco-Rumanian Pact being signed on June 10th; Signor Mussolini succeeded in concluding a Treaty of Co-operation and Friendship, on the Italian model, on September 16, 1926.[2]

Such is the tortuous history of the first six years of Central European efforts to preserve the *status quo*, efforts which were inextricably mingled with the rival desires of France and Italy to dominate the Little Entente, and which consequently involved the States concerned in an intricate *reseau* of treaties. In the long run it would seem that France has been the more successful, for though Italy succeeded in concluding treaties with each of the Little Entente Powers, her later relations with Yugoslavia were such as to make the idea of close co-operation between the two States improbable,[3] whereas Czechoslovakia has definitely returned to her old allegiance, leaving Rumania the only uncertain factor.

Meanwhile the League of Nations was recovering from the unexpected defection of the United States. This recovery

[1] As an immediate *riposte* to the Franco-Yugoslav Treaty came the signature of the Italo-Albanian Agreement of November 22, 1927.
[2] See *Security*, pp. 198–199.
[3] The Italo-Yugoslav Treaty of 1924 has lapsed and has not been renewed.

occupied nearly three years, for not only had the absence of America influenced the attitude of Great Britain towards the League, but also that of the Latin-American States, and a period of readjustment was necessary. It was felt very emphatically that not only must the prestige of the League be reestablished, but reparation must be made for the damage done to the League's guarantee of security, which, it was hoped, would be the forerunner of the complete reduction of armaments, and would supplant the system of bilateral alliances.

A beginning was made towards disarmament as early as November 1920, when the First Assembly had discovered that the problem was a political and not a technical one and had set up the Temporary Mixed Commission, "composed of persons possessing the requisite competence in matters of a political, social and economic nature," to study the matter.[1] The Second Assembly, which met in September 1921, requested this Commission to prepare a draft treaty, and as a result, in the course of its Second, Third, Fourth and Fifth Sessions (February–September 1922), the Commission considered a plan for disarmament submitted by Lord Esher and based upon the ratio system, which had proved so successful at the Washington Conference in the matter of naval limitation.

For a variety of technical reasons the Commission considered the Esher Scheme unacceptable, but in their discussions it became more and more clear that security must precede disarmament—that is to say, that before a State can reduce its armaments it must have some form of guarantee that the other States will assist it in the event of aggression.[2] The Commission reported in this vein to the Third Assembly (September 1922), and that body, as a result of the discussions on the Report in the Third Committee, adopted the famous Resolution XIV definitely declaring the principles of disarmament and security to be inseparable and instructing the Temporary Commission to continue its researches on this basis.[3]

[1] See *Armaments*, p. 34.
[2] See *Ibid.*, pp. 58-61.
[3] See *Security*, pp. 91-94.

It was a definite step forward, and the Commission found itself faced with the problem of discovering some practical method of implementing the guarantees contained in Articles X and XVI of the Covenant in order to bring about the execution of Article VIII. The result of its labours was the adoption by the Fourth Assembly in September 1923 of the Treaty of Mutual Assistance, of which the principal provision was the agreement of all the Contracting Parties to come to the assistance of anyone of their number who was the victim of aggression. In return for this assurance the Contracting Parties were to reduce their armaments to "a point compatible with national security."[1]

Closer examination of the Treaty by national Governments disclosed certain grave drawbacks. No provision was made within its terms for the definition of "aggression" or "aggressor," and, further, there was provided no alternative to war for the settlement of disputes arising between Contracting Parties. For these and other reasons the Treaty was generally considered as unacceptable, and no Member of the League signed it, while it was definitely repudiated by many, including Great Britain.

When, however, the Fifth Assembly met in 1924, the united socialist idealism of Mr. Ramsay MacDonald and M. Herriot discovered a further element to those of security and disarmament, which had constituted the formula hitherto. Arbitration was introduced both as a substitute for war and a test of aggression, it being assumed that the State with the guilty conscience would be unwilling to submit its disputes to arbitration and would thereby brand itself as the aggressor.

This triple formula was embodied in the Protocol for the Pacific Settlement of International Disputes, which was unanimously adopted by the Assembly, who also voted to "welcome it warmly" and recommended its acceptance. Indeed, so sure were the authors of the Protocol that they had devised an instrument acceptable to the Powers and that the technical work of disarmament could now proceed, that Article XVII

[1] See *Armaments*, pp. 61–81; *Security*, pp. 95–100.

actually provided for the convening of a Disarmament Conference at Geneva on June 15, 1925.[1]

But the failure of the Protocol and the Treaty of Mutual Assistance was due to the same fundamental reason. Many Powers, but more especially Great Britain, were unshakably opposed to undertaking military obligations of an indefinite nature. They were prepared to furnish guarantees in those particular quarters of the globe wherein their interests lay, but the idea of so definitely interpreting the Covenant as to bind them in any event was unpalatable to them. So the Protocol was accorded the same fate at the hands of the national Governments as the Treaty of Mutual Assistance.

But though the Protocol failed in its initial purpose, it marked an important stage in and made an invaluable contribution to the work for disarmament. The triple formula which had inspired the Protocol was accepted as the basis of all future research. The problem now became that of finding the right vehicle for its conveyance. Agreements for security no longer took the form of multi- or bi-lateral agreements against any one State or group of States. From 1924 onwards the principle was one of guarantee against a potential aggressor, whoever he might be, and when Sir Austen Chamberlain enunciated his formula of "Special arrangements to meet special needs," it was only a supplement to the triple basic principle of "Arbitration, Security and Disarmament."

[1] See *Armaments*, pp. 89–132; *Security*, pp. 101–110.

CHAPTER II

THE LOCARNO AGREEMENT

THE Locarno Agreement of October-December 1925 marks the close of the first phase of post-War European history. Taken together with its natural corollary, the entry of Germany into the League of Nations, it marks also the opening of the second phase, a phase of rehabilitation and of return of confidence. This period may be said to extend to the liquidation of the war problems achieved by the Young Plan and the Hague Agreements of 1929–30.

In the field of Disarmament and Security the Locarno Agreement also forms a landmark. The Treaty of Mutual Assistance and the Geneva Protocol, put forward by the League of Nations in 1923 and 1924, had had the underlying principle of reciprocity. For whereas the bilateral and multilateral treaties of security previously concluded since the War had all been negotiated with the object of guaranteeing the signatories against future aggression on the part of Germany and her former allies, the new spirit introduced by the League was of mutual guarantee, not against any one specified State, but against any potential aggressor, whoever he might be. To this principle the Geneva Protocol had added the three-fold formula of Disarmament, Security and Arbitration, though the order in which the three elements of the formula should be placed varied according to the views of the different European Governments.

Though it included within its composition the principle of mutual guarantee and the three-fold formula, and was indeed the first instrument in which they found concrete form, the Locarno Agreement was fundamentally based upon the dictum fathered by Sir Austen Chamberlain, "Special agreements to meet special needs," and by this means it materially strengthened the guarantee involved by limiting the obligations of the Contracting Parties to a minimum which all conceived to be to their common interest to undertake.

The Agreement consisted of two distinct series of treaties forming a Western and an Eastern Pact. In the first of these Germany recognized as definite and final the frontier drawn by the Treaty of Versailles as between herself and France and Belgium. Great Britain and Italy guaranteed to come at once to the assistance of either party which was the victim of unprovoked aggression. For the settlement of disputes arising between the two parties treaties of arbitration and conciliation were negotiated between Germany and France, and Germany and Belgium.

In the Eastern Pact Germany gave no such undertaking regarding the permanency of her frontier, but concluded with Poland and Czechoslovakia treaties of arbitration and conciliation similar to those concluded with France and Belgium. In addition to these, France signed treaties of mutual guarantee with Poland and Czechoslovakia. By these it was agreed that in the event of France, or Poland (or Czechoslovakia), being the victim of the violation of their agreements with Germany, France and reciprocally Poland (or Czechoslovakia) would at once give immediate assistance.[1]

The Eastern Locarno Pact is thus made interdependent on the Western, but not *vice versa*. That is to say, that if Germany makes an act of unprovoked aggression against France she automatically finds herself at war with Great Britain, France, Italy, Belgium, Poland and Czechoslovakia, whereas if France is the aggressor, it is assumed that under the Pact, Poland and Czechoslovakia would remain neutral.[2] In the event, however, of Poland or Czechoslovakia being the victim of aggression, France alone is pledged to come to their assistance.[3]

[1] The Locarno Pact was rounded off by a Czecho-Polish Treaty of Arbitration (April 1925), and a similar Treaty between Italy and Germany (December 1926). Though one of these Treaties preceded Locarno and the other followed it, they are complementary in nature.
[2] This statement is made in reference only to the Locarno Agreement and does not take into consideration the Franco-Polish Alliance of 1921, nor the Franco-Czechoslovak Treaty of 1924.
[3] The Polish-Rumanian Treaty, originally concluded in March 1921, was renewed in March 1926 and its scope widened to admit of a Rumanian guarantee of Poland's western frontier against German aggression. In view of this Rumania would now be pledged to come to the assistance of Poland in the event of the Eastern Locarno Pact being called into operation.

The Western Locarno Pact was the first guarantee of the
status quo created by the Treaty of Versailles in which victor
and vanquished in the Great War negotiated on equal terms.
In the Eastern Pact the *status quo* was neither accepted nor
guaranteed, but the right to upset it by means of war was
renounced. In no way, however, did Germany accept her
eastern frontier as permanent.[1]

Such, then, was the concrete form of the Locarno Agreement.
What, however, was its inner meaning? What had the principal
countries concerned gained or lost? What, above all, was the
gain to Europe as a whole?

In the case of Great Britain there was both gain and loss.
Under the new agreement she had assumed considerable
additional obligations. She had made the Franco-Belgian
frontier with Germany her own, and by so doing had advanced
her own boundaries from the cliffs of Dover to the Rhine.
Nor had there been any tangible return for this. The Treaty
of Mutual Guarantee was not reciprocal as far as the Guaranteeing Powers were concerned, and Great Britain shared with
Italy that honourable but onerous position. Lord D'Abernon,
whose diary provides one of the most important and intimate
documents of the period, records that at one point in the
negotiations he felt prompted to suggest to the British Foreign
Office the inclusion of the security of the English Channel
within the scope of the Western Pact. He finally renounced
the idea on the grounds that it would weaken Great Britain's
position as a guarantor if she demanded this condition.[2] It
is more than probable, moreover, that had such a proposal
been made, Italy, too, would have claimed some *quid pro quo*
for her guarantee, and would have pressed for the inclusion of
the Brenner frontier.

For France the result was one of qualified success. She had
succeeded in securing the final acceptance by Germany of
their mutual frontier, and, in addition, the guarantee of this

[1] For full details of the negotiations leading up to the Locarno Agreement, and
for an analysis of the Treaties themselves, see *Security*, pp. 115–156.
[2] See *An Ambassador of Peace*, by Viscount D'Abernon (London, Hodder &
Stoughton, 3 vols., 1929–1930), Vol. III, pp. 177–178.

status quo by Great Britain and Italy. Even this achievement was not without its drawbacks, for it is difficult to imagine France, except in circumstances of the direst necessity, regarding with complacency her rival Italy in the exalted position of potential guarantor of her own security. In the light of more recent events the position is not without its ironies.

In the East French diplomacy had had only a minor degree of success. France had failed to achieve the acknowledgment by Germany of the permanency of her Polish frontier, and had been equally unsuccessful in her efforts to secure the extension of the Anglo-Italian guarantee to the German frontiers with Poland and Czechoslovakia. Her achievement was limited to the agreement by Germany not to rectify her Eastern boundaries by means of war, and she had herself to shoulder the responsibility of guaranteeing her two satellites against a possible breach of this undertaking.[1]

For Germany the Locarno Agreement was mainly another stage along the road to the complete evacuation of the Rhineland and the long-delayed reduction of armaments on the part of the former Allied Powers to a degree similar to that to which Germany had been compulsorily reduced under the Treaty of Versailles. These two aims were consistently in the mind of the great German statesman, Dr. Gustav Stresemann, since the day in September 1923 when he began his seven years' control of German foreign policy by taking the courageous step of advising President Ebert to call off passive resistance in the Ruhr, thereby paving the way for the Dawes Plan and the London Agreement. Throughout his ministry Herr Stresemann was actuated by the desire to free his country from occupation by foreign troops and to persuade the Allies to fulfil their disarmament pledges. For this reason he was

---

[1] France has never lessened her efforts to persuade Germany to accept her Eastern frontier as definite and final and to extend the term of the Eastern Pact for this purpose. Notable attempts to secure this were made during the preliminary negotiations preceding the setting-up of the Young Committee in the autumn and winter of 1929, and the terms on which France was prepared to grant a long-term loan to Germany during the economic and financial crisis of the summer of 1931.

prepared to accept as irrevocable the situation on Germany's Western frontier, and to go as far as he believed it to be compatible with his country's honour in securing a settlement in the East.

Indeed Germany may be said to have been the first of the Contracting Parties to derive a concrete advantage from the Locarno Agreement, since the evacuation by the British Forces of the Cologne Zone of Occupation was made coincident with the signing of the Locarno Agreement in London on December 5, 1925. In a Note to the German Ambassador in Paris, announcing the decision of the Allied Powers to evacuate, M. Briand made the following statement which was eloquent of what at the time was called the Locarno Spirit:

"In thus making the beginning of the evacuation coincident with the signature of the Locarno Agreements, the Conference [of Ambassadors] expresses the confidence of the Governments represented upon it that the signature will inaugurate a new era in their relations with Germany."[1]

It has been said that the Locarno Agreement was founded upon the triple formula of Arbitration, Security and Disarmament. Full provision for the first and second of these elements was made in the various treaties of which the Agreement is composed, but disarmament is dismissed in a few words. Yet the few words are significant and important. They occur in the final paragraph of the covering protocol and are as follows:

"They [the Contracting Parties] undertake to give their sincere cooperation to the work relating to disarmament already undertaken by the League of Nations and to seek the realization thereof in a general agreement."[2]

---

[1] See British White Paper, *Correspondence between the Ambassadors' Conference and the German Ambassador in Paris respecting German Disarmament, Evacuation of the Cologne Zone and Modification of the Rhineland Régime*, Cmd. 2527, p. 14.

[2] See British White Paper, *Final Protocol of the Locarno Conference, 1925 (and annexes), together with treaties with France and Poland, and France and Czechoslovakia*, Locarno, October 16, 1925 (Cmd. 2525). The reference to the "work already undertaken by the League" is of course to the resolution adopted by the Assembly on September 24, 1925, and which formed the genesis of the work of the Preparatory Commission. See below, pp. 44–45.

It may fairly be said from the above that although no general provision for disarmament is contained in the Locarno Agreement yet disarmament is the fundamental underlying principle of the whole structure, towards the fulfilment of which the whole agreement is directed and designed. How it comes about that in 1932, seven years after the signing of the Locarno Treaties, despite the concentrated efforts of the League of Nations, there has been no real progress towards the reduction of land armaments and only partial success in the reduction of naval armaments, it is the object of this book to chronicle and explain. Let it suffice to say here that at the time the treaties were signed they were honestly regarded as a step towards that general reduction of armaments to which the Allies were pledged by the Treaty of Versailles.

British diplomacy has been criticized for not having secured the inclusion of some definite pledge or plan for disarmament within the scope of the Locarno Agreement. It has been said that while Great Britain was asking nothing for herself in return for her guarantee of the Western Pact, yet she might have demanded, as a *quid pro quo*, some commitment or the acceptance of some formula by the other Contracting Powers for the general reduction of armaments.

It cannot be denied that the inclusion of some such provision within the scope of the Agreement would have enhanced its value very greatly. At the same time it is equally true to say that the inclusion of any such a provision was at the time virtually impossible of achievement. Any such proposal on the part of the British Government would inevitably have been met by a counter-proposal from the French to the effect that if there were to be an agreement on reduction of armaments among the Contracting Parties it must be preceded by the acceptance by Germany of her Polish and Czechoslovakian frontier as final and definite. This manifestly Herr Stresemann could not do, and even if he had done so he would not have remained in power a week.

Moreover, the question of Polish security is not dependent on Germany alone. There is the Soviet Union. Throughout the disarmament discussion of the six subsequent years there has always been the Soviet Union, sitting like a death's head at a banquet and watching amusedly the efforts of the "capitalist" Powers. Neither in 1925 nor in 1930 could Poland or her fellow Border States enter into an agreement to disarm to which the U.S.S.R. was not a party.

In addition it should be remembered that it was not until more than a year later that Germany was pronounced as having satisfactorily carried out her disarmament treaty obligations. Parallel with the Locarno discussions, an official, and at times an acrid, correspondence was being carried on between Germany and the Allied Powers as to the non-fulfilment of certain of these pledges by Germany.

It is indeed not a matter for criticism that so little was gained at Locarno, but for satisfaction and congratulation that so much was achieved.

CHAPTER III

DISARMAMENT

A. THE PREPARATORY COMMISSION

1. Origins, Composition and Functions

THE Sixth Assembly of the League of Nations met in September 1925 under somewhat peculiar circumstances. To begin with it was conscious of the fact that it did not hold the centre of the international political stage and that the world's interest was concentrated not so much upon its deliberations as on the negotiations for a European Pact of Security which had reached their penultimate stage at the Conference of Jurists just concluded. (August 31st–September 4th.)[1]

Within the Assembly itself the principal question was what to do with the Geneva Protocol. Ever since Mr. Austen Chamberlain had given this instrument the *coup de grâce* at Geneva in the previous March[2] its supporters had piously waited for some miracle of phœnix-like resurrection, and its opponents had clamoured for a decent burial. This had not heightened the reputation of the League in the public mind. The fact that for two years in succession the Assembly had solemnly adopted a general instrument for the indirect reduction of armaments, which had been repudiated in the interval by the respective Governments of the States Members of the League, had increased the disbelief of many and had seemed to justify the sceptics in their original mistrust of the League's efficiency.

Thus in September 1925 the League of Nations had reached a very crucial point in its history. Its efforts towards eradicating the causes of war by substituting the pacific instead of the belligerent settlement of international disputes had been distinguished for their failures and good intentions. It was

---

[1] See *Security*, p. 132.
[2] For text of Mr. Austen Chamberlain's speech in the Council on March 12, 1925, see *Armaments*, pp. 132–145. See also *Security*, pp. 108–110.

realized that if the League was to get a grip upon popular imagination, without which it could not hope to succeed, it must take some definite step forward at the Sixth Assembly, a step so generally approved and with so close an appeal to common interest that it could not receive the same fate as the Treaty of Mutual Assistance and the Protocol. The result of the common recognition of the necessity of definite action was the abandonment of the indirect treatment of the problem of disarmament and the adoption of a policy of direct approach.

The Assembly was faced, therefore, with a number of problems. That which was good in the Geneva Protocol, namely the fundamental principle of arbitration, security and disarmament, must be saved from the wreck and reconciled with the Chamberlain formula of "special agreements to meet special needs," which had now become an outstanding principle of British foreign policy and a fundamental of the security pact negotiations, about to be concluded. To the amalgam thus formed must be added some definite step towards the reduction, or at least the limitation, of armaments, the general feeling being that the disarmament conference provided for in Article XVII of the Protocol should be called without delay.

As a result of conversations held outside the Assembly Hall, in which Professor James T. Shotwell, of the Carnegie Endowment, and M. Christian Lange, of the Inter-Parliamentary Union, took a prominent part, the head of the Spanish Delegation, Señor Quiñónes de Léon, supported by Mr. Chamberlain and M. Briand, introduced a Resolution on September 12th, of which the principal features were four:

1. It declared once more that a war of aggression was an international crime.[1]
2. It approved the efforts being made by certain nations to attain the objects of the Protocol by concluding treaties of Mutual Security and Arbitration conceived in the spirit of the Covenant and in harmony with the principles of the Protocol.
3. It recommended that when such Agreements had been concluded, the Council should examine them and report to the Seventh Assembly as to what degree of progress to general security had been thus effected.

---

[1] This was taken from paragraph 3 of the preamble of the Protocol.

Its concluding words were as follows:

"And [the Assembly] requests the Council to make preparatory arrangements for a conference on the reduction of armaments, as soon as, in its opinion, satisfactory conditions have been achieved from the point of view of general security as provided for in Resolution XIV of the Third Assembly."[1]

This section of the Resolution was referred to the Assembly's Third (Disarmament) Committee, where it at once became the centre of a spirited discussion. The small Powers, notably Hungary and the Netherlands, were anxious to strengthen the Spanish proposal in order to instruct the Council to convene at an early date a general disarmament conference, and to begin the necessary preparatory work forthwith. Opposition to such precipitate action came from Great Britain and Italy. Sir Cecil Hurst deprecated the raising of false hopes of disarmament at a moment when no immediate prospect of disarmament was in sight and said that the intricacies of the problem "rendered it essential to have the support of the Home Military Department." The Italian delegate, Signor Coppola, went even further and declared that a disarmament conference would "impinge unnecessarily upon national sovereignty."

It was left to the suave agility of Dr. Benès of Czechoslovakia, President of the Commission, to effect a compromise between the two divergent views, and his efforts were rewarded by the final adoption by the Assembly, on September 25, of an amended Resolution, the final paragraph of which ran as follows:

"And in conformity with Article VIII of the Covenant[2], [the Assembly] requests the Council to make a preparatory study with a view to a Conference for the Reduction and Limitation of Armaments in order that, as soon as satisfactory conditions have been assured from the

---

[1] Resolution XIV, adopted by the Third Assembly in September 1922, definitely linked security with disarmament and became the basis of the Treaty of Mutual Assistance. See *Armaments*, pp. 59–61, and *Security*, pp. 91–94.
[2] It is interesting to note that at this stage the primary obligation to disarm is taken to be Article VIII, and no mention is made of Peace Treaties and Allied pledges to the ex-enemy States. These latter obligations received greater attention after Germany's entry into the League in September 1926.

point of view of Resolution XIV of the Third Assembly, the said Conference may be convened and a general reduction and limitation of armaments may be realized."[1]

It will be noticed that the Resolution was so worded as to leave the Council free in its choice of time in beginning these preparatory studies, but an accompanying memorandum from the Third Committee made it quite clear, in no uncertain terms, that "any inactivity of the Council in this respect would fail to meet the ideas of the Sixth Assembly."[2]

Spurred on by this hint the Council on the following day (September 26th) requested a Committee of Enquiry, under the chairmanship of M. Paul Boncour, to submit to it proposals for setting up an organ entrusted with the preparation for a Conference for the Reduction and Limitation of Armaments, and to draft definite proposals.[3]

The Council received the report of this Committee of Enquiry at its session in December and adopted the recommendations almost in their entirety.[4] The organ in question was to be known as the "Preparatory Commission for the Disarmament Conference." Its composition was to consist of

1. Representatives of States Members of the Council.
2. Representatives of countries chosen amongst those which, by reason of their geographical situation, occupy a special position as regards the problem of disarmament and which are not otherwise represented on the Commission.

Under this second section it was agreed to invite, from among the Members of the League, Bulgaria, Finland, the Netherlands, Poland, Rumania and Yugoslavia, and from among the non-member States, Germany, the United States of America and the U.S.S.R.[5] Any State not represented on the Commission could submit its views in memoranda and was entitled to be heard in support of them.

---

[1] League of Nations Document C.P.D. 1, *Documents of the Preparatory Disarmament Conference*. Series I, p. 5.
[2] *Ibid.*, p. 56.   [3] *Ibid.*, p. 6.   [4] *Ibid.*, pp. 44–46.
[5] The Composition of the Commission was subsequently amended to allow retiring Members of the Council to retain their membership of the Commission. The Argentine and Chilean Republics were invited to become members in 1926, Greece in 1927, and Turkey in 1928.

Moreover, the Commission had at its disposal for co-operation in drawing up the proposals for the Conference, two advisory bodies:

1. The Permanent Advisory Commission of military experts appointed under Article IX of the Covenant, in the matter of military, naval and air questions.
2. A Joint Commission to advise on economic questions consisting of
   (a) Two Members each of the Economic, Financial and Transit Organizations.
   (b) Two Members of the Employers' Group and two Members of the Workers' Group of the Governing Body of the International Labour Office.[1]

In view of the importance of the task before the Commission the Council felt called upon to determine not only the composition and working of the new organ, but to some extent the direction of its work. It, therefore, submitted to the Commission for its consideration at its first session a *Questionnaire* based upon suggestions put forward by the British, French and Spanish Members of the Committee of Enquiry. It was considered that the questions contained therein required consideration and constructive reply as a preliminary to the drawing up of any draft convention for disarmament.[2]

With the exception of the U.S.S.R., all the States who received the invitation of the Council to become members of the Preparatory Commission notified their willingness to do so. But M. Chicherin, in a note dated January 16, 1926, notified the President of the Council that despite the fact that the Soviet Government welcomed every step towards disarmament and was genuinely anxious to be represented at the Disarmament Conference, the state of her relations with Switzerland made it impossible for her to become a member of the Preparatory Commission unless that body held it sessions outside Swiss territory.[3] M. Chicherin indicated that if the League Council

---

[1] In accordance with a suggestion made by Dr. Beneš at the March 1926 session of the Council, there were added to the Joint Committee four members "specially competent to deal with industry and transport," and also a national each from Germany, the U.S.A., Japan and the U.S.S.R. Later an expert in chemical warfare was also added.
[2] For text of *Questionnaire*, see below, pp. 50–52.
[3] The Soviet Government severed diplomatic relations with Switzerland after the assassination of M. Vorovsky, Soviet delegate to the first Lausanne

were really anxious for Soviet co-operation, they would summon
the Commission to meet elsewhere.

At its session in March 1926 the Council replied to M.
Chicherin, drawing his attention to the fact that the Swiss
Government had, in the previous December, given him assurances that the Soviet Delegation to the Commission would
receive "the same treatment as the Delegates of any other
Governments, and, in particular, would enjoy the same facilities
for entering Switzerland, the same privileges and immunities
in the conduct of their mission, and the same measures for
protection as the Swiss authorities might think it necessary to
take in order to ensure their safety." In view of this fact and
of the Soviet Government's expressed desire to co-operate, the
Council declared its conviction that M. Chicherin would not
insist on "exceptional treatment" being accorded to his Government in regard to the work of the Preparatory Commission,
and expressed the hope that Soviet representatives would be
present at the opening session of the Commission to be held in
Geneva on May 18th.

This suggestion was, however, far from agreeable to M.
Chicherin, who replied acidly on April 7th, that the assurances
of the Swiss Government were already before him when he
wrote his original note of January 16th, and that they "did not
constitute any new fact from which it could be concluded that
the Swiss Government had changed its attitude." He went on
to accuse the Council of lack of sincerity in their anxiety for
Soviet participation or in their desire for disarmament, in view
of their refusal to meet the Soviet objections to coming to
Geneva. As a parting shot he observed that as the Soviet
Government could not be represented on the Preparatory
Commission it would be equally unable to take part in the
Disarmament Conference, and would "await the day on which
the initiative will be taken in some other quarter before parti-
cipating in a Conference convened for the same purpose."

Conference of 1922, by a White Russian refugee. The dispute was not settled
until 1927, and hence the Soviet representatives only participated in the work
of the Commission from the Fourth Session in November 1927.

Thus a note of ominous presage was struck at the outset, for the hopes of the success of the Commission were considerably diminished by the absence of the U.S.S.R. from its discussions, which as far as Eastern Europe was concerned, were thereby rendered practically useless. It must be admitted, however, that even when in 1927 the Soviet delegation did begin participation it did not materially assist matters, though M. Litvinoff has never allowed the world to forget that the U.S.S.R. alone, of the States represented on the Commission, produced a plan for complete and universal disarmament.

To a certain extent the disappointment caused by Soviet abstention was offset by the representation of the United States in the person of the Hon. Hugh Gibson, whose presence marked the beginning of official American co-operation with the League of Nations in dealing with the question of disarmament.

In addition to this, the balance was the more redressed on December 1, 1925, when the Treaties constituting the Locarno Agreement were finally signed in London. As has already been indicated, the Agreement contained a definite commitment on the part of the Contracting Parties "to give their sincere co-operation to the work relating to disarmament already undertaken by the League of Nations and to seek the realization thereof in a general agreement."

2. THE FIRST AND SECOND SESSIONS
MAY–SEPTEMBER 1926

In making its plans for the organization of the Preparatory Commission in December 1925 it had been the original intention of the Council that the first session should be called for February 15, 1926. On January 30th, however, the Secretary-General received a joint note from the French, Italian, Japanese, Czechoslovak and Uruguayan Governments asking that, in the general interest, the date of the opening meeting might be postponed on the understanding that the Council at its March session should fix another date to be not later than May 15th.

General agreement was secured to this proposal, which was made with the dual hope that by the summer Germany would have entered the League of Nations and the U.S.S.R. might be persuaded to modify its attitude. Neither of these hopes was fulfilled, for the extraordinary session of the Assembly convened for March adjourned with Germany still outside the League, and, as has already been recorded, the Soviet Government displayed no signs of a change of heart. The Council, therefore, summoned the Commission to meet on May 18th.

At the opening session the Commission elected as its President H. E. Jonkheer Loudon, the Netherlands representative, and as Vice-Presidents, Señor Cobian (Spain) and Señor Buero (Uruguay).[1] Jonkheer Loudon was only elected after a proposal by Lord Cecil to put the French delegate, M. Paul Boncour, into the chair. But M. Boncour astutely side-stepped this somewhat ambiguous honour on the ground that France was too closely concerned with the question of disarmament.

The Agenda of the Commission consisted of the *Questionnaire*, already prepared by the Council in the previous December, which read as follows:

QUESTION I

What is to be understood by the expression "armaments"?

    (a) Definition of the various factors—military, economic, geographical, etc.—upon which the power of a country in time of war depends.

    (b) Definition and special characteristics of the various factors which constitute the armaments of a country in time of peace; the different categories of armaments—military, naval and air—the methods of recruiting, training, organizations capable of immediate military employment, etc.

QUESTION II (a)

Is it practicable to limit the ultimate war strength of a country, or must any measures of disarmament be confined to the peace strength?

---

[1] Owing to resignations the composition of the Bureau of the Commission underwent changes. MM. de Brouckère (Belgium) and Veverka (Czechoslovakia) acted temporarily as Vice-Presidents, and at the final session the Vice-Presidents were M. Politis (Greece) and M. Cobian.

QUESTION II (b)

What is to be understood by the expression "reduction and limitation of armaments"?

The various forms which reduction or limitation may take in the case of land, sea, and air forces; the relative advantages or disadvantages of each of the different forms or methods—for example, the reduction of the larger peace-time units or of their establishment and their equipment, or of any immediately mobilizable forces; the reduction of the length of active service, the reduction of the quantity of military equipment, the reduction of expenditure on national defence, etc.

QUESTION III

By what standards is it possible to measure the armaments of one country against the armaments of another, e.g. numbers, period of service, equipment, expenditure, etc.?

QUESTION IV

Can there be said to be "offensive" and "defensive" armaments?

Is there any method of ascertaining whether a certain force is organized for purely defensive purposes (no matter what use may be made of it in time of war), or whether, on the contrary, it is established in a spirit of aggression?

QUESTION V (a)

On what principle will it be possible to draw up a scale of armaments permissible to the various countries, taking into account particularly:

1. Population;
2. Resources;
3. Geographical situation;
4. Length and nature of maritime communications;
5. Density and character of railways;
6. Vulnerability of the frontiers and of the important vital centres near the frontiers;
7. The time required, varying with different States, to transform peace armaments into war armaments?

QUESTION V (b)

Can the reduction of armaments be promoted by examining possible means for ensuring that the neutral assistance, economic and military, contemplated in Article XVI of the Covenant, shall be brought quickly into operation as soon as an act of aggression has been committed?

QUESTION VI

(a) Is there any device by which civil and military aircraft can be distinguished for purposes of disarmament?

If this is not practicable, how can the value of civil aircraft be computed in estimating the air strength of any country?

(*b*) Is it possible or desirable to apply the conclusions arrived at in (*a*) above to parts of aircraft and aircraft engines?

(*c*) Is it possible to attach military value to commercial fleets in estimating the naval armaments of a country?

QUESTION VII

Admitting that disarmament depends on security, to what extent is regional disarmament possible in return for regional security? Or is any scheme of disarmament impracticable unless it is general? If regional disarmament is practicable, would it promote or lead up to general disarmament?

In considering the questions the Commission early arrived at the decision that the task of answering them would be materially facilitated by the constitution of two Sub-Commissions, "A" to deal with military, naval and air questions, and "B" to consider non-military matters. The presiding officers of these Sub-Commissions were the Commission's own Vice-Presidents, and it was made clear in their terms of reference, that the Sub-Commissions were purely expert bodies constituted to deal with the technical aspect of the questions. The Commission alone was competent to discuss the political aspect.

Between these two Sub-Commissions the Commission apportioned the Council's *Questionnaire* as follows:

QUESTION I

Referred to Sub-Commission "A."

QUESTION II (*a*)

Referred to Sub-Commission "A," with the additional request for definition of land, sea, and air forces maintained permanently in peace-time or capable of immediate use without preliminary mobilization measures.

QUESTIONS II (*b*) AND III

Referred to Sub-Commission "A," with two additional questions:

(i) What are the standards by which it is possible to measure: (*a*) military, (*b*) naval, and (*c*) air armaments of one country against the corresponding armaments of another country?

(ii) What are the methods by which reduction and limitation of each of these armaments can be effected? (with the comparative advantages and disadvantages of each method).

The opinions of Sub-Commissions "A" and "B" were requested on the method of limiting armed forces by limiting or reducing expenditure on national defence.

QUESTION IV

Referred to Sub-Commission "A" with two additional questions:

(i) Are there any armaments (and, if so, what) which are only capable of being used for the defence of a State's territory.

(ii) Is there any method of ascertaining whether a certain force is organized for purely defensive purposes or established in a spirit of aggression?

QUESTION V (a), 1, 2, 3, 4, 5, and 7

Referred to Sub-Commissions "A" and "B," to decide the effect of these factors upon armaments in general.

QUESTION V (a), 6

Referred to Sub-Commission "A."

QUESTIONS V (a) and V (b)

In regard to these questions the Commission received proposals:

1. By the French representative, for an investigation of methods to ensure prompt aid to a State when attacked.

2. By the Polish representative, for the study of the machinery, form and procedure of regional assistance.

3. By the Finnish representative for financial assistance to States the victims of the aggression.

The Commission referred these three proposals to the Council for consideration.

QUESTION VI

Referred to Sub-Commission "A."

QUESTION VII

Referred to Sub-Commissions "A" and "B."

In addition to these questions the Commission referred to the Sub-Commissions a proposal from the Belgian representative, for the supervision of disarmament, the Italian delegate asking that he should be placed on record as maintaining that supervision would be ineffective and was inadmissible. Lord Cecil also put forward a series of questions relative to the adaptation of chemical factories for the manufacture of poison gases, which were referred to Sub-Commissions "A" and "B," and a series of questions relative to the use and distribution of poison gas, which was referred to Sub-Commission "A." This

Sub-Commission was also invited to consider what effective sanctions could be proposed for the enforcement of the international undertaking not to employ gas or bacteria in war-time.

Having thus apportioned out its agenda the Preparatory Commission adjourned on May 26th. On the same day Sub-Commission "B" met for the first time, and still further subdivided the work. It referred to the Joint Commission appointed by the Council to advise the Preparatory Commission on economic and commercial subjects, the enquiry, under Question II (b) and III, "Can the magnitude of the armaments of the various States be compared by comparing their military expenditure, and, if so, what method should be followed?" It also referred to the Joint Commission the Belgian and British proposals relative to supervision and chemical warfare. The Joint Commission held its first session on June 28th, and in its turn appointed three sub-committees to deal with the three questions referred to it by Sub-Commission "B." Well might the procedure of the Preparatory Commission be called a Study in Devolution.

Sub-Commission "A" began what proved to be the first of fifty-one meetings on May 28th, and the report of the discussions disclosed the wide divergence of opinion upon a number of subjects, but more prominently upon the questions of the inclusion of trained reserves in peace-time armaments, the choice between total tonnage and tonnage by classes as the standard of naval armaments, and the proposal for a permanent organ for the supervision of armaments. In regard to this last suggestion, the United States Naval representative, Admiral Hilary Jones, declared that in no case would his country accept international supervision in any shape or form.[1]

When the Seventh Assembly met in September 1926 its Third Committee displayed, if not impatience, at least disappointment at the slow progress of the work of disarmament. At the moment the Preparatory Commission was in a state of

[1] Compare this statement with Mr. Hugh Gibson's concession, during the third session of the Commission, to the effect that the United States would agree to sit on a supervising commission provided that the United States was excluded from its jurisdiction. See below, p. 64.

suspended animation pending the reports of its Sub-Commissions. Of these Sub-Commissions "A" had still a number of questions untouched on its agenda and could get no further in its deliberations until it received the report of the Joint Commission. This body, in its turn, was waiting the reports of its three sub-committees.

It is possible that the presence in the Preparatory Commission of so important a non-member of the League as the United States of America kept within the bounds of discretion the criticism of many members of the Third Committee. A number felt that, even when full allowance had been made for the magnitude of the undertaking, progress had been too slow and it was clear that among the experts themselves there was little unanimity. Although Jonkheer Loudon pointed out to the Committee that "the differences of opinion which had been manifested within this Sub-Commission ("A") were only the reflection in the technical field of differences of a political character," this was scarcely an explanation of such a fact as, for example, that in naval questions a majority vote was frequently secured by the support of small States without a yard of coast-line, against the opinions of experts from such maritime powers as Great Britain and the United States.

Within the Third Committee itself there soon developed two parties on disarmament; one, led by France, advocating that the general disarmament conference should be summoned for 1927, and another, led by Great Britain, in the person of Lord Cecil, who, taking warning from the Geneva Protocol which had fixed the date of the Conference for June 5, 1925, laid stress on the possible unfortunate consequences of again announcing a definite date, and stood for further and more searching preparation.

M. Paul Boncour introduced into the Committee a draft resolution calling on the Preparatory Commission "to take steps to hasten the completion of the technical work" so that the Disarmament Conference might be convened "before the Eighth Session of the Assembly." After a process of modification in deference to the opposition of the British (supported by the

Italian) view, this resolution was finally adopted by the
Assembly on September 24th in the following form:

THE ASSEMBLY

"Requests the Council to call upon the Preparatory Commission to
take steps to hasten the completion of the technical work and thus
be able to draw up, at the beginning of the next year, the programme
for a conference on the limitation and reduction of armaments
corresponding to existing conditions in regard to regional and general
security, and it asks the Council to convene this Conference before
the Eighth Ordinary Session of the Assembly unless material
difficulties render this impossible."

Not even M. Paul Boncour, the champion of increased celerity,
believed that the Conference for which this resolution made
provision would reach a final agreement on disarmament.

"As security increases disarmament will increase," he told the Assembly
in presenting the Third Committee's report. "The Disarmament Conference will, therefore, be only the first of a series, and even apart from
the importance of the reductions and limitations which it may bring
about it must, in any case, have the immense advantage of transforming
into an international contract the degree of the different States, and of
thus putting a stop for a definite period to any possibility of competition
in armaments "

In taking its final decision to adopt this resolution the Assembly
was influenced by two important factors, both of them being
direct results of the Locarno Agreement. The first of these was
the vital change in the European situation which had resulted
from the Agreement, and the second was the entry of Germany
into the League of Nations. Now for the first time Germany
could state her case to the world from the rostrum of the
Assembly, and her delegates were not slow to take advantage
of this opportunity.

The last speaker in the debate on the report of the Third
Committee was Dr. von Schubert, and in a short and simple
speech he put the German point of view. M. Paul Boncour, he
said, had stated that an international convention for the reduction of armaments would in itself constitute a considerable
advance, even if it amounted merely to the fixing and acceptance
of the *status quo*.

"We consider that the fixing of the *status quo* cannot be regarded as a genuine advance, for we contend that the preparatory work should be directed from this moment towards the final object, which is to reduce the existing disproportion between the armaments of the States Members of the League, and thereby to fit the League more perfectly for the accomplishment of its mission."

Mild though these words may seem as compared with subsequent presentations of the same case in similar circumstances, they nevertheless enunciated a fundamental principle from which German delegates to the Assembly and the Preparatory Commission never departed, namely, the fulfilment by the Allies of the pledges they assumed under the Preamble to Part V of the Treaty of Versailles and in M. Clemenceau's letter of June 16, 1919.[1]

Partly as a result of the discussions in the Third Committee and partly in order to settle questions concerning the changes in its composition necessitated by the changes on the Council, it was decided to hold the second plenary session of the Preparatory Commission on September 22nd and 27th, during the last week of the Assembly. At the first of these meetings Mr. Gibson took the initiative and put forward proposals calculated to accelerate the work of Sub-Commission "A." This body, he declared, had not adhered sufficiently closely to its original terms of reference, which were to examine the questions referred to it from a purely *technical* aspect. Instead, such replies as the Sub-Commission had already submitted showed that in reaching its decisions it had been unduly influenced by the political and economic factors. The replies themselves, moreover, were limited to the views of the majority, without adequately informing the Commission of the opinions of the minority vote.

Mr. Gibson, therefore, proposed a resolution which should instruct Sub-Commission "A" to revise, at the second reading, the answers to the questions already dealt with in such a manner that the answers should be prepared on purely technical grounds, uninfluenced by political and economic considerations. The same instructions were to guide the consideration by the

[1] See above, pp. 26–27.

Sub-Commission of those questions not already dealt with. In each case the Preparatory Commission was to be furnished with all divergent views, accompanied by a clear statement of the relative advantages and disadvantages of each.

This resolution in a slightly modified form was adopted by the Commission on September 27th, and had the desired effect of enabling Sub-Commission "A" to complete and present its report by November 5th. Sub-Commission "B" completed its work on March 17, 1927. The replies of these two bodies, that of Sub-Commission "A" a massive volume of 176 folio pages, and that of Sub-Commission "B" in three parts, were circulated to the Governments represented on the Commission.[1]

Meanwhile, on December 8, 1926 the Council, acting on the instruction of the Assembly, directed the Preparatory Commission to make suggestions for the date of the General Disarmament Conference and also to draw up an agenda. So that the first phase of the work of the Commission closed with the year 1926.

3. THE DRAFT CONVENTION, 1927–1930

(a) THE FIRST DRAFT, 1927

When the British Government had completed its study of the reports of Sub-Commissions "A" and "B," it decided that it was then in possession of sufficient preliminary data to justify the taking of a definite and decisive step forward. Accordingly, when the Preparatory Commission met for its third session on March 21, 1927, Lord Cecil submitted a Draft Convention which was intended to serve as a basis for discussion.[2] M. Paul Boncour expressed the view that his Government would have preferred to have proceeded to the stage of a Draft Convention after a general discussion of the reports of the Sub-Commissions, but that Lord Cecil's action left him no other alternative than to present the views of France in a similar form.

[1] For text of the Report of Sub-Commission "A," see League Document, C. 739, M. 278, 1926, IX (C.P.D. 28). Sub-Commission "B's" report is as follows: Part I, C.P.D. 29; Part II, C.P.D. 39; Part III, C.P.D. 40. It is impossible to give even a brief summary of these reports here.
[2] League Document, C.P.D. 41 (1).

Just to what degree the French were taken by surprise, however, may be gauged from the fact that by the evening of March 22nd, M. Paul Boncour had circulated a counter-draft treaty, much longer and more complex than that presented by Lord Cecil.[1]

On the morning of March 22nd, that is to say, during the period in which the Commission was awaiting the French Draft, Count Bernstorff took the opportunity to remind his colleagues of the principle which Dr. von Schubert had laid down in the Seventh Assembly. Speaking of the States which had been already disarmed, he said:

"Those States demand, and with good reason, that they shall not suffer a disappointment, a disappointment for which none of us would desire to shoulder the responsibility. . . . The States which have been disarmed by international treaties . . . are perfectly entitled to demand that general disarmament should be achieved. The disarmament of the country which I have the honour to represent is complete. You are well aware that, according to the Treaty of Versailles, this disarmament should only be a prelude to general disarmament."

The Commission devoted five days, March 21st–25th, to a general discussion of the British and French drafts, of which the main principles are summarized as follows:

BRITISH DRAFT	FRENCH DRAFT
1. Agreement to limit military, naval and air armaments to figures agreed upon.	1. Land, sea and air armaments are interdependent.
2. Such limited armaments might be increased by a State, if	2. Limitation of naval armaments should be applied only to total tonnage, and not to various categories in detail.
(i) a war in which it is a belligerent has broken out;	
(ii) it is threatened with:	
(a) a rebellion,	
(b) an emergency involving serious military operations;	
(iii) such an increase is effected with the concurrence of the League.	

---

[1] League Document, C.P.D. 43 (1).

BRITISH DRAFT	FRENCH DRAFT
3. The forces increased under 2 must be reduced to the figure established in 1 as soon as normal conditions are restored.	3. Limitation of land forces to be restricted to limitation of forces with the colours. The system of the composition and training of reserves should not be interfered with.
4. An annual statement to be made to the Secretary-General showing the proposed expenditure on military, naval and air armaments in the current financial year.	4. The "war potentialities" of a country—such factors as geographical position, natural resources and industrial power should be taken into account.
5. An annual statement to be made to the Secretary-General showing actual expenditure during the preceding financial year.	5. Limitation of armaments to be limitation of engine-power. In calculating resources in air armaments, military and civil aviation should be regarded as interdependent.
6. Limitation of land armaments to be achieved by limitation of effectives.	6. Budgetary expenditure for military purposes should be used as a basis of comparison.
7. Limitation of naval armaments to be achieved by limitation of tonnage of any one ship, the number and tonnage of all ships in that class and the calibre of the guns mounted in such ship. General acceptance of Articles 13–18 (inclusive) of the Washington Treaty.	7. There should be some form of international supervision to ensure the carrying out of the terms of the proposed Convention.
8. Limitation of air armaments to be effected by limiting the number of aircraft attached to shore bases.	

It will be seen at once that, while both of these sets of proposals aimed at limitation and not at reduction, this was almost their only point in common, and that the work of reconciling the two drafts would indeed be a Herculean labour. As a beginning, and to facilitate the simultaneous consideration of the British and French proposals, a synoptic table was prepared and this formed the general basis of the ensuing discussions.

It is not proposed to deal, here, with the draft proposals *ad seriatim* but to concentrate on the three main points, of land armaments, the limitation of naval armaments and the question of international supervision or control. As far as possible the record of the discussions is given in the words of Lord Cecil's report to Sir Austen Chamberlain.[1]

(i) LAND ARMAMENTS

It was generally agreed that limitation of effectives was the main method of limiting land armaments. The chief problem was how to estimate the number of effectives.

"Since it is evident," wrote Lord Cecil, "that a man who has just completed his training with the colours is at least as efficient as any of those who are still undergoing training, the British delegation contend that the real test was the number of men who could be put into the front line within, say, a week of the outbreak of war."

"This view, however, was hotly contested by all, or almost all, of the conscriptionist countries, mainly on the ground that it was impossible to draw a line between those reserves which were sufficiently trained to take the field immediately, and those which would require some training before they could be so employed."[2]

The view of the United States on this matter was expressed by Mr. Hugh Gibson as being that the conditions were so different in various regions of the world, and the factors entering into the situation so divergent, that a constructive achievement could only be aimed at by regional agreement rather than by any effort to work out a general plan for the whole world.

In the end it was agreed, subject to reservations by certain States' representatives, that limitation should only apply to troops actually with the colours; but that there should be an

---

[1] British White Paper, *Report of the British Representative to Secretary of State for Foreign Affairs, Preparatory Committee for the Disarmament Conference. Third Session, Geneva, March 21–April 26, 1927.* Miscellaneous No. 4 (1927), Cmd. 2888. The verbatim report of the discussion will be found in the Minutes of Third Session of P.D.C. League Document C. 310, M. 109, 1927, IX.
[2] It was also pointed out that the limitation of the number of men actually with the colours would automatically limit the number of trained reserves.

added limitation of the proportion of officers and N.C.O.'s to other ranks, so as to render the sudden expansion of any army beyond its nominal strength impracticable. It was further agreed that in conscriptionist countries a limit should be put on the period of service with the colours.

The reservations referred to were made by Great Britain, the United States and Germany. Of these the German was the most specific, declaring that the agreed text

"does not contain any limitation of reserves given military training, registered and compelled by law to serve in case of war, although in its (the German delegation's) opinion these reserves, while non-existent in professional armies, form the decisive factor as regards *personnel* in war in countries having a conscript system."

(ii) NAVAL ARMAMENTS

"In regard to sea armaments," Lord Cecil continued, "again the main method of limitation was agreed to, i.e. by tonnage, for the strength of the fleet depends primarily on the number and power of its ships. The three great maritime countries—America, Japan and Great Britain—desired to apply the principles accepted at Washington to all classes of war vessels. That is to say, they proposed that there should be a limit in each class of warship, viz. battleships, cruisers, submarines, destroyers, etc., to the size of the individual ship, to the number of ships in the class, and to the calibre of the guns carried. There can be little doubt that this system of limitation is workable and effective."

"France and Italy, together with several other Powers, contended for a much greater liberty; namely, that the limit to the fleet should be only to its total tonnage, and within that total each Power should be entitled to build as many or as few of each class of warship as they pleased, with a superior limit to the size of the largest ship and the largest gun, subject, however, to the preservation of the engagements entered into at Washington with regard to battleships, aircraft carriers and cruisers.

"It was pointed out that so lax a system of limitation might, at any rate in theory, enable a Power to concentrate on some particular class of warship, such as commerce destroyers, and so either obtain an unforeseen advantage over a rival, or start in a modified form a competition in naval armaments. After prolonged discussion, the French made a compromise proposal to the effect that each Power should state at the outset of the period governed by the treaty the amount of tonnage that it intended to devote to each class of warship, and that if any change in this programme was desired, a year's notice must be given. And they suggested that this would preclude all possibility of surprise, and that particularly Great Britain with her great superiority in building speed would be amply protected."[1]

There was an additional reason why any alteration in the Washington principles was undesirable at this moment. On February 10, 1927, President Coolidge had issued an invitation to the other great naval Powers for a Conference for the limitation of those classes of warships unaffected by the Washington Treaty.[2] In view of this it was considered injudicious to take any steps which might be prejudicial to the success of the Conference.

On the question of naval limitation there was, therefore, no conclusion, and the matter was adjourned until the second reading. The Italian delegation declared that it could not accept even the French modification, because it was too favourable towards the British proposals. On the other hand, the British, who had at first opposed any limitation of naval effectives, agreed to do so, though the American and Japanese were unable to agree to the limitation of officers and non-commissioned officers, as well as to the total number of *personnel*. In view of this objection the French replied that if this were the case they would not accept the limitation of officers and non-commissioned officers in their land armies.

(iii) INTERNATIONAL SUPERVISION

It was upon this subject that the most serious division of opinion arose.

"To the Delegations of a certain number of States represented on the commission, including the British Delegation," wrote Lord Cecil, "it seemed clear that the main reliance for the enforcement of a disarmament treaty must be on the good faith of the parties to the treaty. This school of thought could not bring itself to believe that any international

---

[1] It was this compromise proposal which was accepted by Mr. Gibson in his historic speech two years later (April 22, 1929) as a basis of discussion. In the negotiations begun as a consequence of Mr. Gibson's speech, and which ultimately resulted in the London Naval Treaty of 1930, the French Thesis, with certain modifications, became the Transactional Proposal accepted by the Conference. See below, pp. 174, etc.
[2] For the history of the Conference and its subsequent failure, see below, pp. 103, etc.

supervision short of proposals so drastic as to be unacceptable under existing circumstances could really restrain an international and deliberate evasion of the provisions of the treaty. International supervision might, indeed, prevent carelessness or the like, but could not protect the other signatories against the international fraud of one of their number.

"Other countries, however, took a very different view. The French, in particular, were most anxious to set up an elaborate system of international control. They proposed the creation of a Permanent Commission of some twenty to twenty-five members, whose duty it would be to exercise a kind of oversight over all the armaments of the High Contracting Parties. If there were reasons to suppose that any of them were violating their engagements, then they could be brought before this Commission in one way or another, and the Commission by a two-thirds majority could give its opinion as to whether such a violation had taken place. The decision of the Commission would then be brought to the Council of the League, who could order an investigation by an international commission."

Mr. Hugh Gibson went so far as to review the policy of the American representative on Sub-Commission "A,"[1] to the extent of agreeing to provisions for an International Commission of Control provided that the United States were excluded from its jurisdiction. He emphasized, however, that the United States could never accept a Convention which put America under the jurisdiction of the League, or a Convention which did not confine itself to the provisions of disarmament pure and simple, leaving enforcement to the good faith of each Government.

M. Paul Boncour accepted this American reservation and proposed that the provisions for supervision should only be binding for the members of the League among themselves. Lord Cecil went so far as to concede acceptance of some form of investigatory machinery, particularly in order to give a State suspected of violation of the Disarmament Convention a chance to clear itself. This machinery was closely modelled on Article XI of the Covenant, and would ensure the "friendly right" of any of the States Parties to the Convention to bring before a body consisting of representatives of these States who were members of the Council and of the United States any

---

[1] See above, p. 54.

violation of the Convention or, indeed, any changes of armament which were likely to disturb international relations.

Agreement on these lines seemed to be in view, but all chance of it was destroyed by the Italian representative, General de Marinis, who declared that his Government could accept no Convention containing any provision of control. The deadlock thus reached was not solved during this session of the Commission.

On the question of budgetary expenditure on armaments there was general agreement that its limitation was not only desirable but formed the only effective way of limiting the material employed in land armaments, but this unanimity of opinion did not extend to the means by which such limitation should be carried out. While the British, Italian and Japanese representatives considered that budgetary limitation should be effected solely by publicity, the French, and their followers, maintained that the total budgetary expenditure should be limited to a definite figure, and that if that figure were not reached in any particular year, the surplus should be carried forward to the next year. Here, again, no definite decision was reached.

Thus it will be seen from the foregoing narrative that though there was general agreement in principle on a large number of matters, a unanimous decision was reached on none of the major practical points. In land armaments the question of trained reserves remained unsettled; a deadlock existed in the matter of naval armaments, and the problem of supervision remained unsolved.

The Commission, which adjourned on April 26, 1927, drew up a draft Convention of which their recent deliberations formed the first reading. This draft demonstrated very clearly what degree of agreement was reached, and where there was no agreement the alternative texts of the articles were printed synoptically. The second reading was fixed provisionally by the President, M. Loudon, for November of the same year, but he asked complete freedom in this matter. "You will understand," he said, "that we must not meet again too soon, for we must allow our Governments time to reflect and agree, and we must allow public opinion . . . to weigh the facts of the situation and come to our assistance."

Elsewhere in his closing speech M. Loudon, speaking of the use to which the Report and Minutes of the Commission should be put, said:

"We thought that, with the help of these documents and the Minutes of our debates, our Governments would be able to examine all the points raised during the discussion and give them the close study which is indispensable if the negotiations and exchange of views between the various Foreign Offices are to result in our drawing up, at the second reading, a single text which may be submitted to the proposed Conference."

It was mainly in this passage in the President's address that the French and British Governments found the *raison d'être* for the negotiations in the following summer which terminated in the unfortunate Naval Compromise which, in its turn, perhaps more than any other individual factor, contributed towards the ill feeling between Great Britain and the United States over the naval question.[1]

If the first three sessions of the Preparatory Commission did little else but emphasize the differences of opinion on the matter of disarmament, they at least gave further abundant proof, if further proof were necessary, of the futility of attempting to solve the problem of disarmament without giving parallel considerations to the questions of security and arbitration.

The Assembly of 1927 met in what may be called a "back-to-the-Protocol" spirit. While not advocating the resuscitation of the Protocol in its original form, there was a general desire for a definite reaffirmation of the fundamental principles of security, arbitration and disarmament. As a result of the debate in the Third Committee and in the plenary session the Preparatory Commission was directed to create a new Committee to consider "the measures capable of giving to all States the guarantees of arbitration and security necessary to enable

---

[1] See below, pp. 127, etc.

them to fix the level of their armaments at the lowest possible figures in an international disarmament agreement."

In accordance with these instructions the Commission at its Fourth Session (November–December 1927) set up this new Committee, and an account of its labours and their results is given on a later page.[1]

(b) THE SECOND DRAFT, 1929

IT was not until April 1929, at the Sixth Session of the Preparatory Commission[2] and two years after its first reading, that the Draft Convention was again considered. The intervening years had not been productive of any prospect of the solution of the fundamental difficulties which had faced the Commission in 1927. Indeed, the reverse was the case; in naval matters the rift in the lute was even wider, not, as before, between Great Britain and France, but between Great Britain and the United States. The complete failure of the Three-Power Conference of 1927[3] and the unfortunate episode of the Anglo-French Compromise of 1928,[4] so excellent in intention yet so disastrous in effect, had resulted in a most regrettable atmosphere of mutual distrust and suspicion on both sides of the Atlantic.

There were, however, certain factors on the credit side of the balance sheet. The conclusion of the Kellogg Pact[5] and its corollary, the Litvinoff Protocol,[6] taken in conjunction with the work of the Commission's own Committee on Security and Arbitration,[7] had done a certain amount of good, though, it must be confessed, not very much, towards creating that psychological state of mind which is a necessary preliminary to disarmament.

It was, however, under scarcely ideal conditions that the Commission met to take the second reading, and few at the

---

[1] See below, pp. 279, etc.
[2] The Fourth and Fifth Sessions (in November 1927 and March 1928) had been chiefly occupied with discussion on the Soviet proposals, for details of which, see below, pp. 234, etc.
[3] See below, p. 103.
[4] See below, p. 127.
[5] See below, p. 245.
[6] See below, p. 249.
[7] See below, p. 279.

opening of the session could have predicted the fortunate outcome which brought about its premature adjournment.

At the opening of the session on April 15th, the President, M. Loudon, suggested that the time was not yet ripe for taking the second reading; no agreement had been reached between the groups of Powers mainly concerned as to naval limitation, and until this was done this part at least of the Convention could not be usefully discussed; moreover, they still had before them the second Soviet Proposal of 1928.

With this suggestion, however, Count Bernstorff (Germany) would in no way agree. It had been the expressed intention of the Commission itself in March 1928 and the desire of the Ninth Assembly (September 1928)[1] that the second reading should be taken at this session, and he urged that this should be proceeded with at once and the essential questions—effectives and material—dealt with.

It was accordingly agreed to conclude consideration of the Soviet proposals and then to proceed with the second reading of the Draft Convention. When three days had been spent in fruitless discussion, the Commission decided, with only two dissentient votes,[2] to proceed immediately to the second reading but to annex to its final report the Soviet Draft Convention.

The discussion on the 1927 Draft was but two days old when Mr. Hugh Gibson, on April 22nd, made a speech embodying a declaration on behalf of the United States Government, of great historical importance, which contained the seed which, just twelve months later, on April 22, 1930, bore fruit in the shape of the London Naval Treaty.[3]

[1] The Ninth Assembly had adopted a resolution on September 22, 1928, expressing the hope that "Governments among which differences of opinion still subsist as to the conditions for the reduction and limitation of armaments will seek . . . agreed solutions which will enable the work of the Preparatory Commission to be brought to a successful issue." The Assembly further instructed the President of the Commission "to keep in contact with the Governments concerned so that he may be apprised of the progress of their negotiations and may be able to convene the Commission at the end of the present year, or in any case, at the beginning of 1929." The resolution was adopted before the Anglo-French Compromise had received its *quietus* from Washington. This actually occurred just six days later (September 28th).

[2] The U.S.S.R. and China.

[3] For the immediate results of Mr. Gibson's speech, see below, pp. 143, etc., and for the Anglo-American *rapprochement* which it inaugurated, see p. 142.

Only the Great Powers, said Mr. Gibson, could initiate measures of reduction, and it must be "reduction" rather than "limitation." Above all, what was essential was a state of mind—the psychology of peace—to match the new situation caused by the Kellogg Pact. "Disarmament will only follow from a change of attitude towards the use of force in the settlement of international disputes."

Mr. Gibson then made this important statement:

"My Government is disposed to give full and friendly consideration to any supplementary methods of limitation which may be calculated to make our proposals, the French thesis or any other acceptable to other Powers, and if such a course appears desirable my Government will be prepared to give consideration to a method of estimating equivalent naval values which takes account of other factors than displacement tonnage alone. In order to arrive at a basis of comparison in the case of categories in which there are marked variations as to unit characteristics it might be desirable in arriving at a formula for estimating equivalent tonnage to consider certain factors which produce these variations, such as age, unit displacement and calibre of guns. My Government has given careful consideration to various methods of comparison, and the American delegation will be in a position to discuss the subject whenever it comes before the Commission."

The French thesis to which Mr. Gibson gave his approval was that put forward at the end of the Third Session of the Commission in April 1927, and it aimed at the limitation of total tonnage, and also at the division of the total tonnage stated by each contracting party into total tonnage by groups. These groups would apply to four classes: capital ships, aircraft carriers, surface vessels under 10,000 tons and submarines. Each contracting party would undertake to fix a maximum tonnage for each of the categories during the period of validity of the Convention. But, within the limits of the total tonnage stated, each party could alter its allocations to each class, within a certain margin, subject to informing the Secretariat of the League at least once a year before laying down the portion of the tonnage to be transferred.[1]

[1] See above, p. 62. This thesis, with modifications, was the same as the Transactional Proposal accepted by the London Naval Conference in 1930. See below, pp. 172, 174, etc.

In conclusion, and turning to broader principles, Mr. Gibson declared:

"My Government has always felt that we need no exact balance of ships and guns, which can be based only on the idea of conflict—what is really wanted is a common-sense agreement, based on the idea that we are going to be friends and settle our problems by peaceful means. . . . It feels that genuine disarmament will follow only from a change of attitude towards the use of force in the settlement of international disputes."

The American delegate's speech was hailed with satisfaction by the British, Japanese, Canadian and Italian representatives, all of whom welcomed this new departure, promising to communicate it at once to their respective Governments. Even the ranks of Tuscany, as represented by M. Litvinoff, could scarce forbear to cheer, and the Soviet delegate declared that he was glad to identify in it a certain number of theories and arguments which he himself had advocated in connection with the Soviet proposals.

1. LAND ARMAMENTS

The Commission then passed to a detailed consideration of the articles of the 1927 Draft. It will be remembered that this Draft had contained reservations made by the British, German and United States delegations concerning the non-inclusion of the limitation of trained reserves. When, however, this matter came up at the second reading, the British delegate, Lord Cushendun (who had replaced Lord Cecil in the British Cabinet, on the latter's resignation after the Geneva Naval Conference of 1927[1]), was placed in something of a difficult position. The essence of the ill-fated Anglo-French Compromise of 1928[2] had been that the British Government would withdraw its opposition to the French desire to exclude trained reserves from limitation in return for certain concessions on the part of the French to the British point of view in the matter of naval limitation. It was this aspect of the "deal" which had called forth the loudest protest in America and Germany, and indeed in Great Britain itself.

[1] See below, pp. 103, etc.　　　　[2] See below, pp. 127, etc.

The British attitude in 1929 was that the Compromise had failed and must, therefore, be regarded as cancelled in all its aspects, and Mr. Baldwin had made it clear that the British Government regarded itself as in no way obligated to the French. Such, however, was not the view in Paris, where it was felt that the abandonment of the naval part of the Compromise did not release the British from their pledge in regard to trained reserves.

In his opening statement, therefore, Lord Cushendun walked warily, only hinting that he would not be likely to place obstacles in the way of an agreement which the principal Powers concerned in land armaments regarded as satisfactory. When, however, Mr. Gibson stated that, in order that the work of the Commission might achieve some degree of success in the matter of land armament, his Government would support, as regards the question of trained reserves, the opinion of the majority of the countries where land forces constituted their chief military interest, Lord Cushendun came forward with an explicit statement to the same effect on behalf of the British Government.

In making these concessions both the British and American delegates made it clear that their fundamental objection to the principle involved had not abated but that the method of concession was the only method by which the Commission could advance its work not only speedily but effectively, and offer to the Governments and peoples represented a positive accomplishment; or, in other words, as Professor Toynbee interprets it, "any agreement for the limitation of land armament would be better than none."[1]

Thus, in spite of protests by German, Soviet and other delegations, it was declared by the President to be the desire of a large majority of the Commission that the Convention should not deal with the limitation of trained reserves.

2. Limitation of Material

This was one of the points on which no agreement could be reached at the first meeting, and the 1927 Draft consisted of

[1] See *Survey of International Affairs*, 1929, p. 28.

two proposals, one submitted by the German delegation, aiming at direct limitation of material in service and in stock and based upon tables giving a numerical list of authorized material,[1] the other, presented by the French delegation, aiming at indirect limitation and based on the limitation of budget expenditure. The Commission had still to reach a conclusion on this point and the arguments of both sides were again paraded.

The supporters of direct limitation, amongst whom, in addition to Germany, were the U.S.S.R., the Netherlands and Sweden, claimed that this method alone enabled States to know the armaments in respect of material possessed by other States and to restrict the possibilities of aggression. It was claimed for the method that it prevented the compensation by material factor of a reduction of effectives and this, it was said, was perfectly feasible because it had been applied in execution of the provisions of the Peace Treaties concerning disarmament.

On the other hand the French, supported by the Japanese, Italians and Little Entente delegations, held that direct limitation was only feasible if accompanied (as in the Peace Treaties) by some system of international control, but this suggestion had been declared unpalatable to the United States. Instead, the French representative, M. Massigli, proposed the method of indirect limitation, a system extremely elastic and making it possible to take account of general economic conditions or any special conditions in each country. It was, moreover, a method easy to understand, its progress easy to follow with the help of public documents, and one which was free from any necessity of provisions for control.

Mr. Gibson, however, declared that the United States could accept no convention which envisaged any restriction on budgetary expenditure, a method which would meet with insuperable opposition in America and which was indeed a constitutional impossibility for that country. He, therefore, proposed the even more indirect system of limitation by giving

---

[1] The German proposal was based on the method imposed upon Germany under the Disarmament Clauses of the Treaty of Versailles.

the utmost publicity to budgetary expenditure on armaments, and this was finally accepted by the French and adopted by the Commission by a majority vote of 22 to 2. The minority were the U.S.S.R. and China.

Though he would not oppose the resolution, Count Bernstorff, on behalf of Germany, abstained from voting and issued a general statement dissociating himself from this part of the Commission's work:

"The Commission," he said, "has lost sight of its task at any rate as far as land forces are concerned. . . . My Government has never left it for one moment in doubt . . . that it could not accept, even as a first stage, a solution which would not include *all* the forms of armaments, and which would not bring about an appreciable reduction in the excessive armaments of the present. Such a solution would not correspond with the principles either of the Treaties or of the Covenant. I, therefore, find myself obliged to dissociate myself definitely from the programme which the majority of this Commission has just drawn up and to leave it henceforth with the sole responsibility for the preparation of the Conference as its course is being shaped at the present moment."

This statement of Count Bernstorff's is important as indicating the growing impatience of Germany with the lack of progress on the part of the Commission, and her dissatisfaction with the League of Nations in general and its disarmament policy in particular. This dissatisfaction reached a greater height after the Reichstag elections in September 1930, which resulted in a great gain for the Nationalist Socialist (Nazi) Party. It was manifested very strongly during the meeting of the Eleventh Assembly and when the Sixth Session of the Commission was resumed in November 1930.[1]

3. CHEMICAL WARFARE

At the first reading of the Convention in 1927 a joint draft had been put forward by the delegations of Belgium, Czecho-slovakia, Poland, Rumania and Yugoslavia, but discussion on it had been postponed until the second reading. Now it was agreed that, subject to reciprocity, the parties to the Convention would refrain from using in war poisonous or asphyxiating

[1] See below, pp. 89, etc.

gases and "all analogous liquids, substances or processes." In
any case they would abstain from all bacteriological methods of
warfare.

4. Naval Armaments

It was when the Commission reached this part of the Draft
Convention in their discussions that the full effects of Mr.
Gibson's proposals of April 22nd began to be felt.[1] Communications had passed between the representatives on the Commission
of the other great Naval Powers and their respective Governments, with the result that the American proposal to enter into
fresh discussions had been accorded a warm welcome by all.
Clearly, however, the most careful study must be given to Mr.
Gibson's suggestion and the representatives asked the Commission to allow their Governments time to study the question.
Accordingly the Commission decided to postpone the discussion
both on the naval question and on the remaining articles of
the 1927 Draft. It adjourned on May 6th, instructing its
President to fix the date of its next meeting and asking the
Naval Powers concerned to keep him in touch with the progress
of their negotiations, so as to facilitate his task and enable
him to convene the Commission with a full knowledge of the
facts.[2]

What, then, had emerged from the second reading? First
and foremost in importance was the statement of Mr. Gibson
that the United States was prepared to reopen negotiations
on the naval question. This was undoubtedly a great and
valuable mark of progress. There was an agreement with
regard to chemical warfare, and this was not unimportant. In
addition, there had been agreements reached on the exemption
of trained reserves from the limitation of land armaments, and
on the indirect limitation of material for publicity in budgeting

---

[1] See above, p. 69.
[2] In view of the fact that the Sixth Session of the Commission adjourned
sine die, no report was drawn up on this first part of its work. The verbatim
report of the discussions is to be found in League Document C. 195, M. 74,
1929, IX, to which are annexed the text of the articles adopted at the second
reading.

expenditure. But these latter agreements had been reached only after great concessions on the part of Great Britain and the United States, and had resulted in the estrangement of Germany.

Both inside and outside the Commission there were those who believed that the agreements reached regarding trained reserves and the limitation of material had been bought at too dear a price and that in gaining them the spirit of conciliation had been carried to the point of sacrificing fundamental principles. It was pointed out, indeed, that if the second at least of these decisions was not reversed the Draft Convention would be practically valueless as far as land armaments were concerned.

With the arrival in office (but not in power) of Mr. MacDonald's second Labour Government after the British elections in June 1929 it became evident that the question of disarmament was to play the foremost rôle in British foreign policy. Not only did the Prime Minister himself take charge of naval negotiations with the United States, but he persuaded Lord Cecil, though not a member of his party, to attend the Tenth Assembly of the League (September 1929) as a non-party expert on disarmament and to represent Great Britain on the Third Committee. It at once became apparent from Lord Cecil's statements that the attitude of the Labour Government towards the agreements reached on the second reading was very different from that of its Conservative predecessor.

In a speech in the Third Committee on September 19th Lord Cecil delivered a trenchant attack on the agreements reached during the second reading of the Draft Convention, but more particularly that over the limitation of material, which he described as "profoundly unsatisfactory." He considered that the process of dropping sound proposals because someone disliked them had been carried too far. "It is easy to agree to nothing"—and he accordingly moved the following Resolution:

"The Assembly, being convinced that a progressive and gereral reduction of armaments is urgently needed throughout the world, expresses the hope that the Preparatory Commission will finish its labours at the earliest possible moment, and considers that in concluding the Draft Disarmament Convention it should consider how far the following principles have been, or ought to be, adopted:

(a) "The application of the same principles to the reduction and limitation of *personnel* and material, whether in sea, land or air forces;

(b) "The limitation of the strength of a force either by limiting its numbers or its period of training, or both;

(c) "The limitation of material either directly by enumeration or indirectly by budgetary limitation, or by both methods;

(d) "The recognition of a competent international authority to watch and report upon the execution of the treaty."

The introduction of this resolution produced acute controversy in London, Paris and Geneva. The terms of the resolution were naturally warmly supported by Germany but were attacked with great bitterness by the French Press, and a storm of obloquy broke over the devoted head of Lord Cecil himself. He was held up to scorn and contumely as wishing to throw the whole question into the melting-pot and go back on the decision arrived at. He was accused—and in this charge certain British newspapers joined—of wishing to reopen the much-vexed question of trained reserves, a point to which he had drawn only passing attention in his speech, and all kinds of forms of retaliation were projected in the French Press, some papers even advocating a boycott of the Five-Power Naval Conference, for which the preliminary negotiations were then in progress. In answer to this accusation Lord Cecil replied at a plenary session of the Assembly on September 24th, when he categorically denied that he had ever had the intention of raising again the controversy on trained reserves.

For two days the liveliest of debates raged around the British proposals. The Great Powers, Italy, Japan and France, together with some of the latter's *cortège habituel* (Poland, Yugoslavia and Rumania), opposed the Resolution, and to them was added M. Loudon, President of the Preparatory Commission. Germany and most of the smaller Powers, led by the Scandinavians, supported the British, and M. Loudon, speaking on this occasion as a Dutchman, proceeded to demolish the case which he himself had built up as President of the Commission!

Finally resort was had to the way of compromise and an alternative Resolution the work of that indefatigable pair of compromisors, Dr. Benès and M. Politis, was introduced by the latter, as follows:

"The Assembly, having taken cognizance with interest of the work of the last session of the Preparatory Commission for the Disarmament Conference;

"Cordially welcoming the prospect of an early agreement between the Naval Powers with a view to the reduction and limitation of naval armaments, which agreement may enable the Preparatory Commission to secure general agreement on the methods to be adopted for the reduction and limitation of naval armaments;

"Taking note of the statements made in the Third Committee with regard to the principles on which, in the opinion of various delegations, the final work of the Preparatory Commission should be based;

"Noting that the solution of the disarmament problem can be attained only through mutual concessions by Governments in regard to the proposals they prefer;

"Urging, in accordance with its resolution of 1928, the necessity of accomplishing the first step towards the reduction and limitation of armaments with as little delay as possible;

"Confidently hopes that the Preparatory Commission will shortly be able to resume the work interrupted at its last session, with a view to framing a preliminary Draft Convention as soon as possible for the reduction and limitation of land, naval and air armaments;

"And decides that the Minutes of the plenary meetings of the Assembly and of the Third Committee shall be communicated to the Preparatory Commission for any necessary action."

Had Lord Cecil pressed his own resolution to a vote it is possible that he might have carried it by a small majority, but he admitted that this would be completely unsatisfactory and out of keeping with the spirit of the League. He, therefore, withdrew his own motion in favour of that of M. Politis, which was unanimously adopted.

In so doing he incurred further odium, this time from the zealots of his own cause, who would have liked him to press his original proposal to a division, but Lord Cecil considered— and in this view it is important to note that Count Bernstorff concurred—that the Politis Resolution, though somewhat vaguely worded, gave him all the scope he desired at the forth-coming meeting of the Commission, whenever that might be. He so interpreted the Resolution to the Third Committee in accepting it, saying that "his Majesty's Government desire to have liberty to present their views on these subjects; that liberty is now preserved." He further emphasized this view in speaking on the Resolution at a plenary meeting of the Assembly. "I do not think it (the Resolution) shuts my mouth. It does not preclude me from raising these questions, as I shall raise them in the Preparatory Commission."

Thus at the close of 1929 the stage was set ready for the curtain to ring up on the final session of the Preparatory Commission as soon as the conclusion of the naval agreement should complete the list of properties. But when the curtain did rise it was found that though the wings of the scenery remained the same, the back-cloth had been changed in the interval.

(c) THE THIRD DRAFT, 1930

During the interval between the Tenth and Eleventh Assemblies (September 1929—September 1930) no more important event occurred in Europe than the death of Herr Gustav Stresemann on October 3, 1929. With his death there closed a period of European history and a new phase opened, that in which we now live and of which we can at the moment only appreciate the gravity. The Stresemann period began with his Chancellor-ship in August–September 1923, when he initiated the Policy of Fulfilment in calling off the campaign of passive resistance in the Ruhr. During the seven years through which he guided German foreign policy, Herr Stresemann kept before him two great primary objects—the speedy evacuation of the Rhineland, and the honouring by the former Allied Powers of the disarma-ment pledges which they had given to Germany in the Covenant of the League and in the Treaty of Versailles.

To this end he agreed first to the Dawes and later to the Young Plan, though he may in his own heart have doubted

Germany's capacity to carry out in full the obligations of the latter. To this end he proposed the Locarno Agreement, accepting as definite Germany's western frontier and renouncing war as a method of altering her eastern border. To this end he persuaded a somewhat reluctant and suspicious Germany to enter the League of Nations even after the initial rebuff of March 1926, saying that through the League alone could come disarmament and the protection of minorities.

Throughout his tenure of office Herr Stresemann preached to his countrymen the gospel that fulfilment would beget fulfilment.[1] He lived to see the achievement of one of his dreams. The evacuation of the Rhineland was achieved at The Hague Conference of August 1929, six years before the ultimate period specified in the Treaty of Versailles. The fulfilment of the second dream depends largely upon the result of the Disarmament Conference of February 1932.

The effect of the withdrawal of Herr Stresemann's control from Germany's foreign policy was early perceptible, and was marked by a waning confidence in the League of Nations. The estrangement which had resulted from the first part of the Sixth Session of the Preparatory Commission, though partially counteracted at the Tenth Assembly, had nevertheless gone deep into the heart of the people, who had been wholeheartedly behind Count Bernstorff in his dissociation from the findings of the Commission.

As the year drew on this feeling of distrust became intensified and with it, perhaps as a natural corollary, there arose a great national movement for treaty revision. As this movement gained in popularity so did its chief protagonists the Nazis (National Socialists) gain in power. Throughout Germany there was a stir as of a great awakening, as if the eyes of the German people were at last opened to the futility of the Policy of Fulfilment, the policy which had meant only unilateral fulfilment on the part of Germany. Now, ten years after the Treaty of

---

[1] An account of another phase of Stresemann's foreign policy will be found in *Information on the Reparation Settlement*, by J. W. Wheeler-Bennett and H. Latimer (Allen & Unwin, London, 1930).

Versailles, the disarmament of the Allies was as far away as ever and the League, that agency through which Stresemann had told them justice would come, stood at last revealed in its true form, a covering for the Anglo-French Entente, a "joint stock company for administering the loot of Versailles." So at least it seemed to the disgruntled Germans, and the flames of discontent were fanned by Hitler and his Nazis.

Nor was the situation improved by the failure of the London Naval Conference to reach a Five-Power Agreement.[1] For, whereas, on the basis of the Transactional Proposal the three Ocean Powers, Great Britain, the United States and Japan, reached an agreement on limitation, the two Continental Powers, France and Italy, partly due to the refusal of the first to disarm further without guarantees of security, and partly on account of the latter's demand of parity with France, had refused to be bound by the Treaty and remained as before in a state of rivalry. In this way the naval dispute which had originated in 1927 between Great Britain and France and had passed, as a result of the Geneva Conference and the Anglo-French Naval Compromise, into Anglo-American relations, now took fresh form as between France and Italy, and seemed to intensify the jealous rivalry which already existed between these two States.

To meet the state of European uneasiness thus produced M. Briand proposed in May 1930 a United States of Europe based primarily upon a political system outside the League of Nations. This was immediately diagnosed by many as a last throw on the part of France to secure a general acceptance of the *status quo* created by the Peace Treaties, and it was accorded, on the whole, a lukewarm, if not actually adverse, reception. It had, however, the effect of crystallizing into definite form much of the loose thought which had been circulating around Europe. Italy at once declared herself as the leader of the revisionist *bloc*, and rallied about her the States of the former Quadruple Alliance (Germany, Austro–Hungary, Turkey and Bulgaria) and a motley following which included the U.S.S.R., Greece and

---

[1] See below, pp. 194–205, etc.

Albania. France as the leading opponent of revision was supported by her faithful adherents, Belgium and Poland, together with the States of the Little Entente, though of those Rumania showed an unsettling tendency towards an Italian orientation.

In the late summer of 1930, therefore, Europe was sharply divided, if not into armed camps, at least into two well-defined and antagonistic schools of thought, and when the Eleventh Assembly met in September it did so under the shadow of the forthcoming German general elections. The campaign which preceded the voting was marked by a bitter feeling of resentment against France. Of the twenty-four parties of all shades of political opinion which went to the poll, all, without exception, from Communists to Nazis, placed Treaty revision in the forefront of their programmes. On September 14th there came the amazing news that Herr Hitler's National Socialists, the extreme Right, had increased their representation in the Reichstag from 12 to 107 seats and were in fact the second largest party in the House.

Considering the tenseness of the European situation at the moment and the emphasis which many of the delegates in the general discussion laid on the urgent need for some effective action in the matter of disarmament, that question gave rise to less actual discussion in the Third Committee of the Assembly than usual. Indeed, there was little to discuss. The Preparatory Commission had not met since the last Assembly, though it stood convened for November 6th. The Agreement reached at the London Conference between the three Ocean Powers had been communicated to the Secretary-General of the League by the President of the Conference, Mr. Ramsay MacDonald, while the President of the Preparatory Commission, M. Loudon, had kept in personal touch with the Conference whilst it was in session.

Such discussion as there was in the Third Committee looked beyond the work of the resumed Sixth Session and turned rather on the date on which the actual Disarmament Conference should be summoned. Count Bernstorff, consistently both with

the views he has expressed throughout the past four years and
with the present sentiments of Germany, pressed for the Conference to be called before the end of 1931. With a bitterness
which characterized much of the German attitude towards the
Eleventh Assembly and for which the reason is not far to seek,
Count Bernstorff recalled to the Committee how disarmament
had been postponed year after year and how the Preparatory
Commission, after four years work, had achieved virtually
nothing. He brought forward a resolution calling on the Council
to convene the Conference before the close of 1931.

Lord Cecil replied to the German resolution with a repetition
of the arguments which British representatives had used since
1926. He deprecated undue haste which might by its own
precipitancy jeopardize the success it so anxiously sought. He
emphasized the need for further preparation, saying with truth
that for the Conference to meet and fail would be much worse
than for it not to meet at all. He would not have the Committee
recommend any date at all for the Conference, but would leave
it entirely to the Council to summon it at such time as it saw fit.

Caution won the day, though many of the representatives
sympathized with German anxiety for action, and the Committee
adopted the following resolution, which was subsequently
endorsed by the Assembly:

"The Assembly,

"Has noted with satisfaction the results obtained at the London
Conference and communicated to it by a letter from the President of
the Conference dated the 21st of April, 1930:

"It considers that the results are of a nature to facilitate a general
agreement on the occasion of the next meeting of the Preparatory
Commission regarding the methods to be applied in the matter of the
reduction and limitation of naval armaments.

"It trusts that negotiations, pursued in a spirit of conciliation and
mutual confidence, and with the determination to arrive at practical
solutions, will make it possible to complete and extend the work of
the Naval Conference.

"The Assembly accordingly expresses the conviction that, during
its session next November, the Preparatory Commission will be able
to finish the drawing up of a preliminary Draft Convention and will
thus enable the Council to convene, as soon as possible, a Conference
for the reduction and limitation of armaments.

"The Assembly decides that the proceedings and the report of the Assembly regarding disarmament shall be forwarded to the Preparatory Commission."

Before passing to a consideration of the work of the second part of the Sixth Session of the Preparatory Commission, it is necessary to take note of a series of speeches which occurred in the Reichstag and Chambre des Députés during the course of the meeting of the Commission. These speeches by leaders of Germany and France demonstrate the complete divergence of opinion which exists in the two countries on the question of Allied obligations to disarm. The speeches themselves form the political background against which the more technical discussion of the Commission stands out, and go far to explain the success and failure of that body's efforts.

This exchange of political salvos began on October 29th, when the Foreign Affairs Committee of the Reichstag passed a strongly worded resolution calling upon the Government to use the utmost pressure to secure the disarmament of other States in equal measure with Germany.[1] This was followed by a three-day debate on foreign affairs in the French Chamber on November 12th, 13th and 14th, during which M. Briand had to withstand a very formidable attack on his policy.

One of the first speakers, M. Franklin Bouillon, made no secret of his belief that Germany was guilty of bad faith in her relations with the ex-Allies. After pointing out that, in any case, the disarmament of other nations could only follow on the complete fulfilment by Germany of her obligations in that respect, he quoted figures to show that her expenditure on armaments was out of all proportion to the size of the army allowed to her, and actually constituted a violation of the Treaty. For example, for an army limited to 100,000 men she had spent: in 1924, 2,700 million francs; in 1926, 4,032 millions; and in 1930, 4,728 millions; while the cost of maintaining a navy with a personnel limited to 15,000 had risen from 600 million francs in 1924 to 1,200 millions in the current year. He also stated

[1] The greater part of the following account of the speeches in the Reichstag and the Chamber is taken from the issue of the *Bulletin of International News* for December 4, 1930 (Vol. VII, No. 12).

that credits had been voted for 1,952 guns and for 20,000 machine-guns, though the numbers of these had been strictly limited by the Treaty to 255 and 1,926 respectively. She had hidden her armaments expenditure in all sorts of ways, and was actually spending more on military preparations than France. Referring also to the results of the German General Election, M. Franklin Bouillon said that there were two Germanies, the prudent and the cynical, but both were united in their determination to repudiate their obligations under the Young Plan, to revise treaties and frontiers, to demand the disarmament of France, to remilitarize the Rhine, and to deny responsibility for the War.

An equally bitter tone characterized the speech of M. Scapini, who complained that to the concessions made by France Germany had replied by the double-faced policy denounced by the previous speaker. There could be no question of disarmament until the two prerequisites, arbitration and security, had been achieved, and of that there was as yet no sign. The General Act had been signed by only four nations, and as for the organization of sanctions, France was the only country which had not backed out when it came to the point. The League of Nations had, in fact, done nothing to "organize peace on solid foundations," the Kellogg Treaty had three serious *lacunæ*, and when M. Briand had published his plan for a Federal Union of Europe it had at once been revealed that the Governments were divided into two camps, which he described as revisionist and anti-revisionist. M. Briand, he concluded, was undoubtedly sincere, but he had been duped.

M. Briand, who replied on November 13th, was mainly concerned to show that any reversal of his policy was impossible. Germany was a nation of 60 million intelligent people, and a Foreign Minister who did not seek to diminish the danger of such a neighbour by agreements and understandings would fail in his duty. The Versailles Treaty had been made in very different conditions, and they could not now prevent countries which it affected from using its provisions. To tear up treaties would lead to social as well as international chaos, and if he were to go back to the old alliances it would mean the end of the League; it would mean tearing up the Covenant.[1]

In the small hours of November 14th, the Premier, M. Tardieu, closed the debate with a trenchant commentary on his colleague's policy of conciliation.[2] He laid special emphasis on the point that on the subject of disarmament France was in a conflict both of doctrine and of fact with the German Government. As regards the first point, that of principle, Germany maintained that the Treaty had imposed on the ex-Allies the obligation to disarm at the same time as herself. France maintained, on the contrary, that it had obliged Germany to disarm first, *"cette réduction étant considérée par les ex-Alliés comme susceptible d'entrainer pas la suite leur propre désarmement."*[3]

The Premier went on to warn Germany that if she continued, at Geneva, to emphasize the doctrine that both countries had been placed by the Treaty under the same obligation as regards disarmament, the French Government would be compelled to ask the Council of the League, on the basis of Article 213, to order an investigation of the military establishment of Germany, which, he believed, had in all probability developed far beyond the limits laid down by the Treaty. He also reminded the German Government that Article 19 of the Covenant, providing for the possiblity of a revision of any treaty, required unanimity for its application, and as to treaty revision generally, the mere alteration of frontiers would not cure Europe's present troubles; on the contrary, to throw the frontiers into the melting-pot, to reopen the endless ethnological researches of 1919 would be fatal. It would be followed by war and revolution.

To this statement the speech of Herr Curtius on November 20th was a formal reply.[4] The German Foreign Minister began

[1] For M. Briand's speech, see *Documents on International Affairs*, 1930, edited by J. W. Wheeler-Bennett (Oxford, 1931), pp. 80–88.
[2] For M. Tardieu's speech, see *ibid.*, pp. 89–92.
[3] It is interesting to note that a week later the *Temps* referred to the Premier as having here used the words, *"cette réduction étant considérée librement par les ex-Alliés comme un moyen de parvenir à une réduction des armements,"* while in its own comment on the speech that paper stated that the position was that the obligatory disarmament of Germany was *"considéré comme susceptible de faciliter la réduction des armements des autres nations."*
[4] For Herr Curtius's speech, see *Documents on International Affairs*, 1930, pp. 94–98.

by assuring foreign opinion that it need have no apprehension
that the Government contemplated departing from the Treaty
limits, or putting the German signature of the Young Plan in
question. He then turned to the question of direct relations
with France, and said that a Franco-German understanding
was a matter of the greatest moment for German and for
European policy, but they had not neglected to cultivate
relations with the Powers outside the circle of Versailles, such
as the United States and Soviet Russia. They aimed at no
system of alliances after the pre-War pattern, "but when
opposing views emerge between Governments about the guiding
principles of international policy, we shall always be found on
the side of those who are for equality of rights and a progressive
development of affairs."

This brought Herr Curtius to the question of disarmament.
While, he said, Germany logically and steadily pursued a
straight course, and in doing so found the increasing accord
and support of other countries, the French Government
"apparently intends completely to change course. It is leaving,
to judge from the words of its head, the ground which, since
1919, has formed the basis of all disarmament negotiations.
How else can I interpret it when from so authoritative a
French source it is maintained that there can be no question of
a German Treaty right to general disarmament; that the obligation of the conquered is a matter for the free choice of the
victor?"

Having quoted, amongst other documents, the Locarno
Treaties and the Covenant of the League, Herr Curtius said:
"If the wording of treaties has any meaning all this can
only mean that, after Germany has fulfilled the preliminary
condition, the prescribed sequel, general disarmament, must
follow."

He then referred to the negotiations preliminary to the
signature of the Versailles Treaty, and in especial to the statement handed to the German representatives in Paris in reply
to their observations, to which reference has been made above,
and said: "It there stands clearly and in binding form that

the object of German disarmament is the bringing about of a general process of disarmament."

It was all so clear, he continued, that it should not be necessary even to recall that the official French representatives at Geneva had constantly affirmed these principles and admitted, not only the moral, but also the legal obligation of France and the other States to disarm. He could not think that the French Prime Minister, now that the disarmament problem was pressing to its final decision, would strike at the basis of all negotiations of the last ten years. It was not only a question of the legal claim of Germany, but of one of the most vital tasks of the League, whose future and very existence would be endangered if it proved incapable of solving the disarmament problem. Herr Curtius said he could not believe that Germany's claim would be seriously disputed. Never, even in the time of absolute military might, when France and her Allies dictated the Versailles Treaty, had the despotism of the victor demanded that the one-sided disarmament of Germany should be perpetuated. The raising of such demands twelve years after peace would have incalculable results. "We demand the early convocation of the General Disarmament Conference itself, at which every country will have to show itself in its true colours, and where the final decision will be taken whether Germany's claim to a disarmament which will yield equal security for all is to be acknowledged or not."

The tenour of these speeches on the part of responsible statesmen illustrates startlingly the lack of confidence and understanding without which no disarmament agreement is possible. The tone, as will be seen later, was reflected inside the Preparatory Commission, and it is scarcely surprising, therefore, that the Commission could not achieve a more effective agreement.

The position at the opening of the second part of the Sixth Session of the Preparatory Commission was one of credit and debit. On the one hand, the respective dangers of naval rivalry between Great Britain and the United States, Great Britain and Japan, and Japan and the United States had been settled, or at least appreciably lessened, by the London Naval Treaty of April 22, 1930. On the other hand, the fact that this Treaty had originally been intended as a Five-Power instrument and had been emasculated by the inability of France and Italy to compose their differences, took much from the moral effect of the agreement; more especially as all subsequent attempts to bring about a Franco-Italian *rapprochement* had proved fruitless.

A more alarming factor was the changed attitude of the German delegation. Already in 1929 German dissatisfaction with the lack of achievement of the Commission had been voiced, and warnings had been given of the possible effect of this continued policy of delay upon the German people.[1] In September 1930 these warnings had unfortunately been proved fully justified and the presence of 107 Nazi deputies in the Reichstag was the outward and visible sign of German discontent and disappointment both as regards disarmament and reparations. Thus, although the *personnel* of both the German Government and the delegation at Geneva remained unchanged, Dr. Brüning, Herr Curtius and Count Bernstorff were now fighting a political battle on two fronts and a change on the Berlin front made it inevitable, but none the less regrettable, that they should pursue a less conciliatory policy on the Geneva front.

In the case of Count Bernstorff it was a losing battle he was fighting. Confronted at Geneva with the impossibility of securing for his country an equality with other Powers in the matter of disarmament, and faced with the knowledge that he dared not give German consent to even a draft agreement which did not give Germany this equality, he was placed in the most unenviable position. History of the past twelve years offered the fate which overtook Erzberger in the Black Forest and Rathenau in the suburbs of Berlin, as examples of the penalty meted out to those suspected of bartering away Germany's honour; and apart from this personal threat there was the added danger that acceptance of an unsatisfactory Convention might provide the excuse for an attempted Nazi *coup d'état*.

[1] See above, p. 73.

These considerations resulted in the adoption by the German delegation of an obstructive policy of endless *caveats* and reservations. And it is important to note that even this was regarded as not sufficiently in keeping with the prevailing spirit of the times, since on December 2nd the Foreign Affairs Committee of the Reichstag adopted a Nazi resolution calling upon the Government to recall Count Bernstorff from Geneva. Such a resolution, though it had no effective force, was an indication of the state of mind at home of which the German representative had to take account. A state of mind that was not fully appreciated either by many of the delegates at the Commission or by the public opinion of the various countries.

Perhaps the most important political development of the session was the new alignment of Italy, who now appeared openly for the first time as the leader of a minority *bloc* composed of herself, Germany and the U.S.S.R., with the fluctuating support of such other disgruntled revisionist States as Bulgaria and Turkey. This *volte face* from the policy of 1929, which had manifested itself during the Eleventh Assembly when Italy had begun to vote with Germany, was explained by the Italian delegate as actuated by the realization of the need for progress in the work of disarmament, but was generally attributed to the widening breach in Franco-Italian relations.

It is not proposed to give, here, a detailed account of the discussion of the latter part of the Sixth Session, but to present as clearly as possible the results achieved by the Commission.[1]

When the second part of the Sixth Session opened on November 3, 1930, it was agreed on the suggestion of Lord Cecil that the texts of Articles adopted at the readings of 1927 and 1929 might be reconsidered should Governments desire to reopen questions already decided. In this way the door was left open for further debate on the contentious questions of trained reserves, direct limitation of land war material and the method of budgetary limitation.

[1] The text of the Draft Convention forms an appendix to this book (see page 366). A most admirable discussion of the work of the Session is to be found in Professor Toynbee's *Survey of International Affairs, 1930* (Oxford University Press, 1931), Part I, A.

TRAINED RESERVES

Count Bernstorff made an effort to reopen this question and to secure a reversal of the Commission's decision of 1929[1] by proposing the limitation of the size of the annual contingent as well as the period of service for conscript armies. This proposal was rejected by a vote of 12 to 6 with 14 abstentions,[2] and the draft adopted in 1929 was adhered to. CountBernstorff's comment on this decision was that without some such limitation the Draft Convention "would not be worth the ink with which it is written."

Thus the Draft Convention limits only the effectives on active service together with formations organized on a military basis. This limitation is extended to all three arms, the United States and Great Britain having withdrawn in 1930 the objection which they had advanced in 1927 and 1929 against the limitation of naval and air effectives.

Articles II–IV, which provide for the limitation of effectives, are followed by blank tables in which the totals of the forces of the three arms are to be filled in at the Disarmament Conference. There are in addition other provisions (Articles V–IX) which apply only to effectives recruited by conscription. A maximum period of service, which no country is permitted to exceed, is stipulated.[3]

In view of their decision, the German Government made a general objection to Part I of the Convention on the ground that "the stipulations do not provide . . . for a reduction or limitation of trained reserves who, after having completed their service, continue to be registered and liable for military service."

---

[1] See above, p. 73.

[2] One of the characteristic features of this Session of the Commission was the large number of abstentions in the votes. It is difficult to know whether to attribute this disinclination to register an opinion to an inability on the part of the delegates to make up their minds or a desire to keep an entirely free hand for the Disarmament Conference itself. Professor Toynbee suggests as a third alternative reason the fact that the discussion was often extremely confused, and that some delegates may well have been in doubt as to which amendment was being put to the vote. (See *Survey for 1930*, p. 103.)

[3] See *The Draft Treaty for the World Disarmament Conference*, Foreign Policy Association, Information Series, Vol. VI, No. 25, February 18, 1931.

LIMITATION OF MATERIAL

1. *Land Armaments*

It will be remembered that in 1929 there had been three conflicting views on the subject of limitation of material. The German delegation had favoured the method of direct limitation as imposed upon Germany by the Treaty of Versailles; the British, on the other hand, had advocated the principle of budgetary limitation, but this had met with uncompromising opposition from the United States delegate, who declared that under no circumstances whatever could his country accept a control of its expenditure.[1] Mr. Gibson, however, put forward the third alternative method of limitation by means of the fullest publicity possible, and this proposal was adopted by the Commission somewhat reluctantly. A protest against this decision was raised by Lord Cecil in the Tenth Assembly (September 1929) and the right to reopen the question was secured.

This position still maintained in 1930, and Count Bernstorff earnestly pleaded the justice of his contention that what the Allies had imposed on Germany they should accept themselves. Though warmly supported by the Italians, the United States, the Soviet Union, Turkey and others, the proposal was rejected, the following resolution being adopted:

"The majority of the Commission associates itself with the principle of limitation by budgetary methods of land war material, while recognizing that certain members would prefer the direct method by specific enumeration and that certain members would desire to see some combination of the two methods."[2]

This resolution was finally incorporated in principle as Article X of the Convention:

---

[1] See above, p. 72.
[2] The instance of the new German "pocket-battleship" *Deutschland* was used by Lord Cecil in pointing his argument in favour of budgetary limitation. These 10,000-ton battleships, he pointed out, were infinitely stronger than the 10,000-ton cruisers of other Powers, and yet complied with all the conditions laid down by the Treaty of Versailles. By unlimited expenditure Germany had been able to produce a more effective fighting unit. He pointed out that even if tonnage and effectives were limited, there yet remained competition in expenditure. Count Bernstorff at once made a spirited defence of the German policy in constructing the "pocket" class of fighting vessel.

"The annual expenditure of each High Contracting Party on the upkeep, purchase and manufacture of war material of land armaments shall be limited to the figure laid down for such Party and in accordance with the conditions prescribed in the annex . . . to this Article."

The conditions referred to were to be drawn up by a Committee of Budgetary Experts, appointed by the President of the Preparatory Commission.[1] It should be noted that the United

[1] This Committee held two sessions at Geneva in December 1930 and February 1931, at the latter of which it adopted a report of which the following is the official summary:

"In accordance with the instructions of the Preparatory Commission for the Disarmament Conference, the Experts have established a model statement of expenditure on national defence. This model statement is intended to show in simple and comprehensible form, from an international point of view, both as regards publicity and as regards limitation, the military expenditure of all countries, notwithstanding the diversity of their methods of presenting their budget and accounts.

"The report constitutes a reply to certain preoccupations stressed by the Preparatory Commission which concern the necessity:

(a) of limiting the total expenditure in question;
(b) of taking into account the diversity of methods of presentation and discussion of the budgets customary in the various countries;
(c) of adapting the methods of limitation contemplated to the possible differences in the purchasing power of the various currencies with particular reference to the cost of war material;
(d) of determining the condition under which the carrying forward of credits from one budgetary year to the next or following years might be effected.

"The Committee proposes that, without prejudice to the budget estimates of the various States, limitation and publicity should be based on the payments made in the course of each financial year.

"The Committee had endeavoured to suggest a system which would enable the various Governments to agree to a fixation of their limits at a level corresponding as closely as possible to realities.

"In the first place, therefore, it recommends that the limits should apply to the average expenditure of four consecutive years rather than they should be measured on the requirements of a peak year, on the understanding that the expenditure of one year should not exceed a certain percentage to be fixed by agreement for each country.

"The Committee noted that statements of credits voted by Parliament would have no direct bearing upon the internal practice of each country as regards the limitation of expenditure, since such limitation should be applied to the payments made each year, whatever might be, from a constitutional point of view, the authorization under which these payments were made.

"The Committee further considered that Governments should not support all the risks of fluctuations in price levels. In this connection, it has submitted a system which would allow of a readjustment of the limits fixed in the event of a considerable change in prices.

"In view of the difficulty of giving an accurate definition of expenditure affecting the armaments level in the different countries, the Committee proposes entire publicity in doubtful cases. In its opinion these measures

States has not withdrawn her opposition to this method of limitation and has entered a general reservation regarding this Article.

2. *Naval Armaments*

With regard to naval material the method adopted on the proposal of the Powers signatory to the London Agreement (Great Britain and the Dominions, the United States and Japan) was on the principle of direct limitation of tonnage. The system followed very closely that agreed upon in London and there are annexed three blank Tables, viz. Table I, specifying tonnage; Table II, specifying distribution by categories; and Table III, specifying transfer from one category to another.[1] For purposes of illustration only (this fact is emphasized in the Commission's report) the figures of the Washington and London Agreements were inserted.

In the matter of expenditure it was agreed on the proposal of Lord Cecil to apply the same method of budgetary limitation which had already been adopted in the case of land armaments. When, however, the United States repeated its objection on this point, both the British and Italian delegations made reservations to the effect that their final acceptance depended on the attitude adopted by "the other Naval Powers." The Italians also made a general reservation, saying that they could not agree finally to any specific method of naval limitation before "all the Powers had agreed on the proportions and levels of maximum tonnage"; this was generally interpreted to mean that Italy's agreement must be made dependent on her arriving at an understanding with France.

would contribute to inspiring confidence in the system of financial limitation.

"The Committee has tried to indicate as fairly as possible both the technical shortcomings of the system it has suggested, and also the technical advantages which are inherent in that system. If the Governments are not only fully aware of those advantages, but also on their guard against the difficulties, and prepared to apply the system loyally, the Committee is unanimous in considering that from a technical point of view a satisfactory working of the system can be obtained."

[1] In order to meet the objections of the lesser naval Powers, it was agreed in principle that they should be entitled to more freedom in the matter of transfer than those Powers with larger navies.

3. *Air Armaments*

One of the most unsatisfactory aspects of the Convention is its provision for the limitation of air material. The method to be employed is the direct limitation by number of aircraft and horse-power. Dirigibles are to be limited by number, total horse-power and total volume. A British proposal for the application of the system of budgetary limitation for material in this arm was negatived by six votes to five with thirteen abstentions, and this drew forth the criticism from Lord Cecil that without such limitation "the air arm, potentially the most destructive to civilization, will be the most free for competitive international development."

Count Bernstorff also protested against the omission from the Convention of any limitation of stocks of aircraft in reserve and aircraft which had not yet been assembled. There was nothing to prevent countries from increasing their stocks in reserve without any limit.

A further disappointment was contained in that part of the Draft Convention referring to the relation between civil and military aircraft. No prohibition is placed on Governments as to the construction or adaptation of commercial machines for military purposes, but the Draft merely prohibited them from encouraging or "prescribing" military features in civilian aircraft and from subsidizing "air lines principally established for military purposes."

BUDGETARY LIMITATION

In spite of the opposition of both the United States and Germany the Commission agreed upon the application of the method of budgetary expenditure to the *total* expenditure on land, sea and air forces, including *personnel*, maintenance, etc. as well as to expenditure on military and naval material. The actual drafting of the provisions was postponed until after the Committee of Budgetary Experts already referred to had reported.[1]

---

[1] For Summary of the Report, see above, p. 92.

EXCHANGE OF INFORMATION

In an attempt to implement paragraph 6 of Article VIII of the Covenant,

"The Members of the League undertake to interchange full and fresh information as to the scale of their armaments, their military, naval and air programmes and the condition of such of their industries as are adaptable to warlike purposes,"

the Fourth Assembly had in 1923 authorized the publication of an annual volume entitled *The Armaments Year Book of the League of Nations*. Useful as this publication is, it is quite valueless as a method of comparison of armaments since few States have ever made complete returns, particularly in the matter of war stocks, the number of tanks, guns, etc.[1]

At the final session of the Preparatory Commission, Germany, supported by Italy and the Netherlands, urged the fullest possible degree of publicity. As opposed to this, the French proposed that publicity should be given only to expenditure for the upkeep, purchase and manufacture of land war material and despite the fact that this provision would compel no publicity in the matter of stocks of material in existence when the Convention was signed it was adopted.

The Draft Convention, therefore, makes provision for the exchange of information showing:

1. The total number of effectives in the land, naval and air forces.[2]
2. The number of youths who have received compulsory preparatory training.[3]
3. The period of compulsory service in the case of conscripted forces.
4. The total expenditure on upkeep, purchase and manufacture of land and naval (but not air) war material.
5. Details concerning new warships laid down.
6. Details concerning armed merchant vessels.
7. Numbers and total horse-power of aeroplanes and number, total horse-power and total volume of airships in service (but not in reserve).
8. The number and total horse-power of civil aeroplanes registered by

---

[1] In 1930 the only State to submit a return of figures of land war material in service was the Netherlands.
[2] Differentiation to be made between those at home and those overseas.
[3] This provision was insisted on by France and strongly opposed by Italy.

each country and the amounts expended on civil aviation by Governments and local authorities.

9. Total expenditure on land, sea and air armaments (but not total air material or the air material in reserve).

(No provision was made for the exchange of information on the stocks of war material.)

Count Bernstorff protested against the incompleteness of these provisions and the German delegation made reservations calling attention to the failure of the Convention to include publicity for trained reserves, the size of the annual contingent, the total of land and air material and the non-floating material of navies.

CHEMICAL WARFARE

In the matter of the chemical warfare arm the text of the single Article agreed upon in 1929[1] was finally adopted in 1930, to the effect that the contracting parties reciprocally agree to abstain from the use in war of asphyxiating, poisonous or similar gases, and of all analogous liquid substances or processes. They also undertake to refrain from all bacteriological methods of warfare.

PERMANENT DISARMAMENT COMMISSION

This question of control and supervision had, from the earliest sessions of Sub-Committee "A" in 1926,[2] been a matter of controversy. The French were convinced that without some form of supervision the Convention would be useless and had included plans for a Commission of Control in their 1927 Draft.[3] On the other hand, the Americans had pointed out that any form of supervision, particularly if under the League, would be unacceptable to the United States.

In view, however, of the modified plans for the creation of the Commission put forward in 1930, Mr. Gibson, on behalf of the United States, withdrew his objections and voted for the text as finally adopted.

It was agreed, therefore, that a Permanent Disarmament Commission should be established at Geneva composed of members appointed by their Governments but not representing

[1] See above, p. 73.   [2] See above, p. 49.   [3] See above, p. 58.

them.[1] The duties of the Commission were to follow the application of the Convention; to collate information on disarmament and present an annual report to the Council of the League. In addition, it would have authority to hear complaints on the application of the Convention and to examine applications for temporary supervision of the Convention.

THE RIGHT OF SUSPENSION

As in the cases of the Washington and London Naval Treaties, the Draft Convention was provided with a safeguarding clause which provided for the temporary suspension of the obligations incurred by signatory States in the event of a "change of circumstances" arising which in the opinion of a contracting party constituted "a menace to its national security." The State might in the circumstances suspend temporarily all or any of the provisions of the Convention except those expressly designed to apply in case of war, on condition that it notified all the other contracting parties as to the extent of such suspension and of the change of circumstances which had necessitated it. Provision is also made for reduction of the armed forces of the States concerned to the level agreed upon in the Convention when normal conditions had been re-established.

THE POLITICAL ASPECT

Article LIII is more than any other the storm centre of the Draft Convention. It consists of two paragraphs, the first, the outcome of British proposals to ensure that the undertakings given in the Washington and London Treaties should in no way be diminished; the second, representing the only condition upon which France would agree to the Convention. The text of the Article is as follows:

"The present Convention shall not affect the provisions of previous treaties under which certain of the High Contracting Parties have

---

[1] In view of the controversy over the number of members of the Commission —whether all States signatory to the Convention were entitled to nominate members or only certain States, and, if so, which were to enjoy that right— the Preparatory Commission agreed to ask the Disarmament Conference to take a final decision on the question.

agreed to limit their land, sea or air armaments and have thus fixed in relation to one another their respective rights and obligations in this connection.

"The following High Contracting Parties . . . signatories to the said treaties, declare that the limits fixed for their armaments under the present Convention are accepted by them in relation to the obligations referred to in the preceding paragraph, the maintenance of such obligations being for them an essential condition for the observance of the present Convention."

Any doubt that might have existed in the German mind that the Article did not constitute a reaffirmation of Germany's acceptance of the armament obligation imposed upon her at Versailles, and further that such reaffirmation was the price of France's co-operation in the work of the coming Conference, must have been removed by the following words spoken by M. Massigli on November 27th. In speaking of Article LIII he said:

"When the Conference meets, a certain number of Powers including France will submit proposals in figures for the limitation of their armaments. These proposals will be calculated in relation to a given situation; they will correspond to a given degree of security. In determining this situation, this degree of security, the régime which results from the strict application of the military clauses of the Peace Treaties forms an essential factor. . . . By the text (Article LIII) the Powers concerned define the conditions under which they accept the figures for limitation to be inserted, in regard to themselves, in the Convention. It is a reservation, if you will, but one of which the other signatory Powers will be cognisant in advance and which will thus become for those Powers who submit it an essential condition of the obligation they accept."

The hand is the hand of Briand, but the voice is the voice of Poincaré, Clemenceau and Foch.

At no time could a German delegate allow a statement of this importance to go unchallenged. At the actual moment, when none knew the force or strength of the Nazi movement, when none could tell what effect such a statement might have in Berlin, it was inevitable that Count Bernstorff should counter M. Massigli with a final profession of the German disarmament faith. That he did so with such bitterness is regrettable but not incomprehensible since he knew that defeat was inescapable and the responsibility of repudiating the work of the Preparatory Commission would lie at his door. His answer was made in these words, referring to his declaration in 1929:[1]

"Events which have happened during the present session have abundantly convinced me that this formal declaration was justified. In the draft in its present form, the idea of genuine disarmament, as regards land armaments, only survives in the title.

"If the majority of the Commission would only realize this deplorable result of its five years' work, they would avoid placing this artificial work in relationship with the earlier Treaties. . . . It may be that some delegates here are under the impression that my Government might be induced to accede to a Convention which, instead of leading to genuine disarmament, would merely serve as a cloak for the actual state of the world's land armaments, or—even worse—would make it possible to increase these armaments. That in my opinion would be tantamount to renewing the German signature to the disarmament clause of the Treaty of Versailles.

"I beg you, Gentlemen, to renounce any such illusions . . . you are well acquainted with the conditions which the German Government consider essential if this Convention is to be regarded as discharging the obligations incurred by other nations towards disarmed Germany. . . . We consider that Germany cannot recognize anything as a first Disarmament Convention unless the solution which it provides is just and equitable and pays regard to the security of all States."

All the German disillusionment and weary waiting for twelve years, and all the personal disappointment at the failure of the five years' work were vibrant in Count Bernstorff's denunciation. But bitterness begets bitterness and Lord Cecil, in his defence of the Draft Convention against Count Bernstorff's allegation that it would not really amount to any limitation or reduction of land armaments, professed himself as astounded that "any serious and responsible person not carried away by passion and prejudice" should have made such a charge. He reproached Count Bernstorff for his lack of co-operation with the Commission and expressed the hope that his attitude did not betoken a studied policy of opposition on the part of the German Government.

The French thesis was strongly supported by the representatives of the Little Entente, Belgium and Poland, the latter being particularly emphatic that his Government considered

[1] See above, p. 73.

"the maintenance and the strict observation of the disarmament obligations incurred by certain Powers in the Peace Treaties of 1919 as a prerequisite condition for the acceptance . . . of the present Convention by other Powers."

A proposal by the Bulgarian delegation to refer the whole matter to the Conference for decision was lost by twelve votes to five, the minority consisting of Italy, Germany, the U.S.S.R., Bulgaria and Turkey, an interesting and significant quintette. The Commission then proceeded to adopt Article LIII. The German delegation thereupon made the following formal reservation:

"That in so far as it (Article LIII) does not refer to the Washington and London Treaties, the German delegation would vote against the Draft Convention as a whole. The draft, as drawn up by the majority of the Preparatory Commission, excludes essential elements from the limitation and reduction of land armaments. Instead of leading to real disarmament, this draft would serve only to conceal the real state of world armaments or would even allow armaments to be increased. To accept it would be tantamount to a renewal of the German signature to the disarmament clause of the Treaty of Versailles."

There was one further disappointment in store for the German delegation before the Preparatory Commission finally closed its labours on December 9, 1930. In pursuance of the anxiety which the German delegates to the Assembly in September 1930 had shown that a definite date should be set for the convening of the Disarmament Conference, Count Bernstorff proposed that the Commission in drawing up its report should recommend that the Conference be called for November 5, 1931. The Commission, however, considered that this would be exceeding its sphere and that the Council must be left a free hand as to the matter of the date.

Accordingly, when the Council met in January 1931 for its sixty-third session, the German Foreign Minister, Dr. Curtius, while reiterating Count Bernstorff's statement that Germany could not accept the Draft Convention unless it was drastically revised, pressed for the summoning of the Conference in November. Once more Germany was unsuccessful in her plea. The Council considered that this would leave too short an interval for preparation and accordingly fixed the date of the opening of the Conference for February 2, 1932.[1]

The Council was also faced at the same session with the question of appointing a President for the Conference. The name of Dr. Benès, Foreign Minister of Czechoslovakia, had been mentioned, but this suggestion proved unacceptable to a number of Powers, notably Italy and Germany, who once more found themselves drawn together by a mutual dislike. The decision in the matter of the President of the Conference was, therefore, postponed until the next session of the Council, which on May 22nd unanimously offered the position to the then British Foreign Secretary, Mr. Arthur Henderson, who, having obtained the approval of his Government, accepted it with satisfaction.

In passing criticism on the Draft Convention it is essential to remember that it *is* a *draft* Convention. It is but a lay figure as yet, a skeleton lacking flesh and blood. In his despatch to the Secretary of State, Lord Cecil made this point clear:

"Until the figures have been filled in," he wrote, "it is impossible to estimate how complete will be the first Disarmament Treaty. All that can be said now is that within the ambit of the present document almost any degree of reduction is possible. Those who choose to assume now that the Conference will fill in figures that would not, in their view, be satisfactory, should reserve their strictures for use, in case of need, at the Conference; their reproaches cannot justly be aimed at the Convention."[2]

This is indeed the best possible defence of the Convention, and yet it is impossible to overlook or gloss over the *lacunæ* in the framework, notably the omission of any provision for including trained reserves in the totals of effectives of conscription armies; the failure to limit directly the material of armies or navies and the failure to limit the cost of material of air forces. On the other hand, the degree of agreement reached is so much greater than might have been expected that there is still room for congratulation, though it must be remembered that such agreement was only secured at the price of the alienation of

[1] This in itself was not too happy a choice, since in the course of the spring and early summer of 1932 Parliamentary elections are due to take place in France, Prussia and Bavaria, and a Presidential election in Germany.
[2] See Cmd. 3757.

Germany and the U.S.S.R.,[1] and also by reason of many abstentions.

The draft of 1930 is of much greater value than that of 1929, if only by virtue of the substitution of the provision for limitation by means of control of expenditure, for the method of reliance upon publicity which had been all that the 1929 draft had been able to achieve. Apart from the acceptance of the principle of budgetary limitation, there are four other main achievements; the acceptance of limitation of the period of service; the agreement to set up a Permanent Disarmament Commission; the agreement to limit the number of effectives in land, sea and air forces and the acceptance of the method of naval limitation embodied in the London Naval Treaty.

Perhaps the kindest comment which can be passed on the Convention is one made in the French Press:

"Ce document a une grande vertu qui est d'exister."

---

[1] Italy, though she refrained from wholesale rejection of the Convention, may be said to regard the document with considerable reserve and cynicism.

B. NAVAL DISARMAMENT

1. THE GENEVA CONFERENCE, 1927

THE refusal of the United States to become a member of the League of Nations and the changed relations between Great Britain and the League which resulted from this refusal are in a large measure responsible for the fact that the limitation of naval armaments (the only field of disarmament in which any degree of success has been attained) has been effected outside the ægis of the League.

In the movement for naval limitation the palm for initiative must be awarded to the United States, and for a variety of reasons. American initiative was inspired partly by the very real and genuine desire for peace which exists in that great country; partly, for a completely contrary reason, because the nationalist movement in America wished to deprive Great Britain of her naval supremacy, and parity achieved by limitation is a cheaper method than parity achieved by out-building; and partly on account of the desire of each Administration in Washington to achieve some notable contribution in international affairs to which it could point with justifiable pride at the next Presidential election.

This last was particularly true of the Republican Party, which, though it repudiated the League of Nations in 1920, had consistently, in accordance with its enunciated doctrine of an Association of Nations and "peace by conference," made endeavours to further the cause of world peace, and this policy was a contributory factor, no less than a dislike of the Anglo-Japanese Alliance and a fear of Japanese Imperialism in China, to the calling of the Washington Conference.

This same influence must not be disregarded in considering the abortive Geneva Conference of 1927. Mr. Coolidge's Administration had hoped to have achieved an international *coup* in bringing the United States into the World Court on the latter's own terms. The Conference of States Members of the Permanent Court of International Justice which had been called in September 1926 to consider the five American reservations to the Court Protocol had accepted all but one of these, but had suggested that the fifth reservation should be the subject of further negotiation. Mr. Coolidge had said in his Armistice Day Speech (1926) at Kansas City that the American reservations must be accepted as they stood or not at all, and the matter was regarded as closed from that time.[1]

Thus it was not altogether surprising that the United States Government should make another excursion into the arena of international politics with a proposal for further limitation of naval armaments, and when that too failed, that it should make a third, and this time a more successful, effort, in the proposal for the renunciation of war.

The position of the United States with regard to naval disarmament had been made perfectly clear at the First Session of the Preparatory Commission in May 1926.[2] At the opening meeting Mr. Gibson, the United States delegate, had repeated the words used by Mr. Coolidge in his Message to Congress of January 4, 1926, when he said, "The general policy of this Government in favour of disarmament and limitation of armament cannot be emphasized too frequently or too strongly. In accordance with that policy any measure having a reasonable tendency to bring about these results should receive our sympathy and support. . . ." After referring to the fortunate situation of the United States as regards land armaments, Mr. Gibson said:

"With respect to naval armament it may be noted that while a substantial part of the programme presented to the Washington Conference by the American Government was realized, no agreement was reached as to the limitation of competitive building of naval craft other than

[1] *New York Times*, November 12, 1926. See also Chapter VIII, "The United States and the World Court," in *Information on the World Court*, by J. W. Wheeler-Bennett and Maurice Fanshawe (Allen & Unwin, 1929).
[2] The following account of the Geneva Three-Power Conference is reprinted from *Naval Disarmament* by Hugh Latimer, published in 1930 by the Royal Institute of International Affairs. Mr. Latimer's account is based on the more detailed narrative included by Professor Toynbee in his *Survey of International Affairs, 1927*, and is the best concise account of the Conference which has been published.—J. W. W.-B.

capital ships and aircraft carriers. The American Government would welcome any steps which might tend to the further limitation of competitive naval construction."

During the discussions which filled the eight days of the Commission's session it became clear that the distinction between political and technical considerations was fictitious and impossible to sustain; for example, the *Questionnaire* submitted by the Council included such matters as the definition of and distinction between offensive and defensive armaments, and it is not surprising, therefore, that no material progress was made towards clearing the ground for the Disarmament Conference, especially when it is remembered that unanimity was necessary for the adoption of all the Commission's decisions.[1] A great deal was done, however, in showing up the real difficulties and, more especially, the fundamental differences between certain countries as to the principle by which naval tonnage should be limited. France, for example, wished for a total tonnage to be fixed without specifying vessel size, whilst Great Britain and the United States wanted the size of vessels fixed in each category. It was mainly the desire to find a solution for this difficulty that actuated President Coolidge in issuing, in February 1927, invitations for the Conference which was eventually held in the following summer. Before dealing with this, however, reference must be made to a speech by Mr. Kellogg, the United States Secretary of State, on August 18, 1926, which gave a clear indication of the intention of his Government to take up the unfinished task of the Washington Conference in the near future. While expressing goodwill towards the Preparatory Commission, Mr. Kellogg referred to Mr. Gibson's proposal of May 18th, and made the following announcement on behalf of the United States:

"The work on limitation of naval craft has only been partly consummated. There has been a limitation of battleships and aircraft

---

[1] For an account of the First Session of the Preparatory Commission, see above, pp. 49, etc.

carriers alone. There still remains the task of limiting other units of naval strength as well, namely, cruisers, destroyers and submarines. . . .

"I have stated before, and I reiterate, that the United States would be glad to co-operate with the other naval Powers in extending the principles of the Washington Treaty to other classes of naval vessels, and I earnestly hope that such a measure may soon be practicable."

The form which this co-operation was to take was made clear the following February when President Coolidge issued his invitations for an international conference for the limitation of naval armament. On the same day, February 10, 1927, he sent a Message to Congress announcing the presentation of the invitations to the Governments of Great Britain, France, Italy and Japan, and explaining the considerations which had led him to take this action. The Washington Conference, he said, had succeeded in imposing a specific tonnage limitation upon capital ships and aircraft carriers, but agreement had not then been found possible with regard to other classes of ships. Every nation had, therefore, been at complete liberty since 1922 to build any number of cruisers, destroyers and submarines, and "it was only to be expected that the spirit of competition, stifled as regards capital ships and aircraft carriers by the Washington Treaty, would sooner or later show itself with regard to the other vessels not limited under the Treaty." Competitive building, in the President's opinion, had not actually begun, but far-reaching building programmes had been adopted by certain Powers, and there had appeared, both in the United States and in other countries, "a sentiment urging naval construction on the ground that such construction is taking place elsewhere. In such sentiments lie the germ of renewed naval competition." The present moment seemed particularly opportune for negotiations for the conclusion of further agreements covering auxiliary vessels, since the "earnest desire of the nations of the world to relieve themselves in as great a measure as possible of the burden of armaments and to avoid the dangers of competition" had been shown by the establishment of the Preparatory Commission. The problem of naval limitation was not regional in character, as were those of the land and air, and could, the President believed, be definitely dealt with by further agreements among the five leading naval Powers, who had already treated it successfully in part. Finally, it would be "a contribution to the success of the preliminary work now going on at Geneva should the great naval Powers themselves agree upon a further definite limitation of naval armament."

In this way the President made it clear that he envisaged the work of the proposed conference as supplementary to and not in any way as duplicating that of the Preparatory Commission and the League organs generally. In the invitations issued to the four other naval Powers the latter were asked whether they were disposed to empower their representatives at the forthcoming meeting of the Preparatory Commission (that of March 1927) to initiate negotiations looking towards an agreement providing for limitation in the classes of vessels not covered by the Washington Treaty. The policy of the United States Government was outlined in the following passage:

"Although hesitating at this time to put forward rigid proposals as regards the ratios of naval strength to be maintained by the different Powers the American Government, for its part, is disposed to accept, in regard to those classes of vessels not covered by the Washington Treaty, an extension of the 5–5–3 ratio as regards the United States, Great Britain and Japan, and to leave to discussion at Geneva the ratios of France and Italy, taking into full account their special conditions and requirements in regard to the types of vessels in question. Ratios for capital ships and aircraft carriers were established by that Treaty, which would not be affected in any way by an agreement covering other classes of ships."[1]

About a week before this invitation was received in London, Mr. Bridgeman, then First Lord of the Admiralty, submitted to the Prime Minister a plan for limitation of armaments on which the Admiralty had been working for some months, with the request that the Prime Minister would bring it before the Cabinet, and, if it were accepted there, would call an international conference to consider it. This plan was later elaborated in detail by Mr. Bridgeman at the Conference at Geneva on June 20, 1927.

[1] Records of Geneva Naval Conference, 1927, U.S. Senate Document, No. 55.

Mr. Coolidge's invitation was accepted by Great Britain and Japan, but refused by France and Italy. The French Government considered the proposal for a conference to be unacceptable because it threatened to compromise the chances of success of the movement for general disarmament, the French thesis being that the problem of naval disarmament could not be isolated from the general problem for separate treatment. It was felt that the authority of the League of Nations might be weakened if the Preparatory Commission were deprived of part of its programme, and one aspect of the general problem discussed by a conference limited to five Powers.

The Italian Government held the same views as to the interdependence of every type of armament, but in addition to this took occasion, in declining the invitation, to point out that Italy's "unfavourable geographical position" made it impossible for her, without serious risk, to accept a binding limitation of naval armaments. Her naval forces were already inadequate, and she was compelled to consider the problem in relation to other Mediterranean Powers whose geographical situation was more favourable and which were "elaborating naval programmes of great strength."

After consulting the Governments of the Dominions, the British Government accepted the invitation in a Note which contained the following statement regarding Great Britain's position:

"The views of His Majesty's Government upon the special geographical position of the British Empire, the length of inter-imperial communications, and the necessity for the protection of its food supplies are well known, and, together with the special conditions and requirements of the other countries invited to participate in the conversations, must be taken into account. His Majesty's Government are nevertheless prepared to consider to what extent the principles adopted at Washington can be carried further, either as regards the ratio in different classes of ships between the various Powers, or in other important ways."

In spite, however, of the refusal of two of the interested Powers it was decided after further consultation to hold a Three-Power Conference at Geneva in June 1927, and, at the request of the other Governments, Italy and France agreed to be represented by observers.

The Conference accordingly opened at Geneva on June 20th and Mr. Hugh Gibson, who headed the American delegation, was elected President.[1] The work began by each party tabling its proposals, the United States coming first. Mr. Gibson outlined his Government's scheme in great detail, the main principle being that the ratios of the Washington Treaty should be extended to apply to auxiliary vessels, which should be divided into four categories. Of these, three, i.e. cruisers, destroyers and submarines, should be subject to limitation, while the fourth would not be limited, but would consist only of vessels of negligible combatant value, "the definition of vessels falling in this class to be subject to technical agreement."

The United States, said Mr. Gibson, was prepared to accept a general programme providing for as low a total tonnage in each class of auxiliary vessels on the basis of the Washington Treaty ratio as would be acceptable to the other Powers. The delegation had come to the Conference with an estimate of what they considered equitable tonnage allocation in the various classes of vessels, but with no rigid quantitative proposals. These tonnage allocations were as follows:

Cruiser class.—Total tonnage limitation: For the British Empire and the United States, 250,000 to 300,000 tons each, and for Japan 150,000 to 180,000 tons.

Destroyer class.—For the British Empire and the United States, 200,000 to 250,000 tons each, and for Japan 120,000 to 150,000 tons.

Submarine class.—For the British Empire and the United States, 60,000 to 90,000 tons each, and for Japan 36,000 to 54,000 tons.

In conclusion, Mr. Gibson stated that if any Power felt justified in proposing still lower tonnage levels his Government would welcome this, and was "not unfavourable" to the consideration of a general agreement for the abolition of submarines, should this be possible.

[1] The Conference sat in the offices of the League of Nations, and the services of the Secretariat were placed at its disposal. It was, however, in no sense a League conference.

The British proposals were next explained by Mr. Bridge-man,[1] who began by drawing attention to the difference between the way in which the problem necessarily presented itself to the British Government and people from that in which it was viewed by the other naval Powers. In a review of the "considerations which governed the position of Great Britain" he said:

"First and foremost there is the insular position of the Mother Country . . . and the fact that she is almost entirely dependent not only for raw material, but also for her food supplies and her very existence upon free passage upon the seas. It is no exaggeration to say that if the seas were closed to ships trading with our country, we should be faced with starvation within a few weeks. . . . The other important factors in our case are the immense lengths of the routes over which our trade is carried, and the very large coast-lines which bound the various parts of the Empire, and the necessity for providing reasonable protection for these extensive shores and long lines of communication. . . ."

Mr. Bridgeman then put forward a list of proposals which were noteworthy, amongst other things, for the fact that they departed, in the American view, from what might be called the terms of reference of the Conference, for they included proposals for the reduction in size and the extension of the life of capital ships, as the following outline of their main heads will show:

1. The extension of the accepted life of existing capital vessels from twenty to twenty-six years, involving a waiver by the three Powers of their full rights under the replacement tables adopted at Washington. The life of 8-inch gun cruisers also to be fixed at twenty-four years.
2. The reduction of the size of future capital ships to a maximum of something under 30,000 tons.
3. Reduction of the maximum calibre of guns in battleships to 13·5 inches.
4. Acceptance of the existing ratio of 5–5–3 for cruisers of 10,000 tons, carrying 8-inch guns.
5. A limitation of 7,500 tons and 6-inch guns to be placed on all future cruisers after the number of 10,000-ton vessels has been decided upon.

---

[1] The texts of Mr. Bridgeman's speeches at this and the following plenary sessions of the Conference are printed in the British White Paper, Cmd. 2964 of 1927.

Proposals were also made for reductions in the maximum tonnage of aircraft carriers, together with a reduction of the calibre of their guns, and limitation of the tonnage of destroyer leaders, while as to submarines it was suggested that the tonnage of the larger type should be limited to 1,600 tons, and of the smaller to 600 tons, with a maximum calibre of 5 inches for the guns of both types. It was explained, however, that this proposal was made owing to recognition of the fact that Powers possessing fewer of the larger vessels of war regarded the possession of submarines as a valuable weapon of defence, but that the British Government itself was still prepared, as at Washington, to agree to the discontinuation of their use altogether.

The Japanese scheme was simpler, though vague in character, and really amounted to the maintenance of the *status quo*. Briefly, it provided that in future no building programme should be adopted and no new ships acquired for the purpose of increasing naval strength, and that the naval strength allowed to each Power should be determined for auxiliary vessels (including submarines) on the basis of the tonnage of the existing effective ships and of the ships under construction.

From a comparison of these proposals it will be noticed that whereas the American delegation came to Geneva prepared to discuss a simple extension to auxiliary vessels of the Washington Treaty principles as regards capital ships, the British Government presented the Conference with a scheme which introduced an entirely new element, to the implications of which the other parties to the discussion had not hitherto given consideration. This was unfortunate, because it, as it were, put the negotiations out of their stride at the very first step, necessitating a readjustment of their ideas on the part of the delegates of the other two Powers; but this alone might not have caused more than a temporary difficulty had it not been that as the British thesis was developed it became clear that it was out of consonance with that of the United States in one important respect, in that it, in effect, excluded from the proposed extension of the Washington ratio to auxiliary vessels all cruisers except those of 10,000 tons, carrying 8-inch guns. As the negotiations proceeded, this point was found to constitute an increasingly serious obstacle to Anglo-American agreement, for the reason that the United States Government was not disposed to accept limitation in the particular type of cruiser to which it attached the greatest value while leaving to Great Britain freedom to build up to a large total tonnage in a different type of cruiser, to which the British Government attached particular value but the United States did not.

The British proposals made no mention of total tonnage of auxiliary vessels, but aimed at achieving limitation by reducing the size and lengthening the life of all naval vessels, capital ships as well as cruisers, destroyers and submarines, though by the terms of the Washington Treaty the maximum displacement and life of the former was not due for reconsideration until 1931.[1]

After the three delegations had submitted their proposals they were handed to a Technical Committee for examination, and the Conference did not meet again in plenary session for over three weeks. During the informal meetings held between the principal delegates, the point that aroused most interest was the British desire to include capital ships in the discussions. This appears to have taken the other delegations genuinely by surprise, and the British contention that it did not involve any actual modification of the Washington Treaty,[2] since the suggestion was merely that the three Powers should agree to renounce their rights under it on certain points, failed to convince the Americans of the wisdom of adopting the proposal.

After reference to their respective Governments, however, the American and Japanese delegates consented to discuss capital ships, but only, in the case of the Americans, after the

---

[1] By Article XXI of the Treaty a second Conference was to be held in eight years to consider what changes, if any, in the Treaty might be necessary to meet technical and scientific developments.

[2] This could not, of course, have been effected in the absence of the other signatories, France and Italy.

objects for which the Conference had been convened had been attained, and at the same time the State Department at Washington expressed the view publicly that the extension of the life and reduction of the tonnage of battleships would prolong the existing disparity in Great Britain's favour.[1] This led Mr. Bridgeman and Lord Cecil to make a personal call on Mr. Gibson in order to assure him that there was no question in the minds of any of the members of the British Government that the United States was not entitled to absolute parity with Great Britain in all classes of vessels. A statement on the same lines was issued to the American press representatives at Geneva, who had been charging the British Government with systematically attempting to secure a superiority of naval strength in all classes, and on the following day Mr. Kellogg, the United States Secretary of State, expressed his satisfaction that the "misapprehension had been cleared away."

Consideration of the question of capital ships was accordingly postponed, and the discussions thenceforth centred on that of cruisers. Here the delegates at once came face to face with a delicate problem presented by the British attitude, of which Mr. Bridgeman had given an indication in his speech on the opening day when he said that the British delegation could only discuss cruisers on the basis of the essential requirements of the British Empire. These requirements were primarily concerned with the protection of commerce, and could best be met by the possession of a large number of vessels of medium size, of a maximum displacement of 7,500 tons armed with nothing larger than 6-inch guns. This type of cruiser the British Government regarded as a defensive rather than an offensive weapon, and wished a distinction to be drawn between it and the larger vessels of 10,000 tons carrying 8-inch guns. The British proposals accordingly included provision for the division of cruisers into two classes, large and small, to the former only of which the Washington ratio of 5–5–3 would be applied. As regards the second, in considering

---

[1] If this view was correct, it would seem to show that the experts at Washington had made an error in their calculations.

the question of limitation the British Government was unable
to lose sight of the "absolute" needs of the Empire, calling
for the patrolling of lines of trade routes and communications
80,000 miles in length, and this led it to take the view that,
whatever the needs of other countries and whatever their
views as to relative strengths, in so far as the commerce protecting cruiser was concerned, the British Empire alone must
be the judge of its own requirements. Having agreed to the
principle of parity with the United States, it was, of course,
quite ready to see that country build up to an equal tonnage in
that class of vessel, but as the estimate of the minimum British
requirements exceeded by a large figure the tonnage proposed
by the United States as a maximum, this did not do much to
lessen the difficulty. It was increased by the fact that not
only did America not want a large number of small cruisers,
but she *did* desire to possess large ones, with a radius of action
which would do something to make up for the absence of naval
bases belonging to her abroad. She was supported by Japan in
her objection to the British suggestion as to the distinction
to be made between the two classes of cruisers: the smaller
vessels were useful only to a Power like the British Empire,
which possessed numerous naval bases, and if they were armed
with only 6-inch guns they would be of even less value to any
other Power, since Great Britain would be able, in case of need,
to convert large numbers of merchant ships into fighting
vessels[1] and so upset any treaty arrangements as to ratios.
Accordingly, when the British plan for the division of cruisers
into two categories was put forward the American and Japanese
delegates asked for time to consider it. When the discussion
of it was renewed some days later in the Technical Committee
the American delegate submitted a statement which he declared
should be "construed as our maximum effort to meet the
British view-point," and he went on to say that he was unable
to discuss cruiser tonnages in excess of 400,000 tons for the

---

[1] By Article XIV of the Washington Treaty the arming of merchantmen with
6-inch guns was permitted. British naval experts deny this argument on the
ground that a merchant vessel armed with 6-inch guns would be no match for
a cruiser with the same armament.

period ending December 31, 1936.[1] During that period the United States would require full liberty of action to build 10,000-ton cruisers up to a total of 250,000 tons, recognizing at the same time the full right of other Powers to build cruisers of similar characteristics up to similar tonnages in accordance with the principles of the Washington Treaty. They were, however, willing, for the period mentioned, "to limit our further construction within a total tonnage limitation of 400,000 tons to vessels of a smaller tonnage, to be agreed upon," but did not see any reason for limiting the calibre of guns in the smaller class of cruisers to anything different from that in the larger class. Finally, they still "ardently" desired that the total tonnage limitation of cruisers to be agreed upon should be very much lower than 400,000 tons, while "any limitation on the basis of a cruiser tonnage in excess of 400,000 tons we regard as so ineffective a limitation as not to justify the conclusion of a treaty at this time."

As the discussions in the Technical Committee had by now revealed that the British Government's estimate of the "absolute" needs of the British Empire involved the possession of 70 cruisers, of which 15 would be of large tonnage, it was obvious that agreement between Great Britain and the United States on the basis of the figure of 400,000 tons was not possible, since even if the 55 smaller British cruisers had been of only 6,000 tons displacement the total tonnage would have worked out at 480,000 tons.[2] An attempt was made by Mr. Bridgeman to effect a compromise by suggesting that the total tonnage agreement for cruisers might be made to apply only to vessels under twenty years of age, and that the British Empire might be allowed to retain, in addition, a certain number of vessels beyond the replacement age; but this was not considered to have got over the difficulty, and the Technical Committee decided that the only course to take was to draw up a report on the results which had so far been achieved.

---

[1] That is, when the Washington Treaty expired.
[2] The figure generally mentioned for the tonnage of the smaller type was actually 7,500 tons.

In this it was stated that while provisional agreement had been reached regarding destroyers and submarines, this had not been found possible in the case of cruisers, and it was decided to hold a plenary session of the Conference on July 11th "to give the British delegation an opportunity of stating their case, in order that it might not be misrepresented."[1]

The second plenary session actually opened on July 14th, when Mr. Bridgeman prefaced a restatement of the British proposals by a reference to the "gross misrepresentations of the British case in certain quarters" which were vitiating the atmosphere in which the discussions were being carried on.[2] He then said that numbers of cruisers were more important to Great Britain than size, and she was prepared not to lay down any more 8-inch gun cruisers until the United States and Japan had built up to the Washington ratio. With regard to smaller cruisers, the American right to parity was not contested, but the British delegation did desire to limit the size and the armament of this class of vessel so that they might be defensive and not offensive weapons. There was no intrinsic objection to accepting a limit of total tonnage, provided other countries made it clear what proportion they wanted of large cruisers armed with 8-inch guns, the offensive strength of which was at least two and a half times as great as that of 6-inch gun vessels. To agree in advance to a total tonnage of 400,000 for cruisers would put the British Empire in the position of accepting "not parity, but definite inferiority in offensive power," unless they were prepared to abandon the number of cruisers regarded as essential for the protection of Imperial communications.[3]

This statement was supplemented by detailed particulars of the duties for which the British cruisers were required, furnished by Lord Jellicoe with the object of making it clear why the British Government was compelled to make its cal-

[1] For some days a campaign had been conducted in the American press accusing Great Britain of aiming at reasserting her supremacy at sea.
[2] The official enquiry instituted in America regarding the activities of Mr. Shearer formed an interesting commentary on this.
[3] The text of Mr. Bridgeman's speech is printed in the British White Paper, Cmd. 2964 of 1927.

culations on the assumption that its needs in cruiser strength were "absolute," and not merely relative to those of other Powers. Lord Jellicoe explained how the figure of 70 vessels as a minimum had been arrived at,[1] but owing to the unwillingness of the American delegation to admit the principle of "absolute" needs as the basis for fixing the ratios, his explanation appears to have had no effect. The light in which the American delegates envisaged the problem was, in fact, in direct opposition to that of the British spokesmen, as was proved when Mr. Gibson declared that he entertained "very serious misgivings in regard to the effort to prepare in time of peace for all possible contingencies of this character in time of war. . . . If in time of peace we are building up forces to perform this duty (of hunting down commerce raiders) it effectively closes the door to any real limitation of cruiser strength." He repeated that the American proposals were based on the belief that naval needs were relative, not absolute, and that the fairest method of limitation was that of total tonnage by classes.[2] On the subject of 10,000-ton cruisers, Mr. Gibson pointed out that if agreement could be reached on the tonnage level advocated by his Government it would obviously not be possible for the United States to add to their existing fleet the 25 cruisers of the largest size, which they had been credited with demanding, and the American delegation was quite ready to discuss the number of large cruisers once a tonnage limitation had been agreed upon.

The position, then, was that the British delegation still refused to consider the problem in terms of total tonnage unless they were sure of their 70 cruisers, while the Americans were determined not to discuss numbers until agreement had been reached on total tonnage. Mr. Gibson suggested that, as the Japanese delegates were in agreement with him on the main issues, Great Britain and Japan should attempt to come

---

[1] It is interesting to note that Lord Jellicoe stated that, although Great Britain had had 114 cruisers in 1914, the amount of shipping sunk by German raiders had shown this number to be inadequate.
[2] That is, counting all cruisers as one class, in contradistinction to the British subdivision of them into two, large and small, or offensive and defensive.

to an agreement between themselves, when, he was sure, America would be able to endorse it, and a compromise scheme was, in fact, drawn up after a series of conversations between the British and Japanese delegates. This did not secure American support, however, owing partly to the inclusion of a provision for the retention of certain vessels beyond the replacement age,[1] and in a statement by Mr. Gibson, the day after the Anglo-Japanese plan had been first considered, the United States delegate "made it quite clear that in his opinion a treaty which deprived the United States of its liberty of action with respect to arming the proposed second class of cruisers as they saw fit would be unacceptable," and that "an attempt to deny the United States their liberty of action would be the best method of arousing popular resentment and driving that country into a big building programme."

Thus matters stood when the principal British delegates were recalled to London for consultation with the Government. The reasons which led to this step became known subsequently, when Lord Cecil had resigned office owing to his inability to identify himself with the policy of the Cabinet. From the statement he made in the House of Lords on November 16, 1927, the fact was made public that Mr. Bridgeman's personal assurance to Mr. Gibson that Great Britain was ready to agree to parity in all classes of vessels had "caused great anxiety" to some of the members of the Cabinet, which thenceforward became divided in opinion as to the policy to be pursued in respect of auxiliary vessels. A section of the Cabinet was prepared to see the Conference break down rather than subscribe to a treaty embodying the principle of parity in all classes and, in addition to this, the majority of the Ministers were for insisting on a 6-inch gun as the maximum calibre armament for the smaller cruisers. When, however, Lord Cecil requested that someone else should be sent to Geneva in his place he was asked to reconsider his decision, and in consenting to do so and return to Geneva he

---

[1] In any case the scheme did not go far towards meeting the American views as to total tonnage, etc.

said that if the negotiations failed on the point about the guns, as he felt sure they would, he would have to reserve his full liberty to resign. And as a matter of fact the attitude maintained by the British Government towards this particular point proved, in Lord Cecil's opinion, to be the final obstacle to agreement and the direct cause of the failure of the Conference.

Before the British delegates returned to Geneva an attempt was made by the Government to remove the suspicions of its motives which had arisen both in the United States and in Japan. On July 27th statements were made by Lord Salisbury in the House of Lords and by Sir Austen Chamberlain in the House of Commons in which the most interesting passages dealt with the complicated nature of the problem of limitation of cruiser strength when it concerned the small vessels which were essential to the British Empire on account of its geographical and economic peculiarities. A simple formula like that adopted at Washington, it was explained, was quite inapplicable to vessels designed for purposes which must vary with the needs of the several Powers concerned. However, in the opinion of the Government "there need be no difficulty in arriving at a temporary arrangement about the immediate future of cruiser building. But the British Empire cannot be asked to give to any such temporary arrangement the appearance of an immutable principle which might be treated as a precedent. Any other course would inevitably be interpreted in the future as involving the formal surrender by the British Empire of maritime equality."

This last statement was understood to be an attempt to convey to the United States the British view that "mathematical parity" meant in practice American superiority, whereas what had been contemplated, and within limits achieved, at Washington was practical or "equitable" parity. The view that mathematical parity meant practical American superiority appears to have been held by the whole Cabinet (and is widely held by expert opinion in Great Britain at the present time), and the division of opinion above referred to was over the question of expediency, the minority considering that acceptance of mathematical parity was preferable to allowing the Conference to break down.

When the British delegates arrived back at Geneva—the day following the statements in Parliament—it was found that the attitude of the Americans had stiffened on the subject of the number of large cruisers to be allowed to the three Powers under the compromise suggested by the Anglo-Japanese scheme, but this obstacle might have been got over if it had been found possible to clear away the difficulty regarding the calibre of gun to be allowed to the smaller type of cruisers. On this both sides[1] proved adamant (though Lord Cecil afterwards placed it on record that without a compromise on this point there was no hope of agreement), and the result was that a new set of British proposals, put forward on the same day— July 28th—had little chance of a favourable reception from the United States, and, in fact, these were rejected on the ground that they would call for a much larger navy than America considered necessary. It is, therefore, of little interest to describe them, except to say that they included the usual provision for the subdivision of cruisers into two classes, the smaller of which was to carry guns of not more than 6 inches calibre, and suggested 590,000 tons as the total tonnage to be allotted to Great Britain and the United States, with 385,000 tons to Japan, for cruisers, destroyers and submarines combined.

In spite of this, however, some further attempts were made by the United States and Japanese delegates to escape from the *impasse*. Mr. Gibson proposed the inclusion in the treaty of a political clause[2] under which, in the event of any of the contracting Powers considering that the tonnage allocation in the cruiser class had been utilized by either of the other Powers in a manner to call for an adjustment of the total tonnage

[1] The Japanese appear to have had no strong objection to a limit of 6 inches for the guns of this class of cruiser, but did not side whole-heartedly with the British delegation.
[2] He had previously suggested the inclusion of a similar provision in respect of the construction of 8-inch gun vessels.

allocation of that class, it would have the right to convoke a special meeting of the signatories to effect this adjustment by mutual agreement. Should this prove impossible, each of the contracting parties would be able to terminate the treaty by giving one year's notice of its desire to do so. The suggestion did not appeal to the British Government, however, and the British delegation was not empowered to discuss it. A more sympathetic reception was given to a Japanese proposal, under which Great Britain and Japan would undertake to confine themselves until 1931 to naval-building programmes already authorized, while the United States would undertake not to exceed, during the same period, the British strength in auxiliary vessels, but to the American delegation this "naval holiday" type of agreement proved equally unacceptable.[1] On August 4th, Mr. Gibson, as President of the Conference, announced the opening of "the final plenary session, which was to give an opportunity to the delegates to make a final survey of the divergencies that had rendered agreement impossible." This meant that all hope of saving the Conference had been abandoned, and it only remained for the heads of the several delegations to recapitulate their Governments' cases.

At this session Mr. Bridgeman spoke first, but added nothing to what had been contained in his previous expositions of British policy. He confessed himself unable to understand the United States' objection to the limitation of the smaller cruisers to guns of 6-inch calibre, but assured the American delegation that the British attitude was "not due to fear of any unfriendly action on their part." He was followed by the Japanese delegate, whose principal point was that, while not assenting in principle to the British preference for 6-inch guns, his Government had consented not to let their own desire for a heavier gun stand in the way of a solution.

Mr. Gibson was more controversial. Referring to the British

[1] The reason for this appears to have been in large part that the British definition of "ships authorized" included ships projected but not yet appropriated for, and involved a cruiser tonnage of about 458,000 tons, a great increase over the existing total. In the United States "authorized" ships only included those already appropriated for (and, of course, those under construction)—often a very different thing.

claim as to the absolute naval needs of the Empire, he said that the American delegation "had never been able to reconcile the conception of absolute naval needs with the negotiation of a treaty to fix limitations on the basis of mutual concessions."[1] The American delegation had agreed to discuss the number of 10,000-ton cruisers and to accept a secondary class of cruisers, provided that the latter should not be of a maximum individual displacement which would preclude the mounting of 8-inch guns, and any further concessions would have involved a complete surrender of the right to build ships responsive to their needs. As they had not contested Britain's argument that her needs could best be met by a number of smaller vessels, they expected her to recognize America's claim that her geographical position and lack of bases necessitated a larger type of cruiser. The repeated expressions of willingness to reduce the total cruiser tonnage to the lowest level acceptable to Great Britain should afford sufficient evidence that no American programme of a kind to cause apprehension was contemplated. As a matter of fact, Great Britain already had five 10,000-ton cruisers practically completed, and six under construction, as well as four in commission of 9,750 tons each,[2] while the United States had only two under construction and six recently contracted for. Turning to broader questions, Mr. Gibson criticized the British description of 6-inch gun cruisers as defensive weapons. These vessels, he was told, were intended to protect British commerce, "but in order to afford effective defence to commerce upon the seas these cruisers must in time of war effectively deny the sea to others." The British Government had at its disposal approximately 888,000 tons of fast merchant ships capable of being readily converted into cruisers and armed with many 6-inch guns, while the United States had only 188,000 tons of such ships, and consideration of this fact should influence the British Government in its attitude towards the question of 8-inch guns. Finally,

[1] The fact was that the British Government was prepared to go all the way with the other two Powers in making "mutual concessions," but with the one qualification, that Britain's "absolute" needs in the "defensive" type of cruiser were first safeguarded.
[2] These four cruisers were armed with 7·5-inch guns.

the American delegation found it difficult "to reconcile the British conviction that war is already outlawed between us with their present unwillingness to recognize our right to build a limited number of the type of ships we would desire or with their willingness to risk the success of this Conference because they fear the problematical possession by us during the life of the Treaty of the small number of 8-inch gun cruisers."

Mr. Gibson closed the session with the reading of an agreed statement, setting forth the point of view of each of the three Powers. According to this the immediate cause of the failure of the Conference was the inability to find an acceptable plan to reconcile "the claim of the British delegation for numbers of vessels, for the most part armed with 6-inch guns, with the desire of the American delegates for the lowest possible total tonnage limitation with freedom of armament within such limitation, subject to the restrictions as to armament already set by the Washington Treaty."

As will have been realized from the foregoing outline of the proceedings, however, other causes entered into the failure of the three Powers to reach agreement. The relative parts played by these various causes in bringing about the breakdown of negotiations have been a matter of discussion and difference of opinion ever since. Lord Cecil appears to have attached more importance to the deadlock which occurred over the question of gun calibre[1] than did the American delegates; in fact the State Department in Washington, as reported in *The Times*, maintained that the specific question regarding the guns in the smaller cruisers was never fully discussed; that it would only have arisen if and when the problem of total cruiser strength had been settled; and that this problem was not only never settled, but was the rock on which the Conference split.

How great a part was played by the press in magnifying the difficulties with which the delegates were continually being confronted is difficult to estimate with any accuracy. It is

[1] Speaking in the House of Commons on March 14, 1929, Mr. Bridgeman said that the Three-Power Conference "failed because we could not find a formula which could equate ships mounting 8-inch guns with ships mounting 6-inch guns. . . . The reason for the breakdown of the Conference was that, although we agree on equality, we could not find a formula for it."

certain that many of the reports of what took place at the private discussions of the Technical Committee were inaccurate and sensational, while, in the case of the American press, influences were believed to have been exerted by the Big Navy Group and certain of the armament firms which were not in the best interests of the cause for which the Conference had been convened. The result was that a good deal of the time and attention of the delegates was taken up with efforts to remove the suspicion which had been engendered by misrepresentations of their respective cases.

The opinion most generally held, however, is that what was more than anything else responsible for the failure of the negotiations was the absence of diplomatic preparation. Speaking at Niagara Falls three days after the Conference had terminated, General Dawes said:

"Perhaps before this Conference was held there was not the preliminary careful appraisement by each conferee of the necessities of the other; perhaps too exclusive concentration of each conferee upon the necessities of his own nation resulted in a predetermined ultimatum before a comparison of views. Perhaps the public announcement of respective programmes early in this Conference produced fears of domestic public repercussion if they were reasonably modified, as would be necessary to effect an agreement."

The chief reason why these programmes could not be "reasonably modified" was that they were the work of technical experts who, in drawing them up, were all along concerned with securing for their respective countries the greatest possible offensive strength within the limits of the formula of parity. Naval experts are necessarily compelled to deal with the armaments problem with all the possible contingencies of war in their minds, and to think of war in terms of the offensive. This is inevitable, owing to their responsibility to the people of their respective countries to see that the national safety is not endangered, and the only way out would appear to be the handing over of the conduct of the negotiations to representatives who are not committed to rigid programmes drawn up to meet "absolute" needs or to secure superiority in offensive power.

In this particular instance it happened that, though politically the British and United States Governments were more or less of the same frame of mind (in agreeing to parity and desiring limitation and reduction of armaments), technically their aims were conflicting, and it was the technical considerations which weighed most heavily in the negotiations. The Americans were aiming at economy and offensive power coupled with parity, the British at economy and offensive power coupled with security, and they were each bent upon effecting their economies in the form that would best serve their other aims, which were conflicting. The elements of naval strength when measured against each other by experts could not be reduced to comparable numerical terms, a fact which had been realized by the French when they raised the question of the "potentials of war" at the meeting of the Preparatory Commission the previous spring. The discussions at Geneva three months later served to substantiate their contention that the fighting force of a nation cannot be measured in terms of armaments and effectives without taking into account the totality of the national resources and geographical position. In respect of these factors the positions of the United States and of the British Empire differ fundamentally, and the corresponding difference in their armament needs makes real parity extremely difficult of attainment. As for mathematical parity, this was considered by the British delegation to involve real inferiority, owing to the necessity of keeping a large number of cruisers in far-distant waters. More than one British statesman in public utterances called in question the wisdom of attempting to reach an agreement with the United States on the basis of parity. Thus Mr. Churchill, speaking two days after the close of the Conference, said:

"The fundamental cause which prevented agreement lay in the different views taken of what constitutes naval equality by the Americans and ourselves. . . . Therefore, we are not able now—and I hope at no future time—to embody in a solemn international agreement any words which would bind us to the principle of mathematical parity in naval strength. . . . The doctrine of naval equality, if it is to be accepted by us, must take into consideration the whole position of the two countries on the sea, and their respective risks and vulnerability."[1]

For a different reason, the acceptance of the principle of parity as the basis of negotiation was criticized by Lord Grey, who, in a letter to *The Times* on August 11, 1927, suggested that the theory of parity itself was "the rock on which the Conference was wrecked at Geneva," and said that it was working badly and that there was every sign that it would cause friction, and not harmony, between the two countries, because, though designed to avoid competition, it did in fact imply rivalry.

In the following November, Mr. Ramsay MacDonald moved a vote of censure against the Government on the ground that the lack of preparation for the Conference and the military character of the British delegation had seriously contributed to the failure at Geneva. This failure he described as a natural one, "a failure in the nature of the case, and I say in pursuing security through peace, security through agreement, we will get round that problem, by trying to discover some means by which America and ourselves can come to an agreement, which means that we need not bother about navies with regard to each other at all."

The British Government was determined not to allow the events at Geneva to affect its decision to follow a policy of limitation in naval armaments, and in November Mr. Bridgeman announced in Parliament that two out of the three cruisers which were due to be laid down in the course of the year 1927 had been dropped. The three vessels in the existing programme included one of 10,000 tons and two smaller vessels, and the former was one of the two which were abandoned.

In the United States it was announced from the White House about the same time that the President did not expect either an increase or a diminution in the number of cruisers due to be built, and in a Message to Congress in December Mr. Coolidge said that "the failure to agree should not cause us to build either more or less than we otherwise should."

[1] On other occasions, also, Mr. Churchill took occasion to denounce the principle of mathematical parity.

Thus, far from alleviating international rivalry in naval armaments the Geneva Conference closed with the relations between Great Britain and the United States considerably acerbated. Nor was the position improved by the resignation of Lord Cecil from the Conservative Cabinet and the launching by the League of Nations Union of a monster disarmament campaign, coupled with a very trenchant attack on the British Government. Both these events were interpreted in the United States as being further justification of the stand adopted by the American delegation at the Conference and a corroboration of the strong suspicion already existing that all European statesmen were motivated by a desire to outwit the United States.[1] American public opinion congratulated itself on the avoidance of a repetition of the policy of renunciation adopted at Washington in 1922, when an American building programme which would have reached parity with Great Britain, had it been carried out, melted like snow before the benignity of Lord Balfour's smile.

At the close of the year 1927, Anglo-American relations were undergoing a severe strain which in the following year became tenser and more dangerous, before the welcome relaxation in 1929.

2. THE ANGLO-FRENCH COMPROMISE

The story of the Anglo-French Naval Compromise forms one of the most unfortunate chapters in the history of disarmament. No formula could have been conceived with better intentions, yet none could have been arrived at with more culpable clumsiness. The Compromise of 1928 was formulated in the best traditions of concession which the New Diplomacy has made popular; it was brought about in the best traditions of secrecy for which the Old Diplomacy had been famous.

It will be remembered that at the close of the Third Session

[1] The author was in New York at the time of the launching in London of the disarmament campaign at the Caxton Hall on October 21, 1927, and was deeply impressed with the unfortunate effect which it had on the average American, who at once took it as a confirmation of the correctness of the American view as expressed at Geneva.

of the Preparatory Commission, in April 1927, at which the first reading of the Draft Convention was taken, there arose a complete deadlock between the rival British and French theses as regards the limitation of both land and naval forces.[1] At the close of that session the President, M. Loudon, had recommended an attempt at compromise between the two conflicting formulæ. During the year 1928 no attempt at such compromise was made,[2] but the Coolidge Conference, if it had no positive effect, at least demonstrated the views and standpoint of the United States beyond question, and should have left the British and French Governments in no doubt at all as what would prove acceptable to that country.

The first real step in the negotiations which resulted in the Compromise was taken by Sir Austen Chamberlain during a meeting of the Council (March 9, 1928) which took place just prior to the Fifth Session of the Preparatory Commission. The British Foreign Secretary put before M. Briand a draft of "modified proposals drawn up by the Admiralty," modified, that is, as compared with the position taken up in the Preparatory Commission in the previous spring. This draft suggested that limitation should be effected by classes as follows:

(1) Capital ships;
(2) Aircraft carriers;
(3) Cruisers between 10,000 and 7,000 tons;
(4) Surface vessels under 7,000 tons;
(5) Submarines; and
(6) Small vessels exempt from limitation.

In a letter accompanying this proposal, Sir Austen Chamberlain said that public opinion realized that concessions were necessary from all parties for a general settlement to be reached, and if he could point to a concession by the French in naval matters, it would probably acquiesce in his yielding a point on the military side.

---

[1] See above, pp. 58, etc.
[2] There had, however, been conversations between the Chief of the French Naval Staff and the senior British naval expert during the fourth session of the Preparatory Commission (November–December 1927). No record of these conversations has been published, but they are referred to in a despatch from M. Briand to M. Claudel, French Ambassador in Washington, dated December 31, 1927. See French Blue Book, *Limitations des Armements Navals* of 1928, No. 14, p. 33.

In reply, M. Briand asked for a personal copy of the revised Admiralty proposals and said he would put them before the French naval authorities.

In the course of the Fifth Session of the Commission the general public were given the first hint that bilateral negotiations were in progress. The French delegate, the Comte Clauzel, on March 22nd spoke of conversations which were in progress on "certain delicate matters which have hitherto caused difficulties," and proposed that discussion on the naval clauses of the Draft Convention be postponed until the result of the conversations should be known. This statement was confirmed next day by the British representative, Lord Cushendun, and although it was evident that the disclosure came as a surprise to the other great naval Powers, the American delegate, Mr. Gibson, spoke in favour of "direct negotiation between the various Governments and between groups of Governments to find a way, through mutual concession, to eliminate existing divergencies," and was supported by the Italian delegate, General de Marinis.

In view of the remarks of the American and Italian delegates it was natural that the British Foreign Secretary should wish to follow up the step taken by him on March 9th, and on June 26th he addressed a letter to the Ambassador in Paris from which it appears that the French Admiral Violette had earlier in the month made a suggestion to Admiral Kelly proposing that the only surface vessels subject to limitation should be those mounting a gun of greater calibre than 6-inch. This would have produced a classification for the Preparatory Disarmament Commission as follows:

(A) Capital ships.
(B) Aircraft carriers.
(C) Surface vessels of 10,000 tons and under, mounting a gun above 6-inch.
(D) Submarines.[1]

---

[1] It is not quite clear why cruisers carrying 6-inch guns were not included in the classification, unless it was because, according to this proposal, they were not to be subject to limitation.

Sir Austen said that the British Government was ready to accept this suggestion, and would instruct its representatives to support it, if put forward by the French. He concluded the letter by saying: "You should add that the adoption of this suggestion, which his Majesty's Government recognize would be a concession to their views on naval classification, would enable them to meet the French Government by withdrawing their opposition to the French standpoint in regard to army-trained reserves."

This communication was passed on to the French Foreign Minister integrally on June 28th, and in reply M. Briand addressed a long communication to the British Embassy under date July 20, 1928. The chief points in this were the following:

The French Government, while prepared to accept in principle the proposals put forward in the British Note, considered that the method of their application should be defined. With this end in view Admiral Violette had asked Admiral Kelly whether the British Government proposed that submarines should be limited by fixing the same maximum tonnage for all the great naval Powers, "the advantage of such a system being to avoid the possibility of engaging on delicate discussions concerning the relative needs and importance of different navies." He had also asked whether the same method could be applied to the cruisers which fell within the scope of the British Note, it being understood, of course, that the Conference on Disarmament would have eventually to record, below the theoretical maximum tonnage allowed, the actual figures which in practice the High Contracting Parties would undertake not to exceed for the duration of the Convention. Finally, Admiral Violette had also asked whether submarines could not be divided into two classes, coastal submarines being exempt from all limitation "in view of their strictly defensive character."

The French Government expressed itself as willing to accept the British proposals as a whole if these suggestions were incorporated in them, and added, "this arrangement would have the effect of avoiding at Geneva awkward discussions more likely to increase the existing mistrust between the Powers than to create the atmosphere of mutual confidence essential to a general limitation of armaments."

The Note concluded by reminding the British Government that the agreement so earnestly desired could only bear fruit if the United States Government, in particular, agreed to accept it. After this it is somewhat surprising to read that: "The Government of the Republic are convinced that the concerted action of France and Great Britain will enable the two Governments to obtain the approval of the naval Powers concerned." But should this hope prove illusory, "the two Governments would, none the less, be under the urgent obligation (*l'impérieux devoir*) to concert either to ensure success by other means, or to adopt a common policy so as to deal with the difficulties which would inevitably arise from a check to the work of the Preparatory Commission."[1]

The British Government's reply of July 28th contained only one important point. This was the endorsement of the French claim that France should be allotted the same maximum tonnage as Great Britain and America for the classes of vessels still to be limited, i.e. (c) and (d) in the classification mentioned in the British Government's first Note of June 28th. The actual words were as follows: "His Majesty's Government, in their anxious desire to reach such an agreement with France and other Powers as will lead to the successful conclusion of the labours of the Preparatory Commission, and believing that the proposals now made by the French Government are of a character to achieve this result, are prepared to accept the supplementary proposals made in the French Note, namely, that an equal maximum tonnage for submarines and cruisers

---

[1] In the course of the debate on the Compromise in the House of Lords on November 7, 1928, Lord Cushendun, Acting Foreign Secretary, stated that this paragraph in the French Note had been purposely left unanswered by the British Government for the reason that "it might appear to suggest something in the nature of a closer political alliance, a formal political alliance, rather than a mere attitude of friendliness or entente which existed between the two countries." He added that "H.M. Government thought that this silence would be perfectly understood in that manner, and he did not doubt that it had been understood."

should be fixed for the great naval Powers, and that submarines should be divided up into two classes, the smaller class being exempt from all limitation."

On July 30th Sir Austen Chamberlain made the following statement in the House of Commons:

"As has been publicly announced, conversations have been proceeding between ourselves and the French with the hope of reducing the difference between us, indeed in the hope of finding some compromise upon which we could both agree, and which we might then submit to the Powers and, perhaps, by our proposals, facilitate progress in the Commission. Those conversations have been successful between the French and ourselves, and I am about to communicate to the other principal naval Powers the compromise at which we have arrived, with the hope that it may be acceptable to them also, and that thus a great obstacle to progress will have been removed and a step made in advance. Until those proposals have been communicated to the other Governments, I do not like to say more about them."

In reply to a question whether these were purely naval proposals, the Foreign Secretary said:

"Yes. The proposals I want to communicate are dealing with the disagreements that arise in regard to the naval issue, in which, of course, we take a particular interest. . . . Our Navy has always been the principal defence of our country, and, therefore, naval questions are the ones that interest us most, and it is upon them that we have been seeking to reconcile our differences, and this is the method of making progress."

Apart from the statements made by Comte Clauzel and Lord Cushendun at Geneva in March, this was the first official statement to be made on the Compromise, and certainly the first intimation that the negotiations had resulted in an agreement. Though he gave no details, it is significant that, in answering his questioner, Sir Austen Chamberlain made no reference to the fact that a deal had been struck with the French on the matter of trained reserves, and he left the House under the impression that the proposals were purely naval in character. One can only attribute this amazing lapse of memory to the fact that the British Foreign Secretary was himself on the verge of a nervous breakdown and shortly afterwards left England for a long sea voyage.

It is less easy, however, to explain the same omission in the telegram to which Sir Austen had referred and which was in fact despatched to the Embassies in Washington, Tokyo and Rome on the same day as that on which he made his statement (July 30th). The telegram gave details of the Compromise arrived at, but made no mention of the question of trained reserves. The Naval Compromise was described as a "substantial modification of the positions" which the British and French Governments had respectively taken up at the Preparatory Commission in April 1927.

The impression made by Sir Austen Chamberlain's statement on the public opinion of Great Britain, Germany and the United States was, to say the least, unfavourable. It was impossible to ignore the far-reaching importance of the agreement, yet the complete ignorance of its terms was alarming. Nor was it public opinion only that was alarmed. In Germany the Wilhelmstrasse scented a possible abandonment by Great Britain of her opposition to the exclusion of trained reserves from the Draft Disarmament Convention, and on August 4th the British Ambassador in Berlin telegraphed to London:

"German Government seem somewhat disconcerted by news of Franco-British Naval Compromise, and fear that it may imply some concession on the part of his Majesty's Government in regard to the question of the limitation of the land forces . . . I propose to see the Secretary of State shortly, and I presume that if he refers to the question I may refer him to the statement which you recently made in the House of Commons, and point out that there is nothing in the Compromise inconsistent with the Locarno Treaties."

In reply to this the Foreign Secretary wired, on August 5th:

"You are authorized to give Secretary of State proposed assurance. The text of the Compromise itself refers exclusively to naval limitation, but there is an understanding with the French Government, made before the text of the Compromise was actually drawn up, that if they could meet his Majesty's Government on the question of naval limitation the latter would be prepared to withdraw their opposition to the views of the French and most other Governments on the question of trained reserves, which caused the deadlock in the Preparatory Commission in March 1927."

Copies of both this telegram and the one to which it was a reply were sent to Washington, and were followed up, a few days later (August 10th), by a lengthy one giving a detailed explanation of the reasons which had led to the British Government taking the course it had done. After referring to the divergence of view between the British and French Governments which had prevented progress being made by the Preparatory Commission, the despatch said that the Compromise represented a successful attempt to arrive at an accord between the two Governments, and continued,

"but we realize that it is no more than the first step which we hope may lead to general agreement among the Powers represented on the Preparatory Commission. . . . In the divergence of views which appeared at the outset between the British and French Governments the view of the United States was in principle in agreement with that of Great Britain, and as the Compromise now reached with the French goes a considerable way towards meeting the views of the United States and ourselves, we entertain the hope that it will have the approval and support of the American Government. But we desire to emphasize the fact that this Anglo-French agreement is not a treaty or even a final binding agreement in regard to naval disarmament."

On the subject of the British undertaking to support the French thesis regarding army reserves, the telegram said:

"It has been stated in press telegrams that this naval agreement with the French represents a bargain, one part of which is that his Majesty's Government agree to support the contention of the French Government in the matter of military reserves. Here, again, there is some misapprehension. His Majesty's Government have reluctantly reached the conclusion that it will be impossible to move the French and the majority of other European Governments from the attitude which they have consistently adopted on this question, and that, in present conditions, no further progress in regard to land disarmament will be possible as long as this stumbling-block remains in the way. They do not, therefore, propose to offer any further resistance to the French contention at the present time. It is not believed that any American interest can be prejudiced by the withdrawal of his Majesty's Government's opposition on the military reservist question. An agreement on land disarmament, even if it is in our view not entirely satisfactory in the matter of military reservists, would represent an important stage in the general progress of disarmament, and would be far better than no agreement at all. Moreover, an acceptance of the French Government's thesis on the reservist question will have the important effect of winning the French Government over to the British and American side in the matter of the classification to be adopted as a basis for naval limitation."

There is one serious point with regard to the question of trained army reserves. This is Sir Austen Chamberlain's admission that the British undertaking to support the French view was given prior to the drawing up of the text of the Naval Compromise, since this is considered to give grounds for the French contention that the undertaking must stand, whatever might be the fate of the agreement on naval limitation.

The rising tide of public opinion both in Great Britain, the United States and Europe forced the British and French Governments to adopt a policy of explanation and apology. At Geneva, both before the Council and in interviews given to the press, Lord Cushendun, on August 30th, said that the Compromise was "not an agreement at all in the ordinary sense of the word, as applied to international negotiations resulting in an accord. It is not a treaty and it is not final." There were no secret clauses and no arrangement for pooling the two navies. This was endorsed both by the French Ministry of Marine and by M. Paul Boncour in a statement to the press.

On September 10th M. Briand, before the Assembly, said that the Compromise only represented a certain *rapprochement* of points of view, which should have been welcomed, as showing that France and Great Britain had agreed to help disarmament, instead of being regarded with so much suspicion. He complained bitterly that when two nations made an honest attempt to arrive at a compromise between their mutually conflicting national points of view, the world immediately demanded *"pas pour qui, mais, contre qui ?"*

Despite their protestations, however, neither of the contracting parties seemed anxious to take the surest way of allaying public and official suspicion, that is to say, by publishing the terms of the agreement. At this moment, however, a *deus ex machinâ* appeared unexpectedly in the power of the press, and public curiosity and anxiety were gratified if not allayed by the publication on September 21st in the *New York American*, an organ of that section of the American press controlled by Mr. William Randolph Hearst, of "the authenticated text of a letter distributed by the Quai d'Orsay to French Ambassadors in the principal countries," dated August 3rd, and giving a *résumé* of the negotiations which had terminated in the Anglo-French Naval Compromise.[1]

Through what channels this important document came into the possession of the Hearst press has never been disclosed. The authenticity of the letter has never been questioned, and though it is not printed in the French Blue Book it is referred to in a footnote on page 50. The French Government arrested, cross-examined, and ultimately deported the Hearst representative in Paris, Mr. Horan, who declared that he had received the document from Mr. Hearst himself in the Hotel Crillon. Two subordinate officials of the Quai d'Orsay were suspended, and two years later the Government took its final revenge when, in the summer of 1930, it had the temerity to deport Mr. Hearst himself as "an enemy of the Republic."

If public opinion had been disturbed on account of its ignorance, it was stirred to its depths on being possessed of the facts through the journalistic scoop of the *New York American*. At once the greatest indignation was manifested in Great Britain and in Germany, but by far the worst reaction was in the United States. Apart from the fact that the Compromise itself was based upon a formula which had already been rejected by United States representatives, American opinion was profoundly shocked to learn that, simultaneously with the negotiations for the Kellogg Pact, conversations of a very different nature had been in progress between France and Great Britain. It was indeed unfortunate that M. Briand's invitations to the

[1] Two days later, on September 23rd, the *Red Star*, the organ of the Soviet Army, published a statement regarding the Compromise to the effect that France and Great Britain had also concluded secret agreements for the pooling of their air forces, for the concordance of their "military instructive" services and intelligence services in the Far East and in the U.S.S.R., and for concerted action in their policies towards the Rhineland and Reparation questions, in Balkan Affairs, and in countries bordering on the U.S.S.R.

ceremony of signing the General Treaty for the Renunciation
of War should have been issued just the day before he signed
the Note of July 28th, which completed the Anglo-French
Compromise, and that Sir Austen Chamberlain should have
announced the fact of the Compromise on July 30th during
the same sitting of the House of Commons at which he made
his official statement on the Kellogg Pact after its acceptance
by the British Government.

These coincidences produced the effect on the American
mind of a fresh manifestation of the Old Adam, and as Professor Toynbee has pointed out, "fitted in with the traditional
American vision of a great gulf fixed between the Old World
and the New—the Old World a City of Destruction whose
denizens were fast bound in the misery and iron of a Machia-
vellian 'Old Diplomacy,' and the New World, a 'City of God'
where a Chosen People were assured of a happier dispensation
so long as they kept clear of entanglements with their less
fortunate European fellow-creatures."

In view of the storm raised by the unexpected contribution
of the Hearst press the British Foreign Office decided to
communicate to the American, Italian and Japanese Governments the texts of the Notes of June 28th and July 20th and
28th, and to state that no other Notes had passed between
the British and French Governments. But even this communication was only made in confidence (in the version to the
United States the word "confidentially" is printed in italics)
and was not intended for publication, so that apart from the
Hearst text the world was still in ignorance of details when,
on September 29th, the American Ambassador in London
made public the text of his Government's Reply to the British
Note of July 30th containing the proposals embodied in the
Compromise.

It is to be assumed that the French Government at this
moment either became alarmed at the opposition conjured
up or desired for other reasons to wash its hands of the whole
affair. It accordingly brought pressure to bear on the British
Government to publish the texts of the three Notes, and

when Whitehall demurred, the Quai d'Orsay authorized the publication on October 5th in the *Echo de Paris* of a very full summary of their contents. Its hand thus forced, the British Government could hold back no longer, but it was not until October 22nd that the simultaneous publication in London and Paris of a British White Paper and French Blue Book gave to the world the whole story of the Compromise.

The Compromise itself, moribund from birth, was now defunct and buried, having received its *coup de grâce* in the American Reply.

This Reply, delivered in London on September 28th, contained an unqualified rejection of the Compromise, on the ground that it imposed restrictions only on types peculiarly suited to the United States. It was pointed out that the Washington Treaty of 1922 regulated the first two classes of vessels mentioned in the Compromise, i.e. capital ships and aircraft carriers, and the Preparatory Commission for the Disarmament Conference would, therefore, only have to consider cruisers of 10,000 tons and under, with guns of 6-inch to 8-inch calibre, and ocean-going submarines of over 600 tons. The United States Government had always taken the line that limitation, to be effective, should apply to all classes of combatant vessels; the Compromise, however, provided for the limitation only of the 10,000-ton 8-inch gun type of cruiser, and this would mean the imposition of restrictions only on types peculiarly suited to the needs of the United States.

With regard to the suggestion that there should be no restriction on 6-inch-gun cruisers, this was regarded as even more unacceptable than the proposals made by Great Britain at Geneva, and the United States Government made it clear it could not accept these cruisers as a separate class, since they were capable of being made into highly efficient offensive vessels. As 6-inch guns could be mounted on merchant ships, the proposal would place the United States at a "decided disadvantage," and was "contrary to the principle of limitation as applied to important combatant types of vessels."

As regards submarines, the United States Government would gladly see them abolished, but if this were not done, they should be limited to a reasonable tonnage or number.

Dealing with the question of limitation generally, the United States Government could not "consent to proposals which would still allow the unlimited building of certain types of highly efficient fighting ships, while imposing restrictions on types peculiarly suitable to American needs."

The Note then recapitulated the proposals put forward by the United States Government at the Geneva Conference, and stated that it remained willing to use its best efforts to obtain a basis of further limitations satisfactory to all the Powers, and was willing to take into consideration the special needs of France, Italy and any other Power for the particular class of vessels deemed by them most suitable for their defence. For instance, the Powers might be permitted to vary the percentage of tonnage in classes within the total tonnage, a certain percentage to be agreed upon. "If there were an increase in one class it should be deducted from the tonnage to be used in other classes . . . a proposal along these lines made by Great Britain . . . would be sympathetically considered by the United States."

The Japanese Reply, received on September 29th, expressed "concurrence to the purport of the Agreement," but the Reply of the Italian Government on October 6th destroyed what few hopes the American Note may have left unshattered. It began by making it very clear that that Government could not concur in a separate discussion of the naval problem, but only in one which considered limitation "in the broadest and most logical manner from its three aspects, military, naval, aerial." Nor could armaments and their limitation be considered absolutely, "but only in relation to those of other nations." As regards limitation generally, the Italian Government were "disposed *a priori* to accept as the limit of their own armaments any figures, however low they may be, provided that they are not exceeded by any other European Continental Power," but considered that the adoption of the formula of global limitation of tonnage would, in the case of naval armaments, be the most suitable means for the application of this principle. One reason given for this was that each State, owing to the greater elasticity and adaptability of the system, would find itself able to accept a lower limit, a consideration which had not previously been put forward. A further reason advanced was that the States with greater financial resources would have in limitation by categories the means of creating and maintaining an absolute superiority in each of the different types of ships over those States with smaller resources. Whereas global tonnage, by leaving each State free to adopt and choose those types which best suited its needs, would, in the Italian view, allow the less fully armed States to find in such choice and adoption a certain compensation for the superiority of the others.

The special exigencies of national defence were then described in some detail, emphasis being laid on the fact that Italy was dependent on outlets through the Straits of Gibraltar and the Suez Canal for her communications with the outside world. Her coastline was long, and she was unable to "ignore other nations which touch, or may touch, the Mediterranean, and which are particularly favoured by their geographical position on essential lines of communication."

The Reply concluded with a suggestion in the following terms: That the five signatory Powers of the Washington Treaty should undertake to postpone until after the year 1936 the construction of those capital ships which the Treaty would allow them to lay down during the period 1931–1936. Such an agreement would provide the world with a tangible proof of their pacific sentiments, whilst leaving their fleets in the conditions of the same relative situation as that laid down by the Washington Treaty for the year 1931.

In a final endeavour to explain away its position abroad, the British Government on October 9th addressed a long recapitulatory circular despatch to his Majesty's Representatives in all countries represented on the Preparatory Disarmament Commission. But at home there still lurked an uneasy feeling that some new commitment had been given to France, an impression which was increased rather than otherwise by Lord Cushendun's statement on October 25th that "there was no new entente with France, for the old one had never been dissolved."

The Prime Minister took the opportunity to destroy any illusions on this point in the course of a speech at the Albert Hall on October 26th. Mr. Baldwin said:

"I must contradict an idea that has gained currency in some quarters that we have to some extent abandoned our position of impartiality and conciliation, which we assumed at the time of the Locarno Pact. It is not so; we have made no new engagements, and there is no change in the orientation of our policy. Our interests and our inclination alike prompt us to preserve and even strengthen the cordiality of our relations with Germany, as well as with France. I regret profoundly the temporary failure to come to an agreement with America on naval matters . . . our policy in naval building is, and has been for the last few years, to go slow. We have no intention of building in competition with the United States of America."

The Compromise was the subject of debates in the House of Lords on November 7th and in the House of Commons on November 13th. In both Houses the Government Speakers made it clear that they regarded the Compromise as dead, and with reference to the question of trained reserves, Lord Cushendun declared that his Majesty's Government in Great Britain "were under no obligation in the matter and could if they liked alter their attitude and insist upon their own view"; a statement which was equally forcefully endorsed by Mr. Bridgeman in the Commons. This view, as has already been seen,[1] was not shared by the French Government, which confidently hoped for British support in the matter of trained reserves despite the collapse of the Compromise.

Thus concluded an affair which Lord Grey accurately described as "a very small thing" which "had the most tremendous consequences." Its effect was lamentable both at home and abroad, where it bred suspicion and fear. Acting upon the public opinion of the United States, already exacer-

[1] See above, p. 135.

bated at the results of the Coolidge Conference, it produced a
state of mind intensely antagonistic towards Great Britain, a
state of mind which had almost immediate tangible expression
in the passage through Congress on February 13, 1929, of a
Bill authorizing the President of the United States to undertake the construction of fifteen 10,000-ton "light" cruisers
and one aircraft carrier at a total cost of some two hundred
and seventy-four million dollars.

Thus an agreement concluded to facilitate the reduction of
armaments resulted indirectly in the launching of the largest
post-war building programme in the world.

3. THE ANGLO-AMERICAN *RAPPROCHEMENT* 1929[1]

The year 1929 opened as inauspiciously for the future of disarmament as it was possible to conceive. Both in England and
America the most detrimental effect had been produced by the
failure of the Coolidge Conference and of the Anglo-French
Naval Compromise. In England a latent dislike of all things
transatlantic blazed up afresh and produced a state of mind
vis-à-vis the United States comparable only to that manifested towards Germany in the years 1908–1914. In America
this antagonism and suspicion was keenly reciprocated and
found expression during the Congressional debates on the
ratification of the Kellogg Pact and the passage of the Cruiser
Bill. In both countries men of goodwill declared war between
them to be "unthinkable," a sure sign that they had already
begun to think about it.

A new note was struck, however, by President Hoover in
his Inaugural Address on March 4, 1929. "Peace"—he declared—
"can be contributed to by respect for our ability in defence.
Peace can be promoted by the limitation of arms, and by the
creation of the instrumentalities for the peaceful settlement
of controversies. I covet for this administration a record

---

[1] The greater part of this section appeared in the form of articles by Mr.
Latimer and the author in the *Bulletin of International News* for July 6, 1929,
and October 24, 1929.—J. W. W.-B.

of having further contributed to advance the cause of peace."

It was generally believed and hoped that this statement was but the prelude to some *démarche* which might effect a solution of the deadlock which existed, and these hopes were unexpectedly quickly fulfilled at the Sixth Session of the Preparatory Disarmament Commission.

The story of Mr. Gibson's dramatic intervention on April 22nd has already been told elsewhere in this book,[1] and it will suffice here to say that he accepted on the part of the United States as a basis of discussion the French thesis on naval disarmament put forward at the Third Session of the Commission in 1927. This thesis, it will be remembered, aimed at the limitation of total tonnage, and also at the division of total tonnage declared by each contracting party into total tonnage by groups. These groups would apply to four classes, capital ships, aircraft carriers, surface vessels under 10,000 tons and submarines. Each contracting party would undertake to fix a maximum tonnage for each of the categories during the period of validity of the Convention. But, within the limits of the total tonnage stated, each party could alter its allocation to each class, within a certain margin, subject to informing the Secretariat of the League at least one year before laying down the portion of the tonnage to be transferred.

This declaration of policy on the part of the United States was not only most welcome but also most timely, for it was made on the eve of the British General Election and undoubtedly influenced very strongly the leaders of the three political parties in the conduct of their campaigns. Emphasis was laid by all three on the necessity for the reduction of naval armaments and for the maintenance of Anglo-American friendship.

The next direct step, however, came from President Hoover, who took the opportunity in his Memorial Day Speech (May 30th) at the Arlington National Cemetery to develop still further his plans for naval reduction. If the Kellogg Treaty was to

[1] See above, p. 69.

fulfil its high purpose, said Mr. Hoover, the nations of the
world would have to "clothe faith and idealism with action,"
which would have to "march with the inexorable tread of
common sense and realism to accomplishment." He then
added:

"But to arrive at any agreement through which we can, marching in
company with our brother nations, secure a reduction of armament but
at the same time maintain a just preparedness for the protection of our
peoples we must find a rational yardstick with which to make reasonable
comparisons of their naval units and ours and thus maintain an agreed
relativity.

"So far the world has failed to find such a yardstick. To say that
such a measure cannot be found is the counsel of despair; it is a challenge
to the naval authorities of the world; it is the condemnation of the
world to the Sisyphean toil of competitive armaments.

"The present Administration of the United States has undertaken to
approach this vital problem with a new programme. We feel that it is
useless for us to talk of the limitation of arms if such limitations are to
be set so high as virtually to be an incitement to increase armament."

Fresh support for the President was given on the following
day by the Secretary of State, Colonel Stimson, who in a
public statement laid stress upon the economic as well as the
moral aspect of the armaments question, drawing attention
to the fact that a modern capital ship cost between $30,000,000
and $40,000,000 and the cost of the programme recommended
by the Navy Department in case the policy of naval reduction
was not adopted was, for new ships alone, $1,170,800,000
(£234,100,000).

The British elections resulted in the Labour Party's being
returned to power though without an absolute majority, and
immediately rumours became current that Mr. Ramsay Mac-
Donald proposed to visit Washington at the end of July for a
personal and direct conference with President Hoover on Anglo-
American relations in general and naval reduction in particular.
Though it is uncertain whether this statement had any official
foundation, it gave a further fillip to the increase of goodwill
between the two countries.

The appearance of Brigadier-General Charles Dawes upon
the scene as the new American Ambassador to St. James's

introduced a new, and almost lightning, element into the proceedings. From mid-Atlantic General Dawes made radio arrangements to present his credentials to the King on the day after his arrival in England, which occurred on June 14th. Accordingly he was received at Windsor on the 15th, and that same evening left London for Scotland to confer with Mr. MacDonald at Forres, and the result of their conversation was described in a joint *communiqué* as "informal and general and most satisfactory."

Both the Prime Minister and the American Ambassador subsequently referred at greater length to their conversations. In a speech at Lossiemouth on June 18th, Mr. MacDonald declared that they had met "in the hope that they might be instrumental in preparing a board around which the other nations might ultimately sit in co-operative fellowship, studying the arts and ways of peace, gaining a sense of security not by arms, but by the absence of them."

On the same evening General Dawes was entertained in London by the Pilgrims Society and discussed the proposed agreement in greater detail. The procedure, as he outlined it, fell into three stages:

(1) That the naval experts of each country should work out separate formulæ for the "yardstick"—to which President Hoover had already referred—for the valuation of the comparative fighting strength of naval units.

(2) That the experts should report each to his respective Government and that a conference of statesmen would then be called to frame an agreed formula applicable to all fleets.

(3) This formula would then be written into a diplomatic agreement for the reduction of naval armaments. General Dawes particularly emphasized the necessity that the final agreement on naval reduction should be couched in terms understandable by the ordinary man in the street.

The general reaction abroad to General Dawes' speech was not unfavourable. In Japan the anxiety which had at first arisen at the news of the Forres conference was dispelled and satisfaction was expressed that there was no intention of presenting to the world an Anglo-American *fait accompli*. With regard to the "yardstick," Japanese naval authorities described it as "not impossible, but very difficult." As was to be expected, opinion in Germany expressed great satisfaction at this new step towards international disarmament, but there was some considerable reserve about its reception in France and Italy, "Pertinax" declaring in the *Echo de Paris* that:

"We gather from all this flow of words that the United States is asking Great Britain to give up her supremacy in battle cruisers on the understanding that Great Britain obtains all the smaller cruisers necessary to police her trade routes."

The United States Government showed no sign of allowing the question to lapse, and on June 24th Mr. Gibson arrived in London to confer with General Dawes on the question of giving practical form to the proposals already made. That Great Britain was equally anxious for the immediate putting into effect of the new proposals was evident from the following passage from the King's Speech read to Parliament on July 2nd:

"Conversations have commenced with the Ambassador of the United States of America on the subject of naval disarmament in consequence of which it is the earnest hope of my Government to ensure, in co-operation with my Governments in the Dominions, the Government of India and the Governments of foreign Powers, an early reduction of armaments throughout the world.

In the course of conversations the spokesmen on both sides had continually to keep before them the necessity of neither saying nor doing anything which could possibly give the impression abroad that they contemplated any form of alliance between America and Great Britain, or that they were aiming at presenting to the other naval Powers a *fait accompli* as regards a programme of naval limitation. They had to be careful, too, to keep before their minds the fact that the other Powers regard many of the aspects of the problem of disarmament from a point of view very different from their own. To give only two instances, the French Government made a great point of the necessity, in its view, of dealing with the question of naval disarmament only as part of the whole problem of disarmament on land, sea and in the air, for which reason it regarded the work of the forthcoming naval conference merely as a preliminary to the meeting of the Preparatory Disarmament Commission at Geneva. Again, French opinion was supported by that of Italy and Japan in declining to consider any scheme of naval reduction which would deprive those countries of the right to maintain a fleet of submarines sufficiently large to be effective, in their view, for the defence of their coasts, and the conversations were accordingly carefully confined to consideration of the particular differences of view that had in the past prevented agreement between Great Britain and America as regards cruisers. Throughout the conversations, therefore, one of the chief tasks, on both sides of the Atlantic, was to prevent and correct wrong impressions given by statements in the press and elsewhere such as might be calculated to mislead public opinion at home, as well as abroad, as to the real purpose of the conversations. Thus, on July 1st, Mr. Stimson, the United States Secretary of State, took occasion to emphasize that no agreement was aimed at which could possibly have the air of an exclusively Anglo-American arrangement, and at the same time answered a report which, according to the New York press, was being circulated in England—"a considerable feeling," was the description given of it—that, after the creation of an atmosphere excluding Anglo-American war, "to turn to an effort to establish that, in the case of a next war—which is never to occur—the warships of the two countries should be able to shoot on a parity, seems to be little in the spirit of the occasion," since "it is no way to begin discussions of future perpetual peace by arguing about the tools of war."

Mr. Stimson stated that, in his opinion, the doctrine of parity was of very great importance, not as a means of determining how the nations were to shoot at each other, but as a means of helping them to agree not to do so, since the minute they agreed not to outbuild each other they were taking one of the longest steps possible towards not having a war. Later he developed the same idea in a statement issued to the press on

July 25th with the object of defining the attitude of the Administration towards the principle of parity. This, he said, should not be regarded in the light of a military doctrine at all, but as a doctrine of statesmanship, which contemplated the preclusion of any conflict between the two countries, and aimed at effecting the reduction of their respective naval power.

On another occasion, on July 12th, he found it necessary to issue an emphatic denial that anything in the nature of a fiat was to be despatched to the other naval Powers insisting that the principle of parity should be honoured in any disarmament agreement that might be arrived at. In this, he said, there was not one iota of truth.

The last occasion in which he was compelled to intervene was on October 11th, when a statement was published in Europe suggesting that Great Britain and the United States had arranged to pool their fleets in the event of war. Mr. Stimson said that this report so completely misconceived and misrepresented the actual facts and the spirit of their conference that he could not let it pass without reply. The tenor of their conversations had been exactly the reverse; the understanding aimed at was a moral one, as the influence they were seeking to exert was a moral, and not a military influence. He concluded by saying that the basis of all their discussions was the Kellogg Peace Treaty.

Enough has been said to make clear some of the difficulties met with by the heads of the two Governments, quite apart from those inherent in the problem of reconciling the British and American views as to the lines on which parity should be reached in cruiser strength, and as to the method by which armaments reduction should be effected.

Conversations between Mr. MacDonald, on the one hand, and General Dawes and Mr. Gibson, on the other, continued until the third week of July, when two statements were made which marked a landmark in the negotiations. On July 23rd Mr. Hoover issued a statement on military expenditure in which he reminded the country that "our whole situation is certainly modified" by the existence of the Kellogg Treaty, and said that "the American people should understand that the current expenditure on the strictly military activities (i.e., omitting pensions, etc.) of the army and navy constitutes the largest military Budget of any nation in the world to-day." He added that the total cost of the army and navy was increasing at the rate of approximately $50 millions a year.

On the following day Mr. MacDonald announced in the House of Commons that it had been decided to suspend all work on the 10,000-ton cruisers *Surrey* and *Northumberland*, to cancel the submarine depot ship *Maidstone*, as also two contract submarines, and to slow down all Government dockyard work. As regards the 1929–30 construction programme no decisions were yet to be made, and in any case no commitments for building were to be entered into before the autumn. In explanation of these decisions the Prime Minister said that material progress had been made towards agreement with America. The British Government had definitely agreed to the principle of parity, on the allowance of a measure of elasticity to meet the differing peace requirements of the two nations, and upon determining that technical points should not be allowed to override great public issues. He added that the other naval Powers were being kept informed of the trend of the talks he had been having with the United States Ambassador.

On the same day Mr. Hoover proclaimed the Kellogg Treaty effective, and immediately on learning of Mr. MacDonald's statement announced that though the "actual construction of three 10,000-ton cruisers due to be begun this fall would not be likely in themselves to produce inequality in the final result, we do not wish to have any misunderstanding of our actions, and therefore we shall not lay these keels until there has been an opportunity for full consideration of their effect upon the final agreement for parity which we expect to reach." Mr. Hoover continued, "Mr. MacDonald has introduced the principle of parity, which we have now adopted, and its consummation means that Great Britain and the United States henceforth are not to compete in armaments as potential opponents, but to co-operate as friends in their reduction."

References to Mr. MacDonald's statement were also made the next day by Mr. Stimson, who characterized the British Government's decision as "an immense and tremendous step forward toward an accord between the two nations," adding that the "explicit and formal" concession now made for the first time by the British Government was the first step in the forward progress. The two statements together, those of the Prime Minister and the President, were considered by the press to "tend to create a new atmosphere in Anglo-American relations."

Only a few days later, on July 31st, Mr. Hoover addressed a letter to the American Legion in which he explained that "parity with Great Britain is enunciated by our naval authorities as a complete defence of the United States in any contingency, and defence is all we seek."

Meanwhile, further conversations had been held between Mr. MacDonald and General Dawes, whose reports were considered at length at several meetings called by the President at the White House. Mr. Hoover now had to deal with considerable criticism at home. On August 2nd, Senator Borah published a statement in which he said that nothing but "parity coupled with reduction" would satisfy him; in other words, that this must *not* be obtained by building up to Great Britain. As the statement was issued the day following a prolonged conversation between the Senator and the President it was assumed that the latter probably shared this view, but his gesture as to the postponement of the building of the three 1929–30 cruisers was met by charges by Senator Swanson, among others, that this action was contrary to law. A few days later, on August 8th, Admiral Hussey, speaking at the meeting of the Institute of Politics at Williamstown, claimed that between the Washington Treaty and October 1928 the United States had scrapped 842,000 tons, as compared with only 447,000 tons scrapped by Great Britain,[1] while she had built only 157,000 tons, as compared with Great Britain's 393,000 tons.

[1] This figure omitted, however, 4 blue-print *Hoods*.

On August 20th a further statement was published by Mr. MacDonald, in the form of a report on a further series of meetings he had had with General Dawes in Scotland. The Premier said they had been working at the question of how to reconcile three positions : American claims to parity; British necessities, "which have no relation at all with American building"; and the desire, common to both Governments, to reduce armaments. Considerable progress had been made, but "both of us are fully aware," he concluded, "that no agreement between us two can carry us very far unless other Powers agree, and that conditions all our work."

This statement was supplemented three days later by a speech by General Dawes at Elgin, in which he said that though the negotiations had been progressing favourably they had not yet reached the proper stage for useful discussion in detail in the press. He continued:

"The arbitrators of the ultimate fate of this naval effort will be the respective public sentiments of the naval Powers. Time must be taken to reduce to their simplest terms, before their public discussion, the problems it involves, so that the average man can then understand better what it is all about. If the problem is not mastered so that its final solution is clear and satisfactory to the average man, Parliaments and Congresses may not ratify it in the end . . . the one unforgivable thing would be an inadequate preparation for the proposed naval conference."

On the same day the press in the United States professed to have good authority for stating that Mr. MacDonald was leaving England for New York on September 28th, and that the proposed naval conference would be held in London in December. At the same time the announcement was made semi-officially that any reports as to agreement having been reached were entirely premature.

The next stage was marked by Mr. MacDonald's speech before the Assembly of the League of Nations on September 3rd. After outlining the principles which were guiding British foreign policy, he said that he hoped within a few days to be able to publish the details of a projected naval agreement with the United States Government, since 17 out of the 20 points under discussion had already been settled, but this, he was careful to add, was to be regarded merely as a preliminary to the calling of a five-Power naval conference, at which all would be free to negotiate as though no conversations had taken place between Great Britain and America. This announcement was apparently looked upon as slightly too optimistic by the United States Secretary of State, for on the following day he issued a statement in which he said "we have been making hopeful progress, but we feel it will still require a considerable period of hard work on details before an agreement on parity can be concluded."

On the same day, September 4th, the press at Geneva published details of a number of points on which agreement was believed, on trustworthy authority, to have been reached in principle. These were:

The whole accord was to be definitely linked to the Kellogg Treaty, and to assume naval co-operation, and not naval antagonism.

Parity or equality to be applicable to every class of vessel.

Reduction of naval strength and not merely its limitation.

Progressive reduction over a period of years, to be effected by the non-replacement of obsolete vessels.

Prolongation of the active life of all warships.

A total tonnage limitation for destroyers and submarines.

Application of the "yardstick" to cruisers only.

The definite relegation of small cruisers to a "police" class, which would not be computed in naval strength, or not, at any rate, by the same measurement as of the large cruisers.

Speculation as to the exact nature of the points *not* yet settled was somewhat overshadowed, in the United States at least, by the appearance in the press of a somewhat sensational story regarding the activities of a certain Mr. Shearer, who had been employed by three prominent shipbuilding firms as an observer at the Geneva Naval Conference of 1927. On September 6th a semi-official statement was issued in Washington intimating that Great Britain had acknowledged the right of the United States to have more 10,000-ton cruisers than herself, and that the United States had, on her side, recognized the British right to have a larger total cruiser tonnage, but on the same day the President himself issued a statement denouncing Mr. Shearer's actions in strong terms, and explaining that he wished to make quite clear his determination that the Administration's international negotiations should not be interfered with from such sources or through such methods. The immediate result of this was the decision of the Naval Affairs Committee of Congress, announced on September 10th, to hold an investigation into Mr. Shearer's activities at Geneva and his connection with shipbuilding companies, followed by a further statement by the President urging that the question "should be gone into to the very bottom." On September 11th the Senate ordered an official investigation of the activities of American shipbuilding corporations at the Geneva Naval Conference of 1927.

Meanwhile, another glimpse of the progress of the negotiations had been given to the public by the appearance on September 9th of a semi-official statement in Washington reporting the receipt of proposals from Great Britain suggesting the adoption of the figure of 340,000 tons as her maximum total cruiser strength, and of 295,000 to 305,000 tons for the United States, which would be allowed 18 10,000-ton vessels, or three more than Great Britain. The statement also announced that the two nations had reached agreement regarding the postponement of the replacement of battleships and the fixing of the total tonnage for destroyers and submarines. On September 11th a further conference was held at the White House to consider the British proposal.

In Great Britain, Mr. MacDonald had taken the opportunity to refer to the progress of the conversations in a speech to his constituency at Seaham on September 10th, and two days later, after studying the United States' reply to the proposals just mentioned, he stated that the margin of difference between the views of the two Governments related to three 8-inch-gun 10,000-ton cruisers. On the same day the official announcement was made that he would leave England for New York on September 28th.

The negotiations had now been narrowed down to a point at

which Mr. Stimson was able to say that they were not even discussing tonnage, but only the question of a type of gun, which, he said, "gives an idea of how near we are together on the broad side of the picture." In a statement issued on September 13th the Secretary of State said the Government was now ready for a conference with the other four Powers. The main differences with Great Britain would be "ironed out" at the conference, and he again reminded the country that if the programme already sanctioned for the Navy were completed, it would cost the equivalent of over £234 millions, not counting vastly increased expenses of operation.

On the same day Mr. MacDonald gave an interviewer a statement for the *Petit Parisien*, emphasizing that the British Government's aim was to maintain the closest co-operation with France, who was assured that there could never be an alliance of any kind whatever from which she would be excluded.

It was on September 16th that the official announcement was made regarding the British Prime Minister's programme during his visit to the United States, which was to last from October 4th until he should leave for Canada on October 15th. On the same day it was allowed to be understood that the British Government did not claim the right to possess more than 50 cruisers,[1] of which 15 should be of 10,000 tons with 8-inch guns, and an announcement was made that the proposed naval conference would probably not be held until the third week in January; and that the United States delegation would probably be headed by Mr. Stimson.

On September 17th the British Premier informed the French, Italian and Japanese Governments that invitations were to be sent to them to attend a conference to be held in London on January 20th or 21st, and a day or two later it was stated in Washington that the Secretary of State had been in personal touch with the Ambassadors of those countries regarding the progress of events, and had all along kept the European Governments concerned, including that of Spain, informed of the

---

[1] The number mentioned as the minimum necessary for Imperial defence in 1927 was seventy.

results of the Anglo-American conversations. The necessity, equally important, of keeping their own people informed was not lost sight of by him or by the President, and on September 18th Mr. Hoover broadcast by wireless a statement regarding the policy of the Government. This he described as actuated by the conviction that naval and military "preparedness must not exceed the barest necessity for defence or it becomes a threat against others and thus a cause of fear and animosity of the world." He concluded his message with the words, "Confidence that there will be peace is the first necessity of human progress."

Mr. MacDonald also issued two statements, one on September 27th and the other on the following day, on his departure from Southampton. In the first he emphasized the importance of terminating the deadlock arrived at at Geneva in 1927 as an essential preliminary to progress in naval disarmament, and in the second he took equal care to reassure the Continental countries and Japan regarding the conversations he had been having with General Dawes, and said:

> "Any agreement we achieve can only be, and is only intended to be, a preliminary to the larger agreement which must be reached in conference with the other naval Powers, and later on in the Preparatory Disarmament Commission sitting at Geneva . . . we are not trying to present any other nation or nations with a *fait accompli* which they must take or leave."

Mr. MacDonald reached New York on October 4th and, in his speech replying to an address of welcome, emphasized the fact that he came to the United States not as the leader of a political party, but as the representative of the British people and of a united nation. Two days later appeared the announcement regarding the invitations to the Naval Conference, which were being issued on October 7th to the other three Powers, and the text of these was published on October 8th.[1] Meanwhile, Mr. MacDonald had spent the week-end of October 5th–7th as Mr. Hoover's guest in the country, and on his return to

---

[1] For text see *Documents on International Affairs*, 1929, edited by J. W. Wheeler-Bennett (Oxford, 1930), p. 15.

Washington a joint *communiqué* was issued in which the two statesmen confined themselves to reporting that they had made gratifying progress in their frank review of all the questions which might give rise to friction between their two peoples. Mr. Hoover supplemented this the next day by a statement to the press in which he said that they were fortunate in not having any controversies between the two countries to be settled and they were therefore able to discuss their mutual problems "in the long-distance view, and solely in the broad aspect of human welfare in the largest sense." Mr. MacDonald, on his side, had sought to make clear to the American public the British Government's conception of the lines on which its foreign policy was to be conducted by a speech before the Senate on October 7th, in which he said that when Britain signed the Kellogg Treaty, she meant it to be the guiding idea in future policy, and he went on "if we do our duty in making it effective, it can only mean that no section of our arms on sea, on land or in the air can ever come into hostile conflict again."

A more detailed joint statement was issued on October 9th. This was received with much satisfaction on both sides of the Atlantic, *The Times*, for example, describing it as "a hopeful preface to a more intensive study of international relations in which disarmament will be linked with a fundamental re-survey of the functions of fleets in the future and of the conceptions of security that should properly determine them."

The formal acceptance by the United States Government of the British Government's invitation to the Naval Conference was received on October 10th, and was followed by that of Italy on October 15th, and of France and Japan the following day. Meanwhile, on October 11th, Mr. MacDonald had made another speech in New York which was broadcast throughout the country, and was notable for the appeal he made to the American people to make allowances for the great importance attached to the Navy by the British people.

[1] For text of Joint Statement see *Documents on International Affairs, 1929*, p. 17.

"In our case," he said, "the Navy is the very life of our nation. We have romance surrounding it; we are a people of the sea; we are a small island; Europe is at our doors; for good or for ill the lines of our Empire have been thrown all over the face of the earth; we have to import our food; a month's blockade, effectively carried out, would starve us all . . . in the event of any conflict Britain's Navy is Britain itself."

The British Premier's stay in the United States came to an end on October 15th, when he left for Canada. His visit was described in the press as having definitely established the co-operative, as distinct from the competitive, method as that to be followed in the discussion of future Anglo-American problems.

4. The London Naval Conference, 1930[1]

The conversations in America between Mr. MacDonald and the President resulted, then, in sufficient progress being made to justify the convening of an international conference, the invitations to which were sent by the British Government to the Governments of the United States, France, Italy and Japan on October 7th. Mr. MacDonald left the United States for Canada on October 15th, and on his return to England at once took steps to carry out the exchange of views with the Governments of France, Italy and Japan which he had previously declared to be an essential preliminary to the actual meeting round the Conference table. Before he left Canada he had referred to this in a speech at Ottawa, when he said that on his return to London he would begin conversations with the other interested Powers "in the same frank, free and open way that has characterized the conversations between the United States and ourselves . . . the world is not the United States plus ourselves. Had that been the case we should have come to an agreement a week after the negotiations started."

The exchange of views which was carried on during the last

---

[1] This account of the London Conference is reprinted almost entirely from articles by Mr. Hugh Latimer in the *Bulletin of International News*, appearing in the issues of January 16, 1930, March 27, 1930, April 10, 1930, and May 8, 1930.

two months of 1929 was the occasion of very definite expressions of opinion by the French and Japanese Governments as to the attitude they intended to take up at the Conference, the former, in particular, having taken the precaution to set on record, in a Memorandum presented to the British Government on December 20th, its considered views as to the exact function which the Conference should fulfil in the general scheme for dealing with the whole question of disarmament. The Italian and Japanese Governments also gave clear indications of the claims which they intended to put forward, but before referring to these something must be said of the course of events following on Mr. MacDonald's return to England in so far as it concerned the question under review.

The Prime Minister signalized his reappearance in Parliament by a statement on November 5th regarding his activities in America. In this he said that one of the principal landmarks of his visit to the United States was Mr. Hoover's agreement with him to examine frankly and jointly with the British Government the questions of belligerent powers and fortified naval bases. A few days later, however, speaking at the Lord Mayor's Banquet on November 9th, he stated that the question of the freedom of the seas would not be raised at the London Conference, and he later confirmed this in the House of Commons on December 3rd, when, in answer to a question as to the agenda of the Conference, he replied that only one subject would be dealt with, namely, how best the five Powers could agree upon the reduction and limitation of war vessels on the basis of mutually accepted strength.

Accordingly, when Mr. Hoover put forward a suggestion in his Armistice Day Speech that food ships might be placed on the same footing as hospital ships in time of war, the varied expressions of view which the proposal called forth had an academic rather than a practical interest, and more attention was paid to his statement, later in the Speech, that the people of the United States did not wish to have one gun or one armed man beyond what was necessary for defence alone, and they would reduce their naval strength in proportion to any other; "it only remains for the others to say how low they will go. It cannot be too low for us."

In London during the same week two other references were made to the forthcoming Naval Conference. On November 13th the First Lord of the Admiralty informed Parliament that, pending the results of the work of the Conference, no new work would be embarked upon at the Singapore Naval Base, while the work already contracted for would be slowed down as much as possible. Three days later General Dawes, speaking in London, said that as the result of the preliminary discussions of the previous four months a difference of opinion between the British and United States Governments remained on only a minor matter of 30,000 tons, out of an aggregate of 2,400,000 tons.

It was on the same day, November 16, 1929, that the first official intimation was received from the Japanese Government as to the claims it intended putting forward in London. In a communication to the State Department in Washington it was explained that Japan, while ready to support any scheme for reduction of naval armaments, considered that the existing ratio of 5–5–3 for capital ships ought to be changed, in respect of 10,000-ton cruisers mounting 8-inch guns, to a ratio of 10–10–7, as representing Japan's minimum requirement for defence. Shortly afterwards the Japanese delegation to the Conference arrived in Washington on its way to London, and prolonged discussions took place with the Secretary of State with a view to clarifying the positions of the two countries. At the end of November it was semi-officially announced in Tokyo that the delegation had received instructions to claim a 70 per cent. ratio for "treaty" cruisers,[1] and to maintain the right to retain the existing submarine tonnage,[2] and oppose the abolition of that form of naval vessel. It was also understood that Japan favoured a reduction in the size of capital ships to a maximum displacement of 25,000 tons, and in the calibre

---

[1] That is, cruisers of 10,000 tons. These are described as "light cruisers" in the United States Naval Construction (Cruiser) Bill of February 13, 1929.
[2] This amounted at January 1, 1930, to approximately 78,000 tons.

of guns to a maximum of 14 inches. She also approved the establishment of age limits as follows: for capital ships, 25 years; for cruisers, 20 years; for destroyers, 16 years; and for submarines, 13 years.

The results of the conversations with the State Department were made public on December 19th, when a joint *communiqué* was issued in which it was stated that the discussion had been concerned with

"the general philosophy underlying naval agreement, and the opportunities of the coming Conference. It took up the good results between the United States and Japan of the Washington Conference, and the possibilities of continuing and increasing these results. Agreement on the objectives of both countries was established. Then, in a very frank and friendly way, each delegation presented the broad outlines of its position. The discussion did not go into details or figures, which is the province of the Conference, and should be done there, where all participating nations will be represented."

Mr. Wakatsuki, the leader of the Japanese delegation, supplemented this by a statement to the American press on the same day. He said that Japan was prepared to support a proposal for a complete holiday in capital ship construction until 1936,[1] and replied to the suggestion that uneasiness might be caused in Australia if the 10–10–7 ratio were adopted for 10,000-ton cruisers by saying that if the composition of Japan's whole fleet were taken into account Australia could have no fear of aggression. On reaching England on December 27th he made a further reference to the same subject, and after pointing out that Japan was anxious that not only limitation but actual reduction of naval armaments should be effected, he said that all she asked was the security of the Empire, and she had never thought of aggression.

Meanwhile, the French and Italian Governments had been equally fully occupied in an exchange of views. Towards the end of November the question of the French Naval Estimates for 1930 came up for consideration in Parliament.[2] On November

---

[1] That is, the date of the expiry of the Washington Treaty.
[2] The programme for the year included one 10,000-ton cruiser, the seventh of a series begun in 1924, six destroyers, six submarines, etc.

21st the Naval Committee of the Senate had placed on record its opinion that the Government's existing naval construction programme (which dated from 1922) was inadequate for the overseas and coastal requirements of the country, and that freedom to build for defensive purposes ought not to be abandoned. A week later the Report on the Naval Estimates was published, and this declared that France could not go below the tonnage fixed by her naval programme of 1928.[1] The Estimates for 1930 amounted to 2,583 million francs (£20,664,000) or 22 per cent. less than those of 1914. France, it stated, had accepted the invitation to the London Conference, but should maintain the principles of the interdependence of armaments, the final decision to be taken at Geneva; refusal to consent to the abolition of submarines; and recognition of the obligations imposed by the defence of her own coasts and of her Colonial Empire.

A few days later a report was placed before the Naval Committee of the Senate which purported to show the latest estimates of the naval requirements of the five principal Powers. According to the figures given the needs of France, based on length of coastal line, distances separating the various colonies, and the volume of sea-borne trade, were three times as great as those of Italy, and nearly twice as great as those of Japan.

The next official pronouncement on the subject of the attitude of the French Government was, however, a statement made by M. Tardieu before the Foreign Affairs and Naval Committee of the Chamber on December 18th. In this the Premier said that at the London Conference France would adhere to the standpoint that naval disarmament could not be settled separately, and that the decisions arrived at would have to form the basis of the League of Nations' Conference on the Limitation of All Armaments. The next two or three days were devoted to consideration of the Naval Estimates, the debate on which opened on December 19th, being followed

---

[1] This provided for the laying down of one 10,000-ton cruiser and six submarines.

the next day by the communication to the British Government
of a lengthy memorandum setting forth the French point of
view. Simultaneously the Minister of Marine outlined the
Government's naval policy in a statement to the Chamber in
which he said that the London Conference would be only
preparatory, its object being to aid the Disarmament Conference
of the League. France, he added, would not agree to any
arbitrary standard of measurement of naval strength. Each
country had the right to ensure its own security—so long as
the League had not assumed the responsibility—with adequate
forces, and France would state her needs in the ratio of her
Colonial Empire, not arithmetically, but politically. Before
the end of December the Naval Estimates were adopted,
providing for the construction of a 10,000-ton cruiser, as
mentioned above.

If any uncertainty still existed as to the standpoint to be
maintained by the French delegation at the Conference table,
this was removed when the terms of the Government's Memorandum of December 20th were made public.[1] Many of the
points elaborated in this were repetitions of the contentions
mentioned above, but in addition the following must be noticed.
The French Government, it was stated, would have preferred
to base the negotiations for naval disarmament, not upon the
Kellogg Treaty, but on the League Covenant, since the Treaty's
application had not yet been organized, and it could not,
therefore, be looked upon yet as sufficient to guarantee the
security of the signatory nations. Accordingly, France proposed
to base the reduction of her armaments on Article 8 of the
Covenant, which did not imply the *a priori* application of
mathematical ratios. In the French view, also, a complete
naval agreement presupposed an understanding regarding the
freedom of the seas, defining the rights of belligerents and
neutrals respectively, and providing for the co-operation of
other fleets against that of an aggressor country.

As regards details, it was stated that the French Government

[1] The text of the Memorandum was published in *The Times* of December 27,
1929.

still objected to limitation of naval forces by classes of ships, but it was willing to accept the compromise put forward in April 1927 at Geneva.[1] Finally, it was asked whether it would not be possible for the Mediterranean Powers to conclude a mutual guarantee and non-aggression agreement, to include Powers not represented at the London Conference, on the lines of the Four-Power Treaty concluded at Washington regarding the Pacific.

The contents of the Memorandum were closely scrutinized on both sides of the Atlantic, certain sections of the press professing to see in it an attempt by France to torpedo the Conference. The value of the action of that country in placing all her cards on the table was, however, generally recognized, and more immediate attention was directed to the discussion which arose between the French Government and that of Italy following the latter's claim for parity with France in auxiliary vessels. Direct conversations had been opened between the two Governments in October, almost immediately following the receipt of the invitations to the Conference, and both in communications to the French Government and in statements appearing in the press the Italian claim to parity had been repeatedly ventilated. This claim is understood to be based primarily upon the dependence of that country upon sources of supply outside the Mediterranean for a large proportion of its needs in foodstuffs and raw materials, a situation which renders the possible closing of the approaches to that sea a matter of extreme seriousness to the Italian people. "Even if Italy had naval superiority in the Mediterranean," said the *Popolo d'Italia*, "it would be enough to blockade from outside the approaches to this sea in order to starve the whole Italian population. The situation presents aspects and problems which no other great naval Power has to face." It was added that Italy's mercantile marine of over 3,000,000 tons was nearly as large as that of France, and in case of mobilization the Navy would have to protect not only the merchant fleet but the return

[1] For particulars of this, see the *Bulletin* of October 13, 1928, Vol. V, No. 7, p. 6, etc.

home of hundreds of thousands of Italians resident on the other side of the Atlantic.

The French case was equally clear. Owing to the fact that France has coastal frontiers on three seas, parity with Italy in auxiliary vessel strength would involve inferiority in the Mediterranean. In addition, the possession of colonies in the Far East as well as in West Africa necessitates the distribution of her commerce-protecting forces over a wide area, apart from the need of guarding trade routes and lines of communication which are far longer than those of Italy.[1] By reducing her term of military service to one year France claimed that she had reduced her military strength to a point at which it was insufficient to defeat an invasion from the east unless it was reinforced by colonial troops, and attention was drawn to the fact that normally one-third of the French army serves in Africa, so that it is not a question of transporting an army of black battalions to Europe, but rather of bringing home the trained Colonial troops.

At the beginning of December statements were made in Paris from which it was understood that France would be prepared to accept parity with Italy in the Mediterranean, with a margin for home defence elsewhere and for the defence of her colonies, but this, of course, did not answer the Italian arguments on which the claim to parity was based. To the suggestion as to the conclusion of a Mediterranean agreement, which was communicated to the Italian Government at the same time as to that of Great Britain, Italy replied expressing willingness to follow up the proposal, but took the opportunity of repeating her claim to *de jure* parity with France in all auxiliary naval vessels. An intimation was also given, in an unofficial statement made in Rome on December 11th, that the Italian Government was now in favour of the abolition of submarines, and would support any move made by the British and United States Governments to that effect.

---

[1] The population of the French Empire was stated to be 60 millions, and its area 11 million square kilometres. The trade of the Empire was valued at 32 thousand million francs.

On January 3rd the French Government communicated to the Italian Ambassador in Paris its final views as to the Italian claim to parity. The contents of the Note have not been published and nothing was known as to its receipt until January 9th, but on that day it was unofficially stated in Rome that France had rejected the Italian suggestions and insisted upon a limitation of naval forces based on a statement by each Power outlining its construction programme for the period of any agreement which might be concluded in London.

The impression made by this communication was unfortunate, and it was felt in Rome that the policy of France in calculating her naval needs on an absolute basis, irrespective of other factors, and of declaring in advance her intended programme of construction during the years to be covered by the agreement reached in London would lead in practice to an increase rather than a reduction in armaments, and would tend to divert the Conference from its fundamental objectives.

The British Government's intentions regarding the work to be undertaken by the Conference were made known sufficiently clearly by the terms of the invitation issued to the other four Powers and by the contents of the joint *communiqué* published in Washington on October 9, 1929.[1] Reference has already been made to Mr. MacDonald's statement regarding the agenda of the Conference, and it may be added that on January 8th he informed the press that they would "deal with every class of ship, from the dreadnoughts to the submarines. . . . Great Britain, with the full consent of the Admiralty up to now, is prepared to make proposals which will mean considerable reductions in naval programmes without, in any degree, impairing the security of the Empire. But everybody, both at home and abroad, must very clearly understand that these reductions will depend upon an international agreement."

The British Government's standpoint was set forth in greater detail in the reply to the French Government's Memorandum of December 20th, the text of which was communicated to the

[1] For the text of this and of the invitation, see the *Bulletin* of October 24, 1929, Vol. VI, No. 8.

press on January 12th, and published the following day. This took up point by point each of the considerations put forward by the French Government and, while admitting their force, endeavoured to show that they were in no sense incompatible with the objects held in view by the British Government. It was pointed out that the latter considered that it would not conduce to the success of the Conference if the various Governments were to entrench themselves, before it opened, in positions —based, perhaps on misunderstandings—from which they could not recede, nor, in the invitations, had the Government referred to the obligations contracted under the Covenant or to questions of national security, because they were clearly inherent in all disarmament negotiations and must be in the mind of every nation taking part in the Conference. The considerations set forth in the French Memorandum would, of course, be in the minds of all the delegates.

As regards the absence of complete machinery of sanctions to enforce the peace agreements already in existence, the Government, it was stated:

"place considerable trust in the fact that 56 countries have declared their intention to renounce war as an instrument of national policy. . . . Unless a beginning in the reduction of naval armament is held to be justified by the measure of security already achieved through the Covenant of the League, the Treaties of Locarno, the signature of the Optional Clause . . . by thirty-three countries, and, finally, the Treaty for the Renunciation of War, public expectation will be disappointed, the tendency towards an expansion in arms, which is only too evident already, will develop, and the nations will be taught once more in practice to trust only to military preparations for their security. His Majesty's Government earnestly hope that the nations attending the London Conference may, by agreement on reduced naval strengths, register their confidence in the great advance made since the War in the provision of national security by political agreement."

On the subject of the distinction drawn between the League Covenant and the Kellogg Treaty the Government suggested that the two documents might also be regarded as complementary one of another; that is, the latter might be held by the members of the League to have completed the structure of peace which the more restricted language of the Covenant had for the time left unfinished, and acceptance of the obligations of the Covenant must not be held to involve a delay in progressive steps for disarmament, for which the Kellogg Treaty was a justification.

After pointing out that the British Government's proposals provided for a very considerable reduction in the strength which the Empire had considered necessary in all categories of combatant vessels the reply reiterated the British preference for limitation by categories as the method by which naval reduction should be carried out, but expressed readiness to study carefully the French suggestion, or "transactional proposal," put forward at Geneva in April 1927.

The interdependence of all armaments was admitted by the British Government, but it was pointed out that this fact did not imply that no attempt should be made to deal with one form of armament unless all were being dealt with simultaneously. On the contrary, it was considered that the approach to disarmament could best be facilitated by attacking the problem in detail, as would be done in London.

The suggestion of a non-aggression agreement regarding the Mediterranean was received with the criticism that a treaty such as that proposed by the French Government appeared to go considerably farther than the Pacific Treaty concluded at Washington, since the latter only provided for the summoning of a Conference for the settlement of controversies and for joint consultation in the face of aggressive action, and "inasmuch as all the Mediterranean Powers are members of the League of Nations it would appear that facilities already exist for joint consultation in the event of need."

The British proposals, which provided for "a very considerable reduction in the strength which the Empire has considered necessary," referred in part to the acceptance by the Admiralty of a total of 50 cruisers as the minimum number required for the needs of Imperial defence. It will be remembered that the lowest figure considered acceptable as a basis of negotiation at Geneva in 1927 was 70, and a certain amount of surprise was expressed in the press at the change to a figure so

much lower, without, as far as was known, any explanation
having been given as to the reasons which had led the Admiralty
to revise its ideas. Considerable interest attached, therefore,
to a statement made by the First Lord of the Admiralty on
January 10th, in which he supplied the answer to this question.
After pointing out that in the decision of policy on matters of
this kind it was the Government which was responsible, he said
that it would be opportune to explain the Admiralty's view.
This was based on the maintenance of a one-Power standard,
a matter which in the case of capital ships was very simply
expressed in the form of parity with the greatest other naval
Power. In the matter of cruisers it was not so simple, and one
of the most important aims of the Conference would be to
reconcile their defence needs in the matter of cruisers with the
requirements of international agreement.

In 1927 the number, based on the needs of the defence of
the Empire, was fixed at 70, but "to-day we have to take
account of a new situation which has arisen through the
signature of the Pact of Paris outlawing war by most of the
nations of the world. . . ." They now felt justified in looking
forward to a period in which armed conflicts need not be expected, and the Admiralty were, therefore, prepared to agree
to 50 cruisers as the minimum needs of the Empire "up to
the next date for conference and revision, which we expect will
be near 1936," and later he said, "the proposed reduction in
the number to 50 is, of course, dependent upon agreement at
the forthcoming Conference on adequate limitation of projected
building programmes being made by other Powers."

Mr. Alexander then referred to the Government's wish to see
a reduction in the size and cost of capital ships, and concluded
by pointing out how difficult it was to achieve effective parity
in auxiliary vessels and to get agreement as to what should be
the proper equation, even when the general principle of parity
had been fully accepted, as it had been by the British and
United States Governments.

In the United States reference to the work of the Conference
was made by Mr. Hoover in his Message to Congress on Decem-

ber 3rd, 1929. After referring to the fact that by the ratification
of the Kellogg Treaty "a great moral standard" had been raised
in the world, the President said that they held high hopes that
success would attend the effort which would be made in London
towards eliminating "the dangerous forces which produce controversies among the nations." On the results of the Conference
depended such moderation in naval outlay as could be practised,
since if the United States were compelled "to undertake the
naval construction implied in the Washington Treaty, as well
as other construction which would appear to be necessary if
no international agreement can be completed, we shall be committed during the next six years to a construction expenditure
of upwards of $1,200,000,000, besides the necessary further
increase in costs for annual upkeep."

The President made this statement at the moment the Navy
Estimates for the year ending June 30, 1931, were being
considered by Congress. They provided for an expenditure of
the equivalent of £76,078,000, or £3,180,000 more than in the
previous year, and included the cost of carrying forward the
work on the two 10,000-ton cruisers laid down in the summer
of 1929 (under the Bill of February 13, 1929) and for com-
mencing construction on three more to be laid down late in
1930–31 and of ten more to be laid down late in 1931–32.
A few days later the annual Report of the Secretary of the
Navy was published, and contained the interesting statement
that while existing plans called for the completion of all the
first five of the fifteen "treaty" cruisers by June 30, 1933, the
three of the first five which still remained to be laid down
would not be begun until after the London Conference.

Subsequently Mr. Stimson made one or two references to
the work to be undertaken in London which were no doubt
meant to receive notice abroad. Thus on December 21st he
said that the battleship was still the "core" of the fleet at sea,
but he hoped a reduction would be made in the size of all
capital ships through a reduction in maximum displacement
tonnage and an extension of the life of these vessels. On the
same occasion he emphasized that the attitude of the United

States Government was that any agreement concluded in London should have a separate and unconditional validity and ought to stand as a complete achievement free of merely contingent effectiveness. At the moment of sailing for Europe he added some further information as to the aims of the United States delegation when he said that as they had now come to the time when battleship building was about to begin again, "not competitive, but mutually agreed-on building," it seemed a most opportune time for the United States to meet with the same Powers with whom they had consulted at Washington in 1922 to see if they could not still further delay or decrease the expenses of battleship fleets, and he added, "At the same time we shall endeavour to find a mutually satisfactory arrangement for the building of cruisers, destroyers and submarines . . ."

As a final send-off to the delegation, Mr. Hoover issued a statement to the press warning the country against expecting a quick settlement of the difficulties confronting the Conference. To complete the Conference in three or four months would in itself be a great accomplishment, he considered, and he concluded by appealing to the American people to co-operate in the progress of the work by "patience, encouragement and freedom from criticism."

The Conference was opened by H.M. the King on January 21st, with a formal speech of welcome and of confidence in the good results to be attained if each nation was equally determined to make some sacrifice as a contribution to the common good. On his Majesty's departure the British Prime Minister was voted to the Chair, and the remainder of the session was given up to the speeches of the heads of the several delegations, who took advantage of the opportunity of putting forward their respective national views, which were recapitulated in the subsequent discussions.

The first business meeting of the Conference was not held till two days later, but on January 22nd the Prime Minister broadcast a statement to the people of the United States in which he said they would strive to bring to the lowest common level all the programmes of the five countries concerned, so that two things would happen: (1) there would be no more competition between them in building ships, and (2) the programmes would be reduced to the very lowest possible level. Mr. MacDonald also gave some figures showing that in the British Navy, as compared with 1914, the number of capital ships had been reduced from 69 to 20, cruisers with 8-inch guns from 27 to 11, smaller cruisers from 81 to 43, and submarines from 74 to 53.

It should be said at once that the first weeks of the Conference were taken up in preparing the agenda, the first business meeting being chiefly notable for the detailed statement made by M. Tardieu regarding the extent of the French Colonial Empire, with a view to explaining the absolute needs of his country. These needs, he emphasized, could only be modified by the consideration that if the sense of security were increased throughout the world it would to that extent be easier for France to reduce her naval commitments. After referring to the French Memorandum of December 20, 1929,[1] the Premier quoted figures to show that the protection of the French Colonies necessitated keeping open lines of communication very much longer than those of any other Power except Great Britain; the area of the territories overseas was 12 million kilometres, and their population 60 millions, while the length of coast of these territories and of the mother country totalled over 18,000 miles.

Signor Grandi also entered into some detail in describing the position of Italy. While not making the claim to parity with France the whole burden of his statement, he gave a very definite intimation of the attitude taken up by the Fascist Government. Since Italy depended upon her maritime communications for securing over three-fourths of the imports essential to the life of her population she was fully justified, said the Italian delegate, in claiming not to be asked to deprive herself of her present right to naval armaments on a level with those of any other continental European Power, and he con-

---

[1] For a summary of the contents of this, see the *Bulletin* of January 2nd, Vol. VI, No. 13, p. 15, under December 21st.

cluded by saying that, confirming the statements made several times by the head of the Fascist Government, Italy was ready to reduce her armaments to any level, no matter how low, providing it would not be exceeded by any other continental European Power.

The first plenary meeting was closed with the setting up of a committee composed of all the members of the Conference, and with the adoption of a resolution that sub-committees should be appointed on the decision of the whole Conference.

The following two or three days were devoted to private meetings between the principal delegates, at which methods of procedure were discussed,[1] and on January 27th it was understood that the French delegation had secured the insertion in the agenda of the question of global tonnage and that of the so-called compromise proposal of 1927 for the limitation of each category of ship according to national "needs," including the right to transfer from one category to another within certain limits and provided notice were given to the other Powers. At the same meeting the Italian delegation put forward a suggestion that the question of maximum levels on the basis of global tonnage should be dealt with first, but this was not adopted.

Mr. Wakatsuki broadcast a statement to the American people, and Mr. Stimson gave up to the press three of the seats occupied at the Conference by the United States' advisers, while the contribution to the proceedings from the British Government's side was an official announcement that the two 8-inch gun cruisers, the laying down of which had been suspended in July 1929,[2] had definitely been taken off the building programme. Nothing of importance transpired as to the results of the discussions of the following few days, but Viscount Grey spoke in optimistic terms of the outlook when presiding at a dinner at which the delegates were entertained by the

[1] The chief task was to find an acceptable compromise between the French view that limitation should be by total or global tonnage and the British view that it should be by categories of ships. The basis of discussion was the French suggestion put forward as a compromise (known later as the "transactional" proposal) at Geneva in April 1927.
[2] *Vide* the Prime Minister's statement in Parliament on July 24, 1929.

Pilgrims of Great Britain on January 28th. That day was also noteworthy for an interesting message broadcast to the people of both Great Britain and the United States by Mr. Stimson, who, after describing the main objects of the Conference, gave some figures to show the sacrifices America had made in her naval building programme as a result of the Washington Treaty. On the present occasion they wished, besides putting an end to competition in auxiliary vessels, to reduce the battleship programmes below the levels provided for in 1922, more especially since, unless this were done, they would be faced in the United States with an expenditure of $300 millions on battleships alone during the next six years.

The next plenary meeting was fixed for January 30th, but meanwhile a certain amount of information was made available as to the progress of the discussions between the heads of the British and French delegations. According to this, the latter were understood to have abandoned their contention that discussions on methods of limitation should be on the basis of global tonnage, and to have accepted the principle that they should proceed by categories, subject, however, to the reservation that light cruisers and destroyers should be merged into one category as cruisers carrying guns of less than 8 inches calibre.

An outline of the Japanese attitude was also made public in amplification of what was already known as to the claim of that country to a 70 per cent. ratio in auxiliary vessels. Japan, it was explained, would be satisfied with an inferior position as compared with the largest fleet, and was ready to accept a smaller percentage—down to under 50 per cent.—of the small cruisers, provided her demand for a 70 per cent. ratio of large 8-inch gun cruisers were agreed to. She also claimed the right to retain her existing strength in submarines, i.e. about 78,000 tons.

When the next plenary meeting opened the Italian delegation again made an attempt to obtain consideration of the questions which it had tabled for discussion, on the ground that these raised an important matter of principle. These questions were described as (1) the determination of ratios, and (2) the determination of the levels of the total tonnage of the several countries. Signor Grandi said that as some of the delegates appeared to wish to refrain in the meantime from discussing them he was prepared to wait, but could not commit himself on any special point of the naval disarmament problem until the two fundamental questions in the Italian proposal had been settled. It was eventually agreed that they should not be dealt with at that juncture, and Mr. Stimson proposed that the remaining subjects should be examined by a committee, with instructions to report on them to the full Conference. These subjects were: first, the French proposal for limitation of global tonnage, including that country's "transactional" or compromise proposal[1] and the question as to the classification to be adopted and the amount and conditions of transfer, and, secondly, the British proposal for limitation by categories of vessels. The American delegation intimated that while believing in the British system, it recognized that smaller navies necessarily had a tendency towards specialization and accordingly was ready to accept the compromise proposal as a basis for discussion. The British view was again explained by the First Lord of the Admiralty, who stated, however, that he did not object to some system of transfer being adopted, providing that confidence and stability were not impaired. Transfer of tonnage should, therefore, be restricted to the less powerful type of vessels, and the maximum tonnage of the individual unit in each category should be strictly limited. As regards the British classification of vessels the essential point was that cruisers should be considered under two categories; those carrying guns above 6 inches, and those with guns 6 inches in calibre or less.

On the following day the official text of the French compromise proposal was published, and, as consideration of this and of the British counter-suggestion occupied the attention of the Committee for some time, the main heads of it may be

[1] For the text of this, see the *Bulletin* of February 13th, Vol. VI, No. 16, p. 12.

enumerated. All naval vessels were to be divided into the following classes:

(1) Vessels exceeding 10,000 tons displacement, or with guns of more than 8 inches calibre[1];
(2) Light surface vessels with guns exceeding 6 inches calibre;
(3) Light surface vessels whose guns did not exceed 6 inches.
(4) Submarines;
(5) Aircraft carriers; and
(6) Special vessels, i.e. minelayers, training-ships, etc.

It was not proposed that transfers should be restricted to the smaller classes, but the amount of transfer was to be limited, and a year's notice was to be given to the other Powers whenever the right was exercised.

With this may be compared the British proposal, put forward at the beginning of February as a counter-suggestion. This divided vessels into the following categories:

(1) Capital ships;
(2) Aircraft carriers;
(3) Cruisers:
    (a) with guns of 8 inches or larger calibre, and
    (b) with guns of 6 inches calibre or less;
(4) Destroyers; and
(5) Submarines.

In the first two no transfers would be allowed, but in the heavy cruisers a limited transfer downwards, and in the small cruisers and destroyers unlimited transfer up or down would be permitted. Submarines were not mentioned.

The French proposal appears to have been taken as the basis of discussion, but this was more or less confined to the British and French members of the Committee, because the American delegates intimated that they reserved their comments in the meantime, while the Italians repeated their previous statement that they regarded any decision on the subject as provisional upon the discussion at a later stage of the two questions the settlement of which they regarded as an essential preliminary to the work of the Conference in arranging technical details.

[1] This was presumably a reference to the fact that the new German cruiser, then under construction, was to carry six 11-inch guns.

In spite of this warning, however, the Committee appears to have continued to confine its work to a discussion of methods of limitation and of ascertaining the naval tonnage of the five Powers, while relegating what the Italian delegation described as the fundamental questions to later consideration.

The next questions dealt with by the Conference as a whole were those of the life of capital ships and the policy to be adopted regarding submarines, but meanwhile questions asked in the House of Commons elicited replies which revealed the fact that the British Government was making renewed attempts to lead the way by example to further limitation of naval construction. On February 3rd it was made known semi-officially that a statement made some days earlier in Parliament regarding the cancelling of two cruisers of the 1929–30 programme referred to two further vessels, in addition to the two of the 1928-29 programme, the definite cancelling of which had been announced on January 27th. This made four cancelled (i.e. three of 10,000 tons and one of smaller size) since the previous summer, and in addition three submarines and four destroyers were taken off the original programme laid before Parliament for 1929–30. It might be added here that some weeks later (March 12th), in reply to a further question in the House of Commons as to what was the total tonnage of warship construction which had been cancelled since January 1, 1928 by each of the five Powers represented at the Conference, Mr. Alexander replied that the figure for the British Empire was approximately 66,000 tons, but that no tonnage had been cancelled by any of the other Powers.

To return to the question of battleships, proposals were understood to have been made for a prolongation of the life of these vessels and for a reduction of the largest guns carried by them from 16 to 14 inches, but no definite progress was made towards arriving at any decisions on these lines as far as the public was aware. More encouraging reports were in circulation, however, as to the discussion of the relative cruiser strengths proposed for the British and American Navies. On February 6th Mr. Stimson issued a statement setting on record the views of the United States delegation according to which America would be content with 18 10,000-ton cruisers, as compared with Great Britain's 15, while the latter country would be allowed an excess of tonnage in 6-inch gun smaller cruisers to the extent of 42,000 tons. In order to ensure exact equality of opportunity, however, each country would "have the option of duplicating exactly the cruiser fleet of the other," if so desired.

Nothing transpired as to the reception which these proposals were given by the British delegation, and the energies of the Conference appear to have been largely given up to the attempt to reconcile the British and French points of view regarding methods of limitation. The British Government chose this moment to communicate to the other delegations a memorandum regarding its policy, and a summary of this was published on February 7th. The general policy of the British Empire was, it was explained, to keep the highway of the seas open for trade and communication, and it was pointed out that if naval establishments were not to be a menace, an equilibrium would have to be maintained between them through international agreement. It was proposed that any agreement resulting from the Conference should run until 1936, and a further conference should be called in 1935. The need for agreement as to limitation by categories was insisted upon, and the categories proposed were five only: capital ships, aircraft carriers, cruisers, destroyers and submarines. Transfers might be allowed, but were not advisable in the case of the first two and the last, and the previous suggestions were repeated regarding the transfers of cruisers.[1]

Taking the categories separately the memorandum proposed:

Reduction of capital ships to the Washington Treaty figure within 18 months of the ratification of the agreement resulting from the Conference.

No replacement until the 1935 Conference. Reduction of maximum tonnage to 25,000 tons and of gun calibre to 12 inches. Increase of life of vessels to 26 years.

---

[1] The text of this memorandum was published on February 10th as a White Paper, Cmd. 3485.

The complete disappearance of the battleship in due time.

Aircraft carriers to be limited in tonnage and gun calibre to 25,000 tons maximum displacement. Life to be increased to 26 years. Total tonnage for the British and United States Navies to be 100,000 instead of 135,000 tons.

Cruisers to be in one category, but subdivided according to gun calibre. Great Britain to have 339,000 tons (50 vessels). Tonnage limit for small vessels to be 6,000 or 7,000 tons. The life of cruisers to be 20 years.

Destroyer tonnage to be limited to 1,850 for leaders and 1,500 for others, with a maximum gun calibre of 5 inches. Existing building programme of 200,000 tons could be reduced if submarine programmes of other Powers were reduced.

Submarines to be limited to the lowest possible size and total number, should their abolition be impracticable.

The question of the submarine was next dealt with and on February 11th the First Lord of the Admiralty gave to a meeting of the Conference in plenary session five distinct reasons why the British Government advocated its abolition. He was supported by Mr. Stimson, who proposed a resolution asking for the appointment of a committee to study three specific questions: (1) the abolition of the submarine; (2) regulation of its use through subjecting it to the rules of war governing the use of surface craft, and (3) regulation of the unit size of submarines. The Italian delegation gave qualified support to the principle of abolition—there was no objection in principle to abolition on Italy's part if all the naval Powers concurred in this—but both France and Japan put forward reasons why they considered the submarine to be an essential element of their fleets. M. Leygues set forth the French standpoint under three heads: (1) the submarine was a warship like the others; (2) it was a defensive weapon which all the naval Powers could not dispense with; and (3) its use should be and could be regulated like that of any other warship, and he maintained that any motion tending to abolish it would involve three questions of principle: (1) the measure of lawfulness of any weapons of war deriving from the progress of science and technical improvements; (2) the right of smaller naval Powers to possess, as sovereign States, a navy corresponding to their requirements and their means of defence; and (3) the question of the freedom of the seas.

The Japanese delegates based their attitude on the fact that the geographical condition of their country, which consists of many scattered islands, made the submarine the most convenient means of defence of its waterways and vulnerable points, but apart from this, they were not ready to admit that the submarine should be condemned as a ruthless weapon of war, since most weapons could be put to merciless use—aeroplanes for example. Japan, however, associated herself heartily with the proposal to make the submarine subject to a strict control by law, and as the French and Italian delegations expressed the same views it was decided to entrust to a special committee of experts the task of working out ways and means of providing for such control.

So far the Japanese delegation had not issued any official statement of their general position towards the work of the Conference, but on February 13th a memorandum was published[1] which made no mention of the claim to a 70 per cent. ratio in cruiser strength with the United States. Proposals were made for a holiday in battleship construction, for prolongation of the life of existing ships, and for a reduction of their maximum size, but as to cruisers the only point made was the importance Japan attached to 8-inch gun vessels, of which she desired "to maintain a minimum strength sufficient for national defence, taking into consideration the strengths held by other Powers." The previous arguments regarding submarines were repeated, and the strength considered as essential to Japan's needs was given as that of her existing fleet, i.e. about 78,000 tons.

On the same day there appeared a lengthy French memorandum,[2] supplementary to that published by the French Government on December 20th, giving detailed figures of the naval tonnages regarded as essential to that country's needs. The existing strength of the French Navy was shown as 681,808

[1] The text of this was published in the *Bulletin* of February 13th, Vol. VI, No. 16, p. 17.
[2] For the text of this, see the *Bulletin* of February 27th, Vol. VI, No. 17, p. 11.

tons, and some surprise was felt when it was seen that the French
Government proposed to increase this total to 724,479 tons by
1936. This building programme was justified by the consideration that of the 240,000 tons proposed to be built, no less than
196,800 tons would be merely for replacement, most of which
was already overdue. The number of 10,000-ton cruisers required
was put at 10, so as to give a total large cruiser strength of
124,850 tons, with the inclusion of some old cruisers with guns
over 6 inches in calibre, while the total tonnage of submarines
claimed was 99,629 tons, as compared with an existing total
of 97,875 tons. It should be noted that smaller cruisers were
not specified separately, but a total of 258,597 tons of "light
ships" was included in the 1936 figure of 724,479 tons, this
quantity to be made up of small cruisers, destroyers, torpedo-
boats, etc. Other passages in the memorandum dealt with the
question of a holiday in battleship construction and a reduction
in the maximum tonnage of such vessels, but more interest
was shown in the concluding sentences, in which it was again
insisted that any decisions taken in London should be taken
in relation to the problems of the limitation of land and air
armaments, and in which the statement was made that, "Just
as the American and British Governments were . . . able to
declare that war between the two nations was unthinkable, so
France, too, is happy to declare her profound conviction that
between her people and those of the United States and of the
British Empire any armed conflict is equally unthinkable."[1]
Equally interesting to the other delegations was the concluding
passage in which it was repeated that France remained "ready
to consider favourably any form of agreement for a mutual
guarantee of security the effect of which would be to transform
the absolute requirements of each Power into relative requirements."

A few days after the appearance of this document the French
Government was defeated on a vote of confidence in the Chamber,
and on M. Tardieu handing in his resignation a period of nearly

[1] The absence of any mention of Italy was subsequently commented on
unfavourably by the press of that country.

three weeks followed during which France was not in possession
of a Government capable of representing the country in London.
The Premier's resignation occurred on February 17th, and by
the 25th his successor, M. Chautemps, had also been defeated
on his first appearance before the Chamber, and it was not
until March 2nd that a new Cabinet was formed, this time under
M. Tardieu again, who obtained the necessary vote of confidence
on March 5th. On the following day M. Briand and the other
members of the delegation were able to return to London.

Meanwhile the Conference had confined its work to technical
details, such as the drafting of schedules of exempted ships,
though progress was also made in the examination of the
figures in the Japanese memorandum of February 13th. Though
they did not appear in the published text it was afterwards
understood that the Japanese delegation had made too alternative tonnage proposals regarding the respective strengths of
the Japanese and the United States Navies. If the United
States possessed 18 10,000-ton cruisers, Japan, it was suggested,
should have 126,000 tons of this class (i.e. mounting 8-inch
guns), while the figures for smaller cruisers would be 147,000
tons for America and 81,700 tons for Japan. If, however,
America only possessed 15 10,000-ton cruisers, Japan would be
content with her existing strength of 108,400 tons, and the
figure for small cruisers would then be, for America 189,000
tons, and for Japan 107,700 tons.

Of more importance was the appearance, on February 19th,
of an Italian memorandum defining the policy of that country
at the Conference.[1] This had several interesting features, apart
from the fact that it repeated, in two distinct passages, Italy's
readiness to accept any figure of armaments, however low,
provided this were not exceeded by any other continental
European Power. It also stated that the idea of an armed
conflict with any Power, whether represented at the Conference
or not, was totally foreign to the established naval policy of
Italy, and then proceeded to give detailed figures of the strengths
of the navies of Great Britain, France and Italy in vessels not

[1] For the text of this, see the *Bulletin* of February 27th, Vol. VI, No. 17. p. 14.

covered by the Washington Treaty, with the object of showing
that the existing strength of the Italian fleet in auxiliary
vessels (excluding submarines) was approximately of the
same total tonnage as the French.[1] The figures came in for
some criticism, particularly in French circles, owing to the fact
that they excluded vessels projected, as also cruisers over 20
years of age, destroyers over 16, and submarines over 13 years
old. The equivalent figures which appeared in the French
statement of six days earlier showed the total tonnage of French
auxiliary vessels (excluding submarines) at 365,860 tons, or
134,555 tons more than in the Italian statement, the difference
being accounted for by the inclusion of all ships in service,
building, or authorised, without reference to age. The divergence
was important in view of the French Government's refusal to
admit the justice of Italy's claim to parity in auxiliary vessels.
France was, however, not represented at the Conference at the
time the Italian statement appeared, and until the return of
M. Briand to London work was confined to the task of defining
special ships exempt from limitation, and to an inquiry by
legal experts into the question of humanizing the submarine.
On the former point agreement was reported to have been
reached on February 25th, and on the following day a *communiqué* was issued intimating that pending the return of the
French delegation private conversations were continuing, at
which French interests were entrusted to the French ambassador;
a few days later Mr. Charles Adams broadcast a message to the
United States in which he gave it as his opinion that nothing
had been lost by the fall of the French Government except time.

This was the position at the end of February, 1930.

Early in March there were indications that a definite step
forward might be expected in the negotiations towards an
agreement for limitation, and not merely reduction, of naval
armaments. The interruption caused by the French political
crisis was ended by the return of M. Briand to London on
March 6th, but the day previous to that Mr. Stimson had issued

---

[1] The totals of all cruisers and destroyers completed and building were shown
as France 231,305 tons, and Italy 227,846 tons.

a statement for publication in the United States which gave the first official intimation of the details of the plan of reduction to which the British and American delegations were understood to be working. The American Secretary of State said:

"There seems to be an impression that the work of the American delegation at this Conference is likely to result in an increase instead of a reduction of the navies of the world. The surest way to answer that is to give such results as seem to be within reach up to date. The plan which, in its essentials, appears to be acceptable to the American and British delegations provides for a net reduction in tonnage of the American fleet, in capital ships, cruisers, destroyers and submarines, built, building and appropriated for, of over 200,000 tons, and an even larger reduction on the part of the British fleet. If vessels authorized but not commenced were included in existing fleets the amount of the reductions would be much larger. Of course, these reductions are contingent on some reductions being made in the fleets of other Powers."

On the same day the Committee of Experts began consideration of the question of the submarine, on the basis of the American resolution suggesting total abolition, or failing this, the adoption of a more humane method of using it as a weapon of war,[1] coupled with limitations of total tonnage and the size of individual vessels. It was understood that both the British and United States delegations wished to take as the basis of discussion a figure of 1,800 tons as the maximum unit displacement for these craft, and that Italy was ready to agree to this, but Japan wished for the maximum to be fixed at 2,000 tons.[2] France made a reservation that she would be prepared to accept the figure which suited the other four Powers, provided she were allowed to retain a certain number of vessels of more than 2,000 tons, up to a maximum of 3,000 tons, as she felt this to be necessary owing to the length of her lines of communication. It was understood that the French Government's idea was that submarines should be divided into two classes, those of over 2,000 tons, of which she should be allowed a limited number, and those of 2,000 tons or less.[3] In the first class the number and

[1] For details of the American resolution, see the *Bulletin* of March 27th, Vol. VI, No. 19, p. 8.
[2] Owing to the depth of the water round her coasts Japan was understood to favour a larger type of submarine as the normal type for coastal defence.
[3] The *Surcouf*, the largest French vessel, is of 2,880 tons displacement.

tonnage of the individual vessels to be retained or built would be specified, while in the second the total tonnage only would be fixed and notified to the Powers, who would decide the tonnage of the individual vessels according to their special requirements.

M. Briand's first week-end in England was spent in close touch with the heads of the British and American delegations in an attempt to explain the French point of view as to the necessity of fresh political guarantees as a preliminary to any reduction in the building programme already adopted by the Government. Presumably it was by design that in a message broadcast on the Sunday (March 9th) to the people of the United States Mr. MacDonald referred to this aspect of the work of the Conference in the following words:

"We shall not agree to base any treaty which may result from this Conference on entangling military alliances. That would undo in spirit and in policy the work of the Conference; but some of us will strive to secure as an essential part of the agreement a pledge of goodwill and pacific intention similar to that made by the President and myself after we had convinced ourselves that a naval agreement was possible. The bonds of war are not, and cannot be, the security of peace."

Two days later Mr. Stimson was understood to have intimated clearly to the heads of the other delegations that on no account could the United States Government contemplate being party to any form of undertaking even to consult with the other Powers in face of a danger of war. Simultaneously a statement of the American delegation's position was published in the American press making it clear that the delegation had come to the conclusion that it could not assent to any proposal for a political pact, a decision which was understood to rule out a consultative pact just as much as a Mediterranean Locarno.

Meanwhile, in view of the admitted difficulties of the political question, special efforts were now made to see whether the tonnage figures in the French memorandum of February 13th really constituted as serious an obstacle to agreement as had at first appeared. The French programme was examined in detail, and the global tonnage shown was cut down to some extent by the omission of a number of special ships which had been included in the original statement, but the total was still large, and the maintenance of the Italian claim to parity, coupled with the French refusal to admit this claim, nullified the efforts of the French and British delegations to solve the difficulty. Further efforts were made two days later to explain the French figures by the Minister of Marine, who issued a statement in which the total tonnage for 1936 was shown as 713,532 tons,[1] but any effect this may have had in improving the situation was neutralized by the appearance in Paris on the same day of a semi-official Note declining, in the absence of a Mediterranean pact, either to make reductions in the naval armaments programme or to admit parity with Italy.

M. Dumesnil's figures must be further referred to. He showed the existing tonnage, including special vessels but not exempt ships, as 670,861 tons, but this included ships building and appropriated for, the existing strength in vessels in commission being only 492,407 tons. The figure given for 1936, 713,532 tons, was the total of the ships which would be in commission before the end of that year. From 1931 to 1933 France proposed to build 120,000 tons, i.e. 77,329 tons of replacement and 42,671 tons of supplementary construction, and the latter figure included 23,330 tons in replacement of the battleship *France*, lost in 1922, and 19,341 tons of actual supplementary building, but the rest was entirely replacement tonnage already overdue. These 120,000 additional tons would be in commission in 1936, and the total strength of the fleet in commission would then be—allowing for scrappings—713,532 tons.

During the following three years 1934 to 1936, France was to build a further 120,000 tons, all for replacement, and it was pointed out that the French delegation had already specified, on February 13th, that the tonnage thus built (which would be in commission after December 31, 1936), would be entirely balanced by the scrapping of an equal quantity of over-age tonnage. At the end of 1939, as at the end of 1936, the total

---

[1] The total shown in the memorandum was 724,479 tons, the difference presumably being the amount taken off for exempt ships.

strength of the ships in commission would, therefore, be 713,532 tons.

It cannot be said that the publication of these figures did anything to improve the situation, while, even had the totals shown been lower than they were, the Italian insistence on the claim to parity proved an insuperable obstacle to agreement. While maintaining its attitude on the question of principle, the Italian delegation offered, it was understood, to build no more capital ships during the ensuing six years, provided that France gave a similar undertaking, but M. Briand was reported to have refused to consider this proposal, on the ground that it would involve a departure from the existing building programme of the French Government.[1] Any settlement based on the figures shown in that programme was, however, unacceptable to Italy owing to the low level of existing tonnage of that country; an agreement with France on that basis would either stabilize Italy's inferiority or involve her in further naval expenditure on a large scale. Matters appeared to have reached a deadlock, since France maintained her refusal to curtail her building programme except in return for political guarantees, and at the same time refused to admit the claim of Italy to maintain a naval strength equal to that programme, whether it was cut down or not. If, it was pointed out, Italy based her claim on her position as a world Power, why did she not claim parity with Great Britain or the United States, or even Japan? If, however, she based it on her position in the Mediterranean, then she was claiming, not parity, but marked superiority in that area over the naval strength of any other Power.

On March 18th reports were current that something in the nature of a concession had been made by Signor Grandi in proposals put forward during conversations with M. Tardieu. The latter was understood to have suggested that France might agree to some reduction in her tonnage total—to something over 600,000 tons—if she could be guaranteed a permanent

---

[1] This provided for building the whole 175,000 tons of capital ships allowed to France under the Washington Treaty and six 10,000-ton cruisers carrying 8-inch guns.

superiority of strength over Italy.[1] In reply, the Italian delegate
was reported to have intimated that his Government was prepared to leave France with her existing superiority in battleships,[2] and to forego strict parity in submarines, on the condition
that her claim to theoretical parity over the whole field of naval
armaments was admitted. Signor Grandi suggested that in the
comparative tables of naval strength for the years 1930 to
1936 only really effective tonnage should be included, i.e. under-
age vessels and vessels under construction, and claimed that
this arrangement would give France a temporary superiority
of nearly 150,000 tons; numerical equality estimated on that
basis would, he maintained, mean Italian inferiority, since
France possessed several ships which, though over age, were
still serviceable and in commission, while Italy had very few.

The French delegation does not appear to have given this
suggestion much consideration, partly on the ground that it
was the duty of the Italians to put forward concrete figures
of tonnage, and the prospects of reconciling the two points of
view were made even more remote by the appearance in Rome
of an official *communiqué*, on March 20th, stating that the
Fascist Grand Council had "entirely approved the work done
by the delegates at the Naval Conference in defence of Italy's
right to maritime parity with the most strongly armed Power
on the Continent." M. Tardieu and M. Briand were both back
in Paris, and on March 21st it was understood that the former
had fixed no date for his return to London, while M. Briand's
departure was described by the Paris press as "marking the
decision of the French Government to take no active part in
the Conference so long as the present group of circumstances
is unchanged."

Nor was much more success met with in dealing with the
question of the French figures. After careful examination of
these during several days it was found impossible to induce the
French delegation to reduce them to any material extent,

---

[1] The figure of difference mentioned was believed to be 200,000 tons.
[2] Italy was entitled to 175,000 tons of battleships by the Washington ratio,
but she had only utilized about 75,000 tons of this.

except in return for the assurance of political guarantees, and the efforts of the British and French delegations were accordingly concentrated on an attempt to find a formula which would satisfy the desire of France for security while not involving Great Britain in any obligations beyond those already undertaken under the terms of the League Covenant and the Locarno Treaty. Into this discussion the United States delegation was also drawn owing to the inclusion in the scope of inquiry of the idea of a consultative pact—similar to that signed at Washington in February 1922 regarding the Pacific—as being possibly acceptable to France as a guarantee of security. On March 25th the American delegation issued an official statement with the object of making the attitude of the United States Government clear, in which it was pointed out that it had already been explained some weeks earlier that

"America had no objection to entering a consultative pact as such. On the contrary, the United States is already a party to a number of treaties involving the obligation of consulting with other Powers. It will not, however, enter into any treaty, whether consultative or otherwise, where there is danger of its obligation being misunderstood as involving a promise to render military assistance or guaranteeing protection by military force to another nation."

It was felt, the statement continued, that such a misunderstanding might arise if the United States entered into such a treaty as a *quid pro quo* for the reduction of the naval forces of another Power, and that that danger had hitherto inhered in the existing situation and in the French attitude,

"but if the demand for security could be satisfied in some other way, then the danger of misunderstanding a consultative pact would be eliminated, and in such case the question would be approached from an entirely different standpoint. In such a case the American delegation would consider the matter with an entirely open mind."

This announcement appears to have caused some surprise in the United States, and on the following day Mr. Cotton, the acting Secretary of State, felt it necessary to reassure public opinion in the country with the statement that no change had taken place in the attitude of the delegation in London. The *communiqué* was nothing more than a clarification of the position which the United States has maintained throughout; that is, that they were unwilling to enter into any treaty promising to give military or other sanctions to other Powers. Mr. Cotton added that, in his own opinion, a consultative pact would not mean a material reduction in tonnage, though it might have some slight effect.

This official explanation of what was taking place in London does not appear to have cleared up the uncertainty which was now felt as to the American attitude towards the political question. Though responsible opinion did not believe that there could exist any divergence of opinion between the President and the members of the delegation, Mr. Cotton issued a further statement on March 29th on Mr. Hoover's behalf. This was to the effect that there were no differences of view between him and the delegation, and it was generally believed in London by those best in a position to judge that the view actually taken by Mr. Stimson and his colleagues was that the question of a pact would not arise until an agreement had been reached between the European Powers with regard to the Mediterranean and until this had been followed by the signature of a five-Power treaty embodying reductions in naval tonnage. *After* that point had been reached, it was suggested that the United States would be prepared to enter a consultative pact, at a time when it was clear to the world that their action in doing so could not be regarded as a *quid pro quo* for the reduction of tonnage by any other Power.

Support for the idea of participation in a consultative pact was forthcoming in America from those who pointed out that the Senate had not hesitated to ratify the Pacific Pact of 1922, without which the reductions and limitations adopted at Washington could never have been achieved, while another aspect of the matter was put forward by Mr. Kellogg, who, in a speech on March 28th, gave it as his opinion that the principle of consultation was inherent in the Kellogg Treaty, and "any of the signatory Powers may call the attention of belligerents to its provisions and urge its maintenance unimpaired."

At the end of the month it was understood that Mr. Mac-Donald, as President of the Conference, had invited Signor Grandi to take part in the discussions, which were now practically confined to finding an interpretation of Article XVI of the Covenant which would satisfy France, but the Italian delegate was reported to have given it as his opinion that the consideration of any formula which involved the interpretation or clarification of existing covenants or treaties was a matter which ought properly to be done at Geneva, by all the members of the Council; also that the chief questions with which the Conference had to deal were not political but technical, being concerned with naval disarmament as such.

Mr. MacDonald and M. Briand were accordingly left to find a solution of the problem alone. Their efforts were rendered more difficult by the knowledge that, even if successful, the question of Italy's claim would still remain, but apart from this, the attitude taken up by the French Government, as far as could be learnt from the information made public, did not suggest that anything short of a definite undertaking for military support would be regarded as affording the necessary safeguards. M. Briand was understood to be asking not only that the British Government should formally undertake, so far as France and Italy were concerned, to join in any sanctions recommended by the Council of the League under Article XVI; that is, to do, in the event of a Franco-Italian conflict, what it has already undertaken to do in the event of a Franco-German one, but also that Great Britain should agree that under Article XVI sanctions were obligatory and would come into force automatically against the aggressor in a Franco-Italian quarrel.

TEXT OF ARTICLE XVI OF THE COVENANT

(For purposes of reference the text of Article 16 is reprinted here)

ARTICLE XVI

Should any Member of the League resort to war in disregard of its covenants under Article XII, XIII or XIV, it shall *ipso facto* be deemed to have committed an act of war against all other Members of the League, which hereby undertake immediately to subject it to the severance of all trade or financial relations, the prohibition of all intercourse between their nationals and the nationals of the convenant-breaking State, and the prevention of all financial, commercial or personal intercourse between the nationals of the covenant-breaking State and the nationals of any other State, whether a Member of the League or not.

It shall be the duty of the Council in such case to recommend to the several Governments concerned what effective military, naval or air force the Members of the League shall severally contribute to the armed forces to be used to protect the covenants of the League.

The Members of the League agree, further, that they will mutually support one another in the financial and economic measures which are taken under this Article, in order to minimize the loss and inconvenience resulting from the above measures, and that they will mutually support one another in resisting any special measures aimed at one of their number by the covenant-breaking State, and that they will take the necessary steps to afford passage through their territory to the forces of any of the Members of the League which are co-operating to protect the covenants of the League.

Any Member of the League which has violated any covenant of the League may be declared to be no longer a Member of the League by a vote of the Council concurred in by the representatives of all the other Members of the League represented thereon.

On April 1st questions were asked in Parliament which gave evidence of some concern as to the possible implications of any interpretation of Article XVI which would be likely to meet the French views, and Mr. MacDonald was asked whether he would give an assurance that the Government would not enter into any liabilities in the Mediterranean based on a breach of the Kellogg Treaty. He replied that they had no intention of entering into any commitments which went beyond the obligations resulting from the Covenant and the Treaty of Locarno, and added, "the French Government do not ask, and have never asked that the Government should add to the burdens which already devolve upon them as the result of those instruments."

The Prime Minister's position was not made easier by the statements made the next day by the Paris press, which reported that both he and Mr. Henderson had accepted the French thesis as to the obligatory character of the engagements involved in the interpretation of Article XVI according to which Great

Britain would, on the conditions mentioned in that Article, *ipso facto* and automatically put at the disposal of the League the forces recommended by the Council. A semi-official statement issued in Paris on the following day was, perhaps, intended to correct this, since it was to the effect that France had no desire to ask Great Britain to assume any fresh obligations, but was only trying to make clear those which already existed under the Covenant, and it was added that the safeguard for everybody, in the French view, was that no recommendation could be given by the League Council without the unanimous assent of its members.[1]

In London, uneasiness was not confined to opinion which was in opposition to the Government, and in any event, the feeling was general by the end of the first week of April that definite decisions with regard to the future of the Conference would have to be taken very soon. A meeting of the delegations of the British Commonwealth on April 7th was understood to have been the occasion of intimations that Australia, at any rate, did not desire to be a party to any anticipatory declarations, and general support was given to the thesis already given utterance to by the official spokesman of the British delegation a week earlier when he said that further military commitments were absolutely out of the question, since to undertake them would be tantamount to tying the country down to engaging in military operations without being able to control the situation from which they had arisen.

On April 8th M. Briand returned to London with his Government's reply to the latest British proposal as to the interpretation to be given to Article XVI, and after a meeting between him and the Prime Minister a statement was issued that the conversations would be continued the following day "to continue the search for the means of securing a five-Power agreement." Though it was understood that the two Governments were now fairly well agreed in principle as to the interpretation of Article XVI it was also explained that no definite

---

[1] As a member of the Council, Great Britain could thus nullify any attempt at intervention if she so desired.

formula could be said to have been either accepted or rejected in Paris. As a matter of fact all that the French Cabinet had done was to take note of the British declaration, and it was pointed out by the Paris press that the only thing which the Cabinet had to decide was whether the British formula justified any reduction in the total tonnage demanded by France. The reply to this last question was understood to be a definite negative, and the feeling was general that the prospects of a five-Power agreement had not really come any nearer as the result of the discussions on this question of "interpretation."

Of secondary importance only to the political question was the problem of reconciling the Japanese claim to a 70 per cent. ratio in auxiliary vessels with American views. Much interest attached, therefore, to a proposal made by the United States delegation, and communicated to Mr. Matsudaira by Senator Reed in the middle of March, according to which the figures of tonnage would be fixed at the following totals:

	AMERICA	JAPAN
	Tons	Tons
Cruisers with 8-inch guns ..	180,000	108,400
Smaller cruisers	143,500	101,450
Destroyers	150,000	105,500
Submarines	52,700	52,700
Totals	526,200	368,050

These figures were transmitted to Tokio, but it was not until April 1st that a reply was received. Fortunately this amounted to an acceptance of the proposals, accompanied by reservations which were not considered seriously to affect their value. They referred to the following four points:

(1) The construction of 10,000-ton cruisers after 1935, as to which it was assumed Japan would retain her freedom of action;
(2) Earlier replacement of submarines;
(3) Duration of the agreement, which the Japanese Government understood would run until the end of 1936; and
(4) Capital ships, the arrangement as to which Japan considered should be bound up with the agreement regarding auxiliary tonnage.

On the following day an official statement appeared defining the attitude of the Japanese Government, which, it was explained, had recommended acceptance of the proposals as the basis of a treaty owing to its desire to co-operate to the full in promoting the success of the Conference, but also had in mind the fact that the treaty would be in force only up to the end of 1936; as to the arrangements thereafter all the nations concerned would be free to claim all that they deemed necessary to their security, and Japan would naturally be in a position to maintain the claims which she considered to be necessary "from the point of view of national defence as heretofore." It was at the same time understood that as regards the second reservation Japan wished to begin construction of a limited number of submarines before 1936 and before the age limit of existing vessels was reached, for the purpose of keeping her dockyards employed, and as regards the third the desire was that the acceptance of the figures for auxiliary craft should be contingent on the prolongation of the holiday in capital ship building.

The settlement of the points raised by these reservations was considered to be a matter for technical discussion and was accordingly entrusted to a committee of experts. It will be remarked that the total of 108,400 tons of large cruisers allotted to Japan gives her a ratio of only 60 per cent., but as the United States will have only 15 of these vessels (carrying 8-inch guns) completed by 1936 the Japanese ratio until that date will be 72 per cent. In the number of ships also, the Japanese ratio is favourable, since up to 1936 Japan will have 12 8-inch gun cruisers compared to America's 15, owing to the fact that four of the former's vessels of that gun calibre are of only 7,100 tons.

In the 6-inch gun cruiser class the Japanese ratio is 70 per cent. of the American, as it is also in destroyers, while in submarines the figures are equal. In the total tonnage in the four classes of vessels the Japanese figure is 69 per cent. of that of the United States, but as, in fact, the United States will have only 15 8-inch gun cruisers until 1936, the ratio at present is 73 per cent.

The position on April 9th was understood to be that agreement had been reached on all the important points regarding the three-Power proposals, but that very little hope remained of reconciling the points of view of Italy and France in such a way as to render a five-Power agreement of any kind possible.

On April 8th the Committee reported to the Conference that it had been found impossible to arrive at agreement as to the abolition of the submarine, but progress had been made in fixing figures for the maximum displacement of individual units which were acceptable to all five Powers. The ordinary limit adopted was 2,000 tons, but in view of the fact that both France and the United States had vessels already under construction exceeding that tonnage, it was decided that each Power might be permitted to build not more than three vessels of a larger displacement up to 2,800 tons, it being understood that France would complete the *Surcouf*, which was expected to displace approximately 2,880 tons, and to carry two 8-inch guns. Except for this reservation, the maximum limit of gun calibre was fixed at 5 inches for ordinary submarines, and at 6 inches for the three special vessels allowed to each Power.

On the subject of the "humanizing" of submarine warfare, the Committee adopted unanimously a report drafted by the Jurists' Committee regarding the legal aspects of the problem. The text of this may be quoted:

(1) "In their action with regard to merchant ships, submarines must conform to the rules of international law to which surface war vessels are subject."

(2) "In particular, except in cases of persistent refusal to stop on being duly summoned, or of active resistance to visit or search, a warship, whether surface vessel or submarine, may not sink or render incapable of navigation a merchant vessel without having first placed the passengers, crew, and ship's papers in a place of safety. For this purpose the ship's boats are not regarded as a place of safety unless the safety of passengers and crew is assured in the existing sea and weather conditions by the proximity of land, or the presence of another vessel which is in a position to take them on board."

This Report was adopted in its entirety by the Conference and formed Article XXII of the Treaty. Also embodied in the Treaty was a new definition of aircraft carriers, adopted by a Special Committee of Experts,[1] and on April 10th Mr. MacDonald was able to announce that a document would be prepared covering this and certain other points on which general agreement had been reached, which would be signed by all five Powers. He also stated that as far as the three principal naval Powers were concerned an agreement had been arrived at covering all categories of ships, an achievement which he described the following day as "a substantial step in the direction towards which we have been striving in the face of difficulties which at times appeared to be almost insurmountable."

As regards the main objects of the Conference, on which the failure to reconcile the views of the Continental Powers was now officially admitted, it was emphasized by both the Prime Minister and Mr. Henderson that conversations between France and Italy, in which Great Britain would take part whenever she could usefully do so, were to continue after the adjournment of the full Conference, and that the measure of general agreement already reached would permit of the work of the Preparatory Commission for the Disarmament Conference being taken up again. On the financial side, imposing figures as to the savings expected to follow on the agreement between the three principal Powers were forthcoming from official sources on both sides of the Atlantic. The First Lord of the Admiralty stated that during the next five or six years the saving to Great Britain would be at least between £60 and £70 millions, while in the United States the President was reported to have estimated that the amount spent on naval construction before 1936 would total from 900 to 1,000 million dollars less than would have been spent had the "Geneva basis" been retained.[2] Two or three days later (April 14th), in a statement to the Daughters of the American Revolution, Mr. Hoover said that the Conference had brought about an actual reduction in the armaments of the three countries of approximately 25 per

---

[1] *Vide* Article III, p. 17.
[2] Mr. Hoover mentioned $500 to 650 millions as the probable actual expenditure during the period of the Treaty's remaining in force.

cent. as compared with the standards taken as the basis of discussion at Geneva in 1927, and a reduction of 12 per cent. below the existing naval programmes. It should be added, however, that naval opinion was not unanimous in support of these estimates, and a section of the press described the result achieved as "billion dollar parity" on the ground that the United States, in the view of certain naval experts, would have to undertake a building programme costing 1,000 million dollars (£200 millions).

Before leaving this aspect of the subject, mention must be made of the figures quoted by the American Secretary of State in a message broadcast to the United States on April 13th. According to Mr. Stimson's estimate the fact that no battleships were to be laid down before 1936 would enable America to save about 300 million dollars, and the figures he gave of reductions in the total tonnage in this and other classes of war vessels for the three Powers were large enough to suggest that the financial saving involved would run into formidable figures. Thus, taking the total difference for the fleets of Great Britain, the United States and Japan between the Treaty figures and those of Geneva in 1927, the aggregate reduction was 345,000 tons, without counting the 25 per cent. over-age ships which were to be retained under the 1927 proposals. Comparing the tonnage of the fleets as they stood with that of their estimated strength in 1936, the reduction through the scrapping of battleships represented 230,130 tons, while a reduction of 205,000 tons would be effected in destroyers and of 68,000 in submarines. There would be an increase in the total tonnage of American cruisers, but the net total reduction in the fleets of the three Powers would amount to 460,000 tons. Mr. Stimson explained that in the United States they had "been idle in cruiser building for nearly ten years and now find ourselves with less than a quarter of the normal proportion of cruisers which we should have in respect of the rest of the fleet." The increase they were called upon to make was, however, comparatively small, because Great Britain had agreed to reduce her tonnage by 20 cruisers in order to meet them, and Japan had, for the same purpose,

agreed not to increase the number of her cruisers. Mr. Stimson
concluded by stating that in the present agreement "we have
reached the lowest level of limitation that I have ever heard
seriously discussed before. We have reached a lower level than
any of us on any delegation felt confident could be attained
when we came here."

On April 14th a plenary session of the Conference was held—
the first since February 11th. At this Mr. MacDonald announced
that the Treaty would be ready for signature on April 22nd,
and he enumerated the subjects on which full agreement had
been reached by all the five Powers. These were the following:

> Special vessels and vessels not subject to limitation.
> The tonnage of submarines, and their more humane use in war.
> The disposal of over-age ships.
> The replacement rules to cover ships not provided for in the Washing-
> ton Treaty.
> The holiday in capital ship building, and the disposal of surplus
> battleships.

On the subject of the method of limitation of tonnage, on
which agreement had been reached between Great Britain and
France, reservations had been put forward by Italy, said Mr.
MacDonald, which made it impossible for the plenary session
to adopt the First Report of the First Committee which dealt
with this question. The Report was accordingly "noted" only.[1]

On the following day the six Reports of the First Committee
were issued, and these were embodied in a "Memorandum on
the results of the London Naval Conference from January 21
to April 15, 1930," which was published as a White Paper
on April 16th.[2] Besides giving the figures of the auxiliary ship
tonnage agreed upon by the three Powers—the same figures
as appeared subsequently in Part III of the Treaty[3]—this
document quoted figures of expenditure saved based on the
assumption that

[1] This Report was forwarded to Geneva on April 21st, accompanied by a
covering letter from Mr. MacDonald, the text of which was published on
April 26th.
[2] Cmd. 3547.
[3] *Vide* Articles XV, XVI and XVIII.

"but for this agreement, before the end of 1936 Great Britain would, under the Washington Treaty, have completed five new 35,000-ton ships and would have had a further five appropriated for and under construction. This might have necessitated an expenditure in the region of £50 millions up to the end of 1936. Further, the financial saving involved in reducing at once to fifteen capital ships is estimated at about £4 millions."

It was also estimated that the reduction in the total tonnage of auxiliary vessels would result in a saving of some £13 millions.

The text of the Treaty was ready for signature by April 22nd, and a plenary session was held at which Mr. MacDonald reviewed the achievements of the Conference, as to which he said, "Compared with Washington or Geneva we have progressed far; compared with our desires we are still short." One or two other points may be referred to. As regards the safeguarding clause[1] he said this was not put in as an easy way to get round the Treaty.

"I hope it will never be used, but if it has to be, that will only happen after every effort has been made to avoid it. Only when it is apparent that owing to the ships built, building or definitely authorized by any Power or Powers, our naval position is so affected that it is impossible for this country to rest in peace of mind upon the figures embodied in Part III of this Treaty. Only then shall this protection clause be thought about."

The Chairman was followed by Mr. Stimson, who, in the course of his remarks, said that the Treaty established America's naval relationship with "our good neighbour across the Pacific and ensures the continuous growth of our friendship with that great nation towards whom we have grown to look for stability and progress in the Far East."

The only other delegate who entered into questions of principle in his speech at the closing session was M. Briand, who reminded the Conference that in its Memorandum of December 20, 1929, the French Government had stated that "a general technical agreement on armaments must be preceded by a political agreement," thereby indicating the conditions under which France could take a useful part in the work to be carried out in London.

[1] *Vide* Article XXI.

"Was not," he continued, "the fact of connecting a reduction of naval armaments with reciprocal guarantees of security equivalent to bringing back the question loyally to its essential basis ? . . . was it not, in a very large measure, acting for all, in the interest of the community of nations ? France has never asked, never sought guarantees for herself alone; she has always had in mind the security of all nations, which are called upon to lend each other mutual assistance in order to prevent war or to strive against it ; she has always thought that such a mutual guarantee would bring about a simultaneous reduction of armaments, different from former military alliances or groups of alliances which had actually led to an increase of those armaments."

M. Briand went on to contend that his Government had remained true to the ideas which had always guided her pacific action; in particular, those of connecting the work of the Conference with that of the Geneva Preparatory Disarmament Commission.

The Treaty was signed at the conclusion of the statements of the heads of each delegation, and it only remains here to take note of some of the principal results its terms were expected to bring about. Its chief merit is that it arrested for at least six years all competitive building between the three principal naval Powers. It also reduced very materially the existing tonnage in capital ships, through the scrapping of nine vessels, and since five of these were British, Great Britain may be said to have made the largest sacrifice, because all five were comparatively modern and efficient vessels. The result is numerical equality with the United States, which means, in the opinion of many critics, actual inferiority.

With regard to aircraft carriers, the significance of the amendment in the definition of these vessels is that henceforward all ships built for carrying aircraft, irrespective of their tonnage, are reckoned in the aggregate quota of such tonnage, whereas hitherto all ships of less than 10,000 tons displacement had been outside the quota regulations.

The limitation of the tonnage of submarines to 2,000 tons displacement lost part of its value by the reservation by which each of the three Powers was allowed to possess three vessels whose displacement may be not far short of 3,000 tons, but it has been claimed for the measure of limitation secured that it should check the tendency to build very large submarines such as would be capable of operating against merchant shipping at great distances from their base.

As regards cruisers, the main advantages of the Treaty are that it established the concessions made by Great Britain and the United States in respect of the number of these vessels which they regarded it necessary to retain. Great Britain accepted the figure of 50 vessels as the total number of units, and the United States definitely agreed to reduce the number of her 10,000-ton cruisers[1] to 18, with a further understanding—inserted to remove the difficulties caused by the Japanese reservations to the Reed-Matsudaira proposals—that the sixteenth, seventeenth and eighteenth units of these vessels will not be laid down until the years 1933, 1934 and 1935 respectively. In Article XVIII of the Treaty it is stated that the United States contemplated the completion by 1935 of fifteen of these cruisers, but that for each of the three remaining ones which it was entitled to construct it might elect to substitute 15,166 tons of smaller vessels, carrying guns not above 6·1 inches.[2] In case, however, it should construct one or more of these three remaining large cruisers (carrying guns of above 6·1 inches) they will not be laid down until the years mentioned above, for completion in not less than three years in each case.

The effect of the Treaty as regards cruiser strengths was described by the First Lord of the Admiralty in a statement in Parliament on April 30, 1930, as follows:

"As regards ourselves, we will not construct the two 8-inch gun 10,000-ton cruisers of the 1928 programme, or the one 8-inch gun 10,000-ton cruiser of the 1929 programme, and a figure of fifteen 8-inch gun cruisers will constitute the total number for the British Commonwealth of Nations.

"The United States, which entered the Conference with a projected programme of twenty-three 8-inch gun 10,000-ton cruisers, will actually not complete more than fifteen of this type before 1936, retaining only the option to have three more under construction and not to be completed before the years 1936, 1937 and 1938 respectively.

---

[1] These vessels are termed "light cruisers" in the United States, vide the Fifteen Cruiser Bill of February 13, 1929.
[2] These form sub-category (b), vide Article XV of the Treaty.

"Japan will remain at her present figure of twelve 8-inch gun cruisers, and will not embark on fresh construction as previously anticipated.

"As regards 6-inch gun cruisers, the Treaty allows, generally speaking, only for replacement, except that, in the case of the United States, special provision is made for the carrying out of long-postponed cruiser construction."

The actual position as regards the British Empire at the date of signature of the Treaty was as follows:

There is at present[1] an excess of tonnage of cruisers of sub-category (a), i.e. carrying guns of over 6·1 inch calibre, because though there are in commission only eleven 10,000-ton cruisers, the four 9,850-ton vessels of the *Hawkins*[2] class carry guns of 7·5 inches. There are, in fact, 149,400 tons of these cruisers in commission, against 146,800 tons allowed by the Treaty (Article XVI), and in addition two vessels of the *York* class and two of the *Norfolk* class are nearing completion, so that when they are commissioned the total strength in vessels carrying guns above 6·1 inches will be 186,200.[3] By Article XVI, section 2, it is provided that vessels which cause an excess of tonnage in any category shall be "disposed of gradually during the period ending on December 31, 1936," and as two of the vessels of the *Hawkins* class (*Hawkins* and *Vindictive*) will be respectively 17 and 18 years old in that year,[4] they will presumably be the first to be scrapped. Their disappearance will, however, only reduce the total strength by 19,700 tons, and it is, therefore, clear that, as regards this category of cruiser, the Treaty represents a definite reduction of armaments on the part of Great Britain.

The position with regard to the smaller cruisers—sub-category (b)—is as follows: There are in commission 39 vessels, of an aggregate tonnage of 177,685 tons, whereas the Treaty allows to the British Empire 192,200 tons, representing the addition of, say, two more vessels to the existing fleet. Actually, however,

---

[1] This was written in April, 1930.
[2] These four are known officially as the "improved *Birmingham*" class, *vide* "Fleets," 1930, Cmd. 3464.
[3] The *York* class are of 8,400 tons and the *Norfolk* of 10,000 tons. All carry 8-inch guns.
[4] Under the terms of the Washington Treaty parity with the United States was to be achieved in 1936.

it appears as though a considerable amount of construction will be undertaken within the next few years, owing to the fact that several of the units now in commission will shortly reach the age limit.[1] In 1931 *Dartmouth* becomes over age, in 1934 *Birmingham* and *Lowestoft*, in 1935 six vessels of the "C" class,[2] and in 1936 five more of that class, and in addition *Brisbane*[3] of the Royal Australian Navy, so that allowing about two and a half years as the time necessary for building, it is evident that unless six vessels are laid down during the current year there will be a temporary shortage of tonnage in cruisers carrying guns not above 6·1 inches, that is, of sub-category (*b*).

The position in the United States as regards large, or, as they are termed in America, light cruisers, is made clear by the terms of the Treaty itself—*vide* Article XVIII. The number of vessels carrying 8-inch guns was eight only, and actually the construction of all of these had not been completed at the time of the signature of the Treaty. Five more were authorized in the fiscal year 1928–29 and should have been laid down before July 1, 1929, but actually only two had been begun. The Navy Estimates laid before Congress on December 2, 1929, included provision for beginning construction work on the other three some time during the first six months of 1930 and for a further ten to be laid down late in the fiscal year 1930–31. This makes up the fifteen light cruisers sanctioned by the Bill of February 13, 1929.

In cruisers of sub-category (*b*) the United States possessed twelve vessels only, aggregating about 96,000 tons, including *Pittsburg* of 12,715 tons, which is already over age. As the Treaty allows America 143,500 tons, a considerable increase in her armaments in respect of these cruisers is involved if the Treaty figures are to be adhered to.

Japan possessed fourteen 8-inch gun cruisers, or two more than allowed her by the Treaty, but two of these were already over age.[4] Four of the twelve others are of 7,100 tons displace-

---

[1] In this connection see Article XX (*a*) of the Treaty, limiting the replacement tonnage to be completed before the end of 1936 to 91,000 tons.
[2] These vessels are of approximately 3,900 tons displacement.
[3] *Brisbane* is a 5,120-ton vessel.
[4] These are *Nisshin* and *Kasuga*, of 7,080 tons.

ment only, so that the total tonnage amounts to exactly
108,400 tons, which is the Treaty figure.

In the smaller cruisers Japan's strength in April 1930,
omitting obsolete vessels, was approximately 95,000 tons, as
compared with 100,450 tons allowed her by the Treaty.

In conclusion it may be of interest to compare the existing
strengths in submarines in April 1930 with the 52,700 tons
allowed to each of the three Powers, since the adoption of this
figure represented for two of the Powers a real sacrifice and
reduction of armaments in this particular branch of the fleet.
Great Britain actually possessed only 45,524 tons of submarines,
of which a considerable proportion were soon to reach the age
limit, but vessels under construction totalling 8,850 tons were
due to be in commission within the ensuing twelve months,
and with a moderate building programme maintained during
the next two or three years it would appear that the aggregate
strength will remain at a point near the level of the Treaty
allowance.

The United States is in a different position, and the limitation
accepted by her would seem to involve a very serious reduction
of her submarine strength. She possessed 127 vessels, of which
6 were of between 2,000 and 3,000 tons and 52 of between
850 and 1,100 tons, so that a considerable number of vessels
had to be scrapped.

Japan also made a material sacrifice in accepting a figure
which was over 25,000 tons less than the total which she had
hitherto maintained to be the minimum necessary for her
defence. This latter figure is approximately that of her aggregate
tonnage at the time of the Treaty, so that she was compelled
to scrap a large number of vessels.

One further point may be mentioned. It will be remembered
that Japan had maintained the position, ever since she accepted
the invitation to the Conference, that she should have the right
to a 70 per cent. ratio to Great Britain and the United States
in 8-inch gun cruisers. By the terms of Article XVIII of
the Treaty it will be noticed that the United States, while
reserving the right to build eighteen of these vessels by 1936,

was not actually committed to the construction of more than fifteen, and accepted restrictions as to the times of completion of the remaining three. By this compromise Japan was induced to waive her claim and accept the figures shown in Article XVI of the Treaty, and her position in April 1930, *vis-à-vis* America, was better than the aggregate tonnage allowed her would seem to imply.

ANNEX

THE LONDON NAVAL TREATY, 1930

The following is the text of the Naval Treaty which was signed by all the five Powers:

"The President of the United States of America, the President of the French Republic, His Majesty the King of Great Britain, Ireland and the British Dominions beyond the Seas, Emperor of India, His Majesty the King of Italy, and His Majesty the Emperor of Japan,

Desiring to prevent the dangers and reduce the burdens inherent in competitive armaments, and

Desiring to carry forward the work begun by the Washington Naval Conference and to facilitate the progressive realization of general limitation and reduction of armaments,

Have resolved to conclude a Treaty for the limitation and reduction of naval armament, and have accordingly appointed as their Plenipotentiaries:

[Here follow the names of all the delegates.]

Who, having communicated to one another their full powers, found in good and due form, have agreed as follows:

PART I

ARTICLE 1

The High Contracting Parties agree not to exercise their rights to lay down the keels of capital ship replacement tonnage during the years 1931–1936 inclusive as provided in Chapter II, Part 3, of the Treaty for the Limitation of Naval Armament signed between them at Washington on February 6, 1922, and referred to in the present Treaty as the Washington Treaty.

This provision is without prejudice to the disposition relating to the replacement of ships accidentally lost or destroyed contained in Chapter II, Part 3, Section I, paragraph (c) of the said Treaty.

France and Italy may, however, build the replacement tonnage which they were entitled to lay down in 1927 and 1929 in accordance with the provisions of the said Treaty.

ARTICLE 2

SCRAPPING CAPITAL SHIPS

1. The United States, the United Kingdom of Great Britain and Northern Ireland, and Japan shall dispose of the following capital ships as provided in this Article:

United States.—*Florida, Utah, Arkansas* or *Wyoming.*
United Kingdom.—*Benbow, Iron Duke, Marlborough, Emperor of India, Tiger.*
Japan.—*Hiyei.*

(*a*) Subject to the provisions of sub-paragraph (b), the above ships, unless converted to target use exclusively in accordance with Chapter II, Part 2, paragraph II (c) of the Washington Treaty, shall be scrapped in the following manner:

One of the ships to be scrapped by the United States and two of those to be scrapped by the United Kingdom shall be rendered unfit for warlike service, in accordance with Chapter II, Part 2, paragraph III (b) of the Washington Treaty, within twelve months from the coming into force of the present Treaty. These ships shall be finally scrapped, in accordance with paragraph II (a) or (b) of the said Part 2, within twenty-four months from the said coming into force. In the case of the second of the ships to be scrapped by the United States, and of the third and fourth of the ships to be scrapped by the United Kingdom, the said periods shall be eighteen and thirty months respectively from the coming into force of the present Treaty.

(*b*) Of the ships to be disposed of under this Article, the following may be retained for training purposes:

By the United States.—*Arkansas* or *Wyoming.*
By the United Kingdom.—*Iron Duke.*
By Japan.—*Hiyei.*

These ships shall be reduced to the condition prescribed in Section V of Annex II to Part II of the present Treaty. The work of reducing these vessels to the required condition shall begin, in the case of the United States and the United Kingdom, within twelve months, and in the case of Japan within eighteen months from the coming into force of the present Treaty; the work shall be completed within six months of the expiration of the above-mentioned periods.

Any of these ships which are not retained for training purposes shall be rendered unfit for warlike service within eighteen months, and finally scrapped within thirty months of the coming into force of the present Treaty.

2. Subject to any disposal of capital ships which might be necessitated, in accordance with the Washington Treaty, by the building by France

or Italy of the replacement tonnage referred to in Article 1 of the present Treaty all existing capital ships mentioned in Chapter II, Part 3, Section II of the Washington Treaty and not designated above to be disposed of may be retained during the term of the present Treaty.

3. The right of replacement is not lost by delay in laying down replacement tonnage, and the old vessel may be retained until replaced even though due for scrapping under Chapter II, Part 3, Section II of the Washington Treaty.

ARTICLE 3
AIRCRAFT CARRIERS

1. For the purposes of the Washington Treaty the definition of an aircraft carrier given in Chapter II, Part 4, of the said Treaty is hereby replaced by the following definition:

The expression 'aircraft carrier' includes any surface vessel of war, whatever its displacement, designed for the specific and exclusive purpose of carrying aircraft and so constructed that aircraft can be launched therefrom and landed thereon.

2. The fitting of a landing-on or flying-off platform or deck on a capital ship, cruiser or destroyer, provided such vessel was not designed or adapted exclusively as an aircraft carrier, shall not cause any vessel so fitted to be charged against or classified in the category of aircraft carriers.

3. No capital ship in existence on April 1, 1930, shall be fitted with a land-on platform or deck.

ARTICLE 4

1. No aircraft carrier of 10,000 tons (10,160 metric tons) or less standard displacement mounting a gun above 6·1-in. (155-mm.) calibre shall be acquired by or constructed by or for any of the High Contracting Parties.

2. As from the coming into force of the present Treaty in respect of all the High Contracting Parties no aircraft carrier of 10,000 tons (10,160 metric tons) or less standard displacement mounting a gun above 6·1-in. (155-mm.) calibre shall be constructed within the jurisdiction of any of the High Contracting Parties.

ARTICLE 5

An aircraft carrier must not be designed and constructed for carrying a more powerful armament than that authorized by Article IX or Article X of the Washington Treaty or by Article 4 of the present Treaty, as the case may be.

Wherever in the said Articles IX and X the calibre of 6 in. (152 mm.) is mentioned, the calibre of 6·1 in. (155 mm.) is substituted therefor.

PART II

ARTICLE 6

1. The rules for determining standard displacements prescribed in Chapter II, Part 4 of the Washington Treaty shall apply to all surface vessels of war of each of the High Contracting Parties.

2. The standard displacement of a submarine is the surface displacement of the vessel complete (exclusive of the water in non-watertight structure), fully manned, engined and equipped ready for sea, including all armament and ammunition, equipment, outfit, provisions for crew, miscellaneous stores and implements of every description that are intended to be carried in war, but without fuel, lubricating oil, fresh water or ballast water of any kind on board.

3. Each naval combatant vessel shall be rated at its displacement tonnage when in the standard condition. The word "ton," except in the expression "metric tons," shall be understood to be the ton of 2,240 pounds (1,016 kilos).

ARTICLE 7

1. No submarine the standard displacement of which exceeds 2,000 tons (2,032 metric tons) or with a gun above 5·1-inch (130-mm.) calibre shall be acquired or constructed by or for any of the High Contracting Parties.

2. Each of the High Contracting Parties may, however, retain, build or acquire a maximum of three submarines of a standard displacement not exceeding 2,800 tons (2,845 metric tons); these submarines may carry guns not above 6·1-inch (155-mm.) calibre. Within this number, France may retain one unit, already launched, of 2,880 tons (2,926 metric tons), with guns the calibre of which is 8 inches (203 mm.).

3. The High Contracting Parties may retain the submarines which they possessed on April 1, 1930, having a standard displacement not in excess of 2,000 tons (2,032 metric tons) and armed with guns above 5·1-inch (130-mm.) calibre.

4. As from the coming into force of the present Treaty in respect of all the High Contracting Parties, no submarine the standard displacement of which exceeds 2,000 tons (2,032 metric tons) or with a gun above 5·1-inch (130-mm.) calibre shall be constructed within the jurisdiction of any of the High Contracting Parties, except as provided in paragraph 2 of this Article.

ARTICLE 8

Subject to any special agreements which may submit them to limitation, the following vessels are exempt from limitation:

(*a*) naval surface combatant vessels of 600 tons (610 metric tons) standard displacement and under;

(*b*) naval surface combatant vessels exceeding 600 tons (610 metric tons), but not exceeding 2,000 tons (2,032 metric tons) standard displacement, provided they have none of the following characteristics:

(1) mount a gun above 6·1-inch (155-mm.) calibre;
(2) mount more than four guns above 3-inch (76-mm.) calibre;
(3) are designed or fitted to launch torpedoes;
(4) are designed for a speed greater than twenty knots.

(c) Naval surface vessels not specifically built as fighting ships which are employed on fleet duties or as troop transports or in some other way than as fighting ships, provided they have none of the following characteristics:

(1) mount a gun above 6·1-inch (155-mm.) calibre;
(2) mount more than four guns above 3-inch (76-mm.) calibre;
(3) are designed or fitted to launch torpedoes;
(4) are designed for a speed greater than twenty knots;
(5) are protected by armour plate;
(6) are designed or fitted to launch mines;
(7) are fitted to receive aircraft on board from the air;
(8) mount more than one aircraft-launching apparatus on the centre line; or two, one on each broadside;
(9) if fitted with any means of launching aircraft into the air, are designed or adapted to operate at sea more than three aircraft.

ARTICLE 9

REPLACEMENT OF SHIPS

The rules as to replacement contained in Annex I to this Part II are applicable to vessels of war not exceeding 10,000 tons (10,160 metric tons) standard displacement, with the exception of aircraft carriers, whose replacement is governed by the provisions of the Washington Treaty.

ARTICLE 10

Within one month after the date of laying down and the date of completion respectively of each vessel of war, other than capital ships, aircraft carriers and the vessels exempt from limitation under Article 8, laid down or completed by or for them after the coming into force of the present Treaty, the High Contracting Parties shall communicate to each of the other High Contracting Parties the information detailed below:

(a) the date of laying the keel and the following particulars:

classification of the vessel;
standard displacement in tons and metric tons;
principal dimensions, namely: length, water-line, extreme beam at or below water-line;
mean draft at standard displacement;
calibre of the largest gun.

(*b*) the date of completion together with the foregoing particulars relating to the vessel at that date.

The information to be given in the case of capital ships and aircraft carriers is governed by the Washington Treaty.

ARTICLE 11

Subject to the provisions of Article 2 of the present Treaty, the rules for disposal contained in Annex II to this Part II shall be applied to all vessels of war to be disposed of under the said Treaty, and to aircraft carriers as defined in Article 3.

ARTICLE 12

SPECIAL VESSELS

1. Subject to any supplementary agreements which may modify, as between the High Contracting Parties concerned, the lists in Annex III to this Part II, the special vessels shown therein may be retained and their tonnage shall not be included in the tonnage subject to limitation.

2. Any other vessel constructed, adapted, or acquired to serve the purposes for which these special vessels are retained shall be charged against the tonnage of the appropriate combatant category, according to the characteristics of the vessel, unless such vessel conforms to the characteristics of vessels exempt from limitation under Article 8.

3. Japan may, however, replace the minelayers *Aso* and *Tokiwa* by two new minelayers before December 31, 1936. The standard displacement of each of the new vessels shall not exceed 5,000 tons (5,080 metric tons); their speed shall not exceed twenty knots, and their other characteristics shall conform to the provisions of paragraph (B) of Article 8. The new vessels shall be regarded as special vessels and their tonnage shall not be chargeable to the tonnage of any combatant category. The *Aso* and *Tokiwa* shall be disposed of in accordance with Section I or II of Annex II to this Part II, on completion of the replacement vessels.

4. The *Asama, Yakumo, Izumo, Iwate* and *Kasuga* shall be disposed of in accordance with Section I or II of Annex II to this Part II, when the first three vessels of the *Kuma* class have been replaced by new vessels. These three vessels of the *Kuma* class shall be reduced to the condition prescribed in Section V, sub-paragraph (B) 2 of Annex II to this Part II, and are to be used for training ships, and their tonnage shall not thereafter be included in the tonnage subject to limitation.

ARTICLE 13

Existing ships of various types, which, prior to the 1st April, 1930, have been used as stationary training establishments or hulks, may be retained in a non-seagoing condition.

[*Here follow Annexes I, II and III, containing Rules for Replacement, Rules for Disposal of Vessels, and a list of Special Vessels of each Power.*]

PART III

[This Part was signed by the British and Dominions Delegates and the Delegates of the United States of America and Japan.]

ARTICLE 14

The naval combatant vessels of the United States, the British Commonwealth of Nations and Japan, other than capital ships, aircraft carriers and all vessels exempt from limitation under Article 8, shall be limited during the term of the present Treaty as provided in this Part III, and, in the case of special vessels, as provided in Article 12.

ARTICLE 15

For the purpose of this Part III the definition of the cruiser and destroyer categories shall be as follows:

Cruisers

Surface vessels of war, other than capital ships or aircraft carriers, the standard displacement of which exceeds 1,850 tons (1,880 metric tons), or with a gun above 5·1-inch (130-mm.) calibre.

The cruiser category is divided into two sub-categories, as follows:

   (*a*) cruisers carrying a gun above 6·1 inch (155-mm.) calibre;

   (*b*) cruisers carrying a gun not above 6·1-inch (155-mm.) calibre.

Destroyers

Surface vessels of war the standard displacement of which does not exceed 1,850 tons (1,880 metric tons), and with a gun not above 5·1-inch (130-mm.) calibre.

ARTICLE 16

1. The completed tonnage in the cruiser, destroyer and submarine categories which is not to be exceeded on December 31, 1936, is given in the following table:

   Cruisers.—(*a*) with guns of more than 6·1-inch (155-mm.) calibre: United States, 180,000 tons (182,880 metric tons); British Commonwealth of Nations, 146,800 tons (149,149 metric tons); Japan, 108,400 tons (110,134 metric tons. (*b*) with guns of 6·1-inch (155-mm.) calibre or less: United States, 143,500 tons (145,796 metric tons); British Commonwealth of Nations, 192,200 tons (195,275 metric tons); Japan, 100,450 tons (105,057 metric tons).

   Destroyers.—United States, 150,000 tons (152,400 metric tons); British Commonwealth of Nations, 150,000 tons (152,400 metric tons); Japan, 105,000 tons (107,188 metric tons).

   Submarines.—United States, 52,700 tons (53,543 metric tons); British Commonwealth of Nations, 52,700 tons (53,543 metric tons); Japan 52,700 tons (53,543 tons).

2. Vessels which cause the total tonnage in any category to exceed the figures given in the foregoing table shall be disposed of gradually during the period ending on December 31, 1936.

3. The maximum number of cruisers of sub-category (a) shall be as follows:

For the United States, eighteen; for the British Commonwealth of Nations, fifteen; for Japan, twelve.

4. In the destroyer category not more than 16 per cent. of the allowed total tonnage shall be employed in vessels of over 1,500 tons (1,524 metric tons) standard displacement. Destroyers completed or under construction on April 1, 1930 in excess of this percentage may be retained, but no other destroyers exceeding 1,500 tons (1,524 metric tons) standard displacement shall be constructed or acquired until a reduction to such 16 per cent. has been effected.

5. Not more than 25 per cent. of the allowed total tonnage in the cruiser category may be fitted with a landing-on platform or deck for aircraft.

6. It is understood that the submarines referred to in paragraphs 2 and 3 of Article 7 will be counted as part of the total submarine tonnage of the High Contracting Party concerned.

7. The tonnage of any vessels retained under Article 13 or disposed of in accordance with Annex II to Part II of the present Treaty shall not be included in the tonnage subject to limitation.

ARTICLE 17

A transfer not exceeding 10 per cent. of the allowed total tonnage of the category or sub-category into which the transfer is to be made shall be permitted between cruisers of sub-category (b) and destroyers.

ARTICLE 18

The United States contemplates the completion by 1935 of fifteen cruisers of sub-category (a) of an aggregate tonnage of 150,000 tons (152,400 metric tons). For each of the three remaining cruisers of sub-category (a) which it is entitled to construct the United States may elect to substitute 15,166 tons (15,409 metric tons) of cruisers of sub-category (b). In case the United States shall construct one or more of such three remaining cruisers of sub-category (a), the sixteenth unit will not be laid down before 1933 and will not be completed before 1936; the seventeenth will not be laid down before 1934 and will not be completed before 1937; the eighteenth will not be laid down before 1934 and will not be completed before 1938.

ARTICLE 19

Except as provided in Article 20, the tonnage laid down in any category subject to limitation in accordance with Article 16 shall not exceed the amount necessary to reach the maximum allowed tonnage of the category, or to replace vessels that become 'over age' before December 31, 1936. Nevertheless, replacement tonnage may be laid down for cruisers and submarines that become 'over age' in 1937, 1938, and 1939, and for destroyers that become 'over age' in 1937 and 1938.

ARTICLE 20

Notwithstanding the rules for replacement contained in Annex I to Part II:

(*a*) The *Frobisher* and *Effingham* (United Kingdom) may be disposed of during the year 1936. Apart from the cruisers under construction on April 1, 1930, the total replacement tonnage of cruisers to be completed, in the case of the British Commonwealth of Nations, prior to the 31st December, 1936, shall not exceed 91,000 tons (92,456 metric tons).

(*b*) Japan may replace the *Tama* by new construction to be completed during the year 1936.

(*c*) In addition to replacing destroyers becoming 'over age' before December 31, 1936, Japan may lay down, in each of the years 1935 and 1936, not more than 5,200 tons (5,283 metric tons) to replace part of the vessels that become 'over age' in 1938 and 1939.

(*d*) Japan may anticipate replacement during the term of the present Treaty by laying down not more than 19,200 tons (19,507 metric tons) of submarine tonnage, of which not more than 12,000 tons (12,192 metric tons) shall be completed by December 31, 1936.

ARTICLE 21

THE SAFEGUARDING CLAUSE

If, during the term of the present Treaty, the requirements of the national security of any High Contracting Party in respect of vessels of war limited by Part III of the present Treaty are in the opinion of that Party materially affected by new construction of any Power other than those who have joined in Part III of this Treaty, that High Contracting Party will notify the other Parties to Part III as to the increase required to be made in its own tonnages within one or more of the categories of such vessels of war, specifying particularly the proposed increases and the reasons therefor, and shall be entitled to make such increase. Thereupon the other Parties to Part III of this Treaty shall be entitled to make a proportionate increase in the category or categories specified; and the said other Parties shall promptly advise with each other through diplomatic channels as to the situation thus presented.

LAW OF SUBMARINE WARFARE

PART IV

ARTICLE 22

The following are accepted as established rules of International Law:

(1) In their action with regard to merchant ships, submarines must conform to the rules of International Law to which surface vessels are subject.

(2) In particular, except in the case of persistent refusal to stop on being duly summoned, or of active resistance to visit or search, a warship, whether surface vessel or submarine, may not sink or render incapable of navigation a merchant vessel without having first placed passengers, crew and ship's papers in a place of safety. For this purpose the ship's boats are not regarded as a place of safety unless the safety of the passengers and crew is assured, in the existing sea and weather conditions, by the proximity of land, or the presence of another vessel which is in a position to take them on board.

The High Contracting Parties invite all other Powers to express their assent to the above rules.

DURATION OF THE TREATY
PART V

ARTICLE 23

The present Treaty shall remain in force until December 31, 1936, subject to the following exceptions:

(1) Part IV shall remain in force without limit of time;
(2) The provisions of Articles 3, 4 and 5, and of Article 11 and Annex II to Part II so far as they relate to aircraft carriers, shall remain in force for the same period as the Washington Treaty.

Unless the High Contracting Parties should agree otherwise by reason of a more general agreement limiting naval armaments, to which they all become parties, they shall meet in conference in 1935 to frame a new treaty to replace and to carry out the purposes of the present Treaty, it being understood that none of the provisions of the present Treaty shall prejudice the attitude of the High Contracting Parties at the Conference agreed to.

ARTICLE 24

1. The present Treaty shall be ratified by the High Contracting Parties in accordance with their respective constitutional methods and the ratifications shall be deposited at London as soon as possible. Certified copies of all the *procés-verbaux* of the deposit of ratifications will be transmitted to the Governments of the High Contracting Parties.

2. As soon as the ratifications of the United States of America, of his Majesty the King of Great Britain, Ireland and the British Dominions beyond the Seas, Emperor of India, in respect of each and all of the members of the British Commonwealth of Nations as enumerated in the preamble of the present Treaty, and of His Majesty the Emperor of Japan have been deposited, the Treaty shall come into force in respect of the said High Contracting Parties.

3. On the date of the coming into force referred to in the preceding paragraph parts I, II, IV and V of the present Treaty will come into

force in respect of the French Republic and the Kingdom of Italy if their ratifications have been deposited at that date; otherwise these parts will come into force in respect of each of those Powers on the deposit of its ratification.

4. The rights and obligations resulting from Part III of the present Treaty are limited to the High Contracting Parties mentioned in paragraph 2 of this Article. The High Contracting Parties will agree as to the date on which, and the conditions under which, the obligations assumed under the said Part III by the High Contracting Parties mentioned in paragraph 2 of this Article will bind them in relation to France and Italy; such agreement will determine at the same time the corresponding obligations of France and Italy in relation to the other High Contracting parties.

ARTICLE 25

After the deposit of the ratifications of all the High Contracting Parties His Majesty's Government in the United Kingdom of Great Britain and Northern Ireland will communicate the provisions inserted in Part IV of the present Treaty to all Powers which are not signatories of the said Treaty, inviting them to accede thereto definitely and without limit of time.

Such accession shall be effected by a declaration addressed to his Majesty's Government in the United Kingdom of Great Britain and Northern Ireland.

ARTICLE 26

The present Treaty, of which the French and English texts are both authentic, shall remain deposited in the archives of His Majesty's Government in the United Kingdom of Great Britain and Northern Ireland. Duly certified copies thereof shall be transmitted to the Governments of all the High Contracting Parties.

In faith whereof the above-named Plenipotentiaries have signed the present Treaty, and have affixed thereto their seals.

Done at London, the twenty-second day of April, nineteen hundred and thirty."

5. THE FRANCO–ITALIAN CONVERSATIONS, 1930–1931[1]

The London Naval Conference closed on April 22, 1930 with the signature of a three-Power Treaty for naval limitation between Great Britain and the Dominions, the United States and Japan, but with a record of failure so far as any attempt

---

[1] The greater part of this section is reprinted from an article by Mr. Hugh Latimer in the *Bulletin of International News*, Vol. VII, No. 22, April 22, 1931.

at reconciliation of the rival French and Italian theses was concerned. Italy in no way abated her claim to parity with France. France refused to consider a further reduction of her fleet or the question of Italian parity without further material guarantees of security. The position was, therefore, the same as when the two Powers had first stated their respective cases in January, before the Conference met.

The Treaty was signed on April 22nd, and exactly six days later the Italian Cabinet made provision for 42,900 tons of new naval construction, including the laying down, in 1930–31, of one 10,000-ton cruiser (two of these—*Zara* and *Fiume*—were launched early in 1931), also two scout cruisers, four destroyers and twenty-two submarines—the last-named replacements only.

The two Governments had undertaken to keep in touch, with a view to seeing whether they could not find a way out of the *impasse*, and on May 13th M. Briand and Signor Grandi met at Geneva with that object. Signor Mussolini then made three speeches, and in Paris it was said that they had made negotiations impossible. The first at Leghorn on May 11th referred to the great influence which Fascism would exert in the world: in the second at Florence on May 17th the Duce said the naval programme would be carried out "ton by ton," and reminded his hearers that while words were beautiful things, guns and aeroplanes were more beautiful: and the third at Milan on May 24th warned the Italian people not to be lulled to sleep by the bleating of lambs, which in reality were wolves. Accordingly, when, some weeks later, Signor Grandi appeared to hold France responsible for the delay in the negotiations M. Briand pointed out that the Duce's speeches had set everything back. Arnaldo Mussolini retorted in the press that the French military preparations along her eastern frontier, making it into an armed camp from Dunkirk to the Mediterranean, had been begun in 1929, long before any sabre-rattling speeches had been made in Italy.

Signs of progress appeared, at last, in July, when M. Briand announced, on July 10th, that Italy had been informed that not a ship would be laid down before December 31st, with a view to maintaining the *status quo* during the negotiations. As this statement seemed to arouse certain misgivings the Minister of Marine assured the Chamber the very next day that there would be no suspension or delay in carrying out the construction programme, since all the vessels to be laid down in 1930 had already been begun. This did not prevent the Italian Government from signifying, on July 13th, its intention of not laying down any tonnage for the period indicated by M. Briand, and it repeated a suggestion already made by Signor Grandi, that this arrangement should last as long as the negotiations continued. The rest of the summer passed without any progress being made, as far as the outside world was aware, but the situation was not improved by another speech by Signor Mussolini on October 27th, when he said that the object of his previous speeches was to "tear the mask off a hypocritical Europe which babbles of peace at Geneva and prepares for war everywhere."

On the same day Mr. Gibson, the United States Ambassador in Brussels, visited M. Tardieu in Paris and then went on to Rome. He disclaimed any intention of discussing the naval situation, but said he had come to see Signor Grandi as a member of the Preparatory Commission for the Disarmament Conference.

From this time onwards the rôle of go-between was assumed by the British naval expert, Mr. Craigie, who continued to pursue negotiations diligently both in Paris and in Rome.

Despite the fact that on February 7th the French Government published Naval Estimates showing a total for 1931–32 of 191 million francs above the previous year, Mr. Craigie returned to London on February 21st, having, it was said, successfully persuaded the French and Italian Governments to accept a formula to the effect that both their building programmes up to 1936 should be calculated in such a way as to leave the two countries in the same relative position as then existed, and if this had been adopted France would have possessed in modern units a superiority of 150,000 tons.

So important was it considered by the British Cabinet that no stone should be left unturned to secure a Franco-Italian agreement, that the Foreign Secretary, Mr. Henderson, and the First Lord of the Admiralty, Mr. Alexander, left at once for Paris on February 23rd, and having received a certain degree of satisfaction went on to Rome.[1] As a result of their conversations there and of a further conference in Paris, it was believed that an agreement had been reached on the lines suggested by Mr. Craigie.

The terms of the settlement were published on March 1st, in the form of a White Paper,[2] but when this appeared it was seen that the "Bases of Agreement" reproduced did not include detailed figures of the aggregate tonnages and numbers of vessels accepted by the two Governments in respect of cruisers and destroyers, and it would appear that, in actual fact, no definite figures were finally agreed upon as regards the replacement of these vessels. The agreement as published has been described as vague and obscure by the press, both in England and abroad, and this has been variously attributed to the desire to gloss over the delicate question of ratios between France and Italy, and to the need not to make apparent the concessions made by each country. The document should, however, be read as an annex to the London Naval Treaty, and is, in fact, not to be understood without reference to the terms of that Treaty and of the Treaty of Washington; it is thought, therefore, that any filling in of the details of the present agreement—if it can be so called—should be prefaced by a reference to those sections of the two Treaties which form the basis of the points now settled.

The following provisions of the Washington Treaty have a direct bearing on the negotiations:

(1) The total capital ship replacement tonnage was fixed at 175,000 tons each for France and Italy.
(2) The total aircraft carrier tonnage was fixed at 60,000 tons for each country.

---

[1] Mr. Henderson, in a speech at Lowestoft on March 7th, explained this urgent need for haste by the fact that within a few days France and Italy were expected to announce their building programmes for 1931–32.
[2] Cmd. 3812.

(3) France was allowed to retain ten capital vessels, aggregating
221,170 tons, and to lay down one new vessel, of a maximum
tonnage of 35,000 in each of the years 1927, 1929 and 1931.

(4) Italy was allowed to retain ten capital vessels, aggregating
182,800 tons, and to lay down one new vessel, of a maximum
displacement of 35,000 tons, in each of the years 1927, 1929
and 1931.

In the Treaty of London the provisions which directly affect
the points dealt with in the negotiations are the following:·

(1) Both France and Italy were limited to the construction of only
two of the new capital ships accorded them at Washington,
i.e. they were allotted 70,000 tons each, representing the vessels
to be laid down in 1927 and 1929 (not 1931).[1]

(2) All the Powers signatory to the Treaty had the right to replace,
within the limits of the tonnages awarded them, ships becoming
over age during the interval between the date of the conclusion
of the Treaty and its expiry (December 31, 1936).[2]

(3) The three principal Powers limited their new construction of
cruisers and submarines strictly to replacements.[3]

As has already been pointed out, the original object of the
conversations between the two Governments, or rather the three
Governments—for Great Britain has been specially interested
in this—was to secure the adherence of France and Italy to
Part III of the London Treaty. It should, therefore, be made
clear the exact nature and extent of the obligations assumed by
those two countries by their accession to that Part, and these
may now be enumerated. They accept:

(1) The definition of cruisers as all-surface vessels the displacement
of which exceeds 1,850 tons, or which carry a gun of over
5·1-inch calibre.

(2) The division of cruisers into two sub-categories (A) with guns
above 6·1-inch, and (B) with guns not above 6·1-inch calibre.

(3) The definition of destroyers as surface vessels not exceeding
1,850 tons displacement and with guns not over 5·1 inches.

(4) The stipulation that in the case of destroyers not over 16 per cent.
should be of over 1,500 tons displacement.

(5) The stipulation that transfers between cruisers of category (B)
and destroyers are not allowed over 10 per cent. of the allotted
total tonnage of the category or sub-category into which the
transfer is made.

---

[1] *Vide* Article I.
[2] *Vide* Article IX and Annex I to Part II of the Treaty.
[3] *Vide* Article XIX.

(6) The escalator clause (Article XXI of the Treaty), permitting the
signatories to increase their tonnages in the event of their
national security being materially affected by the new construction of any Power other than those who joined in Part III.

In the provisions as to cruiser construction accepted by Great
Britain, the United States and Japan in Part III it is laid down
by Article XIX that:

"The tonnage laid down in any category subject to limitation . . . shall
not exceed the amount necessary to reach the maximum allowed
tonnage of the category, or to replace vessels that become over age
before December 31, 1936. Nevertheless, replacement tonnage may
be laid down for cruisers and submarines that become over age in 1937,
1938 and 1939, and for destroyers that become over age in 1937 and
1938."

Before dealing with the details of the March agreement something must be said as to the French programme of naval
construction. The figures to which that country is working
were drawn up in 1922 and provided for construction for twenty
years, i.e. until 1942, when the programme would be completed.
The total tonnage arrived at was 744,000 tons, and this figure
was slightly raised at the end of 1929 when the French Government reviewed the position in detail, in view of the forthcoming
meeting of the London Naval Conference. Speaking on December 19, 1929, M. Dumesnil, the *rapporteur* of the Naval Budget,
said that their existing strength in new ships, which he described
as alone of military value, was approximately 422,689 metric
tons,[1] but that if they proceeded with their programme as they
then intended their aggregate tonnage at the end of 1936 would
be 625,000 metric tons. About the same time the Government
laid it down that the "absolute need" of the country was a
minimum of 760,407 metric tons, and in the *exposé* of the French
position, published on February 18, 1930 during the London
Conference, a minimum of 684,886 tons was claimed as essential
for the country.

At the time of that Conference the superiority of the French
Navy over that of Italy was calculated at 240,000 metric tons,

[1] A metric ton is 2,204 lbs. as compared with an English ton of 2,240 lbs.
100,000 tons = 101,600 metric tons.

but this included 83,000 tons of old vessels, so that the superiority in new vessels was 157,000 tons, which is approximately the figure accepted in the March agreement (157,441 tons).

To come now to the agreement itself, the only figures available with which to fill in the details of its provisions are those given in the French press on March 12th, 1931. These figures are official, however, and taken in conjunction with the terms published on March 1st, give a fairly complete outline of the position. The main terms of the agreement may be enumerated as follows:

(1) France and Italy are both allowed, before December 31, 1936, to complete two capital ships, the displacement of which will not exceed 23,333 tons, and the gun calibre of which will not exceed 12 inches.

(2) On the completion of each ship France will scrap one ship of the *Diderot*[1] class and Italy will scrap approximately 16,820 tons of first-class over-age cruisers, i.e. 33,640 tons in all.

(3) Without prejudice to a general revision of the capital ship tonnages established by the Treaty of Washington, the total tonnage in this category accorded to France and Italy shall be raised from 175,000 to 181,000 tons.

(4) Before December 31, 1936 France and Italy may complete respectively 34,000 tons of aircraft carriers.

(5) As regards vessels whose tonnage is regulated by the London Naval Treaty, i.e. cruisers, destroyers and submarines, France and Italy will conform to the following rules in preparing their programmes for construction to be completed before December 31, 1936.

(A) Cruisers with guns of more than 6·1 inches. No further construction after completion of the 1930 programme.

(B) Cruisers with guns of 6·1 inches, or less, and destroyers. The tonnage of new construction to be completed shall not exceed the tonnage which is replaceable in this category before December 31, 1936. Vessels already over age and vessels becoming over age during the period of the Treaty shall be scrapped on being replaced.

A declaration was added here on behalf of the British as well as the French and Italian Governments to the effect that the age of destroyers (in respect of those due to be replaced before December 31, 1936) should be extended to sixteen years.

---

[1] The *Diderot*, of 18,890 tons displacement, was placed in commission in September 1911, and is now used as a training ship.

(C) Submarines. No further construction other than for completion of the 1930 programme and for the replacement of tonnage becoming over age after December 31, 1931. Over-age vessels shall be scrapped, except where this would result in the total submarine tonnage falling below the figure mentioned in Article XVI[1] of the London Treaty.

Subject to a general revision of the question in the Disarmament Conference of 1932, the tonnage of French submarines in commission will not exceed, up to December 31, 1936, the figure of 81,989 tons, representing at the present moment the under-age tonnage of vessels built or building.

To this provision a declaration was attached that the

"Members of the British Commonwealth of Nations maintain that this figure of 81,989 tons is too high in relation to their destroyer figure of 150,000 tons under the London Naval Treaty, but they agree to notify the other signatories of Part III of the London Treaty that they will not have recourse to Article XXI of the Treaty pending the general revision of the naval question mentioned above."

(6) General provisions. France and Italy furthermore declare—

(i) that they will accept all the provisions of Part III of the London Naval Treaty in so far as it applies to the Members of the British Commonwealth of Nations, the United States of America and Japan;

(ii) that they will accept, in so far as they are concerned, those provisions which are of general application and which do not conflict with the provisions of the present arrangement.

At the time of the signature of this arrangement a declaration in the following sense would be signed, either by the Members of the British Commonwealth of Nations, France and Italy, or else by all the parties to the London Treaty:

"It is understood that the present arrangement establishes no permanent ratio in any category of ship as between the Members of the British Commonwealth of Nations, France and Italy. In particular, no precedent is being created for the final solution of the question whether, and if so in what manner, tonnage remaining over age on December 31, 1936, may ultimately be replaced."

---

[1] This is in Part III, and accorded to the three signatory Powers 52,700 tons each.

The above provisions, forming the "Bases of Agreement," were prefaced by a Memorandum, dated March 11, 1931, and signed by Mr. Henderson and Mr. Alexander. In this it was explained that the slight increase proposed in the total tonnage of capital ships accorded to France and Italy under the Treaty of Washington would not in itself give rise to any new construction during the period of the agreement.

On the subject of 6-in. gun cruisers the Memorandum states that:

"It is anticipated that the French Government will, in 1936, possess a large over-age tonnage in this category. It was made clear during the negotiations that the temporary retention of this tonnage conferred on France no claim to its ultimate replacement . . "

As to submarines, it was stated that both the French and Italian Governments had agreed not to include any of these vessels in the 1931 programme, and not to lay down any further submarine tonnage before 1933.

As will be seen from the above, the lack of figures of existing and prospective tonnage totals makes the "Bases of Agreement" somewhat obscure, but the official figures of aggregate tonnages published in the French press enable many of the details to be filled in.

The following were the tonnages of the two fleets in March 1931, including vessels under construction and authorized:

	FRANCE Tons	ITALY Tons
Capital ships	133,134	86,527
Over-age capital ships ..	52,791	—
Aircraft carriers	22,146	—
First-class cruisers	124,424	103,640
Light cruisers, destroyers, etc.	198,233[1]	151,363
Submarines	97,875	53,472
	628,603	395,002
	Of which 146,383 are over age.	Of which 85,077 are over age.

[1] Of this total, 52,133 tons are over age.

The following are the figures of new construction, which may be placed in commission before December 31, 1936 (to replace over-age vessels).

	FRANCE Tons	ITALY Tons
Capital ships	46,666	46,666
Aircraft carriers	34,000	34,000
Light cruisers, destroyers, etc.	51,331	46,158
Submarines	4,441	2,791
	136,438	129,615

Finally, the two fleets will at the end of 1936 be made up as follows:

	FRANCE Tons	ITALY Tons
Capital ships	179,800	133,193
Over-age capital ships ..	17,597	—
Aircraft carriers	56,146	34,000
First-class cruisers	70,000	70,000
Over-age first-class cruisers ..	24,851	—
Light cruisers, destroyers, etc.	197,431	143,342
Ditto, whose life has been prolonged	802	8,021
Ditto, over age	42,107	—
Submarines	81,989	47,390
Over-age submarines	—	5,310
	670,723	441,256

From these figures it will be seen that in 1936 the French superiority will be in new vessels, 157,441 tons, and in over-age vessels, 72,026 tons.

When issuing these figures the French Ministry of Marine accompanied them by a *communiqué* stating that the agreement of March 1st had the effect of hindering all race in armaments between the Powers concerned, and stabilized considerably (*sensiblement*), for the period up to the end of 1936, the existing proportions of the present fleets, taking into account the rights acquired and not yet exercised by France and Italy. Speaking in the Chamber in defence of the agreement on March 11th, both M. Briand and M. Dumont maintained that it gave France substantially all that she had ever asked for in the matter of tonnage. Two days later the *Temps*, in a statement which was understood to express the official view, said that the figures in the agreement established in indisputable fashion that the interests of the country had been well defended, and that the door was closed to any unpleasant surprises for both parties. France had, in fact, gained in the acceptance of a tonnage increase from the existing aggregate of 628,603 tons to 670,723 tons, and had established her right to lay down and complete before the end of 1936 two capital ships, of about 23,000 tons, to form that country's reply to the new German "pocket battle-ships." Italy, on her side, obtained from France an undertaking not to make use of her ability still further to increase her superiority, and an undertaking to restrict her submarine tonnage to a figure approximately 15,000 tons lower than she had hitherto claimed. Signor Mussolini expressed himself as satisfied with the result of the negotiations, which he regarded in the light of an extension of the London Naval Treaty, saying that there could be no "doubt that the five-Power Naval Treaty will afford the best possible preparation for the general Disarmament Conference."

As the month went on the news as to the progress made by the Drafting Committee engaged in putting the "Bases of Agreement" into final form suggested that the questions of interpretation remaining to be settled were causing more difficulty than had been anticipated. Though Mr. Henderson was able to say, as late as March 27th,[1] that the difficulties were "simple questions of interpretation," the Foreign Affairs Committee of the Chamber in Paris had decided, on March 18th,[2] that it must await the opinion of the Naval Committee of the Chamber, especially as to the provisions relating to new construction and replacement. It also decided that henceforth it would approve naval agreements only in so far as they were connected with the guarantees of international security already

---

[1] In a statement to the British press representatives in Paris.
[2] It was on this day that the French Government received its first intimation of the conclusion of the Austro-German Customs Union agreement.

obtained or likely to be obtained. Only two days later the French Minister of Marine, in an *exposé* of the agreement before the two Committees of the Chamber, said that:

"Apart from the two cruisers of 23,333 tons, the construction of which is accorded to us for the years 1931, 1932 and 1933, nothing prevents us from constructing whatever we consider necessary in 1934, 1935 and 1936, subject to new agreements and decisions of the Conference of 1932."

Furthermore, in the Senate on March 25th, it was argued that the alleged superiority in French tonnage had only been obtained by the inclusion of old vessels, to which M. Dumont replied that the agreement represented merely a holiday in the augmentation of the fleet, with the object of carrying out immediately an urgent programme, and he concluded:

"Quant aux sous-marins, notre limitation dépasse de 30,000 tonnes la part de toute autre nation. Cette supériorité est trés sensible. Nous avons obtenu d'autres supériorités, dont ce n'est pas l'heure de parler."

While no particular notice appears to have been taken of these statements abroad, by the end of March it was evident that the final drafting of the agreement was being delayed by difficulties which had not originally been foreseen. Reports were current that the French Government were claiming the right to start construction in 1935 and 1936 of ships due to be replaced in 1937 and 1938, and that they had the intention of laying down 66,000 tons of new construction which would come into commission in 1937, thus seriously affecting the balance of strength in new vessels almost immediately after the expiry period of the London Treaty. What the French Government was actually claiming was the right to lay down in 1935 and 1936 whatever cruiser and destroyer tonnage it considered that the needs of the country's security dictated, and to replace certain already over-age vessels whose retention had only been permitted as a special case, instead of limiting construction strictly to the figures necessary to replace the tonnage becoming over age in 1937, 1938 and 1939. This meant that France was now apparently unwilling to subscribe to Article XIX of the

London Naval Treaty, the text of which has been quoted above, in spite of the fact that, under the General Provisions of the "Bases of Agreement" she would declare that she accepted all the provisions of Part III, in which that Article appears. Were her claim to be admitted it would mean that, whereas the British Government is bound until the end of 1936, in that her construction programme for 1935 and 1936 is limited to the laying down of keels necessary to replace vessels becoming over age during the following three years, France would only be bound for four years, or, in other words, would be accepting the terms of the London Treaty for four years instead of six.

It was not until April 21st that M. Massigli, the French expert, left Paris for London carrying fresh proposals, which had been approved by the Cabinet the previous day. These were understood to consist of an offer not to begin the construction of tonnage to replace existing over-age units before the Conference of 1935, but a free hand was insisted upon as to the laying down of such replacement tonnage at once, if the Conference failed to reach an agreement.

After discussion of this suggested compromise between the British and Italian Governments, the British Government put forward a counter-proposal. This suggested that a compromise might be found by agreeing that France, instead of waiting until the expiry of the agreement, might lay down new construction after the 1935 Conference, but only at a rate and to an extent to be agreed upon by the Conference. Failing an agreement there, she would remain bound only to lay down replacement tonnage, as provided for in Article XIX of the London Treaty. The Note containing these proposals was handed to the French Government on April 25th, and the Italian reply as delivered on May 4th. The latter pointed out that the French suggestions went far beyond a mere interpretation of the text of the agreement and constituted absolute variation from that instrument. They would mean an increase in the average annual naval construction of both countries from 27,000 to 40,000 tons, and thus, contrary to the whole spirit of the London Conference and the subsequent negotiations, would entail an increase rather than a reduction of armaments. However, owing to its desire for an understanding with France, the Italian Government declared that it associated itself with the British counter-proposals already under consideration by the French Government.

Reviewing the agreement as a whole the conclusion is reached that though professing to stabilize the position, the figures given for the aggregate tonnages of the two fleets increase considerably during the period of the agreement, that is, the period of the duration of the London Treaty. For example, the tonnage of the French fleet at the beginning of 1931 totalled 628,603, including vessels building and authorized. The figure shown for the end of 1936 is 670,725 tons, an increase of 42,000 odd all sanctioned by the terms of the agreement, and this latter total represents vessels in service only. Further than that, the value of the fleet is increased, because the proportion of over-age vessels is reduced. At the date of the agreement these represented 146,383 tons, and in December 1936 they will amount to only 84,000 tons.

In the case of Italy, the tonnage aggregate shown is 395,000 and this rises to 441,000 odd, all in service, in December 1936. Here again the proportion of new vessels increases, since the over-age tonnage at the time of the agreement was 85,000 odd, while at the end of 1936 it will be 13,000 only. One is tempted to think, in fact, that not much was lost by the failure to stabilize the building programmes on this basis, since when not deprived of their freedom of action there is a good prospect that the Governments concerned may not build up to their authorized programmes. In France especially, insistence has often been laid on the necessity for retaining freedom for building, and to this principle the Government has adhered with noteworthy tenacity. Italy, on the other hand, may be said to have modified her attitude to a very material respect, because her acceptance of the agreement of March 1st amounted, in fact, to virtual abandonment of the claim to parity. Looking back on the negotiations it is evident that the French Government had not moved one inch from the standpoint it took up before the Naval

Conference of January 1930. At the closing session of that gathering M. Briand reminded the delegates that France, in her Memorandum of December 1929, had laid it down that "a general technical agreement on armaments must be preceded by a political agreement," and he would presumably have said this again, as a gentle reminder that the protracted negotiations regarding figures of naval tonnage were, after all, quite beside the point.

No further communication was received from Paris until the beginning of September, when what were described as semi-official proposals were communicated to Rome. An examination of these showed that they did nothing to reconcile the existing differences of view, and on September 20th, during the meeting of the League Assembly, the Italian Delegation issued a *communiqué* stating that it was not easy to see how the naval conservations could be resumed, "seeing that the latest French proposal diverges considerably from the basis of the agreement concluded on March 1, 1931."

6. The Ægean and Black Sea Pacts of Stability, 1930–31

Whilst attempts were being made during the summer and autumn of 1930 to reconcile the naval rivalries of France and Italy in the Western Mediterranean, important events were taking place at the eastern end of the same sea, which drew comparatively little attention at the time. Yet these events were no less than the apparent termination of a hundred years' feud between two States which had always been regarded as implacable enemies, and which less than ten years before were at death grips. Any political prophet who, as late as 1927, had foretold a Greco-Turkish *rapprochement* would have been laughed to scorn, yet the autumn of 1930 saw M. Venizelos and the Ghazi Pasha clasping hands at Angora and announcing to the world: "We have agreed on the future of the Near East."

This surprising change of events was due to a variety of causes, many of which are traceable to the much-abused Peace of Lausanne. The ancient feud between Ottomanism and Hellenism has vanished. Mustapha Kemal Pasha had abolished the one as a decrepit institution and M. Venizelos had abandoned the other as a false ambition. The deportation of the Greek population from Turkey, except from Constantinople, a feat carried out under the ægis of the League of Nations, had freed Turkey from the fear that this minority might prove a channel of intrigue. Moreover, the Patriarchate at Stamboul had ceased to exercise its former powerful influence in Turkish politics, and was no longer a rallying point for disaffected Greek. It had become a purely spiritual body with little or no political aspect.

Thus in Turkey the way was clear for reconciliation. M. Venizelos, however, met with certain opposition in his policy. There was opposition in the Chamber, division in the Ministry, and hostility from the Greek Orthodox Church. Over all these adverse factors, however, M. Venizelos' Cretan guile prevailed and, after negotiations which lasted from February to October, he and his Foreign Minister, M. Michalacopoulos, set out on what proved a triumphal progress from Athens to Angora. There on October 30th in the midst of brilliant fêtes and celebrations they signed with Izmet Pasha and Dr. Tewfik Rushdi a Treaty of Friendship and Arbitration, by which they accepted the territorial arrangements as defined in the post-war treaties, including the Treaty of Lausanne, and pledged themselves to neutrality in the event of a recourse to arms to bring about a revision of these treaties.

It is improbable, however, that even combined Greco-Turkish statesmanship would have brought about this reconciliation had there not been the added external force of Italian diplomacy. In pursuance of a policy which is dealt with in greater detail elsewhere in this book,[1] Italy, who herself had treaties of friendship with both Turkey and Greece, was anxious to bring these two countries to a degree of comradeship by which they might usefully be added to the Central and Eastern European *bloc* which she is forming. Throughout

[1] See below, p. 31.

the negotiations, therefore, Italy played the rôle of an honest broker, and a tribute to the good offices of Signor Mussolini was paid by Mustapha Kemal Pasha during the festivities at Angora.

Attached to the Treaty of Friendship and Arbitration was a Protocol providing for the maintenance of the *status quo* in naval armaments. Each party was required to inform the other six months beforehand of any intention to construct new naval units. The text of the Protocol is sufficiently short to reprint in full:

"Les deux hautes parties contractantes, inbues des principes qui les ont conduites à la signature du pacte d'amitié et d'arbitrage signé en date de ce jour, et désireuses de prévenir de vaines augmentations de leurs dépenses pour des armements navals et de marcher de pair dans la voie de la limitation parallèle de leurs forces respectives en tenant compte des conditions particulières, à chacune d'elles, s'engagent à ne procéder à aucune commande, acquisition ou construction d'unités de guerre ou de leurs armements sans aviser au préalable l'autre partie contractante six mois à l'avance, afin que l'occasion soit ainsi fournie aux deux gouvernements de prévenir éventuellement la course aux armements navals, au moyen d'un échange amical de vues et d'explications de part et d'autre, dans un esprit de parfaite sincérité."[1]

Having thus secured a pact of stability with Greece, Mustapha Kemal Pasha turned his attention to Turkey's other naval neighbour, the Soviet Union. The Soviet-Turkish Pact of Neutrality and Non-Aggression, signed on December 17, 1925, as a counter-blast to Turkey's diplomatic defeat in the Mosul dispute, had been renewed in December 1929 and had had annexed to it a Protocol, of which Article II read as follows:

"The two Contracting Parties mutually affirm that they have not concluded agreements, other than those published, with States contiguous by land or sea to the other Contracting Party. The two Parties further undertake not to enter into any negotiations for the conclusion of political agreements with States contiguous by land or sea to the other Party without notifying the latter, nor shall they conclude any such agreements without the consent of the other Party. It is, however, understood that instruments aiming at the establishment or maintenance of normal relations with such contiguous States, and which are made public, are not subject to the above stipulation.

[1] See *l'Europe Nouvelle*, December 20, 1930.

"The duration of the Treaty shall be two years, and, unless denounced by either Party six months before its expiration, it will automatically remain in force another year."[1]

And it was in pursuance of this engagement that Turkey began negotiations.

There had for some time been indications that the balance of power in the Black Sea was threatened by the Soviet Union and that a race in naval armaments might ensue. In January 1930 a Soviet dreadnought and a cruiser were transferred from the Baltic to the Black Sea fleet, and their passage through the Dardanelles caused a certain flutter in international dovecots and at Angora. In reply to comments raised it was pointed out in Moscow that as the U.S.S.R. had neither signed nor ratified the Lausanne Straits Convention she was not bound by it, and further that, as in any case Article 5 of that Convention provided that States adjacent to the Black Sea could at any time pass their warships through the Straits, the Soviet Government had been entirely within its rights in doing so.[2]

This statement, though justifying the Soviet action, was of little satisfaction to Turkey, and a further cause for trepidation was provided when the Rumanian Government began to construct important new naval works under, it was said, British supervision. It was Turkey's policy to preserve the naval equilibrium in the Black Sea and to prevent any further transfers from the Baltic.

The negotiations with Moscow were begun almost immediately after the signature of the naval pact with Greece on October 30, 1930 and resulted, on March 8, 1931, in the signature of a supplementary Protocol in Angora resembling very closely that already concluded with M. Venizelos. The text of the document is as follows:[3]

"Neither of the High Contracting Parties will, without notifying the other Party six months beforehand, lay down any warship which is intended to strengthen its fleet in the Black Sea or neighbouring seas,

[1] *The Times*, December 19, 1929.
[2] See *Izvestia*, January 23, 1930.
[3] See *Europäische Gespräche*, March 1931. (English translation prepared by the Information Department of the Royal Institute of International Affairs.)

or give an order for the construction of any such ship by foreign dockyards, or take any other measures which would strengthen the present
establishment of their war fleet in the above-named seas. The present
supplementary Protocol requires ratification and will, after ratification,
become an actual part of the Protocol of 17th December, 1929."

Some uncertainty attaches to the words "adjacent seas," it
not being clear whether the Sea of Marmora and the Ægean,
or only the Sea of Azov, are included. In any case, however,
these two agreements may be regarded as diplomatic triumphs
for Turkey. She has obtained the stabilization of naval power
in her two neighbouring seas, and secured herself against
maritime competition with her two most important neighbours.

The implications of the Black Sea Agreement are particularly interesting, for it virtually means that the Black Sea is
neutralized. It is improbable in view of the Soviet-Turkish
Agreement that Rumania will proceed with her construction
projects, which are no longer necessary, and there is little
likelihood of Bulgaria becoming a great naval Power. No
source of rivalry can enter from outside, for under the Straits
Convention no fleet stronger than the strongest fleet in the
Black Sea can pass the Dardanelles and the Bosphorus. Thus,
the neutralization of the Black Sea, imposed after the Crimean
War in 1856, and abrogated by Bismarck in 1871 as the price
of Russian neutrality in the Franco-Prussian War, has at last
been achieved for all practical purposes by the Black Sea
Powers themselves.

In passing it should be observed that the naval agreements
concluded by Turkey with Greece and the Soviet Union, though
described officially as pacts of parity, are more accurately
termed pacts of stability. They provide not for scrapping but
against further construction. They do not level down the
number of units or the gun power of the navies in any way.
In this way Turkey will still have the advantage over Greece
in the Ægean in the possession of the reconstituted *Goeben*,
but will herself remain inferior to the Soviet Union in the
Black Sea.

C. OTHER PROPOSALS FOR DISARMAMENT

1. THE SOVIET PROPOSALS

THE circumstances of the issuing of the original invitation to the Soviet Government to take part in the work of the Preparatory Commission in 1925 and its refusal have already been described.[1] On April 17, 1927 the Soviet and Swiss Governments reached an agreement which, while it did not entail Swiss recognition of the Soviet régime, enabled a delegation from Moscow to participate in the International Economic Conference which opened in May of that year. The ice having been broken, M. Chicherin announced on October 1st that Soviet representatives would also be present at the Fourth Session of the Preparatory Commission which was convened for November 30th.

The appearance of the Soviet delegates at Geneva was no mere gesture of empty participation; they came full-handed with a proposal which took away the breath of their colleagues, for at the first meeting of the Commission, M. Litvinoff announced that he was empowered to propose universal disarmament within one year, or, "in the case of the capitalist States rejecting the immediate abolition of standing armies," within a period of four years.

The measures for the realization of this proposal were simplicity itself:

1. Disbandment of all armed land, air and naval forces.
2. Destruction of all arms, warships, military airships, fortresses, and factories for military production.
3. Abolition of any form of compulsory military service.
4. Suppression of appropriations for war purposes.
5. Abolition of war, naval and military aviation Ministries and Chiefs of Staff.
6. Legislative prohibition of all military propaganda and militarist instruction of the youngest State organizations and public societies.
7. Promulgation of laws according to which the violation of the above-mentioned clauses would be considered a serious crime against the State.

---

[1] See above, p. 47.

As a substitute for national armed forces the Soviet proposals provided for "the maintenance of a protective and police service, the personnel of which shall be engaged by voluntary contracts of service, shall be authorized in the territory of each of the contracting States for the purpose of Customs and Revenue, police supervision, internal police and the protection of the State and private property." There was also to be a maritime police service for the protection of the natural products of the sea and the suppression of piracy and the slave trade.

To give his proposals constitutional form, M. Litvinoff moved a resolution empowering the Commission to

1. Proceed immediately to the working out in detail of a draft convention for complete general disarmament on the principles proposed by the Soviet Union delegation, and
2. Propose the convocation not later than March 1928 of a disarmament conference for the discussion and confirmation of these proposals.[1]

The Soviet proposals, though identical in aim with the objects of Article VIII of the Covenant, ran counter in method of execution to the general principles upon which all the previous disarmament work of the League had been based, namely, the triple formula of Disarmament, Security and Arbitration. There was, moreover, a general feeling amongst many of the delegates of the "Capitalist" Powers of suspicion, not so much of the sincerity of the Soviet proposals, but of what lay beyond them.

Since the war with Poland and the defeat before Warsaw in August 1920, the Soviet Union was believed to have exchanged the *fortiter in re* of armed force for the *suaviter in modo* of subversive propaganda as the requisite method of securing world revolution. Hence Moscow had much to gain and little to lose from world disarmament, more especially as one of the Soviet proposals provided that "the national funds freed

---

[1] By way of supplementing the Soviet proposals, M. Litvinoff circulated a memorandum illustrating the losses caused by the World War both in men and money, and also the growth of armaments since the War. This interesting document is printed as an annex to the Minutes of the Fourth Session of the Preparatory Commission. (League Document, C. 667, M. 225, 1927, IX.)

from war budgets are to be employed by each State at its own discretion, *but exclusively for productive and cultural purposes*. The latter phrase is open to very wide and generous interpretation.

It is only fair to the Soviet Government to mention that, as an earnest of good faith in the matter of disarmament, it declared its readiness to sign immediately the Convention on the prohibition of the application to military purposes of chemical and bacteriological substances and processes, which had been drawn up under the auspices of the League in 1925.

As none of the delegates present felt themselves qualified to discuss the Soviet proposals before they had been submitted to the scrutiny of the various Governments, it was decided, in spite of M. Litvinoff's objection, to postpone the discussion until the next session of the Commission.

Yet one is bound to confess that in presenting these proposals M. Litvinoff had made a very astute move. If the Commission rejected them it placed itself in the position of refusing to consider a constructive plan for disarmament made in apparent good faith from a most unlikely quarter. If, on the other hand, the proposals were accepted it meant the complete abandonment of the original terms of reference of the Commission. M. Litvinoff, fully alive to the delicacies of the situation, pressed his point when the Commission reassembled for its Fifth Session on March 15, 1928.

The Soviet proposals had now been elaborated into a draft convention of 63 articles,[1] and in introducing it M. Litvinoff asked that, before the Commission proceeded to a detailed discussion of the proposals, the various delegations should answer two questions:

Did the Preparatory Commission accept the principle of general disarmament during the period mentioned in the Soviet Draft Convention? and

Did it accept the proposal as to the rate of disarmament which would make war impossible in a year's time?

---

[1] League Document, C.P.D. 117. (See also Annex V to the Minutes of the Fifth Session of the Preparatory Commission, C. 165, M. 50, 1928, IX.)

The effect of thus bringing matters to a direct issue was to produce a situation unique in the annals of the Commission. Whatever else the Soviet proposals may or may not have done, they at least produced a degree of unanimity amongst the other delegates which was never displayed in previous or subsequent sessions. For once an almost complete harmony of accord possessed the Commission, while representatives of nineteen States rose in their places to register their disapproval of M. Litvinoff's convention. Of these speakers, only Lord Cushendun, on behalf of Great Britain, subjected the proposals to a more or less detailed examination, in a speech which the *Temps* described as "crushing," and the *Izvestia* as "a haughty and derisive treatment of the enemy." Only the German and Turkish delegates welcomed a general discussion of the draft convention.

When it became obvious that the original Soviet proposals had no chance of acceptance, M. Litvinoff, with the air of a *prestidigitateur*, produced from his pocket a second draft convention, this time providing for "partial and gradual disarmament,"[1] the main points of which were as follows:[2]

1. The division of the world into four groups according to size of armaments and reduction according to category. That is to say, using the proportional principle, taking as a basis the size of armaments as they are now, those States with the largest forces would reduce the most. The strongest Powers should reduce their armaments by 50 per cent., the medium Powers by 33 per cent., and the weakest Power by 25 per cent. The fourth category consisted of States already disarmed as a result of the Peace Treaties. The same principle was to be applied to the reduction of naval tonnage.
2. The abolition of air warfare, poison gas, tanks, long-range guns, high-calibre artillery, etc.
3. The institution of a permanent international control commission composed of legislative and workers' representatives.

The draft convention also accepted the principles of "pooled security" and of collective responsibility for measures to keep the peace at sea.

[1] See *World Disarmament*, by Maurice Fanshawe, League of Nations Union, 1931.
[2] League Document, C.P.D. 117. (See also Annex V to the Minutes of the Fifth Session of the Preparatory Commission, C. 165, M. 50, 1928, IX.)

Again M. Litvinoff pressed for an immediate discussion and again the Commission required more time for consideration, and finally, in a resolution adopted unanimously (the Soviet and German delegations abstaining), the Commission noted "that the immense majority of its members are of the opinion" that the Soviet proposals for immediate complete and general disarmament submitted by the Soviet Government "cannot be accepted by the Commission as a basis for its work, which must be pursued along the lines already mapped out," and agreed to reserve consideration of the substitute proposal for partial reduction until the next session.

In his closing remarks on March 24th, M. Loudon somewhat prejudiced future discussion of the Soviet proposals by calling upon the Soviet delegation

"in all seriousness to attend our next and any ensuing meetings in a constructive spirit and not with the idea of destroying the work we have already done."

This statement led to an acrimonious exchange of letters between M. Litvinoff and the President of the Commission, in which the former defended his attitude throughout the session, quoting M. Loudon's own statement that the discussion of the Draft Convention for Total Disarmament had been "interesting and valuable," and pointing out that but for this discussion "there would have been nothing left for the Fifth Session of the Preparatory Commission but to disperse after its second or third sitting—a procedure hardly calculated to the raising of its prestige.[1] This statement was indeed true, for when the Commission passed from the discussion of the Soviet proposals to the second reading of its own Draft Convention no progress could be made, a fact which called forth a bitter protest from Count Bernstorff on behalf of Germany.

During the interval which elapsed between the Fifth and Sixth Sessions of the Preparatory Commission (March 1928–April 1929) M. Litvinoff on two occasions, in letters dated August 20 and December 6, 1928, exhorted M. Loudon as

[1] The texts of this correspondence are printed as Annex VI to the Minutes of the Fifth Session.

President of the Commission to summon a new session and adopt the second Soviet draft convention as a basis for discussion.[1]

When in effect the discussion on the Soviet proposals actually began on April 17, 1929, there was clear evidence that the only factor which prevented most of the delegates from rejecting them outright was the desire not to provide the Soviet Government with fresh material for propaganda. Alone in the Commission Count Bernstorff and Tewfik Rushdi Bey were in favour of serious discussion.

And indeed there was much of value and importance in the proposals. They were not, like their original predecessors, outrageously impracticable. They contained suggestions based upon measures for disarmament already in force in the ex-enemy countries. For example, the Soviet proposal for the abolition of tanks and heavy artillery resembles closely the restrictions imposed upon Germany by the Treaty of Versailles.

The issue, however, which was really exercising the minds of the Commission was whether or not they were to continue on the lines on which they had been working for the past four years or whether, with this record of accumulated work behind them, they should start again on a new task and scrap all that had gone before.

After a desultory discussion, which lasted until April 19th, it was recorded, against the votes of the U.S.S.R. and China (with Turkey abstaining), that the Commission could not accept the method of reduction based upon the proportional principle, but that this in no way precluded the Disarmament Conference, when it met, from considering this same principle. It was agreed to annex the Soviet draft convention to the report of the Commission and to lay it subsequently before the Disarmament Conference.

Thus the door remains open in February 1932 for further consideration of that which is valuable and constructive in the Soviet proposals.

[1] Texts of this correspondence printed as Annex I to the Minutes of the First Part of the Sixth Session of the Preparatory Commission. (League Document, C. 195, M. 74, 1929, IX.)

2. THE TURKISH AND CHINESE PROPOSALS

In the course of the first part of the Sixth Session of the Preparatory Commission (April–May 1929) disarmament proposals were put forward on behalf of both the Turkish and Chinese Governments. Though it was the original desire of the delegates of the States concerned to secure discussion of their proposals, they both eventually agreed to forgo this for the moment and to present their plans to the plenary Disarmament Conference.

The official summary of the Turkish proposal, which aimed at fixing a maximum limit for the armed forces of all countries, is as follows:[1]

The solution which the Turkish Government proposes for the problem of disarmament may be briefly indicated as follows:

"The origin of many cases of aggression is to be found, generally speaking, in the inequality of existing forces and the opportunities which the maintenance of large effectives offers for rapidly carrying out attacks which are intended to secure certain objects and to satisfy certain ambitions. The fundamental idea in the system which we propose is to eradicate the war virus from the international community by providing, as far as possible, that all States should have equal peace effectives.

"In essence, the idea which we put forward would therefore take the form of a system of a maximum contingent for all States without distinction.

"Uniformity on these lines would be the ideal system of disarmament, but we consider it might at present be rendered somewhat more elastic by putting that contingent on a higher scale. We have adopted this modified form and we would indicate for your consideration the following scheme:

"Having defined our object, we would propose that the maximum effectives should be the armed forces required by a large State to provide for its legitimate defence against sudden aggression.

"Once the numbers were fixed in this way, States with forces in excess of this contingent would have to reduce to the limit fixed, and States whose effectives were below the limit fixed would not be permitted to increase their contingent, seeing that the basic principle is the reduction of armaments and not their increase, even if only a partial increase.

---

[1] See Annex IV of the Minutes of the First Part of the Sixth Session.

"In practice, it would not appear that the fixing of the maximum contingent on the basis of a large country's requirements for its legitimate defence would present any serious difficulties. We have indeed in this connection experience from which we can draw valuable conclusions.

"To sum up, as the reduction of armed forces taken as a final stage towards disarmament forms the basis of the system we recommend, the maximum armed forces would be calculated on the basis of the legitimate requirements of a large country for its national defence. Armed forces exceeding this limit would be reduced accordingly, and those already below the limit would remain unchanged.

"Such, in its main outlines, is the system of disarmament which we recommend.

"We consider that the special merit of our proposal lies in the great simplicity of its conception and indeed its simplicity of application."

The Chinese proposal was a brief proposition for the abolition of compulsory military service. In putting it forward General Tsiang Tso-ping declared that his Government was "actuated purely by the desire to speed up the Conference . . . by offering a direct and practical solution to some of the questions which have not been successfully dealt with during the last session of this Commission."

The text of the Chinese proposal is as follows:[1]

"Whereas the High Contracting Parties consider that the system of universal military service tends to engender a warlike spirit in the minds of the people, intensify the antagonism of neighbouring States and thereby create so-called 'militaristic nationalism' which is incompatible with the principles of the League of Nations.

"And whereas they recognize that, in view of the conclusion of the multi-lateral Pact for the outlawry of war, whereby the signatory Powers solemnly condemn war and renounce it as a measure for settling international disputes and as the instrument of national policy in their mutual relations, any system which is to militarize the entire population in preparation for war is contrary to the spirit and letter of the said Pact.

"They therefore agree that, henceforth, they will not adopt a universal compulsory military service, either in their home country or in their possessions or colonies, as a means of forming and organizing their armed forces."

---

[1] See Annex III of the Minutes of the First Part of the Sixth Session.

CHAPTER IV

SECURITY

A. THE RENUNCIATION OF WAR

1. THE ASSEMBLY RESOLUTION, 1927

THE renunciation of war may be said to be the fundamental principle of the League of Nations; it is the basis of Article X of the Covenant and every subsequent attempt to elaborate the Covenant has only seemed to emphasize the essential importance of this doctrine. In the early days, however, renunciation was restricted to aggressions only. Thus Article I of the Treaty of Mutual Assistance declared that "aggressive war is an international crime, and (the Contracting Parties) severally undertake that no one of them will be guilty of its commission." Similarly, the preamble of the Geneva Protocol asserts that "a war of aggression constitutes . . . an international crime," though curiously enough it contains no explicit undertaking to refrain from committing this misdemeanour.

These draft declarations are the first steps on the road of renunciation, but with the failure to reach a general agreement on the principles of arbitration, security and disarmament the idea of renunciation too fell somewhat into the background. It was not until the Assembly of 1927, which was characterized by attempts on the part of certain delegations, notably the Dutch, to revive the Geneva Protocol, that it again became prominent.

The Polish delegation were anxious for definite action. They came to the Assembly with the intention of proposing some declaration by which the representatives of each State bound themselves never to engage in war as a means of settling their international disputes. Such a declaration, it was felt, though it would have no juridical force, would be of great moral value. This proposal did not meet with the unqualified approval of the Greater Powers and a period of somewhat hectic negotiation took place before the resolution was finally drafted. When, however, the Polish representative moved it from the tribune, it appeared as a proposal not for the prohibition of all wars between Members of the League but only of "wars of aggression."

"The League is not yet universal," explained M. Sokal, "so that we can only proclaim the outlawry of wars of aggression as between its Members, but it is obvious that by this very act we should be undertaking to introduce the principle throughout the world in our relations with countries which do not yet belong to our community. . . .

"The fact that the nations have not yet definitely reconciled their respective points of view on the question of disarmament by no means precludes the possibility of a declaration proclaiming their final and solemn renunciation of all acts of aggression."

The Resolution in the form finally adopted by the Assembly on September 24, 1927, was as follows:

"THE ASSEMBLY

"Recognizing the solidarity which united the community of nations;

"Being inspired by a firm desire for the maintenance of general peace;

"Being convinced that a war of aggression can never serve as a means of settling international disputes and is, in consequence, an international crime;

"Considering that a solemn renunciation of all wars of aggression would tend to create an atmosphere of general confidence calculated to facilitate the progress of the work undertaken with a view to disarmament;

"Declares:

"(1) That all wars of aggression are, and shall always be, prohibited.
"(2) That every pacific means must be employed to settle disputes, of every description, which may arise between States.

The Assembly declares that the States Members of the League are under an obligation to conform to these principles."

2. THE PAN-AMERICAN RESOLUTIONS, 1928

The policy of renunciation was carried one step further at the Sixth Pan-American Conference at Havana (January and

February 1928). Here the Mexican delegate proposed, and the Conference unanimously adopted, a resolution which, based upon the hypothesis "that war of aggression constitutes an international crime against the human species," declared

1. "All aggression is considered illicit and as such is declared prohibited.
2. "The American States will employ all pacific means to settle conflicts which may arise between them."

In a further resolution, which recorded in its preamble the desire of the American Republics "to express that they condemn war as an instrument of national policy in their mutual relations," the Conference accepted obligatory arbitration as the method for the settlement of juridical disputes arising between them, and agreed to the convening of a Pan-American Arbitration and Conciliation Conference within a year "to give conventional form to the realization of this principle."[1]

This latter Conference met in Washington from December 10, 1928, to January 5, 1929, and there resulted from its discussions three instruments:

A General Convention of Inter-American Conciliation;
A General Treaty of Inter-American Arbitration; and
A Protocol of Progressive Arbitration.

This last document is of particular interest, as it forms the first provision in the form of a definite treaty obligation of machinery for the gradual or complete abandonment of reservations made to a treaty.[2]

This action on the part of the American Republics represents the first pact for the outlawry of war which was consummated by the setting up of machinery for the pacific settlement of international disputes. It is the only existing agreement which, while renouncing war as a method of settling disputes, provides an alternative means of settlement. In this it differs materially

---

[1] For the texts of these resolutions see *Documents on International Affairs,* 1928, edited by J. W. Wheeler-Bennett (Oxford University Press, 1929), pp. 193–194.
[2] For the texts of these instruments see *Documents on International Affairs,* 1929, edited by J. W. Wheeler-Bennett (Oxford University Press, 1930), pp. 249–259.

from both the Kellogg Pact and the Litvinoff Protocol, both of which accept pacific settlement in the abstract but provide no method by which this obligation may be put into effect.

3. THE PACT OF PARIS, 1928

These two achievements already referred to were but links in a chain which led ultimately to the signing on August 27, 1928, of the General Treaty for the Renunciation of War.[1]

The negotiations for this agreement had been initiated by M. Briand in June 1927 in a suggestion to Mr. Kellogg, United States Secretary of State, for a bilateral treaty between France and the United States envisaging a solemn declaration by the two Powers condemning recourse to war, renouncing war as an instrument of national policy and agreeing that a settlement of all disputes between them should be brought about only by pacific means.

Mr. Kellogg, supported by a large section of the public opinion of the world, felt that valuable though this suggestion was its importance would be greatly enhanced if the agreement signed were a multilateral treaty for the outlawry of war. He accordingly proposed to M. Briand that France and the United States should jointly sponsor such a pact and should invite the other Great Powers to become parties to it.

France, however, did not at once see her way free to accept such a proposal. Unlike the United States, she was a Member of the League, a signatory of the Locarno Agreement and a party to some half-dozen European treaties of guarantee, all of which made provision for the use of war in the final emergency. It was one thing to propose the renunciation of war in the relations with a State with whom war was very improbable, and quite another to sponsor a multilateral Pact for the

---

[1] It is not proposed to give here a detailed history of the Pact negotiations. For this the reader is referred to *Information on the Renunciation of War*, by J. W. Wheeler-Bennett (George Allen & Unwin, 1928), which contains a full account of the discussions leading up to the signing of the Pact, together with all the relevant documents and speeches. An excellent account will also be found in Professor Toynbee's *Survey for* 1928 (Oxford University Press, 1929), Part I A, pp. 1–47.

same purpose. M. Briand, therefore, fell back upon the Polish resolution adopted by the League Assembly of 1927 and suggested that if the Pact were to be of a multilateral character the provision for renunciation should be restricted to "wars of aggression."

In face of American objections, M. Briand later abandoned this stand and agreed to Mr. Kellogg's original proposal on the understanding that the four following conditions were observed:

1. That all countries adhere to the treaty, and that the treaty should not come into force until universal adherence was given, unless some special agreement was reached waiving certain abstentions.
2. That each country retained the right of self-defence.
3. That in case one country violated the pledge not to engage in war, all others would automatically be released.
4. That the Pact should not interfere in any way with France's previous obligations under the Covenant of the League of Nations, the Locarno Agreements or her neutrality treaties.

On these conditions France agreed to become with the United States the joint sponsor of a general treaty for the renunciation of war as an instrument of national policy.

Although the Franco-American proposals were transmitted at first only to Great Britain, Germany, Italy and Japan, at a later date in the negotiations the number of the original contracting parties was increased, out of deference to France, to include the three minor Locarno Powers, Belgium, Czecho-slovakia and Poland, and, in deference to Great Britain, the self-governing Dominions of Australia, Canada, the Irish Free State, New Zealand, the Union of South Africa, and also the Government of India.

Apart from the French conditions, all of which were taken into account, either by direct inclusion in the Pact or by implication and agreement, the only other State to make a reservation was Great Britain. The British Government of the day (a Conservative administration) felt that they could not give an unqualified acceptance to the proposal and in due course agreed to become a party to the Pact on the following condition:

"There are certain regions of the world the welfare and integrity of which constitute a special and vital interest for our peace and safety. H.M. Government have been at pains to make it clear in the past that interference in these regions cannot be suffered. Their protection against attack is to the British Empire a measure of self-defence. It must be clearly understood that his Majesty's Government in Great Britain accept the new treaty upon the distinct understanding that it does not prejudice their freedom of action in this respect. The Government of the United States have comparable interests any disregard of which by a foreign Power they have declared that they would regard as an unfriendly act. His Majesty's Government believe, therefore, that in defining their position they are expressing the intention and meaning of the United States."

This declaration of what really amounted to a British "Monroe Doctrine," which was generally believed to relate to British unilateral commitments in Egypt, was made specifically on behalf of his Majesty's Government in Great Britain, and both the Canadian and Irish Free State Governments made statements to the effect that they did not consider themselves bound by it.[1]

On August 27, 1928, therefore, the representatives of the fifteen original Contracting Parties met at the Quai d'Orsay to sign the General Treaty for the Renunciation of War, of which the main provisions were as follows:

Article I.—The High Contracting Parties solemnly declare, in the names of their respective peoples, that they condemn recourse to war for the solution of international controversies and renounce it as an instrument of national policy in their relations with one another.
Article II.—The High Contracting Parties agree that the settlement or solution of all disputes or conflicts, of whatever origin they may be, which may arise among them, shall never be sought except by pacific means.

Immediately after the ceremony of signing the Pact was declared open to the adherence of all States and by the close

[1] The British reservation was the subject of subsequent counter-reservations on the part of the Powers who later adhered to the Pact. The U.S.S.R., Egypt and Persia adhered with the specific proviso that they were not bound by the British reservation.
[2] The inherent weakness of the Pact lies in the fact that, while it makes compulsory pacific settlement of international disputes, it provides no machinery whereby this may be achieved. In this it is inferior to the Pan-American Agreement (see above, p. 244). For a discussion of the possibility of strengthening the Pact, see the section of this Chapter entitled "A Consultative Pact." (See below, p. 272.)

of 1930 it had become binding on sixty-one States, the only important abstentees being Argentine and Brazil.

But though signed in August 1928 the Treaty did not come into operation until nearly a year later. An acrid debate in the Senate had first to take place before the ratification of the United States was obtained on January 14, 1929, and owing to certain opposition in domestic politics Japanese ratification was delayed until June 27th of the same year. The Pact was finally proclaimed in force by President Hoover on July 24, 1929.

Theoretically as a result of the Pact we live to-day in a warless world; but the efficacy of outlawing war was considerably lessened by the qualifications imposed through the interpretation placed upon the text by the various contracting States. In effect, therefore, war is outlawed except when it is declared lawful, and recourse to war is permitted in self-defence; against any treaty-breaking State, in execution of any obligation consequent upon the signing of any treaty of neutrality, or, in the case of Great Britain, in defence of certain places and strategic points which are vital to the safety of the Empire; and in fulfilment of the obligations and responsibilities incurred by membership of the League of Nations and by the signature of the Locarno Agreement.

It will be seen, therefore, that the Pact only effectively outlaws war in what M. Briand in his speech at the ceremony of signature described as "its most specific and dreaded form: selfish and wilful." It had come round to M. Briand's proposal after all, and only war of aggression had been outlawed.

As the enunciation of a new international ethic the Pact of Paris was of the greatest importance but its practical value as an additional guarantee of security may be gauged from the fact that it has changed the French attitude towards disarmament not one iota, as was evident from the policy pursued at the London Naval Conference, in the subsequent negotiations with Italy and during the Sixth Session of the Preparatory Disarmament Commission in 1929 and 1930.

4. THE LITVINOFF PROTOCOL[1]

An unexpected sequel to the signature of the Kellogg Pact was the lively interest which the Government of the Soviet Union evinced in the outlawry of war movement. Having denounced the Pact as merely a new manifestation of the anti-Soviet policy pursued by the capitalist Powers since Locarno, the Soviet Union was the first State to adhere to the Treaty after it had been thrown open for signature on August 27th and the first of all the Contracting Parties, whether original signatories or subsequent adherents, to ratify the Pact. She then proceeded to play a part of her own.

With that unexpectedness with which Soviet diplomacy has come to be associated (one is almost tempted to misquote the Roman historian in saying *ex Russia semper aliquid novi*), the Soviet Government, through its Minister in Warsaw, proposed to the Polish Government on December 29, 1928 that the two Powers, together with Lithuania, should sign a protocol rendering the Peace Pact effective between them as soon as all three had ratified it, without waiting for the general exchange of ratifications between the original signatories.

The Soviet Note began by recalling that as long ago as August 1926 the Government of the U.S.S.R. had initiated negotiations for a treaty of neutrality and non-aggression with Poland, negotiations which, however, "in spite of the most earnest attempts on the part of the Soviet Government to reach an agreement," had not made any advance. The Soviet Government regretted the fruitlessness of its efforts and reiterated its readiness to sign a non-aggression treaty with Poland at any time. After stating that both the U.S.S.R. and Poland had signed the Kellogg Treaty and drawing attention to the reservations made by the Soviet Government in so doing, the Note continued:

"Unfortunately the entry into effect of the Paris Pact is stipulated in Article III to be by way of ratification by fourteen Powers which were

---

[1] Reprinted in part from an article in the *Bulletin of International News* (Vol. V, No. 15), July 2, 1929. See also *Survey* for 1929, p. 63 *et seq.*

mentioned.[1] During the four months which have elapsed since the day of signing the Pact, not one of these fourteen Powers have ratified it, which gives rise to the fear that for a long time to come it may remain a formal document binding no one. Obviously an earlier enforcement of the Pact as between individual States is only possible if they sign a special supplementary obligation.

"Considering that the assurance of peace in Eastern Europe is a matter of paramount importance and that, of the Western countries bordering on the U.S.S.R. the Paris Treaty was signed by Poland, the Soviet Government has decided to address to the Polish Government a proposal to sign the attached Protocol which will render the Paris Treaty against war effective between the Soviet Union and Poland immediately upon its ratification by these two States, regardless of the condition stipulated in Article III of the Pact. By signing the said Protocol the Polish Government will, of course, undertake the moral obligation to ratify as soon as possible both the Paris Treaty and the Protocol itself. As regards the U.S.S.R., its adherence to the Paris Pact has already been ratified by the Presidium of the Central Executive Committee."

The Note continued that the present proposal did not in any way rescind the earlier offer of the Soviet Government for a pact of non-aggression, "the conclusion of which would serve further to strengthen neighbourly relations between the U.S.S.R. and Poland." The Polish Government was further advised that "the Soviet Government is simultaneously addressing an analogous proposal to the Lithuanian Republic as the only Baltic country which has so far adhered to the Kellogg Pact." It was explained that similar proposals had not been addressed to Finland, Estonia or Latvia merely because these States had not formally adhered to the Pact.

The Protocol accompanying this Note was an instrument of six Articles of which the first stated that the Kellogg Pact should enter into effect between the U.S.S.R. and Poland as soon as it had been ratified by their respective legislative bodies. Article II provided for the ratification and the exchange of ratifications of the Protocol itself, while the third Article laid down procedure for its coming into force. Articles IV and V made provision for the adherence of other States to the

[1] The Government of the U.S.S.R. is in error here; the Pact was signed by representatives of *fifteen* States.

Protocol and the procedure for the same. The last Article ran as follows:

"The coming into effect as between the parties to this Protocol, of the Treaty of Paris, as foreseen by the present Protocol, shall be independent of the coming into effect of the Treaty of Paris, as foreseen by Article III of that Treaty."

To the Protocol was appended, as "an inalienable part," a copy of the Kellogg Pact.

This sudden departure on the part of the Soviet Union placed the Polish Government in something of a quandary. From the point of view of Poland alone there was no deep-seated reason why the Soviet offer should not be accepted; but Poland was bound to Rumania by the terms of an alliance concluded originally in 1921, and considerably strengthened in 1926. Between Rumania and the U.S.S.R. not only did diplomatic relations not exist, but the disputed province of Bessarabia (ceded to Rumania by the Allied Powers in 1920, but to which Moscow has never abandoned her claim) forms a permanent bone of contention. Both States, however, had adhered to the Kellogg Pact.

When M. Zaleski, Polish Minister for Foreign Affairs, came to make his reply on January 10th, it was evident that he wished to hedge. The Polish Government accepted the Soviet proposal in principle, but felt that, as one of the original signatories to the Kellogg Pact, it should "first come to an agreement with the initiators and first signatories of the Pact on the subject of a partial putting into force of this Pact by a method different from that proposed." With regard to the Soviet statement that none of the original signatory Powers had as yet ratified the pact, the Polish Note anticipated a "sensible brightening of the situation on this point in the very near future."

The Polish Government further expressed surprise that the Soviet proposal should not have been made to all the border States and that, in addition to Poland, Lithuania should have been singled out, a country which had neither a common frontier with the U.S.S.R. nor diplomatic relations with Poland.

It was imperative to treat "the problem of the security of Eastern Europe conjointly by all the interested States, for only by this means of treating this question can effective guarantees be given for the maintenance of peace in this part of the world."

The importance which the Soviet Government attached to their proposal and their anxiety for its success is indicated by the fact that within four days (on January 14th) of the receipt of the Polish reply, M. Litvinoff had presented his counter-answer. In it he expressed a surprising readiness to fall in with the Polish point of view. He explained that the Soviet Government had so far made a similar proposal only to Lithuania because none of the other Baltic States, according to his information, had notified their adhesion to the Kellogg Pact. With regard to Rumania, M. Litvinoff stated that if Rumania, with whom the Soviet Union has no diplomatic relations, had formally adhered to the Pact, the Soviet Government was prepared to propose that it join the Protocol.

The Polish Government's reply to the second Soviet Note was handed to M. Litvinoff by M. Patek, Polish Minister in Moscow, on January 19th, thus maintaining the unusual celerity of this diplomatic correspondence. The position of Poland had been considerably facilitated by the decision of the United States Senate on January 15th to ratify the Kellogg Pact, and in view of this, M. Zaleski declared that Poland was now in a position to negotiate freely with Soviet Government upon the form of the suggested Protocol and on the procedure to be adopted in signing it. He further expressed great satisfaction that M. Litvinoff had announced so explicitly his readiness for the inclusion of Rumania among the Powers accepting the Protocol, and in confirmation of this, the Rumanian Foreign Office made a statement to foreign journalists on the following day (January 20th) to the effect that Rumania would be prepared to follow Poland's example if that country elected to sign a non-aggression pact with the U.S.S.R.

The next step in this somewhat precipitate course of negotiation was that M. Patek was received by M. Litvinoff on January 21st, and as a result of their conversation a *communiqué* was issued from the Commissariat of Foreign Affairs stating that M. Litvinoff had made the following suggestions for the signing of the Protocol and the subsequent procedure:

1. That the Protocol should be signed at once at Moscow by the accredited representatives of Poland and the U.S.S.R.
2. That immediately after signature, the Government of the U.S.S.R. should invite Finland, Estonia, Latvia and Rumania (the latter presumably through the good offices of Poland) to adhere.
3. The procedure of adherence should be the same as that in use with regard to the Kellogg Pact (i.e. written notification to the Sponsor State, in this case the U.S.S.R.).
4. Signatory and adhering States should pledge themselves to submit both the Pact and the Protocol to their respective Parliaments for ratification as soon as possible.
5. The Protocol should enter into force as between the U.S.S.R. and Poland on the exchange of ratifications and, in the case of adhering States, on the receipt in Moscow of the official notification of ratification.

In recommeding this suggested procedure M. Litvinoff pointed out that it led to the earliest possible operation of the Kellogg Pact among the States of Eastern Europe and at the same time afforded an opportunity to all these States to become equal participants in the Protocol simultaneously. M. Patek referred these proposals to his Government for instructions.

With Lithuania, the U.S.S.R. had been even more rapidly successful. The Government of M. Voldemaras, though Fascist and nationalist in character, had always been more receptive to Soviet suggestions than those of other Baltic States. Alone among her fellow border States Lithuania, then under a semi-socialist régime, negotiated a pact of neutrality and non-aggression with the U.S.S.R. in 1926, and this agreement was maintained after M. Voldemaras had executed his *coup d'état*. This continuity of policy is not necessarily actuated by any deep affection for the Soviet Union, but rather by the fact that a working agreement with Moscow is a strong asset in

Lithuania's seemingly deathless struggle with Poland over the possession of Vilna.

Lithuania received the Soviet proposals on the same date as did Poland (December 29th) and accepted them on January 3rd. She did more. On January 5th the Lithuanian Foreign Office despatched an identic Note to Latvia and Estonia proposing that they too should adhere to the Protocol, and by way of example ratified the Kellogg Pact on January 14th. M. Litvinoff reinforced the Lithuanian *démarche* in interviews with the Latvian and Estonian Ministers in Moscow, and by the end of January had obtained their approval of his proposal.

All attempts to bring Finland into the scope of the Protocol were fruitless, and at the last moment Lithuania refused to be an original party with Poland. The Protocol was, nevertheless, signed on February 9, 1929 at Moscow by representatives of the U.S.S.R., Poland, Latvia, Estonia and Rumania. Lithuania eventually adhered on April 1st and Soviet diplomacy was successful in obtaining the subsequent adherence of Turkey on April 1st and Persia on July 4th. The Free City of Danzig also acceded on April 30th.[1]

This marked the third occasion on which the Soviet Government had sponsored negotiations for pacts of security with her Baltic neighbours. The first occasion was the Moscow Conference of December 1922 to consider disarmament and non-aggression, and though no result was attained, the draft Pact of non-aggression adopted by the Conference was the most comprehensive agreement of its kind. Of particular interest is the fact that Article III of this Pact, drawn up some six years before the Kellogg Treaty, contained the very same formula of paragraph IV of the Preamble of this latter document. Article III ran as follows:

"Should the Pact be violated by one of the High Contracting Parties . . . the other Contracting Parties agree to give no aid or support to the attacking State and are freed from their engagements towards the attacking State under the present Pact."

---

[1] See *Security*, p. 81.

The second occasion was in April 1926, when the U.S.S.R. opened negotiations with Finland, Estonia, Latvia and Lithuania, and subsequently with Poland, for pacts of non-aggression and neutrality. These negotiations were successful only in the case of Lithuania and were allowed to drop in the cases of the other States.[1]

The Litvinoff Protocol provides the second instance (the first was the Pan-American Pact of early 1928, to which reference has already been made) in which the Pact of Paris had been supplemented and reinforced by regional pacts. And in addition there is also the Assembly Resolution of 1927.

The Pact of Paris is binding upon some sixty States, the Pan-American Agreement involves the seventeen American Republics, the Litvinoff Protocol embraces nine States and the League Resolution is binding upon its fifty-six Members, truly a bulwark of renunciation, but unfortunately without very much practical result.

5. The Amendments to the Covenant, 1929–1931[2]

The Covenant of the League of Nations permits resort to war by any Power which has exhausted the mediatory efforts of the League to settle a dispute by peaceful means, while the Pact of Paris renounces war as an instrument of national policy in all circumstances.

Although the Pact did not come into force until July 24, 1929, a proposal was made by the Lithuanian Delegation as early as the Ninth Assembly of 1928, that the Council should examine the question of adapting the provisions of the Covenant to the undertakings of the Pact.

This proposal to bring the Covenant into harmony with the Pact was, in 1928, considered premature. In 1929 the British Delegation, with due support, deposited a draft resolution inviting the Tenth Assembly "to take account of the progress

[1] *Security*, p. 173.
[2] This section is reprinted in part from two articles in *Bulletin of International News*, Vol. VI, No. 18, March 13, 1930, and Vol. VII, No. 9, October 23, 1930, by Mr. Maurice Fanshawe and Mr. Ralph Arnold respectively.

made in the organization of peace and to examine Articles XII
and XV of the Covenant in order to decide whether it seemed
necessary to make any modifications," and on September 24,
1929 the Tenth Assembly, in a resolution, duly declared "that
it is desirable that the terms of the Covenant of the League
should not accord any longer to Members of the League a right
to have recourse to war in cases in which the right has been
renounced by the provisions of the Pact of Paris."

This resolution set the seal of official acquiescence upon the
desirability of amending the Covenant. There remained the
question of the manner in which the text should be amended.
Upon the solution of this problem obviously depended the
secondary question; when should the amended Covenant take
the place of the existing one?

In a nutshell, the British draft text aimed at transforming
Article XII into a simple obligation not to resort to war, and
omitting the words "until three months after the award by
the arbitrators . . . or the report by the Council," and at
making consequential changes in Article XIII, paragraph 4, and
Article XV, paragraphs 6 and 7. It was proposed, in fact, to
bring Covenant and Pact into harmony by leaving out from
these three Articles the phrases which still permitted war in
certain circumstances.

The whole matter was carefully discussed by the First
Committee, and on its proposal, the Assembly decided that
a Committee of Eleven should be chosen by the Council to
meet early in 1930, make the consequential changes in Articles
XII, XIII and XV, and report to the Assembly at its Eleventh
Session. The Assembly declared that "it is desirable that the
terms of the Covenant of the League should not accord any
longer to the Members of the League a right to have recourse
to war in cases in which that right has been renounced by the
provisions of the Kellogg Pact." The text of the British Amendment was meanwhile circulated to all States Members of the
League for their observations.

The Report of the Committee of Eleven[1] is a comprehensive

[1] League document No. A. 8, 1930, V.

document. It contains, in addition to the actual text of the Articles of the Covenant as amended according to the proposals of the Committee, the Committee's report containing their comments on these proposals, their reasons for adopting certain suggestions and rejecting others, and a frank avowal of the principles which guided them to their conclusions. It also contains the text of the amendments proposed by the British Delegation and the observations thereupon of twenty-one foreign Governments.

An examination of the proposals formulated by the Committee of Eleven may be profitably prefaced by a brief survey of these Governmental observations. Such an examination reveals two main tendencies. First, there is to be found a very generally expressed acquiescence in the desirability of and even necessity for the amendment of the Covenant. Secondly, the contention, also widely held, that the British draft did not go far enough. A short extract from the observations of the Austrian Federal Government will illustrate this latter tendency:

"The Covenant of the League of Nations, the Pact of Paris and a large number of multilateral and bilateral agreements made since the great war are due to the ardent desire and firm determination of Governments and peoples to substitute right and justice for force in international relations. This purpose has a double aspect; on the one hand there are efforts to suppress the employment of force and to avoid and even abolish war; on the other hand there are efforts to develop and organize methods of pacific settlement on the basis of right and justice. Great progress has been made in the pursuit of this purpose in its two-fold aspect. The Federal Government does not hesitate to recognize that the British amendments constitute real progress from the point of view of the first aspect, but it cannot but say that, considered from the second aspect, the amendments seem to it hardly calculated to strengthen the possibilities of pacific settlement of disputes on the basis of right and justice, unless they are completed by the provisions which the Federal Government venture to propose."

Thus, while it was generally agreed that it was entirely desirable and necessary that the Covenant should be amended (and, indeed, that question had been decided by the resolution of the Tenth Assembly), it was felt on all sides that the British proposals were inadequate in that, while removing war as an ultimate resort, they did not strengthen the hand of the League as regards alternative procedure for the settlement of disputes by pacific means. In pursuance of these two well-marked tendencies, certain of the Governments consulted formulated definite proposals.

These, tabulated for the sake of brevity, included:

(1) The introduction of the Articles of the Pact of Paris into the text of the Covenant.

> "The British Government has proposed amendments to Articles XII, XIII and XV of the Covenant. One might possibly also contemplate a special amendment to the Covenant containing in their entirety the provisions of the Pact of Paris."[1]

(2) The inclusion in the Covenant of a general prohibition of resort to war.

> "The Members of the League agree that, if there should exist between them any dispute likely to lead to a rupture, they will in no case resort to war for the settlement of the dispute . . ."[2]

These two suggestions emphasized the desirability felt by certain Governments of harmonizing the Covenant and the Pact.

(3) The framing of an amendment to the Covenant designed to render a unanimous report by the Council of the League as binding as an arbitral award or judicial decision.

> "If a report by the Council is unanimously agreed to by the Members thereof, other than the representatives of one or more of the parties to the dispute, the Members of the League agree to comply with the recommendations of the report. If a recommendation is not carried out, the Council shall take steps to give effect thereto."[3]

(4) The framing of an amendment to the Covenant designed to include in the Covenant a ruling establishing (in the event of the failure of the Council to reach a unanimous decision) ultimate recourse to compulsory arbitration.

> "The Danish Government feels that, where the Council fails to reach a unanimous report, it would be preferable to follow

---

[1] Extract from the observations of the Finnish Government.
[2] Amendment to Article XII, suggested by the Greek Government.
[3] Amendment to Article XV, suggested by the Finnish Government.

the method prescribed for this case in Article IV, paragraph 4, of the Protocol of Geneva of 1924."[1] [2]

These two last suggestions emphasized the desirability felt by certain States of strengthening the procedure for settling disputes by pacific means.

In addition to the two major tendencies already noted, two other tendencies are clearly discernible in these observations.

The first, a tendency to draw attention to the fundamental difficulty of harmonizing the two instruments when "the difference between them is not merely one of degree, it is fundamental,"[3] and the second, a tendency to strike a note of caution, to qualify acceptance of the principle of amendment with the rider that any amendments should be so framed as to avoid an extension of States' obligations under sanctions.

"On the other hand, the Norwegian Government must strongly advise against any simultaneous enlargement of the obligations which the Members of the League have, under the Covenant as actually in force, to participate in sanctions against a State which resorts to war. The Norwegian Government would feel that it would be a cause of serious anxiety for Norway to assume an obligation to apply sanctions under Article XVI of the Covenant outside the cases of war to which, under the present system, the provisions of that Article are applicable."[4]

Thus the matter stood when the Committee of Eleven began its sessions and, both in its discussions and in its Report, the influence of all these tendencies, manifested by the observations of the Governments, are clearly discernible.

The amended text as proposed by the Committee of Eleven is appended as an annex to this chapter, and it will be seen in the first place that a general prohibition of war is embodied in Article XII, paragraph 1, a fact emphasized by the change in number of the term "obligations" in the preamble. The so-called gaps in the Covenant, closed by the British draft amendments, remain closed. In the second place, the amended text contains certain innovations designed to facilitate the

[1] Extract from the observations of the Danish Government.
[2] This paragraph reads as follows: "If the Council fails to reach a report which is concurred in by all its members, other than the representatives of any of the parties to the dispute, it shall submit the dispute to arbitration. . . ."
[3] Extract from the observations of the German Government.
[4] Extract from the observations of the Norwegian Government.

settlement of disputes by pacific means. Notably, in Article XV, paragraph 6, the Committee has aimed at strengthening the hands of the Council by giving its unanimous resolutions a binding character, comparable to, if not identical with, that of arbitral awards or judicial decisions. Again, in the event of the failure of the Council to reach a unanimous decision, the Committee did not rest satisfied with the original text of Article XV, paragraph 7, which permitted Members, in this contingency, to reserve to themselves the right to take such action as they shall consider necessary for the maintenance of right and justice. Article XV, paragraph 7, as amended, removes from Members the right of taking independent and probably warlike action and states that the Council shall examine the procedure best suited to meet the case and shall recommend it to the parties, while the Committee framed an entirely new paragraph to this same Article, paragraph 7 *bis*, which encouraged recourse to the Permanent Court of International Justice. Two considerations underlay this draft, the object of which was to remedy the defects of paragraph 7 by ensuring that the legal issues could, in all circumstances, be settled. The first consideration was that it was essential, even in a political conflict, to ensure respect for International Law, and the second that the solution of any kind of dispute would be greatly facilitated if the issues of law raised by the parties could be settled by the competent authority. It is interesting to notice that, in this instance, the Committee of Jurists thought it advisable that the Council should be given the possibility of making a request for an advisory opinion by a decision adopted by a *simple majority*, the question of whether unanimity is required in such a case having never previously been decided, for the point, when it arose very directly over the case of the Rumanian Optants, was evaded.

It will be noted that, in certain respects, the amendments as proposed by the Committee of Eleven fall short of the suggestions contained in the observations of the Governments, and this phenomenon is explained by a reference to the comments embodied in the Committee's Report.

This Report commences by some statements of a general character in which the Committee emphasized its determination to touch the provisions of the League Covenant as little as possible and its insistence, at the same time, on the undesirability of merely reproducing the terms of the Pact of Paris in the Covenant, a procedure which would court contradictions between the added provisions and the old unaltered ones; while a complete incorporation of the Pact in the Covenant would be equally undesirable in that some Members of the League have not acceded to the Pact, while some signatories of the Pact are not Members of the League.

Hence the failure to include the Articles of the Pact of Paris in the text of the amended Covenant. Subsequent comments of a less general nature reveal an interesting discussion which centred round a suggestion, emanating from one of the Committee's members, that, in order to secure execution of the Council's decision in the event of a State proving recalcitrant, an amendment should be made to Article XIII, paragraph 4, allowing the Council to determine *by a simple majority* what means should be taken to give effect to awards or decisions which had been rendered. The Committee found itself unable to concur in this interesting suggestion on the ground that it considered that an award rendered by the Council had so much authority that, in practice, a State would be very unlikely to refuse to comply with it and that the Council's intervention in such matters would, therefore, be exceptional. The Committee also held that this innovation might be construed as violating a fundamental principle embodied in Article V of the Covenant, but it drew the attention of the Assembly and the Council to the necessity of ensuring that effect should be given to awards or judicial decisions in all circumstances whatsoever. Of considerable interest, too, are the comments concerning the amendment of Article XV, paragraph 6, which reveal the importance which the Committee attached to unanimous decisions by the Council, while the commentary on the amendment of Article XV, paragraph 7, discloses the details of a discussion which centred around the question of ultimate recourse to compulsory arbitration. This safeguard evidently had its warm supporters among the members of the Committee and a procedure was formulated and summed up in the three following propositions: a new examination of the case by the Council; an obligatory consultation of the Permanent Court of International Justice upon the legal points material to the dispute; an arbitration organized by the Council. The Committee felt that the true solution of the case covered by paragraph 7 lay in the accession of the Members of the League to the General Act of Arbitration, but since such an accession could, naturally, not be assured, it felt that it was not desirable to make any particular procedure obligatory. It therefore leaves the Council with the task of examining what course would be the most appropriate to the case and of making recommendations accordingly. The Council could recommend arbitration, resort to the Permanent Court of International Justice, or any other procedure for pacific settlement of the dispute. The Committee realized that the solution of the problem was inadequate and emphasized its regret at the impossibility of establishing obligatory arbitration as a last resort.

Two other tendencies were noted in the observations of the Governments; the tendency to draw attention to the fundamental difficulty of harmonizing the two instruments, and the tendency of certain Members to qualify their approval of the project of amending the Covenant by stipulating that there should be no extension of sanctions.

The Report of the Committee of Eleven reveals the fact that the Committee, while calling attention to the political difficulties which might arise in bringing the two instruments into concordance with one another, did not consider them to be fundamentally incompatible. As for sanctions, during the Committee's discussion on Article XVI, an interesting suggestion was brought forward. This proposal envisaged the case of war occurring after the breakdown of the various forms of procedure embodied in Article XV, the suggestion being that in such a case, sanctions should only apply in regard to the period of three months provided for in Article XII of the text. When this period had elapsed, the possibility of sanctions in case of resort to war would disappear. This proposal was completed by the suggestion that Articles I and II of the Pact of Paris should be incorporated in the preamble, and was, in reality, not so much one for amending Article XVI as for framing Article XII in a different way, so as to make it possible to avoid an extension of sanctions.

The Committee examined this proposal, but could not concur in it, for it held that it was impossible to conceive of there being two kinds of obligations, one accompanied by sanctions and the other not, that the new undertakings under Articles XII, XIII and XV would be meaningless if they could remain a dead letter, and that, this being so, it was essential to place them upon the same footing as the obligations previously established by those Articles and covered by the authority of Article XVI. Further, the Committee held that the extension of sanctions brought about by the bringing of the Covenant into line with the Pact would be a theoretical extension rather than a practical one, since, in view of the education of public opinion and as a result of the signing of the Pact of Paris, the likelihood of "Legal Wars" had been greatly lessened.

On September 22, 1930 the First Committee of the Eleventh Assembly of the League began its examination of the Report of the Committee of Eleven, and it became immediately apparent that, just as the British draft amendments had failed to satisfy the Governments of the Members of the League and the Committee of Jurists, so the draft amendments of this same Committee were to be subjected to considerable criticism.

They satisfied on certain points. They included the desired general prohibition of resort to war. They provided a new procedure for the settlement of disputes by pacific means even if, as some thought, this new procedure was open to criticism on the score of its alteration of the true position and functions of the League Council. But the Report was found wanting in that it failed to take sufficiently into account the inherent differences which lawyers held to exist between the Covenant and the Pact and the political and juridical difficulties which might ensue from any attempt to fuse them, and in that it failed to guard against an extension of sanctions.

It was on these lines that the Report of the Committee of Eleven was criticized during its examination by the First Committee, M. Undén (the Swedish Delegate) and M. Ito (the Japanese Delegate) being in the van of the attack. M. Undén, faithful to the Scandinavian viewpoint, stressed the danger of an extension of sanctions, and M. Ito hinted darkly at fundamental incompatibility and the legal and political tangles which would result from the proposed harmonization. It was in vain that Mr. Noel Baker countered these arguments, and it soon became only too apparent that the amendments proposed by the Committee of Jurists would never be adopted as they stood.

On September 26th a Sub-Committee met,[1] its members chosen by the First Committee, to consider the political as well as the juridical aspects of the problem of bringing the League Covenant into harmony with the Paris Pact. The Sub-Committee was also instructed to consider what changes, if any, should be made in the proposals of the Committee of Jurists, and to state in its report whether it considered the question to be ripe for final decision in the current year.

In its turn, the Sub-Committee presented a Report[2] on October 3rd, and yet another text of proposed amendments to the Covenant was given to the world. But, from its terms of reference, it can be seen that the production of a new text was only a part, and even perhaps a secondary part, of the Sub-Committee's task.

As for the textual proposals of the Sub-Committee, reference to the annex of this chapter will show that the hand of com-

[1] The Sub-Committee consisted of the following: M. Cassin (France), Viscount Cecil (Great Britain), M. Chao-Chu Wu (China), M. Erich (Finland), M. Gans (Germany), M. Guani (Uruguay), M. Ito (Japan), M. Limburg (Netherlands), M. Mironesco (Rumania) (replaced by M. Visoiallo), M. Pilotti (Italy), M. Politis (Greece), M. Raestad (Norway), M. Rolin (Belgium), and M. Undén (Sweden).
[2] League document No. A. 85, 1930, V.

promise had been busy, and there had been a definite effort
made to strike a balance between the draft proposals of the
British Government and the text drawn up by the Committee
of Jurists. There is noticeable a certain rearrangement by
phrasing, carried out with a view to rendering the text clearer
and more logical, while the binding character of a unanimous
report by the Council has been done away with and with it
has disappeared paragraph 7 *bis*. For the rest, the Sub-Committee upheld in the main the findings and comments of the
Committee of Eleven, stressed the cardinal importance of
ensuring that an award or decision rendered by the Council
should, whatever the circumstances, be carried out, and, with
this end in view, the word "invite" was introduced into
Article XV, paragraph 6, as also was the undertaking by
Members of the League in no way to support any party in
refusal to comply with recommendations by the Council. The
Sub-Committee only returned to the original principles established by the existing Covenant from a conviction that the
Council was essentially a political organ and, as such, should
retain an elasticity and a freedom of decision which might be
seriously hampered if its recommendations were recognized
as binding.

But it is Part II of the Sub-Committee's Report which is,
perhaps, the more interesting, for in it is given the answer
to the question contained in its terms of reference: did its
members consider the question of amendment to be ripe for
final decision during the current year? The Sub-Committee
answered this question in the negative and Part II of the
Report concludes with the following draft resolution, intended
for submission to the Assembly:

"THE ASSEMBLY:

"Believing it to be necessary to incorporate in the Covenant of the
League of Nations the general prohibition of resort to war and the
principle that the settlement of international disputes should never
be sought except by pacific means;

"Appreciating the great value of the Report made by the Committee of Eleven;

"Taking account of the facts that, on some points, the First Committee has been led to consider changes in the proposed texts and that, in the course of the discussion certain political aspects of the question have come into view which render it desirable for it to be further studied;

"Requests the Secretary-General to submit to the Governments of the Members of the League the Report of the Committee of Eleven and that of the First Committee, asking them to formulate their observations before June 1st, 1931, and to state, if they so desire, what amendments to the Covenant would, in their opinion, be best suited to attain the object in view."

The Sub-Committee counselled postponement and, in explanation, certain considerations were brought forward in its Report.

It was explained that the representatives of those Members of the League which had not acceded to the Pact, Latin-American countries for the most part, had been expressly consulted as to the advisability of the proposed amendment and their reply had been that, while their Governments were in general sympathy with the project, "It did not present itself to them as an urgent matter and they felt its achievement should be conditional upon a very thorough examination of the new methods of pacific settlement which are its corollary."

Further, the Report reveals that, under discussion in the Sub-Committee, the political and juridical difficulties, attendant upon the projected harmonization, crystallized. Suppose the Covenant were amended so as to prohibit the resort to war omitting, at the same time, any specific reference to the Pact of Paris, a consideration rendered almost obligatory by the fact that certain Members of the League had not acceded to the Pact, what would be the result? How would the reservations which certain States Members had made in acceding to the Pact be affected? And again, many existing treaties, either textually or implicitly, contemplate the possibility of war and some even contain definite obligations of military action. It was suggested that such treaties would, on the amendment of the Covenant, become obsolete, for would there not be a manifest contradiction between the old undertakings and the new inhibitions? And lastly, as the Sub-Committee put it in its Report: "The question of the conditions of the applications of the sanctions of Article XVI of the Covenant to the new obligations is a question on which all the Members of the League do not as yet hold the same views."

Accordingly, the Sub-Committee decided that these outstanding questions needed further discussion, and the draft resolution suggesting postponement was adopted in turn by the First Committee and, on October 4th, by the Eleventh Assembly.

In so far as the British Commonwealth was concerned the draft amendments were discussed by the Imperial Conference of 1930. The Conference was agreed that their underlying principle was "one which should receive the support of all the Governments represented at the Conference" and decided therefore to recommend acceptance of the amendments, but that their entry into force "should be made dependent upon the entry into force of a General Treaty for the Reduction and Limitation of Armaments."

By September 1931 twenty out of the fifty-four Governments, States-Members of the League, had sent in their observations on the question of the amendment, and thirty-four had failed to do so.

Fourteen Governments accepted, in principle, the texts drawn up by the Sub-Committee. Of these, however, three, while accepting the Sub-Committee's version, indicated their preference for the proposals of the Committee of Eleven. Two Governments raised objection of principle to the texts of the Sub-Committee, and three others confined themselves to approving the principle of amending the Covenant.

The question of amendment was discussed by the First Committee of the Twelfth Assembly and the debates disclosed the existence of considerable division of opinion. On September 19th M. Politis, the Greek representative, suggested the appointment of a new Committee to take into consideration the two sets of draft amendments already put forward and to indicate the method to be followed in seeking a successful solution of the problem during the year 1932, having regard to the convening of the Disarmament Conference.

The Chairman of the First Committee, M. Motta, considered,

however, that it would be preferable to constitute a Sub-Committee without giving it formal instructions, and this course was adopted.

The Sub-Committee drafted, and the First Committee approved, a Resolution which was finally adopted by the Assembly on September 26th to the effect that a new Committee should be created consisting of representatives of all Members of the League of Nations "for the purpose of seeking unanimous agreement . . . in drafting amendments which may be voted by the Assembly at its next Session." This Committee may meet during the general Disarmament Conference, and if necessary the Members of the League may submit for its consideration their views "as to the nature of the agreement which they think could be obtained."

Tables showing the comparative texts of the amendments to the Covenant will be found on pages 277–280.)

6. A Consultative Pact[1]

When the General Treaty for the Renunciation of War—more commonly known as the Kellogg-Briand Pact or the Pact of Paris—was signed on August 27, 1928 it was generally agreed that as the enunciation of a new international ethic it was of great importance. Opinions differed, however, as to its practical value, the sceptics basing their criticism on the fact that the Pact provided neither the means of coercing any one of its signatories who disregarded Article I (by which war was renounced as an instrument of national policy), nor the machinery for implementing Article II (which provided for the pacific settlement of all international disputes). Behind the scepticism was the all-important and unanswered question, "What will America do in the case of a State which goes to war in disregard of the Pact?"

This problem exercised the minds of many in America as well as in Europe, and a number of resolutions containing

[1] Reprinted from *Bulletin of International News*, Vol. VII, No. 14, January 1 1931.

potential solutions were introduced into both Houses of Congress. These resolutions aimed at the clarification of the attitude to be adopted by the United States in time of war. Some of them declared for the refusal of the United States to give "aid or comfort" to any aggressor State, some suggesting that such an aggressor should be determined by the President, and others, by Congress. Other of the resolutions provided for the refusal of the United States to give support of any kind, directly or indirectly, whether by Governmental or individual action, to any belligerent State, whether the aggressor or the aggressed. These resolutions, however, got no further than the table of the House of Congress into which they were introduced, though the majority of them still lie there, ready to be taken up at any time.

Very soon, however, circumstances arose which demonstrated the necessity of some concerted form of action on the part of the principal signatory Powers, if the Pact was to be taken at all seriously. Early in July 1929 a series of events occurred in Northern Manchuria in connection with the Chinese Eastern Railway which resulted in a virtual state of war existing between China and the Soviet Union. At once the United States Department of State took steps to consult with the representatives in Washington of the original signatories of the Pact as to what should be done in this emergency. Owing to the Japanese delay in ratifying the Pact it was not in force, and nothing could be done at the moment. When, however, this outstanding ratification reached Washington on July 24th, the Pact was proclaimed as being in force as from that date, and six months later, as the belligerent conditions in Manchuria still persisted, Mr. Stimson, United States Secretary of State, once more suggested a consultation as to what should be done. As a result of the deliberations in Washington, identic Notes were despatched to Moscow and Nanking by the United States, British, French and Italian Governments, which, though they arrived at the moment of the termination of the hostilities and therefore lost something of their primary value, demonstrated, nevertheless, the desire of the principal signatories of the Pact to see its pledges preserved.[1]

The lack of regular machinery of consultation and its obvious necessity, which the Manchurian crisis disclosed, moved Mr. Stimson in December 1929 to approach the French Ambassador in Washington, M. Claudel, with the suggestion that the Pact should "be given additional force by setting up machinery for consultation and the moulding of public opinion against an aggressor nation." In view of the forthcoming conference for the limitation of naval armaments the time was unpropitious for exploring the ground further, but the London Conference had not long been in session when it became clear to all that on the problem of security rested the success or failure of the Conference as far as the European nations were concerned. Before she agreed to disarm, France wished to know what interpretation Great Britain placed upon her obligations incurred under Article XVI of the Covenant of the League of Nations, and before she could give an honest answer to that question Great Britain had to know, for her part, what would the United States do in the case of a League blockade imposed on a State acting in defiance of its pledges given under Pact and Covenant. Would America insist on convoying her merchantmen through a League blockade, and thereby aid the aggressor State (not to speak of risking an "incident" which might jeopardize Anglo-American relations)? Or would she agree to support an international boycott of an aggressor State? Would she not perhaps take her part in determining such an aggressor?

The records of the discussions of the London Conference on this crucial point have not yet been given to history, but ultimately the fact emerged that no satisfactory agreement was reached, and as a result France (and therefore Italy) refused to be a party to the London Naval Treaty in its entirety. It is known, however, that the question of a Pact of Consultation was fully discussed at the Conference, and it

---

[1] For texts of the British and United States Notes and the Soviet and Chinese Replies, see *Documents on International Affairs, 1929*, pp. 276–284.

is believed that the United States representatives were not unfavourably inclined towards it, provided that France's demands for guarantees of security could be met in other ways. On this latter point there was failure to reach an agreement, but, in any case, there was a vast body of opinion in America which did not believe it to be possible to find phraseology which would not be interpreted in Europe as meaning more than it said and committing the United States to concerted action against an aggressor nation.

In his 1930 Armistice Day Speech, President Hoover made a reference to the idea of a Pact in terms which were understood to imply that personally, at any rate, he saw possibilities in the adoption of some such principle. The President's words were:

". . . There has been so much discussion as to the desirability of some further extension of the Pact so as to effect a double purpose of assuring methodical development of this machinery of peaceful settlement, and to insure at least the mobilization of world opinion against those who fail when the strain comes. I do not say that some such further step may not some day come about."

Mr. Hoover went on to speak of the idea in his mind as a "formula," saying that "such a formula would be stimulative and would appeal to the dramatic sense of the world as a mark in the progress of peace," and he then turned to describe as "less dramatic and possibly even more sure" the "day to day strengthening and buttressing of the Kellogg Pact by extension from one nation to another of treaties which in times of friction assure resort to the well-tried processes of competent negotiation, of conciliation and of arbitration."

The interest aroused by the President's tentative endorsement of the proposed method of extending the Kellogg Pact was as great in America as in the European countries; and the impression made by his words was deepened when statements appeared in the press, ten days later, that the proposal which Mr. Stimson had made to the French Government in the previous December had taken the form of "an impartial conciliation commission similar to that which investigated the Chaco dispute between Paraguay and Bolivia. This commission would spend several months investigating the rights and wrongs of any dispute, thus providing a cooling-off period similar to that provided for in the Bryan Conciliation Treaties. The commission would endeavour to fix responsibility, and, therefore, tend to mobilize public opinion against any disputant which took the part of the aggressor. No nation would be obliged to take any military preventive action, however."

It was generally agreed that the President had something of the sort in his mind when he made his Armistice Day Speech, but it is equally certain that no further official negotiations have been opened on the subject. Following on these press reports the State Department took occasion, at the end of November 1930, to issue a formal denial to that effect, but it was generally felt that the Administration would not be opposed to discuss an agreement to consult in an emergency (provided it could be guaranteed that the United States would assume no further obligation whatever), and that the responsibility for the next move rested with the Quai d'Orsay.

It was generally believed that the subject of a Consultative Pact would form one of the subjects for discussion during M. Laval's visit to the United States in October 1931. But before his departure a further development had occurred.

The Sino-Japanese dispute with regard to the Japanese occupation of Mukden was brought before the Council of the League during its session in September 1931 and was considered of so grave a nature that the co-operation of the United States was essential in any attempt to bring about a solution.

The first step was taken on the suggestion of Lord Cecil, when the Council agreed to forward to the United States Government for its information all the Minutes and documents on the subject, and this was met by a communication from the United States Secretary of State to the effect that his Government was not only "in whole-hearted sympathy" with the recommendations of the Council to China and Japan, but would also despatch Notes to Tokio and Peking along similar lines. Thus the United States definitely aligned itself with the collective action taken by all the States Members of the League, and from that moment became more intimately identified with the policy pursued by the League in the problem.

Evidence of the desire for close co-operation on the part of the United States was provided on October 9th, when the Secretary of State cabled to Geneva urging the League to "exert all pressure and authority within its competence" towards settling the dispute, and this was followed by a further telegram on October 12th in which the Secretary of State asked the League to continue its efforts to bring pressure on China and Japan to fulfil their obligations and stated that if the time came the United States would not forget to point out to both countries that they had assumed obligations under both the Kellogg Pact and the Nine-Power Treaty of Washington signed in 1922.

As a corollary to this expression of co-operation from the American Government, M. Briand, as President of the Council, issued a formal invitation to the United States Government to be represented at the further meetings of the Council at which the dispute would be discussed. This invitation was sent in spite of the opposition of the Japanese representative, who questioned its legal validity, and was accepted by the United States Government. In transmitting it the Council was influenced by the fact that the dispute concerned the execution of the obligations of the Kellogg Pact as well as of the Covenant.

Accordingly, on October 16th, Mr. Prentiss Gilbert, the United States Consul-General at Geneva, took his seat at the Council table with instructions from Washington "to take part in the discussions when they relate to the possible application of the Kellogg-Briand Pact. You are expected to report on the results of the discussions to the State Department for its determination as to possible action. If you are present at the discussion of any other aspect of the Chinese-Japanese dispute it must only be as an observer and auditor."

The same process was adopted when the Council reassembled for its adjourned session in Paris on November 16th, when Mr. Gilbert's place was taken by General Dawes, United States Ambassador to Great Britain.

These events have gone far to create a *modus vivendi* for discussion on a Consultative Pact, but considerable progress has yet to be made to render the necessary consultation really efficacious. It is necessary to have definite machinery which can immediately be put into operation, and it should not be necessary for the Council of the League to invite the United States to be represented on each occasion, nor is it really satisfactory that the representation of the United States should only be in an observatory or auditory capacity. The two Manchurian disputes of 1929 and 1931 have shown the great importance which must necessarily be attached to unanimous action by the signatories of the Kellogg Pact in the event of a threatened breach of its provisions.

Much depends on the reception which the action of the Administration in Washington receives at the hands of Congress when that body reassembles in December,[1] and there are already signs that this form of co-operation with the League has aroused in the breasts of some 100 per cent. American citizens the fear of the old bogy of "entangling alliances."

The action of the United States Government in sending an observer to the Session of the Council is not so revolutionary a procedure as it might at first seem. American co-operation with the League of Nations, official and unofficial, has increased steadily in the last ten years until there is scarcely a branch of the League's activities in which the United States does not take part, either actively or through observers.

As has been seen, Mr. Hugh Gibson stated that the United States would agree to be represented on the proposed Commission for the control and supervision of disarmament, and the Protocol for the Adherence of the United States to the Permanent Court of International Justice, now before the Senate pending ratification, definitely provides for American representatives to sit on the Council and the Assembly of the League during the election of Judges. If such a representation can be arranged for one specific purpose it is possible that a similar agreement might be reached for other specific purposes,

[1] This was written at the end of November 1931.

always with the understanding that the United States would
not be bound in advance to take the least action in the matter
of sanctions. It is very necessary to emphasize this last point,
for without a full realization of its importance it is useless to
proceed in negotiation with the United States. In that country
Congress alone is responsible for the declaration of war, and
that august body is very jealous of its privileges, and demands
the right to decide every issue upon its own merits.

There remains the possibility that, if a definite agreement for
consultation with regard to the breaches of the Kellogg Pact
were arrived at, the United States might prefer it to be on the
lines of the Four-Power Pacific Pact signed by Great Britain,
U.S.A., Japan and France at the Washington Conference of
1921–22. Article I provides for consultation in the following
terms:

"If there should develop between any of the High Contracting Parties
a controversy arising out of any Pacific question and involving their
said rights which is not satisfactorily settled by diplomacy and is likely
to affect the harmonious accord now happily subsisting between them,
they shall invite the other High Contracting Parties to a joint conference to which the whole subject will be referred for consideration
and adjustment."

In this case, however, the Treaty covers a specific area and is
between a limited number of Powers. The question becomes
more complicated when the whole world is concerned and the
contracting parties number some sixty States. If the United
States insists on consultation apart from the League of Nations,[1]
it is conceivable that a case might arise in which the signatories
of the Pact of Paris consulting in Washington and the Council
of the League deliberating at Geneva might arrive at opposite
conclusions, and any such result might prove to be more of a
hindrance than assistance, though it is possible in certain
circumstances that the Council of the League might not be
unwilling to pass on to a conference in Washington the responsi-

[1] This view was prevalent in the United States before the Sino-Japanese
dispute, but the evident willingness of the Government and the Department
of State to be represented at the Sessions of the Council in Geneva and Paris
render much smaller the probability of American insistence on the policy of
independent consultation.

bility of defining an aggressor and of determining what action should be taken.

It is, however, not outside the bounds of human conception that an agreement may be reached whereby, for purely consultative purposes only, the United States might be willing to send to the Council of the League not merely an observer but a representative, if not with plenary powers, at least with instructions capable of liberal interpretation; it being understood that the results of such consultation would, so far as the United States were concerned, have to be submitted to, and endorsed by, Congress before any action could be taken.

The fate accorded in the Senate to the present policy of the Administration and to the Court Protocols will be an indication as to whether any further progress is possible. It should be understood that some such means of "putting teeth" into the Kellogg Pact would to a certain extent meet some of the French objections to the present lack of adequate guarantees of security.

NOTE

AMENDMENTS TO THE COVENANT

PRESENT TEXT	AMENDMENTS PROPOSED BY THE COMMITTEE OF ELEVEN	TEXT DRAWN UP BY THE SUB-COMMITTEE
PREAMBLE	**PREAMBLE**	**PREAMBLE**
In order to promote international co-operation and to achieve international peace and security by the acceptance of obligations not to resort to war.	In order to promote international co-operation and to achieve international peace and security by accepting the obligation not to resort to war.	In order to promote international co-operation and to achieve international peace and security by accepting the obligation not to resort to war.
ARTICLE 12, paragraph 1	**ARTICLE 12, paragraph 1**	**ARTICLE 12, paragraphs 1 and 2**
The Members of the League agree that, if there should arise between them any dispute likely to lead to a rupture, they will submit the matter either to arbitration or judicial settlement or to inquiry by the Council, and they agree in no case to resort to war until three months after the award	The Members of the League agree that, if there should arise between them any dispute likely to lead to a rupture, they will only employ pacific means for its settlement.	1. The Members of the League agree that, if there should arise between them any dispute likely to lead to a rupture, they will in no case have recourse to war for the settlement of the dispute and will only employ pacific means for this purpose. If the dispute cannot be otherwise settled, it
	If the disagreement continues, the dispute shall be submitted either to arbitration or judicial settlement, or to	

AMENDMENTS TO THE COVENANT

PRESENT TEXT	AMENDMENTS PROPOSED BY THE COMMITTEE OF ELEVEN	TEXT DRAWN UP BY THE SUB-COMMITTEE
by the arbitrators or the judicial decision or the report by the Council.	inquiry by the Council. The Members of the League agree that they will in no case resort to war for the solution of their dispute.	shall be submitted either to arbitration or judicial settlement or to inquiry by the Council. 2. The award of the arbitrators or the judicial decision shall be given and the report of the Council shall be made within a reasonable period.

ARTICLE 13, paragraph 4 (Present Text)

The Members of the League agree that they will carry out in full good faith any award or decision that may be rendered, and that they will not resort to war against a member of the League which complies therewith. In the event of any failure to carry out such an award or decision, the Council shall propose what steps should be taken to give effect thereto.

ARTICLE 13, paragraph 4 (Committee of Eleven)

The Members of the League agree that they will carry out in full good faith any award or decision that may be rendered and that they will not take any action against any Member of the League which complies therewith.

In the event of any failure to carry out such award or decision, the Council shall propose what measures of all kinds should be taken to give effect

ARTICLE 13, paragraph 4 (Sub-Committee)

The Members of the League agree that they will carry out in full good faith the award or decision rendered in a dispute to which they have been parties. They further undertake in no way to support a State in refusal to carry out an award or decision. In the event of any failure to carry out such an award or decision, the Council shall propose what measures of all kinds should be taken to give effect thereto; the votes of the representatives of the parties shall not be counted.

ARTICLE 15, paragraph 6

If the report by the Council is unanimously agreed to by the members thereof, other than the representatives of one or more of the parties to the dispute, the Council shall invite the parties to comply with the recommendations of the report. The Members of the League undertake in no way to support any party in refusal to comply with such recommendations.

ARTICLE 15, paragraph 7

If the Council fails to reach a report which is unanimously agreed to by the members thereof, other than the representatives of one or more of the parties to the dispute, it shall examine the procedure best suited to meet the case and recommend it to the parties.

---

thereto; the votes of the representatives of the parties shall not be counted.

ARTICLE 15, paragraph 6

If the report by the Council is unanimously agreed to by the members thereof, other than the representatives of one or more of the parties to the dispute, the Members of the League agree that they will comply with the recommendations of the report. If the Council's recommendation is not carried out, the Council shall propose suitable measures to give it effect.

ARTICLE 15, paragraph 7

If the Council fails to reach a report which is unanimously agreed to by the members thereof, other than the representatives of one or more of the parties to the dispute, it shall examine the procedure best suited to meet the case and recommend it to the parties.

ARTICLE 15, paragraph 6

If a report by the Council is unanimously agreed to by the members thereof, other than the representatives of one or more of the parties to the dispute, the Members of the League agree that they will not go to war with any party to the dispute which complies with the recommendations of the report.

ARTICLE 15, paragraph 7

If the Council fails to reach a report which is unanimously agreed to by the members thereof, other than the representatives of one or more of the parties to the dispute, the Members of the League reserve to themselves the right to take such action as they shall consider necessary for the maintenance of right and justice.

NOTE—*continued*

AMENDMENTS TO THE COVENANT

PRESENT TEXT	AMENDMENTS PROPOSED BY THE COMMITTEE OF ELEVEN	TEXT DRAWN UP BY THE SUB-COMMITTEE
	ARTICLE 15, paragraph 7 *bis.* (New Paragraph)	ARTICLE 15, paragraph 7 *bis.* (Suppressed)
	At any stage of the examination, the Council may, either at the request of one of the parties or on its own initiative, ask the Permanent Court of International Justice for an advisory opinion on points of law relating to the dispute. Such application shall not require a unanimous vote by the Council.	
ARTICLE 16	ARTICLE 16	ARTICLE 16, paragraph 1, First Sentence
1. Should any Member of the League resort to war in disregard of its covenants under Articles 12, 13 or 15, it shall, *ipso facto*, be deemed to have committed an act of war against all other Members of the League.	(No change proposed)	1. Should any Member of the League resort to war in disregard of its covenants under Articles 12, it shall, *ipso facto*, be deemed to have committed an act of war against all other Members of the League . . . .

B. THE SECURITY AND ARBITRATION COMMITTEE, 1927–1930

1. ORIGINS AND FUNCTIONS[1]

IT was confidently hoped that the Locarno Agreement and the entry of Germany into the League of Nations would provide that added degree of security, particularly in France, which was necessary for the advancement of the limitation and reduction of armaments. Working on this, unfortunately erroneous, hypothesis no provision was made in setting up the Preparatory Disarmament Commission for the discussion of matters of security, which, as a subject, was somewhat pushed into the background.

The need for further security was not actively felt during the first twelve months following the Locarno Agreements, and the Seventh Assembly of the League (1926) contented itself with merely re-emphasizing its approval of this form of treaty and recommending States Members of the League to use them as a model for their future agreements. It further offered the good offices of the Council of the League for "the conclusion of suitable agreements likely to establish confidence and security—and/or a result to facilitate the reduction and limitation of the armaments of all States."

The events of 1927, however, proved conclusively that without an additional degree of increased security disarmament was virtually impossible. In the Preparatory Commission itself a complete deadlock was reached on this very point,[2] and the failure of the Geneva Naval Conference gave further point to the urgent need for the discovery of some further formula.

The effect of these events, as has been seen, was an attempt by France to bring about a revival of the Geneva Protocol at the Assembly of 1927, an attempt which was successfully side-tracked by Great Britain. The Assembly was, however,

---

[1] Part of this section is reprinted from an article appearing in the *Bulletin of International News*, Vol. IV, No. 18, March 3, 1928.
[2] See above, pp. 97 etc.

convinced that something must be done in the matter of security and as a beginning adopted the Polish proposal outlawing aggression.[1] But this additional provision was only of moral value and gave little practical satisfaction to those States who stood in need of protection.

In taking a practical step the Assembly was in something of a quandary. On the one hand stood France firmly refusing to disarm without further guarantees, on the other Germany calling for the honouring of the Allied disarmament pledges given in the Treaty of Versailles. In effect the German contention was that it was useless to delay longer in searching for the security formula satisfactory to France, since nothing would satisfy the French short of the permanent crippling of Germany.

If, however, the Preparatory Commission was to continue its work it was clear that it must be given the authority and machinery to go outside its primary sphere and explore the avenues of security and arbitration. The Eighth Assembly, therefore, adopted a resolution on September 26, 1927, requesting the Council to give the Preparatory Commission "the necessary instructions for the creation without delay of a Committee consisting of all States which have seats on the Commission and are Members of the League of Nations, other States represented on the Commission being invited to sit on it if they so desire." The functions of this Committee were "to consider . . . the measures capable of giving all States the guarantees of arbitration and security necessary to enable them to fix the level of their armaments at the lowest possible figures in an international disarmament agreement."

The Security and Arbitration Committee was duly constituted during the Fourth Session of the Preparatory Commission (November 1927) and held its first session on December 1st, under the Chairmanship of Dr. Beneš of Czechoslovakia. The United States refused to be represented on a Committee whose functions would include the examination and elaboration of the Covenant of the League; and the

[1] See above, pp. 242–43.

U.S.S.R., while declining to be officially represented, agreed to follow the deliberations of the Committee by means of an observer.

The task of the Committee really amounted to the interpretation of the security provisions of the Covenant, namely Articles X, XI and XVI, and reconcile with them the principles of the Locarno Treaties of Guarantee. There was in addition a further factor which had to be taken into account in the form of the treaties of non-aggression and neutrality concluded by the U.S.S.R. with her neighbours in December 1925 and during the following years. The main principle of these agreements is that in the event of one of the Contracting Parties being attacked the other will remain neutral, and further that neither of the Contracting Parties will participate in any alliance or political agreement with a third party against either of them. The particular and unique interest of these treaties, and there are now some eight or ten of them in operation, lies in the fact that they are purely negative, and provide only that neither party will take any measure *against* the other *should it be the victim of an attack*.[1]

The Committee decided that its work could best be furthered by issuing a form of *questionnaire* giving its programme of work to all interested Powers. The programme fell naturally into three categories: questions on arbitration agreements, questions on security agreements, and the study of Articles X, XI and XVI of the Covenant, and for each of these categories a *rapporteur* was appointed.

To co-ordinate its work the Committee appointed its Bureau (the Chairman and two vice-Chairmen, Señor Urrutia of Colombia and M. Undén of Sweden) together with the three *rapporteurs*, MM. Holsti (Finland), Arbitration, Politis (Greece), Security, and Rutgers (The Netherlands), Articles of the Covenant, to meet together and receive and discuss the replies of the Governments to *questionnaires* and the memoranda presented by the *rapporteurs*. The result of their labours should

---

[1] For further details on the Soviet system of Treaties of Neutrality and Non-Aggression, see below, pp. 312 etc.

form the basis of discussion for the second session of the Committee.

Observations on the Security Committee's proposals were received (in order of date) from the Swedish, Norwegian, Belgian, British and German Governments. The Swedish Note confined itself to that portion of the Committee's terms of reference which referred "to promoting, generalizing and coordinating special and collective agreements on arbitration and security," and presented a draft Collective Conciliation and Arbitration Agreement "based on the principles which were adopted in the Locarno Agreement, and which were rightly endorsed by large sections of the public in States Members of the League of Nations."

The Norwegian and Belgian Governments, each in a short Note, also declared themselves in favour of a general Convention of conciliation and arbitration drawn up, *mutatis mutandis*, on the Locarno model. The Norwegian Government further suggested two additional provisions:

(1) That the provisions of the Locarno Treaties concerning the submission of disputes to the Council under Article XVIII should be supplemented by a clause under which the Contracting Parties would undertake to accept as binding the conclusions of the Council's report, if this report was accepted unanimously, the votes of the representatives of the Parties not being counted in reckoning this unanimity.

(2) The addition of an optional clause, acceptance of which would make obligatory among the signatories submission to an arbitral tribunal instead of to the League Council any non-juridical question which had been referred to a permanent conciliation commission and had not proved capable of settlement by this method.

Far more detailed were the observations of the British Government, which went to the heart of the matter at once. "Arbitration treaties have no sanction behind them but the force of public opinion of the world at large. An arbitration award which a Party to the dispute resolutely refused to execute would not merely fail to settle the dispute; it would prejudice the movement in favour of arbitration." Therefore, the Note argued, "an arbitration treaty which goes beyond what the public opinion of a country can be counted upon to support when the interests of that country are in question, and when a decision unfavourable to those interests is pronounced, is a treaty which is useless." Referring to the question of general agreements, conciliation, and arbitration for the settlement of non-justiciable disputes, the Note recommended the working out of such drafts, if "there are any States which feel themselves able to accept and sign such a general agreement."

As regards security agreements, the British Note reiterated the policy of the British Government expressed by Mr. Chamberlain before Locarno, that of "special arrangements in order to meet special needs. . . . These objects can best be attained *by knitting together the nations most immediately concerned, and whose differences might lead to a renewal of strife*, by means of treaties framed with the sole object of maintaining, as between themselves, an unbroken peace."

The German Government's observations were more general in nature. The Committee, it was said, "should not aim at building up a theoretical system, but at framing those practical measures which are both necessary and attainable under present political conditions." It was pointed out that the crux of the question was the avoidance of armed conflicts, and the aim of the Committee should be the endeavour "to find for all conceivable disputes without exception a procedure which is calculated to lead to equitable and peaceful solutions." It was suggested that such a scheme could be embodied both in bilateral and multilateral treaties.

The British and German Notes were at variance over the question of the necessity of sanctions in a system for the pacific settlement of international disputes. The latter declared that "if the bodies which are called upon to pronounce the final decision are invested with sufficient authority, and if the limits of their competence are defined with the requisite exactness, it is hardly likely that a State would dare to disregard such a decision."

On the subject of regional pacts the German Government warned the Committee that in discussing this question it should be remembered that "any increase in the security of particular States at the expense of the security of other States constitutes no progress in the direction of peace." Group alliances within the League which had the object of protecting some State Members against other State Members would be a grave danger, and might easily split the League and render joint action in time of crisis impossible.

The Bureau of the Committee, together with the three *rapporteurs*, met in Prague on January 26th to consider the replies of the Governments, and as a result the reports for the agenda of the second session of the Committee were drawn up. The Prague Memorandum, published at Geneva on February 10th, was noticeable for the attention it paid to the British proposals.

(1) It stressed the fact that the security provided by the Covenant, which in the majority of cases can be applied to prevent war, was not appreciated at its full value.
(2) The absence of a rigid code of procedure encouraged the exercise of the common will for peace.
(3) No alteration in the text of the Covenant, and no new pact was proposed.

Special or collective treaties were the only practical means of a supplementary guarantee.

M. Nicolas Politis, *rapporteur* on security, made the following recommendations:

(1) The conclusion of regional pacts (in preference to separate treaties of non-aggression) for the pacific settlement of disputes and mutual assistance or of non-aggression only.
(2) He advised against the proposal of a general treaty, as a third failure might damage the prestige of the League.
(3) The chief points in any security pact were:
    (A) The exclusion of the recourse to war;
    (B) The provision of pacific procedure; and of
    (C) A system of mutual assistance in co-operation with the Council of the League.
(4) Only wars of aggression were condemned, as force could be applied legally under Article XVI of the Covenant.

Other suggestions were that the League should have power to order belligerents to observe an armistice, the breach of which would form a proof of aggression, and that the provision in the Locarno Rhineland Pact concerning aggression might be adopted, where possible, in regional pacts.

The second session of the Committee on Arbitration and Security was opened by M. Benès on February 20th. The first three days were given over to general observations, and from these it was evident that the general concensus of opinion agreed that the Locarno Treaties should form the model on which all agreements for arbitration, conciliation and security should be drawn up. In the words of M. Paul Boncour, "Everyone pays a tribute to the work done at Locarno, but if the Locarno Treaties are so excellent—which I firmly believe they are—it is essential that we should not keep those treaties for ourselves, but that we should endeavour to frame others."

The Committee then proceeded to take the memoranda of the three *rapporteurs* clause by clause, and to assign the Drafting Committee its tasks. At the outset it was clear that a large number of the Committee agreed with Lord Cushendun that bilateral treaties rather than general treaties were the right avenues of approach, whether in reference to arbitration, conciliation, or security. The difficulty of reducing to one common type the varying practices of existing arbitration treaties, which had been admitted in M. Holsti's memorandum, was clearly illustrated by delegates from Canada and the South American States, who each demonstrated the suitability of their own form of treaty to their own special needs.

On the other hand, the French Government, both through M. Paul Boncour ("I am in a position to state France is entirely won over to the idea of a general arbitration treaty of this kind") and by a circulated memorandum ("The French delegation is in favour of the proposal for a [general] treaty which would cover every kind of dispute, and would apply to all possible relations of the contracting States *inter se*"), expressed its preference for the opposite course, and was in principle supported by Belgium.

As a result, the Drafting Committee was instructed to draw up models for both general and bilateral arbitration treaties.

There was some hesitancy as to whether conciliation should be made a subject of a special treaty or should be annexed to the draft arbitration treaty. The representatives of Italy and Belgium supported the latter course, but this was opposed by Canada, Chile and Germany. The Canadian representative was particularly anxious that the importance of the use of conciliation should not be merged and lost sight of in the provisions for arbitration. The British delegate was emphatic that non-justiciable disputes should be submitted to conciliation and not to arbitration.

In accordance with its instructions the Drafting Committee produced six model treaties:

1. Convention A.—General Convention for the Pacific Settlement of all International Disputes.
2. Convention B.—General Convention for Judicial Settlement, Arbitration and Conciliation.
3. Convention C.—General Conciliation Convention.
4. Convention D.—Collective Treaty of Mutual Assistance.
5. Treaty E.—Collective Treaty of Non-Aggression.
6. Treaty F.—Bilateral Treaty of Non-Aggression.

These treaties passed their first reading before the end of the second session of the Committee on March 1, 1928, and were read again at the third session (June 27th to July 4, 1928), having been previously approved by the Preparatory Commission at its fifth session in March. In the course of the Security Committee's third session, three further model treaties were adopted, this time all of a bilateral character:

1. Convention (a).—Bilateral Convention for the Pacific Settlement of all International Disputes.
2. Convention (b).—Bilateral Convention for Judicial Settlement, Arbitration and Conciliation.
3. Convention (c).—Bilateral Conciliation Convention.

The Committee also adopted a draft Treaty for the Strengthening of the Means of Preventing War, put forward by the German Delegation.

Thus in six months the Committee had prepared no less than ten draft treaties, all of which were forwarded to the Ninth Assembly which met in Geneva in September 1928. The treaties came at a very opportune moment, only a few days before the signing of the Kellogg Pact had proclaimed the outlawry of war as an instrument of national policy and had proclaimed the pacific settlement of international disputes. No machinery had been provided in the Pact for this method of settlement, but here ready to hand for the selection and choice of States so disposed, were the makings of nearly a dozen means.

The Ninth Assembly endorsed the work of the Security and Arbitration Committee with one important modification. It combined, in face of British and Japanese opposition,[1] the three collective treaties for arbitration and conciliation (Conventions A, B, and C) into one General Act which would come into force between any two or more States as soon as they had accepted it in whole or in part, and which would remain open indefinitely for the accession of all States.

The remainder of the draft treaties were approved by the Assembly and recommended to States Members of the League for their consideration and adoption as models.

2. THE GENERAL ACT FOR THE PACIFIC SETTLEMENT OF INTERNATIONAL DISPUTES[2]

The General Act, adopted by the Ninth Assembly in September 1928, was an amalgam of three draft collective treaties of arbitration and conciliation prepared earlier in the year by the Security and Arbitration Committee of the Preparatory Disarmament Commission. It has been described as "a singularly bold and ingenious scheme for uniting all States willing

---

[1] British opposition was withdrawn when it became known that approval by the Assembly of the General Act carried with it no obligation to adhere.
[2] For text of the General Act see *Documents on International Affairs*, 1928, edited by J. W. Wheeler-Bennett (Oxford University Press, 1929), pp. 15–27.

to accede to it by a network of provisions for pacific settlement."[1]

The Act is a document of four chapters.

Chapter I provides for the solution of disputes by conciliation and provides machinery almost identical with that in the Locarno Treaties. Such conciliation procedure can, but only by agreement between the two disputing parties, precede action by the Permanent Court of International Justice.

The judicial settlement of disputes or the arbitration of disputes of a legal character is provided for in Chapter II, whereby it is laid down, in the actual language of the Locarno Treaties, that "questions in regard to which parties are in conflict as to their respective rights," shall be submitted to the Permanent Court, unless the disputing parties agree to go to arbitration.

Chapter III headed "Arbitration," makes provision for the settlements mentioned in Chapter II, which are not submitted to the Permanent Court; such disputes to be settled by a non-permanent arbitral tribunal whose decisions are binding on the parties and which shall function, subject to any special agreement, under the regulations laid down in the Hague Conventions of 1899 and 1907.

The fourth chapter (although labelled somewhat euphemistically "General Provisions") is not without interest, and is remarkable for the guarded manner in which parties are permitted to adhere to the Act and for the elastic forms of reservations which can be made.

States may adhere either to the Act as a whole, or separately either to Chapter I (Conciliation) or Chapters I and II (Conciliation and Judicial Settlement), with addition in each case of the general provision of Chapter IV. With regard to reservations, Contracting Parties may exempt from the scope of the Act:

---

[1] See an Article, "Model Treatise for the Pacific Settlement of International Disputes, Mutual Assistance and Non-Aggression," by Sir John Fischer-Williams in the *Journal of the Royal Institute of International Affairs* for November 1928, Vol. VII, p. 407. This article is recommended as a critical examination of the General Act and the Model Treaties from a technical point of view.

1. Disputes arising out of facts prior to the accession either of the Party making the reservation or of any other Party with whom the said Party may have a dispute.
2. Disputes concerning questions which by international law are solely within the domestic jurisdiction of States.
3. Disputes concerning particular cases or clearly specified subject-matters such as territorial status, or disputes falling within clearly specified categories.

It is also provided that, if one of the Parties to a dispute has made a reservation, the other Parties may enforce the same reservations in regard to that Party.[1]

Though the General Act was adopted unanimously by the Ninth Assembly, there was no immediate haste on the part of States Members of the League to adhere to it. Each seemed to be looking to the other for a lead and by the close of the year the instrument still remained unsigned.

In Great Britain and the other component parts of the British Commonwealth the attitude towards the Act was very much the same as that adopted towards the Optional Clause of the Statute of the Permanent Court of International Justice. The Conservative Government were on principle opposed both to general arbitration agreements and to obligatory jurisdiction.

After the British elections of May 1929, however, and the advent to office of the Labour Party, a new policy was pursued. In the course of the Tenth Assembly (September 1929) the British Government and the Governments of Australia, Canada, India and New Zealand signed the Optional Clause[2]

---

[1] In discussing this provision Signor Scioloja, the Chairman of the First Commission of the Ninth Assembly, somewhat drily remarked that there would obviously be great competition to be the last State to accede to the Act because every State would wish to see what reservations other States were going to make, and profit thereby before making its own! In this connection it is only fair to point out that Article XLI provides for reference to the Permanent Court of International Justice of all disputes relating to the interpretation of the Act, including those concerning the classification of disputes and the scope of reservations.

[2] The text of the Optional Clause and of Article XXXVI, paragraph 2, to which it refers, is as follows:—

The Optional Clause

"The undersigned, being duly authorized thereto, further declare on behalf of their Government that, from this date, they accept as compulsory *ipso facto* and without special Convention the jurisdiction of the Court in with the reservation, however, that the following categories of disputes should be exempted from its scope:

1. Disputes in regard to which the parties to the dispute have agreed or shall agree to have recourse to some other method of peaceful settlement.
2. Disputes with the Government of any other Member of the League which is a member of the British Commonwealth of Nations, all of which disputes shall be settled in such manner as the parties have agreed or shall agree to.
3. Disputes with regard to questions which, by International Law, fall exclusively within the jurisdiction of the United Kingdom.

The South African delegate made a reservation to these reservations to the effect that although his Government believed that disputes between States of the British Commonwealth were justiciable by the Permanent Court, they nevertheless agreed that it was preferable to settle them by other means. Subject to this condition South Africa joined the other five Governments in accepting the obligations of the Optional Clause for a period of ten years. The Irish Free State, on the other hand, adhered independently without any reservations for a period of twenty years.[1]

conformity with Article XXXVI, paragraph 2, of the Statute of the Court under the following conditions:

Article XXXVI, Paragraph 2

"The Members of the League of Nations and the States mentioned in the Annex to the Covenant may, either when signing or ratifying the Protocol to which the present Statute is adjoined or at a later moment, declare that they recognize as compulsory, *ipso facto*, and without special agreement, in relation to any Member or State accepting the same obligation, the jurisdiction of the Court in all or any of the classes of legal disputes concerning:

(a) The interpretation of a Treaty.
(b) Any question of International Law.
(c) The existence of any fact which, if established, would constitute a breach of an international obligation.
(d) The nature or extent of the reparation to be made for the breach of an international obligation.

"The declaration referred to above may be made unconditionally or on condition of reciprocity on the part of several or certain Members or States, or for a certain time.

"In the event of a dispute as to whether the Court has jurisdiction, the matter shall be settled by the decision of the Court."

[1] The texts of the various reservations and the views of His Britannic Majesty's Government on their policy of adherence to the Clause were published in a White Paper on December 12, 1929. See *Documents on International Affairs, 1929*, pp. 38–50.

At the Eleventh Assembly of the League (September 1930) matters were taken a step further and the question was raised as to the adherence of the British Government to the General Act. It was felt that no definite step could be taken before further consultation with the Dominion Governments, and decision was, therefore, postponed until the Imperial Conference which met in the following month.

The question was considered first by the Committee on Arbitration and Disarmament, on whose recommendation the Governments of the United Kingdom, Canada, Australia, New Zealand, the Irish Free State and India agreed

"to commend the General Act to the appropriate authority with a view to accession on conditions mainly similar to those attached to their respective acceptances of the Optional Clause; in particular, the reservation regarding questions which by International Law fall within the domestic jurisdiction of the parties would be retained . . . in view of the importance attached by many of his Majesty's Governments to certain matters, such as immigration, which are solely within their domestic jurisdiction."

This view did not entirely satisfy South Africa, and her representatives expressed themselves as not being opposed to the principle of the General Act, but requiring more time for further consideration before arriving at a final decision.

As in the previous case, his Britannic Majesty's Government published on February 25, 1931 a Memorandum giving its reasons for adhering to the General Act, explaining that while the signing of the Optional Clause was a first step towards a completion and settlement of international disputes, the signing of the General Act completed "an organized system of all-in arbitration."[1]

3. THE MODEL TREATIES

The six model treaties, drawn up by the Security and Arbitration Committee during its Second and Third Sessions, fall naturally into two categories, one dealing with conciliation,

[1] See British White Paper, Cmd. 3803. At the close of 1931, 17 States had signed and ratified the General Act in whole or in part.

arbitration and judicial settlement, and the other with undertakings for non-aggression and mutual assistance. In all of
them, as in the General Act itself, the predominating influence
is that of the Locarno Treaties.

In the first category are the Bilateral Conventions for
Pacific Settlement of all International Disputes, the Bilateral
Convention for Judicial Settlement, Arbitration and Conciliation, and the Bilateral Conciliation Convention. These instruments are designed on the lines of the General Act and are in
substance the General Act modified so as to apply to an agreement between two parties. In each case the arrangement is
somewhat different and this is particularly noticeable in the
case of the second Convention—which, in comparison with
the corresponding provisions of the General Act, has been
described by a commentator as "less extensive, less ambitious,
and possibly, in a sense, more orthodox."[1]

The three treaties falling within the second category consist
of a Collective Treaty of Mutual Assistance, and a Collective
and Bilateral Treaty of Non-Aggression, the last two being
mutatis mutandis identical in wording.

The Collective Treaty of Mutual Assistance, called in draft
Treaty D, combined the three elements of non-aggression,
peaceful settlement of disputes and mutual assistance. Of
these the provisions affecting the first and third followed
closely those of the Locarno Treaty of Mutual Assistance,
the Rhineland Pact, but differed in the important particulars
that no provision was made for mutual assistance before
reference to the Council nor for guarantees by third parties.
The machinery for the pacific settlement is also modelled on
that of the Locarno Treaties.

The two remaining instruments, the Collective and Bilateral
Treaties of Non-Aggression, are almost word for word identical
with the preceding document save that the clauses relating to
mutual assistance were omitted. They provided a regional or
bilateral means of reaffirming and re-emphasizing the principle

---

[1] See *Journal of the Royal Institute of International Affairs*, already cited,
p. 413.

of the Kellogg Pact, with the added advantage of the arbitration machinery of the Locarno Agreements.

At the moment of writing, the only one of these treaties which has been used in practice as a model is the Bilateral Treaty of Non-Aggression and Arbitration, Treaty F. Before the text of the Treaty had been finally adopted by the Ninth Assembly (September 1928), Greece and Rumania signed at Geneva on March 12, 1928 a Treaty of Non-Aggression and Arbitration based entirely on the model Treaty F.[1]

4. The Convention for Financial Assistance

When the Preparatory Disarmament Commission at its first session in May 1926 was discussing and arranging its agenda it received from the Finnish representative a proposal for the rendering of financial assistance to States victims of aggression. It was pointed out that certain small States—more particularly the Border States of theU.S.S.R.—felt a diffidence about reducing their armaments and particularly about restricting their right to build up stocks of material unless they could be certain of being able to obtain immediate supplies of munitions, etc., from abroad in time of war. The Commission was, therefore, asked to examine "the practical means by which small States in need of special security . . . could obtain sufficient guarantees as regards immediate financial assistance to enable them, in the event of their becoming the victims of an unprovoked aggression, to purchase war materials and other supplies necessary for a successful defence until, in accordance with Article XVI of the Covenant, general assistance by the League is forthcoming."

The Preparatory Commission, feeling it to be somewhat outside their terms of reference, referred this matter to the Council of the League, and for four and a half years it was the subject of discussion and debate in one League Committee or another until in September 1930 it blossomed forth into a full-blown Convention.

A Council Committee discussed it during 1926 and at the

[1] For text of this Treaty, see *Documents on International Affairs, 1928*, p. 113.

end of the year referred it to the Financial Committee, who by June 1927 had prepared a draft scheme, which in its turn was submitted to the Eighth Assembly in September 1927. The Assembly decided that the draft proposal fell within the scope of the activities of the Committee on Security and Arbitration which it had decided to set up. Accordingly during 1928 the scheme was further thrashed out by a Joint Committee of the Security and Arbitration Committee and the Financial Committee.

After discussions in the Ninth Assembly (September 1928) three important decisions were reached in connection with the proposal which greatly determined its final form. It was agreed

1. That the scheme should be drafted in the form of a special Convention, within the framework of the League general programme for the limitation and reduction of armaments.
2. That within the text of the Convention, financial assistance should be provided for, not only in the case of war mentioned in Article XVI of the Covenant, but also in the case of war or threat of war mentioned in Article XI.
3. That the responsibility of deciding whether the Convention should be put into force in any given circumstance should be vested in the Council.

By the beginning of March 1929 the Draft Convention was complete and circulated to Members of the League. It formed the subject of heated discussion in the Third Committee of the Tenth Assembly (September 1929), where a number of criticisms were raised, particularly the German objection to the inclusion of cases in which war was threatened, and the British contention that the coming into force of the Convention should be made contingent upon the acceptance of a general disarmament agreement. So great were the divergences of opinion that the Assembly felt bound to postpone taking a final decision until its next session and accordingly referred the Convention back to the Committee on Security and Arbitration and the Financial Committee.

As a result of the labour of these bodies a revised draft, which attempted, somewhat unsuccessfully, to reconcile the points at issue, was presented to the Eleventh Assembly in

September 1930. The Assembly, after discussion in its Third Committee, adopted the amended draft, which now contained the provision that the Convention might be called into operation in the event of a threat of war "provided it (the Council) considers that peace cannot be safeguarded otherwise." There was also a specific provision that "the entry into force and maintenance in force of the Convention was made conditional, in respect of each of the High Contracting Parties, upon the entry into force and maintenance in force in respect of that Party of a plan for the reduction of armaments adopted in execution of Article VIII of the Covenant of the League of Nations."

The Assembly having adopted the Convention on September 29th, it was declared open for signature and by the end of the year had been signed by thirty States, including Great Britain, France, Germany and Italy.[1]

As regards the provisions for granting financial assistance contained in the Convention, the best summary available is one made by Sir Henry Strakosh, a Member of the League Financial Committee, and one who played a leading rôle in drafting the Convention. Though the summary refers to the scheme as it stood in 1929, the subsequent amendments did not affect this materially.[2]

"The plan provides that the Convention shall be put into operation in favour of any member of the League who had become a signatory to the Convention, and who, *by the unanimous vote of the* Council, is held to be a victim of, or threatened by, aggression. The financial aid is to be obtained in the international money markets in the ordinary way, the Government concerned contracting for a loan on the general security of its revenues. To fortify its own credit there is to be associated with it, by way of guarantee of the service of the loan, the credit of all the other signatories to the Convention. To meet the difficulties and delays involved by reason of these guarantees being widely distributed—a serious disadvantage in circumstances where promptness of action is

---

[1] For text of the Convention, see *Documents on International Affairs, 1930*, pp. 45–60.
[2] See *Times*, August 10, 1929. For a further exposition of the Convention by Sir Henry Strakosh, followed by critical discussions, see "International Affairs" (*Journal of the Royal Institute of International Affairs*), Vol. X, No. 2, March 2, 1931, pp. 208–222. See also *Survey of International Affairs, 1930*, Part I, A (iv).

of the very essence—and to endow the operation with added strength, the Convention provides for a system of special or super guarantees. A few of the signatories whose financial standing is so high as to be likely to command confidence in almost all circumstances are to guarantee *vis-à-vis* the investor the whole service of the loan. In this way any such loan would become thrice secured, by the liability of:

(*a*) The borrowing Government;

(*b*) All the signatories to the Convention (ordinary guarantee); and

(*c*) Certain signatories of undoubted financial strength (special guarantee).[1]

When in any particular instance the Council—by a unanimous vote—decides that a certain signatory shall receive financial assistance, it will authorize that signatory to issue a loan (within the total permissible under the Convention) enjoying the above-mentioned ordinary and special guarantees. The maximum annual service of the loan (and therefore, broadly, its amount) will be fixed by the Council. The precise responsibility of each guarantor for each year will then be determined by dividing the service of the particular loan among all the guaranteeing Governments in the proportion of their maximum possible liability. A similar procedure is followed in the determination of the annual liability of each special guarantor Government.

The liability of the ordinary guarantors is a contingent one, and becomes operative to meet its loan charges, and only after a reserve to be provided by the borrowing Government has been exhausted. The liability of the special guarantors is contingent not only upon the failure of the borrowing Government to meet its load charges, but also on the failure of any of the ordinary guarantors to honour their guarantee. These contingent liabilities of both the ordinary and special guarantors are again strictly limited in amount.

The Convention provides for the appointment of trustees, to whom is entrusted the whole management of the loan service, and who will hold the reserve fund which, under the Convention, is to be constituted by the borrowing Government, and who will also undertake the financial settlements as between special and ordinary guarantors."

There arise from an examination of the Convention three main objections; the first psychological, the two latter technical. With regard to the first, the Convention for Financial Assistance is in effect ethically antithetical to the Kellogg Pact, the spirit of which was *si vis pacem para pacem*.[2] In 1928 war was re-

---

[1] The special guarantors were to be the Governments of the States which were permanent members of the League Council, together with such other Governments as the permanent members of the Council might invite to accept the position.

[2] The words engraved on the gold pen presented by the City of Havre to Mr. Kellogg, and with which he subsequently signed the Pact.

nounced as an instrument of national policy, yet in 1930 the same Power who made this act of renunciation accepted a Convention by which its supporters "thought to promote peace by financing war."[1] In spirit it is a retrogression to the principle of *si vis pacem para bellum*,[2] a turning away from the "peace mentality initiated by the Pact" towards the war mentality of the older pre-war European diplomacy.

Of the two technical objections the first is that the whole operation of the Convention turns upon the ability of the Council to define the words "aggressor" and "aggression." The difficulty of this definition has been the rock on which many League proposals for security and disarmament have gone asunder, as for example the Treaty of Mutual Assistance in 1923. Even if the method adopted in the Geneva Protocol be used, the test of arbitration, this would scarcely apply in the case of the U.S.S.R. which has stated in advance that it will not be bound by the agreements for pacific settlement provided by the League and the Permanent Court.

The almost impossibility of defining an aggressor has been amply illustrated during the past twelve years. Who, for example, was the aggressor in the Polish Soviet war of 1920 ? Was the act of aggression the Polish invasion of the Ukraine or was it the increase of Communist propaganda in Poland which forced that country to the conclusion that attack was the only means of defence ?

Or again, what can be done in the quite possible contingency of the Council either disagreeing on the question of defining the aggressor or being frankly unable to make up its mind ?

The second technical objection is that the putting into force of the provisions of the Convention in any given case is dependent on a *unanimous* vote of the Council. The principle of unanimity in Council decisions is too abstruse to discuss here at length, but it is clear that, should there be two disputants "A" and "B," of which "A" has an ally "C," who is also a member of

---

[1] The *Observer*, September 22, 1929.
[2] These words were inscribed on the door of the Imperial Austro-Hungarian War Office in Vienna.

the Council, it would be possible for "C," by refusing its vote, to hold up the putting into force of the provisions of the Convention in favour of "B."

To take a concrete example. Should a State member of the Little Entente, all of which are bound to France by treaties of mutual alliance, become involved in a dispute with a Central European Power, France could (and in the light of past history, probably would) immediately make impossible any unanimous proposal for giving the necessary guarantees to the latter State.

On the other hand, it is claimed for the Convention that it provides the Council with a new and powerful weapon—perhaps more effective and easy of operation than any which it had hitherto possessed—for preventing or stopping a conflict, and that the Convention was almost the first proposal which approached the solution of the problem of security from a practical angle.[1]

5. THE GENERAL CONVENTION TO IMPROVE THE MEANS OF PREVENTING WAR, 1931

Article XI of the Covenant of the League gives the Council wide powers of action in any case of war or threat of war. These powers are most valuable, but they suffer from two limitations. Firstly, no obligation is imposed upon the parties to the dispute to accept the "advice" of the Council, and if they refuse to do so, without taking action which incurs the application of Article XVI, the Council may find itself practically powerless.[2] Secondly, the decisions of the Council, under Article XI, have to be unanimous and the Council will always in such cases include the parties to the dispute as, if affected, they have the right to be summoned to the Council meetings and to vote. A party to the dispute can therefore always vote against the Council's recommendations and thereby stultify their effect.

These considerations led the German Government, at the First Session of the Committee of Security and Arbitration in

[1] At the close of 1931, 30 States had signed the Convention.
[2] This possibility also exercised the minds of the framer of the Amendments to the Covenant, see above, pp. 257, etc.

December 1927 to make certain observations to the effect that Article XI might be supplemented by voluntary agreements between certain parties—if not all the Members of the League, at least a number of them—going beyond the province of the Covenant, as had been done by the parties to the Locarno Treaties.

At the Second Session (February 1928), despite the fact that the Committee were generally of the opinion that "it is impossible at present to contemplate the conclusion of a general agreement—adding to the obligations assured under the Covenant—with a view to giving the nations greater security," the German delegation submitted some draft suggestions which, they indicated, "might constitute the object of an agreement or of a protocol which would be open for signature by all States Members and non-Members of the League of Nations, and which might come into force separately for the several continents in a way similar to that provided for in the Draft Treaty of Mutual Assistance of 1923."

These proposals were as follows:

I

In case of a dispute being submitted to the Council the States might undertake in advance to accept and execute provisional recommendations of the Council for the purpose of preventing any aggravation or extension of the dispute and impeding any measures to be taken by the parties which might exercise an unfavourable reaction on the execution of the settlement to be proposed by the Council.

II

In case of threat of war the States might undertake in advance to accept and to execute the recommendations of the Council to the effect of maintaining or re-establishing the military *status quo* normally existing in time of peace.

III

In the case of hostilities of any kind breaking out without, in the Council's opinion, all possibilities of a pacific settlement having been exhausted, the States might undertake in advance to accept, on the Council's proposal, an armistice on land and sea and in the air, including especially the obligation of the two parties in dispute to withdraw the forces which might have penetrated into foreign territory, and to secure the respect of the sovereignty of the other State.

In his *exposé* Herr von Simson demonstrated the anxiety of Germany to concentrate on preventing the outbreak of hostilities, rather than halting their course once war had broken out.

The Committee referred these proposals to a *rapporteur* whose opinion on them they considered at their Third Session (June–July 1928). Inspired by a spirit of caution in the matter of assuming fresh obligations, the Committee rejected the idea of drawing up a general protocol. On the other hand, it was not considered that bilateral treaties on this basis would be very effective, and there was little support for the German suggestion of an agreement coming into force by continents. The Committee therefore cast its draft in the form of a model multilateral treaty, recording their opinion that its value would be directly proportionate to the number of States adhering to it. The Draft Treaty was submitted to and discussed by the Ninth Assembly (September 1928), who expressed the hope that this model might form a careful basis for States wishing to conclude a treaty of that nature.

For a year nothing was heard of the model draft, except a warm word of praise from the Netherlands Government expressing strong approval of the general principle, and there was danger of its being allowed to recede into the limbo of good intentions. From this fate it was, however, rescued by Lord Cecil, on the part of the British Government, who at the Tenth Assembly (September 1929) sponsored a resolution calling on the Committee of Security and Arbitration to consider the possibility of establishing a Draft General Convention on the broad lines of the model treaty drawn up in the previous year. Meanwhile the 1928 draft was circulated to Governments for their opinions, which were received in considerable quantities.

In the course of the discussions before the Committee it was found impossible to reach an agreement—more particularly on the conservatory measures of a military nature and the means of enforcing them. The Committee was therefore unable to draw up a single text, but their various views were all, however, to be reduced to two main currents of opinion which, with certain reservations, were submitted to the Eleventh Assembly

(September 1930) in the form of alternative texts, with the agreed title of "Draft General Convention to Strengthen the Means of Preventing War."

The Third Committee of the Eleventh Assembly did its best to reconcile the two conflicting schools of thought but with singularly little success, and it became clear that certain "delicate questions of a technical nature" would have to be gone into more thoroughly before there could be any hope of establishing a single text. It was agreed therefore to advise the Assembly to request the Council to appoint a special Committee to continue the study of the question.

At its session in January 1931 the Council invited the Governments of Chile,[1] France, Germany, Great Britain, Greece, Guatemala, Italy, Japan, the Netherlands, Norway, Poland, Spain and Yugoslavia to appoint representatives to form a Special Committee. This body met at Geneva from May 11-15, 1931, with M. Politis (Greece) as Chairman and M. Lange (Norway) as *rapporteur*.

The Special Committee succeeded in drafting and unanimously adopting[2] a single text covering points concerning which the Committee of Security and Arbitration had been unable to reach an agreement—namely, the conservatory measures of a military character which the Council might recommend the parties to a dispute to take under the Convention, the supervision of the execution of such measures, the sanctions to be applied in the event of this violation and the examination applicable should war break out as a consequence of any such violation.

Briefly, the Convention provided that such States as so desired would, subject to reciprocity, agree that their vote should not be taken into consideration in determining unanimity in the Council when they were parties to a dispute, if the Council decided to recommend the adoption of conservatory measures of a non-military character (or, in the event of threat of war, of a military character) specified in the Convention. In the same way, without taking into accord the votes of the disputing

Chile refused.   [2] The Japanese delegate abstained from voting.

parties, the Council might take a decision to ensure the supervision of the execution of the non-military measures, and in case of the violation of these measures, the execution of the Convention. If war were to break out as a consequence of such violation, the Contracting Parties agreed to consider this violation as *prima facie* evidence that the party guilty thereof had resorted to war within the meaning of Article XVI.

The Committee also agreed that the title "General Convention to *Improve* the Means of Preventing War" should be substituted for the title "General Convention to *Strengthen* the Means of Preventing War," as seeming to correspond more exactly with the character of the preferred text, which, it was considered, represented only a modest advance in the direction of strengthening the means of preventing war.

The text of the Convention together with the Special Committee's Report[1] were submitted to the Twelfth Assembly (September 1931) and were referred to the Third Committee, where they were the subject of considerable discussion and further suggested amendment. A Drafting Committee was instructed to prepare a new text, and this was finally adopted on September 25th, the Chinese and Japanese delegations abstaining. Two days later (September 27th) it adopted the text of the General Convention and declared it to be open for signature, with the added hope that a large number of States would adhere before the opening of the forthcoming Disarmament Conference.

As finally adopted the provisions of the Convention are as follows:

All the provisions presuppose the fact that a state of war between the Powers does not exist. The conservatory measures envisaged are of two kinds, non-military and military. Under Article I the High Contracting Parties, in the event of a dispute arising between them and in the event of this dispute being

---

[1] There was also an interesting suggestion put forward by the Polish and Swedish Governments to the effect that the Assembly should "study the possibilities of guarding against the dangers which might arise at a time of international crisis from irresponsible campaigns in the Press and the publication of incorrect and tendencious information."

brought before the Council, undertake to accept and to apply the conservatory measures of a non-military nature which the Council may recommend with a view to preventing the aggravation of the dispute. Article II provides for conservatory measures of a military character if, though the circumstances do not create a state of war between the Powers at issue, the forces of one of those Powers enter the territory or territorial waters of the other or a zone demilitarized in virtue of international agreements, or fly over them. Then the High Contracting Powers undertake to carry out such conservatory measures of a military kind as are prescribed by the Council to ensure evacuation by the forces involved.

Again, given the same circumstances or, if in the event of a threat of war, special conditions, and in particular the possibilities of contact between the forces of the parties to the dispute rendering it necessary, Article III provides the Council with another method of procedure which again envisages the prescription of conservatory measures of a military kind. Under this Article the Council may fix lines which must not be passed by the land, naval or air forces of the Powers at issue. (This to apply, where necessary in order to avoid incidents, to civil aircraft), and the High Contracting Parties undertake to comply with the Council's recommendations in this matter. The lines envisaged are to be fixed, if possible, by agreement with the parties at issue, but, failing such agreement, the lines must be fixed with the consent of the party whose forces are affected. Certain stipulations govern the fixing of such lines, framed to guard against a withdrawal beyond the exterior lines of the defence organizations existing on the frontiers of the High Contracting Parties, and to guard against any disturbance to the "essential works" or communications of the party concerned. It rests with the Council to determine the period within which such lines shall be fixed. In addition, the High Contracting Parties agree to give strict orders to the commanders of their forces, if the Council so recommends, to take all necessary precautions to avoid incidents.

In accordance with the Provisions of Article IV, if the Council

thinks fit or if one of the parties at issue so requests, Commissioners may be appointed for the sole purpose of verifying
on the spot the execution of the conservatory measures of a
military character recommended by the Council under the
conditions specified in Articles II and III. Certain stipulations
govern the appointment and activities of these Commissioners.

Under Article V, if any violation of the measures defined
in Articles II and III is noted by the Council and continued
in despite of its injunctions, the Council shall consider what
means of all kinds are necessary to ensure the execution of the
General Convention. Should war break out as a consequence
of this violation, such violation shall be regarded by the High
Contracting Parties as *prima facie* evidence that the party
guilty of such violation has resorted to war within the meaning
of Article XVI of the Covenant.

Under Article VII the decisions and recommendations of
the Council envisaged in the Articles of the General Convention
are to be considered binding (except as otherwise provided in
these Articles) provided that they are concurred in by all the
other Members voting, other than the parties to the dispute;
the provisions to apply only as between the High Contracting
Parties.

It is emphasized under Article IX that the Convention must
not be interpreted as restricting the task or the powers of the
Council of the League as laid down in the Covenant, nor should
it affect the right of free passage through the Suez Canal
provided for in the Convention on the Free Navigation of the
Suez Maritime Canal (signed at Constantinople on October 29,
1888).

NOTE.—At the end of 1931 no State had signed the General
Convention.

C. OTHER PROVISIONS FOR SECURITY

1. NOTE ON ITALIAN RELATIONS WITH FRANCE AND YUGOSLAVIA

In a previous chapter the story has been told of the race between France and Italy for the establishment of a hegemony in Central Europe. The general result may be said to have left the honours with France, but there is little doubt that Italian influence remained very strong in at least one of the three Powers forming the Little Entente—Rumania.

The subsequent policy of Italy was mainly governed by her relations with France and with France's Balkan satellite, Yugoslavia. With regard to the first, Italy early took the opportunity of securing the friendship of the ex-enemy States, which she gradually welded into a very definite European *bloc*, as a counterbalance to the Little Entente. In dealing with Yugoslavia, Signor Mussolini pursued very much the same tactics as those adopted by France in regard to Germany. He proceeded to surround Yugoslavia not with a network of military alliances but with a ring of neighbouring States in which either Italian influence was paramount, or which were on terms of very good friendship with Italy.

The first steps in this policy were taken immediately after the signature of the Locarno Agreement. One of the complementary treaties to this agreement was the Italo-German Treaty of Arbitration and Conciliation of January 31, 1926, and there is good reason to believe that an offer of an alliance of a more practical nature was refused at the same time by Herr Stresemann as being alien to the spirit of Locarno.

In the following year a Treaty of Friendship, Arbitration and Conciliation with Hungary (April 5, 1927) confirmed the efforts put forward by Signor Mussolini to secure the friendship of that country.[1] With the replacement of Mgr. Seipel by Herr Schober

---

[1] Italian influence at Budapest waxed considerably in 1931, as a result of the financial supremacy of France in Europe. In return for a French loan Hungary forsook her Italian orientation.

as Austrian Federal Chancellor in September 1929 Italo-
Austrian relations improved in a marked manner. Italian
opposition to talk of an *Anschluss* became less violent and with
the sincere efforts of Rome to reach an understanding with the
German-speaking population of the Alto Adige, this cause of
dispute with Austria became less and less acute. Finally during
the visit of the Chancellor to Rome an Italo-Austrian Treaty
of Friendship, Arbitration and Conciliation was signed on
February 6, 1930.

Meantime the rivalry with France had been steadily increasing.
Rivalry in the Mediterranean and in Northern Africa, rivalry
in Central and South-eastern Europe, anti-Fascist plots in Paris,
anti-French speeches in Rome, all contributed to a state of
affairs which was startlingly brought before the public notice
at the London Naval Conference of 1930, when that body failed
to effect its primary object of a five-Power Pact through the
inability of France and Italy to compose their mutual
differences.

This clash of views, at first diplomatic in nature, was thrown
still more strongly into relief in the month of May 1930 by the
series of speeches delivered by Signor Mussolini in Leghorn,
Florence and Milan by which he later declared his intention
of "tearing the mask off a hypocritical Europe which babbles
of peace at Geneva and prepares for war everywhere."[1] The
immediate result of these speeches was to bring about the
rupture of the naval disarmament negotiations then in progress
between Paris and Rome and generally to exacerbate the relations between the two countries.

Nor were these same relations improved when on July 4, 1930
came the Italian Reply to the Briand Memorandum of May 17th
on a European Federal Union. In no way had M. Briand's
desire for a general reaffirmation of the existing European
status quo been misunderstood or underestimated in Rome, and
in the Italian Reply Signor Mussolini came into the arena for
the first time as the openly proclaimed champion of the ex-enemy

---

[1] For texts, see *Documents on International Affairs, 1930*, edited by J. W.
Wheeler-Bennett (Oxford University Press, 1931), pp. 115–118.

Revisionist States. In the view of Italy, said the Note, it was useless to speak of European solidarity until the disarmament provisions of the Peace Treaties had been loyally carried out by both sides.

"The Fascist Government consider that this development [of the organic system for peace provided by the Covenant] at the stage of international organization at which Europe has now arrived, should not consist in building up a rigid system of security, but in carrying out the definite pledges of disarmament given in the Covenant of the League of Nations by the States signatories thereto, pledges which, so long as they remain unfulfilled, threaten that very system of security so laboriously constructed."[1]

Italian support for the German disarmament policy as opposed to the French was still further evidenced when the Preparatory Disarmament Commission met for its final session in November and December 1930, and although the Italian delegates did not go as far as their German and Soviet colleagues and disown the Draft Convention, they at least gave evidence of their sympathy with the German attitude and of their lack of confidence in the value of the document which the Commission finally fathered.[2]

Though Italo-German relations suffered something of a setback in the matter of the Austro-German Customs Union in March 1931, Italian opposition to this proposal was less violent than that of France, and it is important to note that alone of the continental Powers, Italy, with Great Britain, accepted unreservedly President Hoover's offer of June 20, 1931, of a War Debt Moratorium, and put it into operation on July 1st.

It is a regrettable but nevertheless an evident truth that the post-war policy of France has resulted in driving her two most powerful territorial neighbours into each other's arms. Whether there are sufficiently strong grounds for a permanent Italo-German *entente* it is difficult to say. In Germany certainly there exists a romantic alliance with Italy of many years' standing. There is scarcely a German who does not make a visit to the

---

[1] See League Document A, 46, 1930, VII, p. 25.
[2] See above, pp. 97, etc.

Italian Lakes his first journey abroad, and the similarity of their history of union is an added bond. But whether or no this *rapprochement* would long exist if the mutual antagonism ceased to exist is uncertain. Yet it is very true to say that a common distrust of France has bound Germany and Italy in something stronger than a mere diplomatic friendship.[1]

The quarrel between Italy and Yugoslavia dates back originally to the unfortunate Pact of London of 1915, to the well-intentioned but ill-advised appeal of President Wilson to the Italian people over the heads of their delegation to the Peace Conference, and to the subsequent *bragadoccio* and heroics of Gabriele d'Annunzio at Fiume.

For present purposes, however, it is unnecessary to go further back than 1926. In the January of that year, as has already been recorded, Signor Mussolini proposed to M. Ninchitch, the Yugoslav Foreign Minister, a form of Locarno Pact for Central Europe with the particular object of preventing the *Anschluss*. M. Ninchitch agreed provided that France was a party, and on Signor Mussolini's refusal proceeded to Paris there to initial with M. Briand a Franco-Yugoslav Pact of Friendship.

The Italian reply to this move was to sign with Albania on November 27, 1926 a Treaty of Friendship and Security. Despite the Fascist declaration that the Pact emphasized the rigid respect for the independence and integrity of Albania, this new Italian move caused considerable anxiety in Europe, the general feeling being that when a great Power makes such a Treaty with a small and weak neighbour it is not a friendship but a protectorate that is established. This view was strengthened by the fact that Italian penetration of Albania had been so successful as to place the National Bank of that country completely under the control of Italy. In addition, Albania had been persuaded to accept a loan from Italy, the terms of which might be interpreted as ultimately

---

[1] The Entente between the two countries was still further strengthened during the visit of the German Chancellor and Foreign Minister to Rome and of Signor Grandi to Berlin in August and November, 1931 respectively.

leading to the entire economic subjection of the former country.

By reason of the fact that Italy controlled the "Society for the Economic Development of Albania," she exercised the sole right of building roads, bridges, etc., and in virtue of this priority in all public works and undertakings enjoyed a large share of Albania's revenues.

There is little doubt that this economic control of an impoverished and ill-populated country was greatly advantageous to Albania, but when this was accompanied by a form of political protectorate, it was regarded as an overt act against both Yugoslavia and her French patron.

In Belgrade a Cabinet crisis immediately took place and resulted in the fall of M. Ninchitch, who had always been regarded as pro-Italian in sympathy. A change of policy towards Italy was at once noticeable and relations between both countries became less friendly, this in its turn having a natural repercussion in Italo-French relations.

A natural corollary to this new Italo-Yugoslav antagonism was a strengthening of the bonds between Paris and Belgrade, and on November 11, 1927 the Franco-Yugoslav Treaty, which had been initialled in Paris the previous year, was signed and published. At once Signor Mussolini made *riposte* by signing on November 22nd with Albania the second Treaty of Tirana, this time a Military Agreement of Defensive Alliance.

The original Italo-Yugoslav dispute thus became a part of the greater game of political and diplomatic hostilities between Italy and France, and Signor Mussolini set about the dual task of forming a European *bloc* of ex-enemy Revisionist States which would act as a counter-poise to French hegemony in Central and South-eastern Europe, and at the same time creating in the Balkans an iron ring which should checkmate France's Adriatic ally.

In pursuance of this latter policy an Italo-Turkish Treaty of Neutrality, Conciliation and Judicial Settlement was signed on May 30, 1928,[1] and on September 23rd of the same year a

[1] Ratifications exchanged April 29, 1929.

Treaty of Friendship, Conciliation and Judicial Settlement with Greece.[1] But Signor Mussolini was aware that for the future peace of the Balkan Peninsula a *rapprochement* was necessary between the two Ægean Naval Powers. He, therefore, added all the weight of his influence to the negotiations already proceeding between Athens and Angora with the satisfactory result that a Treaty of Neutrality, Conciliation, Arbitration, and Friendship was signed between Greece and Turkey on October 30, 1930.

But in Italian foreign policy the *via obliqua* is as acceptable a method of approach as the *via directa*, and co-operation with certain Balkan States has added to the weight of Italian influence in that quarter. Thus the restoration of King Carol to the weary throne of Rumania was not without its Italian facet and the marriage of the King of Bulgaria to Princess Mafalda in October 1930 created a dynastic alliance between the Houses of Savoy and Coburg.

In the space available it is not possible to discuss the problem of Italy's relations with France and Yugoslavia in greater detail but merely to indicate broadly the general outlines of the respective situations—situations which will play a vastly important rôle at the Disarmament Conference.

2. THE U.S.S.R. SYSTEM OF NEUTRALITY AND NON-AGGRESSION[2]

The success of the Locarno negotiations, which, in spite of the opposition of the Nationalist Party in Germany, culminated in the signing of various Treaties in London on December 1, 1925, was a very severe blow to Soviet diplomacy. This was further aggravated by the lively disappointment felt at the defection of Germany, whose relations with the U.S.S.R. had hitherto been very friendly, and by the thought that, in spite of all M. Chicherin's efforts, Germany had been won over to the

[1] Ratifications exchanged October 1, 1929.
[2] This section is reprinted in part from an article by Mr. Stephen Heald in the *Bulletin of International News*, Vol. IV, No. 25, which in its turn was based on *Security*, pp. 163–186, 209–210.

"Capitalist" Powers. In Soviet Russia the Locarno pact was regarded as an attempt on the part of the capitalist Powers of Western Europe, directed exclusively against the U.S.S.R., to save Germany from the growing orientation of her policy towards the East, and to oppose a united front to the spread of Bolshevism. In the words of Radek, "Germany's subordination under the League of Nations constituted a step on the road to the creation of an alliance of capitalist Powers which is directed against the Soviet Union and against the East." It is not difficult, therefore, to understand why, from a very early stage of the negotiations, Moscow viewed the manœuvres of the capitalist Powers, not only with suspicion, but with a certain apprehension.

In the summer of 1925 M. Chicherin realized that his efforts to frustrate the Locarno programme of the Western Powers were likely to prove vain. Moscow was already becoming alarmed at the favourable progress of the Locarno negotiations, and it was essential for the Soviet Government to prepare some diplomatic success, which could be produced as an offset to the now practically inevitable success of the capitalist Powers. It was to meet this need that the system of the Neutrality and Non-Aggression Treaties was conceived. They were to be the counter-attraction to Locarno in Europe, and the means whereby the U.S.S.R. might prevent the extension of the influence of the capitalist Powers over the countries of the Near and Middle East. A new note was struck. Neutrality, Non-aggression and Moscow were offered as rival attractions to Arbitration, Security and Locarno. Non-aggression and a guarantee of benevolent neutrality to the victim of an unprovoked attack were thus substituted for a promise of active assistance.

This policy was adopted during 1925, and it seemed that it was destined to have an immediately favourable inception in the East, at all events, where the Mosul dispute had already embroiled Turkey with Great Britain, the most dangerous of the "Imperialist" Powers. The moment seemed favourable, and it may be an occasion for surprise that the first of the new series of treaties of neutrality and non-aggression was not concluded until December 17, 1925, and actually after the signature of the Locarno Pact. It would be natural to suppose that the conclusion of such a treaty with the U.S.S.R. before the discussion of the Mosul question at Geneva, and even before the announcement of the award, would have been an important factor in strengthening Turkey's position.

There were, however, reasons which retarded the progress of the negotiations between the U.S.S.R. and Turkey. Mutual suspicion had been aroused by rumours alleging the existence of a secret alliance between the U.S.S.R. and Italy and by the knowledge in Moscow of the *rapprochement* between Turkey and Poland, which had been followed by an exchange of military missions, and by the remembrance of the part played by Turkey during the Georgian Revolution of 1924.

It is not surprising, therefore, that up to the autumn of 1925 very little progress had been made in the negotiations for a Soviet-Turkish treaty. But in October 1925, such faint hopes as the Soviet diplomatists still cherished of the ultimate breakdown of the negotiations for the Locarno Pact were dashed by the discovery of the necessary formula of agreement, and the signature at a special conference in London on December 1, 1925 of the various treaties comprising the Pact.

In the same month Turkey also suffered a severe setback when the decision of the Permanent Court of International Justice on the Mosul case was announced, and the Council of the League of Nations accordingly made its award.

Both Moscow and Angora had suffered a severe reverse, and in their eagerness to gain some immediate diplomatic success which might compensate for their loss of prestige both countries forgot the suspicions which had previously menaced their relations, and Tewfik Rushdi Bey, the Turkish Foreign Minister, took advantage of the presence in Paris of M. Chicherin, on his Western European Tour, to make two flying visits from Geneva, where the Mosul negotiations were in full course, to the Soviet Embassy, where on December 17, 1925, they signed the first of the new Treaties of Neutrality and Non-Aggression.

It is of interest to examine the main points of this Treaty, as it served as a model for those which were subsequently concluded with Germany, Lithuania, Afghanistan and Persia. The Treaty consists of three Articles and three additional explanatory Protocols. The first Article provides for the neutrality of the one Party, if the other Party is the victim of military action by a third Power or third Powers. An annex to this Article states that the expression "military action " does not include manœuvres or military demonstrations, provided that they are not directed against the other Party. In Article II the Parties undertake not to attack one another and not to participate in hostile agreements with third Parties, which are directed against the other Party. Protocol 2 includes agreements for a financial or economic boycott under this head. The second paragraph of Article II provides for complete abstention from joining with hostile third Powers in acts directed against the other Contracting Party. Article III stated that the Treaty shall continue in force for three years, dating from the exchange of the ratifications, and shall enter at once into force. Of the two remaining Protocols, the first reserves to the Contracting Parties complete freedom of action in the sphere of foreign relations, outside the obligations contained in the Treaty, and the third represents an agreement to institute "a modus of settlement" for disputes arising between the Parties, which cannot be solved by the ordinary diplomatic channels.

The Treaty is important, not so much politically, for neither country would be called upon to attack the other and consequently it was of no great significance as a counter-blast to Locarno, but because it represented the initiation of a new policy and of a new system, which contain many interesting characteristics. One point, however, arises for which the Treaty does not clearly provide; as a matter of speculation, what would happen if either Party were the aggressor—if, for example, Turkey invaded Mosul or the U.S.S.R., Besserabia? There is no mention of such a contingency in the text of the Treaty, and M. Litvinoff felt it his duty "to state that there are no secret annexes whatever to the agreement or to the protocols," and further, that "the agreement is not directed against and does not therefore threaten any country." Neither Power, however, is a Member of the League of Nations, and, consequently, neither is bound under Article XVIII of the Covenant to register any treaties concluded by it. It is interesting to notice that the need for a clearer explanation of the question of aggression was felt in the German Treaty, and that the position, in a case where the Soviet might be the aggressor, was carefully examined in the German Note which accompanied the signature of the Soviet-German Treaty.

The successful conclusion of the Soviet-Turkish Treaty had provided the Soviet Commissariat for Foreign Affairs not only with a sorely needed diplomatic success to which it could point as a counter-blast to the success gained by the capitalist Powers at Locarno, but also with a new basis on which to found the continuity of Soviet foreign policy. The new system of treaties had been put to the test and the machinery was working smoothly. Encouraged by this success M. Chicherin set to work once more to undermine the foundations of the Locarno Pact.

The new treaties of neutrality and non-aggression were indeed ingeniously conceived, for, with the aid of a little explanation, there was nothing in them which precluded the accession of States Members of the League of Nations. Germany, Lithuania and Persia were all Members of the League, and no one of them found the signature of the neutrality treaties incompatible with its obligations under the Covenant, although each State considered it advisable to avoid the risk of any misunderstanding by accompanying its signature by a Note, in which it declared definitely that it intended to respect to the full its obligations.

The keynote which the Soviet Government wished to be struck by the new policy was neutrality and the maintenance of peace, and it was in these attractive terms that M. Litvinoff, in a commentary on the Soviet-Turkish Pact, explained the programme of his Government. "The best proof," he wrote, "of the peaceable intentions of the agreement is the fact that the Soviet Government is ready to conclude an analogous

agreement with all countries with which it has normal relations."
It is in this statement, couched in however disinterested and
peaceable terms, that the key to Soviet foreign policy is given
and its true objective revealed. This was to be the means
whereby the U.S.S.R. was to make a final bid to win back
Germany from the ranks of the capitalist Powers of Western
Europe.

Since the *rapprochement* at Rapallo in 1922, the relations
between Germany and the U.S.S.R. had been very friendly,
and the bonds of friendship had been further strengthened by
the exertions of the German Ambassador in Moscow. [In view
of these efforts to foster friendly relations, the policy which
was pursued by the Soviet Government in its handling of the
affair in the Donetz Basin and the many allegations which
were made against Germany during 1928 and subsequently
were all the more surprising.]

It was relying upon this friendship that the U.S.S.R. hoped,
by means of these treaties, if not to win back Germany completely, at least to divide her allegiance between Locarno and
Moscow, for, although all hopes of a Soviet-German Entente
seem to have been dashed to the ground by the successful
conclusion of the Locarno Pact, the U.S.S.R. was not prepared
to abandon Germany without a struggle. In the circumstances
only one policy was open to M. Chicherin—to wait in the hope
that an opportunity would present itself, when, by means of
subtle suggestion, he might be able to transform a molehill of
misunderstanding into a dividing range of dissension.

He did not have long to wait, for in April the failure of the
Locarno Powers to procure the admittance of Germany to the
League of Nations aroused such violent resentment in Germany
that, in the reaction, she was almost thrown into the arms of
Soviet Russia. In accordance with the Locarno Protocol an
extraordinary session of the Assembly had been called in March
1926, at which Germany was formally to be admitted. Unfortunately, Spain and Brazil seized the opportunity to make their
consent conditional on the offer to them of a permanent seat
on the Council of the League. Several Conferences were held,

but without avail. The Assembly broke up with Germany still waiting upon the doorstep of the League of Nations.

Such was the position at the end of March, when on the 26th the announcement of the renewal of the Polish-Rumanian Alliance of March 3, 1921 was an important contributory factor in widening the breach between Germany and the Locarno Powers. It was not surprising, then, that immediately upon the return of the German Delegation from Geneva, Herr Stresemann took steps to conclude the negotiations which had been going on intermittently with Moscow since M. Chicherin's visit to Berlin in September 1925, for the conclusion of a treaty on the model of that signed in December 1925 by the U.S.S.R. with Turkey.

The signature of the Treaty, which was concluded by Herr Stresemann and M. Krestinsky, the Soviet Ambassador in Berlin on April 24, 1926, was accompanied by a Note from the German Foreign Minister, who had been impressed by the surprise publication, owing to a regrettable leak, of an official and confidential *Questionnaire* drawn up by the Czech Foreign Office, with the necessity of making some definite statement of policy. He, therefore, devoted a great part of the Note, which accompanied the signature of the Treaty, to a clear *exposé* by which he hoped to satisfy the suspicions of the U.S.S.R., reassure the Western Powers of Germany's respect for her obligations under the Locarno Pact, and clear himself of any charge of divided allegiance. On the one hand, he had to show that the Locarno policy, by which Germany had associated herself with the Western European Powers, was not directed against the U.S.S.R., and, on the other hand, that nothing in the Treaty was incompatible or at variance with Germany's obligations to the League of Nations. He pointed out that, as the object of the League was the preservation of peace, Germany's intention to collaborate closely with the League in the work of the peaceful settlement of Europe "can constitute no obstacle to the friendly development" of Soviet-German relations. At the same time he assured the Soviet Government that should there be "any efforts within the League

contrary to the fundamental idea of peace" or any movements
with an anti-Soviet tendency, Germany would not fail to oppose
them energetically.

Having thus dealt with the general position, Herr Stresemann
went on to examine the special question of Germany's attitude,
in the event of the League Council deciding to put into operation
the sanctions provided by Articles XVI and XVII of the
Covenant against a recalcitrant State. By these Articles,
States Members are obliged to take part in a financial or
economic blockade and to contribute to the armed forces used
against an aggressor State. In this connection, Herr Stresemann
stated that the attitude of the German Government towards
the U.S.S.R. could not be adversely influenced by the loyal
observation of these obligations, for they could only come into
operation in the event of a war in which the U.S.S.R. was the
aggressor State. It will be remembered that the Treaty provides
for neutrality, only in the event of the other party being the
victim of an unprovoked attack, "in spite of its pacific attitude."

With regard to the determination of the fact of aggression
Germany as a Member of the League Council would have to
concur with the decision and, if she could not, Herr Stresemann
declared that the obligations of Article XVI would not apply.
In a case, however, where the U.S.S.R. was clearly the aggressor
State and not the victim of an unprovoked attack, Germany
would not be bound by the Treaty (as the conditions of
neutrality would not have been fulfilled), but by her obligations
under the Covenant to take part in the sanctions against an
aggressor State. In such a case her action would be based on
the Note of December 1, 1925, by which the Locarno Powers
agreed to pledge themselves to "co-operate loyally and effectively" in resistance to any act of aggression, each to an extent
which was compatible with its military situation and which
took into consideration its geographical position.

This *exposé* of the German point of view cleared up the
question which had been left unanswered in the Soviet-Turkish
Treaty. The addition of the qualifying phrase "in spite of its
pacific attitude" in the Soviet-German Treaty, which makes

neutrality binding only if the other Party is the victim of an unprovoked attack, constitutes an important advance and a valuable addition to the basic idea of the neutrality and non-aggression treaties.

NEGOTIATIONS WITH THE BALTIC STATES

In March 1926, undismayed by the failure of the conferences in 1922, and by the rebuffs with which Poland had met his proposal of a pact of non-aggression in 1924 and 1925,[1] M. Chicherin judged that the time was ripe to renew proposals for a treaty of guarantee to the other and more friendly disposed members of the Baltic *bloc*, Lithuania, Finland, Latvia and Estonia, and a joint Note was despatched at the end of the month to Latvia and Estonia, and identic Notes to Lithuania and Finland. In an interesting statement on Soviet foreign relations, at the end of April 1926, M. Litvinoff declared that good relations with Latvia and Estonia were important to the U.S.S.R., both economically, because they were commercial and transit countries, and politically, because the Soviet was desirous of reaching "a lasting friendship capable of guaranteeing our frontiers with these countries." "Foreign influences," he continued, "have hampered this up to the present. . . ." He went on to say that Poland's unauthorized insistence on speaking in the name of the other States and managing their foreign relations had obstructed all "our efforts to arrive at a full understanding." In conclusion he noted, significantly, "the particularly friendly relations with Lithuania," and considered "that the interests of general peace in Eastern Europe would be greatly promoted by a more definite settlement of our relations with Lithuania." He noted also that the "relations with Finland are steadily improving and becoming closer." It is significant that, with the widening of the breach between Poland and the Baltic States, their relations with the U.S.S.R., for the time, steadily improved.

To the identic Notes presented by the Soviet Government, the Latvian and Estonian Foreign Ministers, after a consulta-

[1] See *urity Sec*, pp. 81–87, 175–176.

tion (in accordance with the terms of the Latvian-Estonian Treaty of November 1, 1923) returned a joint reply, with which Finland later associated herself, and in which, among other things, they insisted on the abandonment of propaganda by the U.S.S.R. It was on this rock that the Moscow Disarmament Conference of 1922 had foundered, when the Soviet Government refused to agree to "moral disarmament."

M. Chicherin replied by submitting to the States a Draft Treaty, to which they responded by a reiteration of their insistence upon all the points raised in their Note, and by a demand for a joint preparatory commission to discuss the details of the Treaty. This demand was rejected out of hand by the U.S.S.R. on the ground that such a commission would be "open to foreign influences."

Meanwhile the original Note of the Soviet Government had met with an immediate reaction on the part of Lithuania, and negotiations had been instituted on the basis of the Soviet Draft Treaty. Lithuania was inclined favourably to separate negotiations not only by reason of her long-standing jealousy of Poland, which had been embittered by the Vilna dispute,[1] but also by the hope of being able to obtain certain political concessions. M. Chicherin, therefore, suitably baited his line with the fly in the ointment by promising to recognize the right of Lithuania to Vilna, in return for an undertaking on the part of Lithuania not to enter a Baltic Coalition.

The anxiety of the Baltic States was inevitably aroused by the advanced stage of these negotiations, and in a final attempt to discover the real intentions of the Soviet Government and prevent, if possible, the imminent defection of Lithuania, the three States decided, as an earnest of sincerity, to withdraw their insistence on the joint preparatory commission. But while the U.S.S.R. regarded the treaty as a political manoeuvre, the Baltic States looked upon it as a juridical instrument intended to enforce the strict observance of the rules of non-aggression. An agreement was consequently delayed.

[1] On October 9, 1920 Polish troops under General Zeligowski seized Vilna. In March, 1921 the Conference of Ambassadors awarded the town to Poland, a decision never accepted by Lithuania.

Every effort made by the Baltic States to prevent the defection of Lithuania proved vain. The negotiations were too far advanced. Even a grudging expression on the part of Poland of her willingness for a diplomatic *rapprochement* with Lithuania and her readiness to receive a draft of a Soviet-Polish Treaty of Non-Aggression could not delay the final negotiations or the signature by MM. Chicherin and Slezewicius in Moscow on September 28, 1926 of a Treaty of Neutrality and Non-Aggression on the lines of that already concluded with Germany.

It is an interesting fact that the Voldemaras Administration which came into power on December 17, 1926 by a *coup d'état*, pledged to an anti-Communist policy, saw no reason to abrogate the Treaty, which is operative for a period of five years.

In January 1927, negotiations for a pact of non-aggression were reopened by the Soviet Government with the new Latvian Socialist Administration, and by March the prospects of reaching some agreement had improved considerably. M. Cielens, the Latvian Minister for Foreign Affairs, after consultation with the Estonian Foreign Minister, drafted certain counter-proposals to the Soviet provisions. The Draft Soviet-Latvian Pact, unlike the previous models of non-aggression treaties, was drawn up in two sections, the first dealing with neutrality, non-aggression and non-participation in hostile coalitions, and the second containing provisions for the pacific settlement of disputes. The two sections were to be ratified simultaneously. The outcome of the discussions was favourable, and when the Soviet representative, M. Aralov, left on March 9th agreement had been reached on most of the points in the first section of the Treaty, and these he had initialled with M. Cielens, on behalf of their respective Governments. M. Cielens, however, declared at the time that he desired to be satisfied more fully by the U.S.S.R. with regard to Latvia's obligations under the Covenant, and that he still hoped that it would be possible to co-ordinate Soviet-Latvian relations with Finland and Estonia.

In spite of the fact that M. Cielens discussed with the Estonian Foreign Minister the subject of the Soviet Draft Non-Aggression Treaty in February and March 1927, and therefore fulfilled his obligations under the Latvian-Estonian Treaty of November 1, 1923, the initialling of the Non-Aggression Pact and the signature of a Commercial Treaty in June 1927 were significant, both because it was feared they might lead to the economic and political dependence of Latvia on the U.S.S.R. and because they marked not only the second defection from the Baltic *bloc*, and the policy of joint negotiations with the U.S.S.R. adopted at the Helsingfors Conference in 1921, but also, in spite of the assurances of M. Cielens, the cooling of Latvian-Estonian relations. The Treaty of Non-Aggression, however, was never signed.

In addition to the Non-Aggression Treaties, it is interesting to note the conclusion of Agreements laying down the procedure to be followed for the settlement of frontier disputes between Poland and the U.S.S.R. on August 3, 1925, between Latvia and the U.S.S.R. on July 19, 1926, and between Estonia and the U.S.S.R. on August 8, 1927. Though these agreements are, perhaps, of minor significance politically, they provide a valuable mode of procedure for the pacific settlement of minor disputes of almost daily occurrence, and thus tend to remove elements of friction between the countries concerned.

NEUTRALITY AND NON-AGGRESSION IN THE MIDDLE EAST

The success of the Soviet-Turkish Treaty of December 17, 1925 induced in the Soviet Commissariat for Foreign Affairs a natural desire to extend the system to include the countries of the Near East and thus to aim another blow at British "Imperialism" in Iraq and India. On February 26, 1921 the U.S.S.R. had concluded a Treaty of recognition and friendship with Persia, which, among other things, provided for the diplomatic settlement of all disputes arising between the two countries, and, on February 28, 1921, a similar Treaty with Afghanistan, which contained a mutual recognition of independence.

It was on this basis of friendship that M. Chicherin planned to found an alliance of the States of the Near East as a bulwark

to the U.S.S.R. and a protection to them against the encroach-
ment and penetration of the "Imperialist" Powers, and in
opposition to the League of Nations. With this object in view,
he was successful in concluding with Afghanistan on August 31,
1926, at Paghman a Treaty of Neutrality and Non-Aggression,
much on the lines of the treaties already signed, based upon
and extending the Treaty of February 28, 1921.

So far, M. Chicherin's diplomacy in the Near East had been
crowned with success, for already, on April 22, 1926, Turkey
under his influence had signed a Treaty of Friendship and
Neutrality[1] with Persia. The next move was to approach Persia
with the offer of a similar treaty with the U.S.S.R. on the basis
of the Treaty of February 26, 1921. This suggestion was received
favourably at Teheran, and the negotiations culminated successfully in the signature, on October 1, 1927, of the Soviet-Persian
Pact of Guarantee, Neutrality and Non-Aggression, thus raising
the number of Soviet Non-Aggression Treaties to five. A Note
which accompanied the signature of the Treaty declared that
the Persian Government intended to respect to the full its
obligations as a member of the League of Nations.

The system of treaties as envisaged by Moscow was con-
summated by the signature on November 28, 1927 of the
Afghan-Persian Pact of Neutrality and Non-Aggression, and on
May 25, 1928, of the Turko-Afghan Treaty of Friendship and
Security. In this way the U.S.S.R. has concluded vertical pacts
with Turkey, Afghanistan and Persia and has completed the
pattern, in accordance with M. Chicherin's plans, by influencing
the signature of the horizontal treaties between Turkey and
Persia, Persia and Afghanistan, and Afghanistan and Turkey.
M. Chicherin, therefore, seems, even if only in theory, to have
achieved his object of lining up the Near East in a united

---

[1] The Treaty of Friendship and Neutrality of April 1926 was supplemented
on June 15, 1928, by the signature of a special agreement consisting of two
Articles. In the first the Parties agreed that in case either of them was the
object of a hostile attack, the other would use "all its efforts to remedy the
situation." If these failed and war should break out, the two Parties should
examine the situation anew with the object of finding "a solution conformable
to their superior interests." In the second, the Parties agreed to regulate as
soon as possible the conditions of their close co-operation in economic matters.

front against Western "Imperialism," with the Soviet guarding the rear, herself securely protected in the event of war with an "Imperialist" Power by a cordon of neutral States.

THE BASIS OF THE TREATIES

The basis of all the Soviet treaties of neutrality and non-aggression is, in general outline, the same. The Soviet-Turkish Treaty of December 17, 1925, with its provisions for neutrality, non-aggression and non-participation in hostile agreements, provided the model on which the subsequent treaties were moulded. There are, however, interesting and important additions to be noticed, such as the addition in the German and Lithuanian treaties of the qualifying phrase "in spite of its pacific attitude," which made neutrality conditional upon the other party being the victim of an unprovoked attack. The importance of this qualification lies in the fact that on it hinges the question of the obligations under the Covenant of Germany and Lithuania, who have concluded these treaties with the U.S.S.R. As Herr Stresemann pointed out, if the Soviet should be proved to be the aggressor State, then the Article in the Treaty imposing neutrality upon Germany does not operate, and Germany can fulfil her obligations to the League. Since unanimity of opinion in the Council of the League is necessary before recourse can be had to the application of sanctions, such action can only be taken with the concurrence of Germany. If, therefore, in the opinion of Germany, the Soviet Government is not guilty of aggression and Germany, therefore, does not concur with the decision of the other Members of the League Council to resort to the sanctions, the Article of the Covenant does not become operative and the provision of neutrality is not violated by her.

In the fifth Article of the Soviet-Lithuanian and Soviet-Persian Treaties and in Article IV of the Soviet-Afghan Treaty it is interesting to notice that an agreement to submit disputes to pacific procedure is incorporated in the text of the Treaty. A similar agreement appeared in Protocol 3 of the Soviet-

Turkish Treaty, and in the Notes which were exchanged at the time of the signature of the German Treaty.[1]

Another addition appears in Articles III and IV respectively of the Soviet-Afghan and Soviet-Persian Treaties, which contain an engagement not to interfere in the domestic affairs of the other Party and the obligation to prohibit, each in its own territory, any activity directed against the security, sovereignty and territorial integrity of the other Party. Further, Persia and Afghanistan undertook not to permit any movement organized by hostile and "Imperialist" Powers against the Soviet and to prevent the transport through their territory of troops or stores destined for use against the Soviet. These conditions are reciprocally binding on the U.S.S.R. In this connection it is perhaps interesting to notice the extension of this obligation in the treaties signed by Persia with Turkey and Afghanistan in April 1926 and November 1927 wherein the neutral Party is bound to defend its neutrality, if necessary by force of arms. The signature of these treaties, unlike the case of the Soviet-Persian Treaty, was not accompanied by any declaration on the part of Persia concerning her desire to respect her obligations to the League of Nations. This omission raises the whole question as to whether a State Member of the League can, by concluding a treaty with a non-member, contract obligations which are at variance with its undertakings under the Covenant. If the point is pressed it becomes evident that, however sincere a State may be, the signature of the Articles making abstention from participation in hostile coalitions and boycotts binding may, in given circumstances, be in direct contravention of a State Member's obligations under Article XVI of the Covenant. The astute way in which the German Foreign Minister was able to reconcile, sincerely, Germany's obligations to the Treaty and the Covenant is a great tribute to the ingenuity of those who devised this system of treaties.

Be it supposed that the Soviet Government is genuinely desirous of peace and friendly relations with her neighbours and

[1] A Treaty of Conciliation was signed between the U.S.S.R. and Germany on January 25, 1929.

is not meditating any acts of aggression, then there is nothing in the treaties really contrary or antagonistic to the Covenant or Locarno. The whole point, and indeed, the unique feature of the treaties, is the provision of neutrality and the consequent avoidance of the spreading of military action and the entanglement in a general conflict of States which are innocent of the initial causes of it. Unlike the Covenant which, *in extremis*, provides certain sanctions against an aggressor State, it seeks to localize a dispute and to confine it to the two original disputants, while providing for an attitude of benevolent neutrality towards the other Party, should it be the victim of an unprovoked attack.

The system is not without certain merits, and if the League of Nations, instead of the U.S.S.R., had been responsible for its conception and initiation, it is hard to believe that it would not have been welcomed as advancing the cause of peace and contributing to the security of Europe. The non-aggression Articles have many advantages, and it is interesting to recall that M. Politis, the *rapporteur* on Security, recommended in his memorandum to the Security Committee on February 10, 1928 the conclusion of regional pacts of non-aggression, agreements for the pacific settlement of disputes and mutual assistance or non-aggression only, and that model treaties of non-aggression, both bilateral and collective, were drawn up by the Committee and approved by the Ninth Assembly.

Conforming to this recommendation, in some of its points, three Pacts were signed during the same year; namely, a Treaty of Neutrality, Non-Aggression and Arbitration between Greece and Rumania on March 12th, a Treaty of Neutrality, Conciliation and Judicial Settlement between Italy and Turkey on May 30th, and a Treaty of Friendship, Neutrality, Conciliation and Judicial Settlement between Italy and Greece on September 23, 1928.[1] A similar treaty was concluded between Italy and Spain on August 7, 1926.

[1] Similar treaties have also been concluded between Turkey and Hungary, January 5, 1929; Turkey and Bulgaria, March 6, 1929; and Turkey and Greece, October 30, 1930.

All the Soviet Neutrality Treaties contain a Non-Aggression clause, and all except the German Treaty[1] and the Treaty between Turkey and Afghanistan include an Agreement to submit disputes to pacific procedure.

But it is not so much the letter of the text as the spirit of the interpretation that is the important consideration. It has been said that treaties are made to be evaded. The question arises as to whether the Soviet Government is really sincere, or whether the initiation of this system of treaties was merely an attempt to break up the Locarno Agreement of Western Europe by the establishment of a rival system of alliances in Eastern Europe and the Near East. Making allowances for a natural prejudice against, and not unfounded suspicions of Soviet policy, it is sometimes rather difficult to regard the Soviet system in the light of a sincere and genuine move for peace and security, though account must be taken of the signature of the Litvinoff Protocol. It is clear that the Soviet Government does not want war, at least not yet, and that it desires peace the better to carry on trade development and to spread its propaganda throughout the world. The refusal by the Soviet Government to renounce propaganda as an instrument of policy has been in each case the cause of the breakdown of the disarmament and security negotiations between the U.S.S.R. and the Baltic States. It appears that the non-aggression treaties are nothing more than a pacific gesture, which is contemporaneous with the declaration of the "breathing-space" in the U.S.S.R. intended to serve as a cloak to the Soviet's real intentions in the future, and the instrument of the re-establishment of the prosperity of Soviet trade. They have also been the means by which the U.S.S.R. has been successful in concluding treaties with its neighbours, States Members and non-members of the League alike, and surrounding itself against the danger of attack with a *cordon sanitaire* of neutral States, which cannot be used as a base of operations against Soviet territory. If such be the case, the addition in the German and subsequent treaties of the qualifying phrase "in spite of

---

[1] A Conciliation Treaty was, however, signed on January 25, 1929.

its pacific attitude," assumes a greater significance, and the obstruction raised by the Soviet's refusal at Moscow, in December 1922, to consider moral disarmament and the renunciation of propaganda reveals itself as the real menace to the establishment of friendly relations between Moscow and the Western Powers.

3. ANALYSIS OF NEUTRALITY AND NON-AGGRESSION TREATIES

I. U.S.S.R. AND TURKEY. 17th December, 1925

1. Neutrality.
2. Non-aggression and non-participation in hostile coalitions.
3. Duration—3 years.
   Prolonged automatically each time for one year if not denounced.

> (Protocols provided for liberty of international relations, outside the obligations of the Treaty, and for pacific settlement of differences.)

On December 17, 1929, a Protocol was signed in Angora by Karakhan and Tewfik Rushdi Bey renewing the Treaty for two years. Unless denounced six months before the expiration of this period it will automatically remain in force for another year. By the second Article of the Protocol the two Contracting Parties declared that they have not concluded any agreements, other than those published, with States contiguous by land or sea to the other Contracting Party. Further the two Contracting Parties undertake not to enter into any negotiations for the conclusion of political agreements with States contiguous by land or sea to the other Party without notifying the latter, nor shall they conclude any such agreements without the consent of the other Party. It is, however, understood that instruments aiming at the establishment or maintenance of normal relations with such contiguous States, and which are made public, are not subject to the above stipulation.

The final Article states that the present Protocol is an extension of the Treaty of Friendship and Neutrality and forms an integral part of it, remaining valid as long as the Treaty remains in force.

II. U.S.S.R. AND GERMANY. *24th April*, 1926

1. Treaty of Rapallo the basis. Still in force.
2. Neutrality, if other victim of unprovoked attack ("in spite of its pacific attitude").
3. Non-participation in hostile coalitions, military, financial or economic, boycotts or blockades.
4. Duration—5 years.
   Prolonged automatically one year if not denounced.

   (Note attached *re* League of Nations obligations and pacific settlement of differences.)

On June 24, 1931, in Moscow, the German Ambassador, Herr von Dicksen and M. Krestinsky, Assistant Foreign Commissar, signed a Protocol renewing the Soviet-German Treaty of 1926, (expiring on June 30, 1931). The Protocol contained and expressed the intention of the two Governments by prolonging the Treaty "to continue the friendly relations existing between the German Reich and the U.S.S.R., to foster collaboration which is in the interest of both countries, and at the same time to contribute to the assurance of general peace."

While the text of the original treaty remains unchanged, the term of the treaty now becomes indefinite in that after June 30, 1933 it may be denounced at one year's notice. and will remain in force until so denounced. The only other new point is that the Treaty of Conciliation between the two countries signed on January 25, 1929 is made to hinge directly on the Pact and will remain in force so long as the Pact remains in operation.

III. U.S.S.R. AND LITHUANIA. *28th September*, 1926

1. Treaty of 12th July 1920 the basis. Still in force.
2. Mutual recognition of territorial integrity as defined in above treaty (i.e. Vilna to Lithuania).
3. Non-aggression.
   Neutrality—if other victim of unprovoked attack ("in spite of its pacific attitude").
4. Non-participation in hostile coalitions.
5. Pacific settlement of disputes (which cannot be settled by ordinary diplomatic channels) by commission of arbitration. Special convention attached.
7. Duration—5 years. Renewed automatically one year if not denounced.

   (Note attached *re* League of Nations obligations.)

On May 7, 1931, MM. Litvinov and Baltrusaitis (Lithuanian Minister in Moscow) signed in Moscow a Protocol renewing the Treaty of 1926 for five years.

IV. U.S.S.R. AND AFGHANISTAN. 31st *August*, 1926

1. Neutrality.
2. Non-aggression and non-participation in hostile coalitions.
3. Non-interference in matters of domestic interest.
   Prohibition of activity (in own territory) directed against the other.
4. Procedure for settlement of differences (which cannot be settled by diplomatic channels).
5. Liberty of international relations outside obligations of the treaty.
6. Duration—3 years.

At Kabul on June 24, 1931, a Treaty of Neutrality, Non-Aggression and Non-Participation in hostile coalitions was signed, replacing the Treaty of 1926 which expired on April 10, 1931. The new Treaty with one or two insignificant amendments is the same as the Treaty of 1926.

V. U.S.S.R. AND PERSIA. 1st *October*, 1927

1. Convention of 26th February 1921 the basis.
2. Non-aggression.
   Neutrality absolute (not to be violated by attacked party regardless of advantages).
3. Non-participation in hostile coalitions, boycotts or blockades.
4. Non-interference in domestic affairs of the other. (Article V. February 26th, 1921.)
   Prohibition of hostile activity by nationals, or by those who have seized territory as a base versus the other.
   Prohibition of enrolment of forces, or transport of munitions versus the other.
5. Pacific settlement of differences (which cannot be settled by diplomatic channels).
6. Liberty of international relations outside these obligations.
7. Duration—3 years. Prolonged automatically one year if not denounced.

(Note attached *re* League of Nations obligations.)

VI. PERSIA AND TURKEY. *22nd April*, 1926

2. Neutrality.
3. Non-aggression.
   *Non-participation in hostile coalitions or boycotts.
4. Neutrality shall be defended by arms if violated.
5. Prohibition of all propaganda and activities (in own territory) against other party.
6. Collective or separate measures for the preservation of tranquillity on frontiers.
8. Procedure for pacific settlement of disputes (which cannot be settled by ordinary diplomatic channels).
9. Full liberty of international relations outside obligations of treaty.
10. Duration—5 years.

> * (No mention of Persia's obligations under Covenant.)

VII. PERSIA AND AFGHANISTAN. *8th November*, 1927

2. Neutrality, absolute.
   Non-aggression.
*3. Non-participation (active or passive) in hostile coalitions, agreements or movements, blockades or boycotts.
4. Neutrality shall be defended by arms if violated.
6. Pacific settlement of differences (which cannot be settled by diplomatic channels) (one national to be appointed from each party—in the event of deadlock a neutral to be elected by common consent whose decision shall be binding).
7. Full liberty of international relations outside obligations of the treaty.
8. Duration—6 years.

> * (No mention is made of Persia's obligations under the Covenant.)

VIII. AFGHANISTAN AND TURKEY. *25th May*, 1928

2. (Neutrality) Promise to use good offices to prevent a conflict between other party and a third party or parties.
3. Non-participation in hostile coalitions.
4 & 5. { Co-operation in re-establishment, progress and development.
6. Reciprocal most-favoured-nation treatment, as regards residence and commerce.
7. Full liberty of international relations outside obligations of the treaty.
9. Duration of Articles (except Art. I)—10 years.

CHAPTER V

THE YEAR 1931

1. Europe in Turmoil (January–August)

It was confidently hoped at its outset that the year 1931 would provide a period of progressive development and preparation towards the great moment when the general Disarmament Conference should convene on February 2, 1932. In effect, however, it would be difficult to find a year in which have occurred more events calculated to render sterile the efforts of such a gathering.

Almost from the beginning of the year there began a series of events all tending towards the aggravation rather than the amelioration of the European situation, until in the autumn a concatenation of circumstances had placed France in a position in which, both from a military and a financial view-point, she could virtually dictate to the rest of Europe. Indeed, even by the summer, the idea of disarmament had been forced into the background of public interests by the more pressing matter of the general economic and financial crisis, which in the course of a few short weeks brought Germany, Austria and Hungary to the brink of bankruptcy, forced Great Britain to abandon the Gold Standard, and involved the £ sterling in a fight for existence such as it had never previously experienced.

Early in 1931 it became evident that the result of German extravagance in State and Municipal Works and Social Insurance, to which the Agent-General for Reparations had called attention in his Reports,[1] taken in conjunction with the effect of the world-wide economic depression, would render Germany unable to meet her reparation obligations and would necessitate a revision of the Young Plan Agreements reached at The Hague in the previous year. A moratorium from her debts and the obtaining of credits or a long-term loan were essential for the

See *Reparations*, pp. 65–66.

preservation of the economic life of Germany, and it was therefore a singularly unpropitious moment to throw a bomb-shell into the camp of those who alone could grant her these necessities.

On March 19, 1931 there was signed and published in Vienna an Austro-German Protocol for the establishment of a Customs Union. It embodied proposals for an Agreement between the two countries under which a single Customs Law and a single Customs Tariff would be put into force in their territory and in accordance with which no Customs duty on imports or exports would be levied on exchanges of goods between them.

The effect on Europe of the announcement of this action was symptomatic of the very real feeling of insecurity lying dormant therein, and it is difficult to over-emphasize the lack of wisdom displayed by the German Foreign Office in taking such a step. The idea of such a Customs Union revived not only the old bogy of the *Anschluss* to terrify the Little Entente but also rekindled in French minds the fear of German economic superiority. At the same time it alienated from Germany a measure of Italian sympathy.

The reaction on the disarmament situation was disastrous. The French Government took the opportunity to break off the naval conversations with Italy[1] on March 28th, and on April 10th the President of the Republic delivered a speech at Nice, the more important because of the rarity of M. Doumergue's political utterances. After reproaching Germany for her latest step, which, the French Government claimed, had taken them completely by surprise, the President struck a note of warning in the matter of disarmament which was maintained in all subsequent French announcements on this subject. "So long as the League of Nations—to which she (France) is so loyally attached—has not at its disposal a military force sufficient to enforce the execution of its decisions on all not willing to accept them voluntarily, she must keep vigilant watch and ward and rely to a large extent upon herself. . . . A country like ours, which has been taught by bitter experience the cruel surprises

[1] See above, p. 229.

to which it may be exposed, must not, so long as no powerful international force has been set on foot, allow itself to reduce its own forces below the level demanded by the needs of the security and integrity of the Mother-country and the Colonies."[1]

The situation was ascerbated rather than palliated by the statement of the German Government that they were prepared to conclude similar Customs agreements with any other country who might wish to do so. In this suggestion the French at once saw a challenge to the plans put forward in M. Briand's European Federation Movement.

So strained did the European situation become, that the advisability of postponing the Disarmament Conference was debated in the English press and was even discussed in official circles.

At the request of the British Government, the question of the Customs Union was placed on the Agenda of the May Session of the Council, on the ground that it might be found to be contrary to the stipulations of certain international instruments, namely, Article LXXXVIII of the Treaty of St. Germain and Protocol No. 1 signed at Geneva on October 4, 1922.[2] On the motion of the British representative the question of the legality of the proposed Austro-German Customs Union was referred to the Permanent Court of International Justice for an advisory opinion, it being understood that there would be no further negotiations until the Court had given its opinion (May 19, 1931).[3]

[1] The hint contained in this speech that France would demand as part of the price of her disarmament the revival in some form of the security of the Geneva Protocol of 1924 became stronger in subsequent speeches as the year grew older and the date of the Conference approached.
[2] Article LXXXVIII of the Treaty of St. Germain (corresponding to Article LXXX of the Treaty of Versailles) declares that the independence of Austria is inalienable, otherwise than with the consent of the Council of the League, and Austria undertakes to abstain from any act which might, directly or indirectly, compromise her independence. The Protocol of October 4, 1922 was the instrument under which Austria was accorded a loan under the auspices of the League to assist in her financial reconstruction. It included an obligation undertaken by Austria not to enter into any negotiations which might, directly or indirectly, compromise her independence, and, further, not to accord to any State a special régime or exclusive advantage calculated to threaten that independence.
[3] For details of the proposed Austro-German *Zollunion* and its results, see *Bulletin of International News*, Vol. VII, No. 21 (April 9, 1931), and No. 25 (June 4, 1931).

A further series of events occurring almost at the same time did little to improve the situation. Towards the end of April it became known that the first of the German 10,000-ton "pocket-battleships," constructed within the scope allowed by the Treaty of Versailles, was nearing the moment of launching, and it was understood that the German naval architects had succeeded in creating a war vessel which was superior in every way to anything in its own class. It could sink anything that could catch it and could escape from anything that could sink it.[1]

Nowhere were the possibilities of this new craft more appreciated than in Paris, where it was realized that, if Germany built up to the full naval strength allowed her by the Treaty, she would, in the event of the General Disarmament Conference abolishing capital ships, become once more a first-class naval Power on a scale very much superior to that of France. The French Reply to this new potential threat was contained in the Naval Budget presented to the Chamber on May 7th, wherein provision was made for a battleship of 23,000 tons. The report on the building programme, issued on June 11th, showed that whereas the previous apportionment had been 70 per cent. of light vessels and 30 per cent. of submarines, the new programme was divided into 60 per cent. of battleships, 40 per cent of light vessels and no submarines. The necessity for this change was attributed to the construction of the *Deutschland*.[2]

The debate which followed the presentation of this report disclosed in the Chamber an unexpectedly friendly attitude

Writing in 1930 on the significance of this vessel, the author said that, "Stimulated by this restriction (Article CXC of the Treaty of Versailles), the German naval architects have designed a 'pocket-battleship,' which, if its theoretical merits are borne out in practice, threatens to revolutionize naval construction and upset the existing balance of naval strength." See *Reparations*, p. 22.

[2] The *Deutschland* was launched at Kiel on May 19th in the presence of President von Hindenburg and the Imperial Chancellor, Dr. Brüning. The circumstances of the actual launching and christening were such as might interest the superstitious reader. At the moment when the Chancellor had reached in his speech a passage containing the words "Disarmament . . . League of Nations" . . . the vessel was inadvertently allowed to slide prematurely from the stocks into the water, leaving the President grasping an unbroken bottle of champagne and the Chancellor with his peroration in mid-air. "Like Germany, she was so tired of phrases," commented an onlooker. The ceremony of christening was performed later from a launch.

towards the policy of disarmament. The full consequences of the projected construction of a 23,000-ton battleship and its probable effect on the construction programme of other naval Powers were fully debated and from more than one quarter came the opinion that such an action on the eve of the Disarmament Conference would be absurd and out of keeping with the spirit of that gathering. On June 18th, therefore, the Chamber passed the budget with a cut of more than 50 per cent. (£4 million instead of £8,799,680) and agreed to refer back the appropriation for the new battleship for further study.

This conciliatory gesture on the part of the Lower House was, however, offset by the action of the Senate, which, on July 2nd (in the midst of the Franco-American negotiations for the adoption of the Hoover proposal), rejected the modified Naval Budget, accepted a motion calling on the Government for the immediate laying down "of a cruiser designed to reply to the construction of the *Deutschland*," and two days later passed an additional appropriation of some £20 million to complete the chain of fortifications on the eastern frontier, a project on which nearly £11½ million had already been spent.

To return now to Germany, where the financial and economic situation had rapidly worsened. No longer was it a question of *will* Germany declare a moratorium, but rather of *when* will a moratorium be declared. The Chancellor and the Foreign Minister were due in England for a conference early in June, and it was felt that, if possible, no irrevocable step should be taken until after this meeting.[1]

Drs. Brüning and Curtius visited England from June 5th to 9th and conferred frankly and freely with Mr. MacDonald and Mr. Arthur Henderson at Chequers. The main advantage of this Conference was that for the first time the German statesmen

[1] The Chequers Conference marked the inauguration of a series of similar meetings between the Chief Ministers of the Great Powers. The German Minister paid subsequent visits to Paris and Rome in July and August, while the British Prime Minister and Foreign Secretary went to Berlin at the end of July. The French Premier and Foreign Minister visited Berlin and Rome in September and October, and in the latter month M. Laval went to confer with President Hoover in Washington. The United States Secretaries of the Treasury and of State were in Europe throughout the summer and conferred with their colleagues in various capitals.

were enabled to explain personally to their British "opposite numbers" the full gravity of their position.[1]

At the same moment the German Government in Berlin issued a new Emergency Decree—the third since July 1930—imposing heavy increased taxation and stringent cuts in salaries and social insurance. This was accompanied by a Manifesto to the Nation signed by President von Hindenburg, designed alike for internal and external consumption, and containing a warning to the world at large that Germany had reached her ultimate capacity to pay:

"We have made every effort to fulfil obligations resulting from a lost war. We have, too, made use of foreign help for this purpose to a large extent. That is no longer possible. The mobilization of the last forces and reserves of all sections of the population gives the German Government the right, and renders it its duty to its own people, to declare to the world: The limit of the privations which we can impose on our nation has been reached! The assumptions upon which the New [Young] Plan was based have been proved erroneous by the course taken by world developments. The alleviation which it was the intention of all concerned that the New Plan should bring to the German nation, and which at first it gave promise of doing, has not been brought by it. It is clear to the Government that the economic and financial situation of the Reich, which is menaced in the extreme, inevitably compels the relief of Germany from the intolerable reparation obligations. The economic recovery of the world is also involved."[2]

It was confidently hoped and believed in Germany that, as a result of the Chequers Conversations, a moratorium would be declared, and it therefore caused the greatest disappointment that, on his return to Berlin, the Chancellor made no statement to this effect. As a result there occurred a political crisis which in its turn so affected foreign confidence in German credit as to occasion very considerable withdrawals of gold. It was estimated that the political uncertainties of June 10th–19th cost the Reichsbank a milliard marks and it seemed certain that a financial crash in Germany was inevitable.

Then on the morning of Sunday, June 21st, appeared those *Extrablätter* containing the welcome news of President Hoover's

[1] The Chequers Conference also met under the shadow of the recent collapse of the important Austrian banking house, the Kreditanstalt.
[2] See *Bulletin of International News*, Vol. VII, No. 26 (June 18, 1931).

proposal for a "War-debt Holiday" and the clouds lifted almost visibly from the German horizon.[1]

In effect Mr. Hoover proposed "the postponement during one year of all payments on inter-Governmental debts, reparations and relief debts, both principal and interest . . ." and gave a lead in that, "subject to confirmation by Congress, the American Government will postpone all payments upon debts of foreign Governments to the American Government, payable during the fiscal year beginning July next, conditional on a like postponement for one year of all payments on inter-Governmental debts owing to the important creditor-Powers."

Great Britain and the Dominions,[2] Italy and Japan gave immediate approval and adhesion to this proposal, but France demurred, being anxious to secure the guarantee of the continuance of the unconditional annuities under the Young Plan and of the return into operation of the full Plan at the conclusion of the Hoover Year. The essential value of the Hoover Proposal clearly lay in its psychological effect, and speedy action was necessary if the full benefit was to be derived from the offer.

For this reason it was the more regrettable that the Franco-American negotiations in Paris relative to the French adherence to the Hoover Plan should have dragged on until July 5th, by which time developments in Germany had so seriously affected that country's financial condition that, within the space of a few days, the problem Mr. Hoover's proposal was intended to solve reappeared in a form even more acute than before.[3]

---

[1] The author was in Berlin and Bremen during these eventful June days, and was greatly impressed by the psychological effect of the announcement of the Hoover Plan. Equally impressive was the return of despair during the prolongation of the subsequent Franco-American negotiations in Paris. It was felt that if the Plan was to have its intended beneficial effect its operation must be immediate, and as the negotiations dragged on (until July 6th) so proportionately did the atmosphere of despair descend once more upon Germany, the more intensified by reason of its brief alleviation.

[2] Great Britain's loss under the Hoover Plan has been estimated by Mr. Snowden at approximately £11 million.

[3] It is obviously impossible in a few lines to do anything but convey the barest outline of the important events of June and July 1931. The full story of the Hoover Proposal and the subsequent Franco-American negotiations is to be found in the *Bulletin of International News*, Vol. VIII, No. 1 (July 2, 1931) and No. 2 (July 16, 1931).

The delay in putting the Hoover Plan into operation resulted in Germany in an increased loss of confidence in the mark and an accentuated flight of capital abroad. The emergency measures taken by the Government failed to have an immediate effect, and an aerial dash by Dr. Luther, President of the Reichsbank, to London and Paris on July 8th–9th, in an attempt to gain further credits abroad, though a complete and signal failure, served to re-emphasize the necessity of further and immediate action.[1]

It was at this moment that a rather more sinister note crept into the course of events. It became known officially that France was prepared to give financial assistance to Germany— but on her own terms, terms which included the giving of certain "political guarantees" by Germany. The German-Austrian *Zollunion* was to be abandoned; all work on the construction of the second "pocket-battleship," the *Ersatz Lothringen*, due to be launched in 1934, must cease; a "political moratorium" must be declared, meaning that all Treaty-revision agitation must stop, and Germany must dissolve (forcibly if need be), such militant organizations as the *Stahlhelm*.[2] Last, but not least, Germany was to guarantee the integrity of her Eastern frontier by the signing of a Pact similar to the Western Locarno Pact of 1925.

The German Government contended that the acceptance of any of these conditions would endanger the Brüning Cabinet and so open the door to the possibility of serious international complications. Moreover, the case of the Customs Union was *sub judice* and the construction of the battleship was already employing a considerable number of men who would be thrown out of employment were it scrapped, while no Government could agree to an Eastern Guarantee Pact and survive in office twenty-four hours. Apart from this, the view in official circles

---

[1] Illustrative of the critical economic situation prevailing in Germany at that moment was the failure of the North German Wool Corporation (*Nordwolle*) on July 8th and the closing of the doors of the Darmstädter und Nationalbank (Danat) on July 13th.
[2] The *Stahlhelm* rallies at Coblentz in the summer of 1930 and at Oels in June 1931 had occasioned considerable anxiety to the French and Polish Foreign Offices respectively.

in Berlin was that Germany was already disarmed to the bone
and that the French demands placed a highly disagreeable extra
burden on her internal policy because they emphasized and
increased the German feeling of helplessness and inequality
with other nations.

Thus matters stood on the eve of the Conferences of Ministers
held in Paris and London (July 18th–22nd). Germany was definitely not prepared to accept the French conditions of assistance
and some other method must be found. As a result no long-term
loan was secured, but the London Conference closed with the
"Stand-still" Agreement whereby no further short-term credits
still with Germany should be withdrawn and that the £20
million credit to the Reichsbank, falling due on August 16th,
should be extended for a further ninety days. It was also agreed
that the Bank for International Settlements should appoint an
expert committee to go into the wider question of the future
financial position of Germany and to examine the question of
the possibility of converting the existing short-term credits
into long-term loans.[1]

It has been necessary to trace the course of events during
the summer of 1931 partly because it is impossible to ignore
the most momentous happenings of the post-war period and
partly because of the very strong though indirect influence which
these happenings have had on the disarmament problem. For
one of the most salient factors which have emerged from the
welter of financial chaos in which the world is still floundering
is the financial and political predominance of France in Europe,
which has had its inevitable effect on the future of disarmament.

France at the close of the London Conference occupied a
position in Europe unequalled since the Great War. A large
portion of the gold of the world lay in the vaults of the Banque
de France,[2] French unemployment was negligible, French

[1] An account of the Paris and London Conferences is given in the *Bulletin of
International News*, Vol. VIII, No. 3 (July 30, 1931). The Expert Committee
appointed by the Bank for International Settlements sat at Basle from
August 8th–17th and produced the Wiggin Report. See *Bulletin of International News*, Vol. VIII, No. 6 (September 10, 1931).
[2] Heavy gold withdrawals from the Bank of England necessitated Great
Britain's accepting a £25 million credit from France in July 1931. In August

currency stable and the French Army and Air Force the largest (with the exception of the Red forces) on the Continent. At a moment when many European States needed financial assistance and needed it desperately and speedily, France, alone, of the Great Powers, was in a position to supply it— but on her own terms. In every case political conditions accompanied the granting of aid. In return for French loans Hungary departed from her Italian and German orientation, dispensed with the services of Count Bethlen and modified her treaty-revision agitation; Austria renounced, in the most humiliating circumstances, the Customs Union with Germany, and Yugoslavia returned from the dictatorial to the constitutional form of Government.

Even before the draining of her reserves forced Great Britain to abandon the gold standard, on September 19th, France had established her dominance in Europe, and if ever she had attained her long dreamed of state of security it was in the summer of 1931.

What then was the effect on the disarmament problem of this attainment by France to the pinnacle of power? Was she urged by the other Great Powers to utilize her unique position by making a gesture? Or did France herself, in the surety of her national security, take the opportunity which presented itself by taking the lead in disarmament? Far from endeavouring to persuade the French to modify their attitude towards the problem at issue, the only publicly expressed views on the subject went in the opposite direction. In the course of the disarmament debate in the House of Commons on June 29th, both the Prime Minister and the then Leader of the Opposition, Mr. Stanley Baldwin, went out of their way to send a remarkable message of sympathy to France in her nervousness regarding disarmament.

No doubt the Quai d'Orsay was greatly pleased with this unsolicited testimonial of appreciation from across the Channel,

a further credit of £40 millions was obtained. Similar agreements were reached by Great Britain with the United States. The rate of interest was 4¼ per cent. Continued withdrawals and the inability to obtain further credits necessitated the abandonment of the gold standard by Great Britain on September 19, 1931.

and any illusions as to whether French policy had undergone any modification must have been shattered on July 21st by the publication of a Memorandum on the reduction and limitation of armaments prepared in response to the request of the Council of the League at its January session.[1]

The Memorandum contained a full statement of the land, sea, and air forces of France, but included sections dealing with the political aspect of the problem, and here the French views were an elaboration of those set forth by President Doumergue on April 9th,[2] or in a word—Back to the Protocol.

"Within a system of international co-operation (*solidarité*) such as the League of Nations, a reduction of armaments might become more important for each State as mutual assistance against aggression became better organized, more certain and more rapid. . . . Insecurity for one State means insecurity for all. . . . By reason of the dangers threatening the weaker or more exposed States, the general reduction of armaments lays upon the stronger or less threatened Powers responsibilities which they cannot elude."

The French Government was convinced of the

"necessity of a security guaranteed to every State by assistance which should be mutual, effective and prompt. . . . By such assistance alone can the League of Nations be given sufficient strength, material and moral, to prevent the launching of an aggression."

Such a revival of the ideals of 1924 is completely at variance with the foreign policy of Great Britain, which has, since Locarno, been based on the Chamberlain formula of "special agreements to meet special needs," and is essentially opposed to the undertaking by this country of fresh security obligations of a general nature.[3]

It was, however, to Germany that the most important passages of the Memorandum referred:

"Reduction of armaments implies confidence. Can that confidence be expected to prevail, so long as the feeling is abroad that, in the eyes of

---

[1] League Document, C. 440, M. 187, 1931, IX.
[2] See above, p. 334.
[3] See an article entitled "Great Britain's International Obligations" in the *Bulletin of International News*, Vol. VI, Nos. 21 and 22 (May 8, 1930).

many, the problem is not so much one of organizing peace for the benefit of all, as of modifying the existing order for the benefit of a few and so long as it is possible for some States to feel that the very existence conferred upon them by the Treaties is threatened ? The decision of the Conference must be based upon respect for the Treaties.

"Should an attempt be made, for instance, in the name of a theoretical principle of equality, to modify the relative situation created by the provisions of Part V of the Peace Treaties, it would prove impossible to maintain the reductions already accomplished and still less practicable would become the general limitation of armaments."

Elsewhere the Memorandum dealt even more definitely with the German theory of equality.

"It by no means follows, however, that the Member States of the League, whose standards of forces have not been expressly defined by the Treaties, are under the obligation of adopting either the methods or the figures laid down in Part V of the Treaties as regards the general limitation of armaments. When the Treaties were framed, at no time and at no place was the agreement advanced either in speech or in writing, that other States should in their turn place their armaments on the level prescribed for certain States. . . . Were it to be admitted that the standards prescribed in Part V of the Treaties for certain States should apply in an equal and uniform manner to other States, Article VIII of the League Covenant would clearly be bereft of all value and all significance."

A week later, addressing a reunion of officers of the National Reserve at Arcachon on July 27th, M. Maginot, French War Minister, further emphasized this latter aspect. At the Disarmament Conference, he said, France would demand that in the military stipulations laid down for certain nations the strength of their respective forces must be excluded from the discussions. France had only been able to reduce her forces owing to the limitation of armaments imposed on Germany by the Treaty, and if Germany were to be free to re-arm, France would be obliged to increase her armaments. In any case, no contribution could be made by France to a general limitation of armaments unless guarantees for the maintenance of international order were to take the place of the guarantees of security represented by military forces.

Taken in conjunction the French Memorandum and M. Maginot's speech represent the most depressing contribution yet made on the subject of disarmament. Here is found the seal of official approval set upon M. Massigli's statement of November 27, 1930, at the last session of the Preparatory Commission.[1]

Of the two conditions demanded as the price of French disarmament, the first, a general guarantee of security, is inacceptable to Great Britain, and the second, the perpetuation of the *status quo* in regard to the disarmament of the ex-enemy States, is impossible for any German Government to agree to, since the granting of the principles of equality is the one concrete achievement which Germany expected to gain from the Conference.

In view of this intransigent attitude officially adopted by France the advisability of holding the Conference at all began to be questioned in various quarters, and indeed rumour began to circulate that the postponement of the Conference was really the aim of the French Government, who had launched their Memorandum in the nature of a torpedo. To many of the more earnest proponents of disarmament, on the other hand, it seemed that it would be better to postpone the Conference rather than to hold it in face of its almost certain failure, a failure which would almost certainly entail the withdrawal of Germany from the League of Nations.

A further complication arose with the fall of the second Labour Administration in England on August 24th and the formation of a National Government. Mr. Arthur Henderson, the President-elect of the Disarmament Conference, led the majority of the Labour Party into opposition and it became a matter for debate whether he would be able or willing to discharge his high office in Geneva in the coming February.

Thus the summer of 1931 closed, and the September Assembly of the League of Nations opened, with a deep depression blanketing the world and the prospects of the Disarmament Conference as dark as they well could be.[2] It seemed that the

[1] See above, p. 98.
[2] One of the principal reasons for the general depression prevalent at the opening of the Assembly was the unfortunate circumstances which attended the closing of the *affaire* of the Austro-German Customs Union. On September 5th, by eight votes to seven, the Permanent Court of International Justice made public their opinion that the proposed Union was not legally compatible

one consideration which might induce the peoples of the world to reduce their armaments would be the sheer inability to find sufficient funds to continue their construction.

2. THE GENEVA ASSEMBLY AND THE ARMS TRUCE[1]

The Twelfth Assembly of the League of Nations held at Geneva in the month of September 1931 made three important contributions to the programme towards disarmament. These were, first the definite statement by M. Briand that France did not propose that the Disarmament Conference should be postponed;[2] secondly, the participation of a United States representative in the discussions of the Third Committee, thereby ending the existing anomaly that that body should discuss the reduction of armaments without the presence of delegates from certain countries which were already associated with the work of the Preparatory Commission and had every intention of taking part in the Disarmament Conference; and, thirdly, the Italian proposal for an Arms Truce until after the close of the Conference.

Though the first and second of these events had their own importance in that, respectively, they ensured the meeting of the Conference and re-emphasized the keen interest of the United States in its work and success, it was around the Italian proposal that the main interest concentrated.

In a speech to the Assembly on September 8th, Signor Grandi, Italian Minister for Foreign Affairs, conveyed the Italian proposal to the League that, from that date, until at

with the Protocol of 1922. Two days before, however, under pressure of the necessity of French financial assistance, the Austrian Chancellor had been forced to make a public announcement abandoning the project on behalf of his country. Though it is believed that the decision of the Court was known in Geneva on September 3rd, Dr. Schober was not allowed to make use of this information in making his statement. Dr. Curtius also made a statement of renunciation on behalf of Germany, and subsequently resigned on this issue on October 6th.

[1] Reprinted in part from an article in *Bulletin of International News*, Vol. VIII, No. 8 (October 8, 1931).

[2] In his speech on September 10th Lord Cecil declared that "No Government, let alone the British Government, would tolerate postponement," and M. Briand was seen to applaud this statement with vigorous hand-clapping. His own speech was made on the following day.

least the end of the Disarmament Conference, there should be a "real and effective truce in armaments." This suggestion, arising in part out of the Conference held earlier in the year (July 9th–14th), between Signor Mussolini and Mr. Stimson, American Secretary of State, was warmly supported in subsequent speeches by Lord Cecil and Dr. Curtius. The latter took the opportunity of recalling to the League its particular responsibility for disarmament and of warning it of its loss of authority if it failed in this task. In fact failure might be disastrous for it—a point which the speaker emphasized and repeated.

The Italian proposal received the general approval in nearly all the speeches made in the earlier Plenary Sessions except that of M. Briand, in which mention of it was conspicuous by its absence.

The first step towards implementing the proposal was taken by the Neutral *bloc* (Denmark, Norway, the Netherlands, Sweden and Switzerland) by putting forward a draft resolution calling on the Assembly to request the Council

"To urge all Governments convened to the said Conference to show their firm determination to support the efforts to ensure peace and re-establish mutual confidence by abstaining, pending the result of the Conference, any measure leading to an increase in the present level of their armaments."

This resolution was referred to the Third Committee for discussion, as a result of which it was agreed to invite the representatives of non-member States to take part in the deliberations of the Committee.[1] After two days' debate, the Italian representative, General de Marinis, in support of his contention that the Resolution of the Neutral *bloc* was inadequate, presented one of his own, which represented the Italian form of the proposal for an Arms Truce.

The Italian draft Resolution contained four main points:

[1] Afghanistan, Argentina, Brazil, Costa Rica, Egypt, Ecuador, Turkey, the United States and the U.S.S.R. were invited, and of these the United States, Costa Rica, Brazil, Egypt and Turkey accepted. The Soviet Government intimated that it was prepared to support the Italian proposal provided it should be adopted in a form obligatory for all countries and concerning all categories of armaments.

1. Each Government undertakes not to increase the expenditure on land armaments already authorized for the current financial year and likewise not to exceed the total of such expenditure during the next financial year until the expiration of the Truce.
2. Each Government undertakes not to place any warships on the stocks, until the expiration of the Truce, provided always that vessels under construction may be continued and completed.[1]
3. Each Government undertakes to suspend the construction of additional military aircraft during the Truce, except to replace machines which are placed out of commission during the Truce.
4. The duration of the Truce shall be one year, dating from November 1, 1931.

In the ensuing discussion on the two draft Resolutions it became clear that while the five original sponsors of the first Resolution preferred their own draft, the remainder of the Committee were principally concerned with the Marinis proposal. The United States and a number of smaller Powers were supported by Italy, while France, with Yugoslavia and Rumania, were opposed. Lord Cecil declared that the British Government favoured the Italian draft, provided that all other countries agreed to it as well. The Japanese, with a certain *naïveté*, advocated the postponement of the whole question until February 1932.

In view of the divergency of views it was at length agreed to refer the two Resolutions to a drafting committee with the hope that a compromise text acceptable to all might thus be evoked. This method proved successful, for on September 29th the Third Committee adopted unanimously the new draft Resolution, which two days later received similar approval from the Assembly.[2]

The Resolution, after its preamble, reads as follows:

"In view of the fact that an undertaking on the part of all States not to increase their armaments would help to create an atmosphere of confidence, to prevent competition in armaments, and to prepare the

---

[1] It will be noted that the Italian Resolution had not been drafted without taking into consideration the Franco-Italian naval discussions which were proceeding during, but outside, the Assembly, between M. Massigli and Signor Rossi. (See above, p. 229.) This clause would also permit Germany to continue work on the second "pocket-battleship."
[2] In the vote on the adoption of the resolution Persia abstained.

ground for the forthcoming Conference, the Assembly requests the
Governments invited to the Disarmament Conference to prepare for
this event by means of an armaments truce and accordingly requests
the Council to urge the Governments convened to the said Conference
to give proof of their earnest desire for the successful issue of the efforts
to ensure an organized peace and without prejudicing the decisions of
the Conference or the programmes or proposals submitted by each
Government, to refrain from any measures involving an increase in
their armaments.

"The Assembly likewise requests the Council to ask the Governments
to state, before November 1, 1931, whether they are prepared for a
period of one year as from this date to accept this truce in armaments."

In its accompanying Report the Third Committee showed
clearly that "this Resolution aims at preventing any increase
of the efforts at present made in respect of the whole of each
country's armaments."

Apart from its value as a mark of progress on the road towards
disarmament, the Arms Truce may be regarded as a high point
scored by Italy in her continuous diplomatic conflict with
France. The fact that Italy was enabled to take the lead for
the first time and to establish her position before the world
as a peace-seeking nation is a considerable achievement for the
diplomacy of Signor Mussolini.

As to the effectiveness of the Truce, this may best be judged
from the fact that on November 30th fifty nations had
accepted the proposal.

In the realm of security the Assembly adopted on the
recommendation of its Third Committee the General Convention
to Improve the Means of Preventing War and agreed, in
accordance with the proposal of the First Committee, to postpone the question of Amending the Covenant in order to bring
it into harmony with the Kellogg Pact until the Disarmament
Conference, when it would be further considered by a special
committee.

3. LATER DEVELOPMENTS (OCTOBER–DECEMBER)

As the year drew on towards its close circumstances became
no more favourable for the Disarmament Conference. The

practical relationship between the reduction of all international War Debts (as a possible solution of the world's economic difficulty) with the reduction of armaments had been equally emphasized by President Hoover in his Address on May 4th to the Congress of the International Chamber of Commerce at Washington. Co-operation between the European countries or between Europe and the United States, undertaken with a view to ameliorating the economic depression, was, he argued, futile, and would be futile, until such a time as action had been successfully taken to reduce armaments.

The acceptance by Europe of the Hoover Moratorium of July 1st was the first material advance on this line of policy, and M. Laval was anxious to be quite clear in his own mind as to the continuance of this policy by the United States. He went to Washington in October, therefore, with the hope of converting official opinion in the United States to the French disarmament thesis and of ensuring the resumption of operation of the Young Plan at the end of the Hoover Year.

The results of the French Premier's mission have never been disclosed, for the joint statement issued on October 25th was a masterpiece of vagueness. It is, however, to be believed that M. Laval regained for France the initiative in the matter of reparations. But he received very little encouragement for his disarmament policy in Washington, since, on his return to Europe, he made a declaration to the press on November 1st to the effect that France would "remain mistress of her own security until the nations of the world shall have found effective means of realizing the organization of peace on a firm and permanent basis," which is nothing more than a repetition of the sentiments contained in the French Memorandum of July 21st.

Indeed, rather than meeting with encouragement, French policy had suffered a definite rebuff at the hands of Senator Borah, Chairman of the Senate Committee on Foreign Relations, who, in a statement on October 25th, the date on which President Hoover and M. Laval issued their joint statement, declared himself in favour of the revision of the Peace Treaties, a sentiment which was re-echoed in a speech at Naples the same day by Signor Mussolini, who put to his audience the poignant question "how is it possible to speak of reconstruction unless there is a modification in certain clauses of certain Peace Treaties which have driven the world to the brink of material disaster and moral despair ?"

These words of the Italian Premier, taken in conjunction with those of Signor Grandi on the following day (October 26th) in Berlin to the effect that the "Head of the Italian Government . . . has more than once declared that the reconstruction of Germany must be regarded as one of the most important elements in the reconstruction of Europe and the whole world," indicate the reaffirmation of Italian support for Germany.

If the visit of M. Laval to America had no direct results, it did, however, convince the French Premier that nothing further was to be secured from the United States and that the time had come for the necessary effort towards a *rapprochement* with Germany. The "Standstill" Agreement terminates on February 29, 1932, and it was necessary to take some steps to meet the circumstances which will arise at the close of the Hoover Moratorium in July of the same year. It was no longer possible to refuse to realize the fact that Germany would not be capable of resuming payments, and that provision must be made for this eventuality.

With this end in view conversations were opened in Paris on November 3rd between M. Briand and Herr von Hoesch, the German Ambassador, which resulted in an agreement on November 19th whereby Germany should apply to the Bank for International Settlements for the putting into operation of the provisions of the Young Plan for the setting up of a special Advisory Committee whose function it is "to consider the circumstances and conditions which have led up to the necessity for postponement or have created a situation in which Germany considers that her exchange and economic life may be seriously endangered by further transfers of the postponable portion of the annuity, and make a full investigation of Germany's position in regard to her obligations."

This Committee began its discussions at Basle on December 7th. Simultaneously with this application for a moratorium, a Committee of the creditor States met in Berlin to consider what should be done at the termination of the "Standstill" Agreement. It was anticipated that when the special Advisory Committee had completed its Report a conference with the creditor Powers of Germany would be held in January to deal with the position.

A further, and much more serious complication, had arisen in the case of the Sino-Japanese dispute in Manchuria. This matter, which involved not only an infringement of the Articles of the Covenant of the League, but also of the provisions of the Kellogg Pact, had come before the Council of the League at its Session in September. The Council had adopted a Resolution calling upon Japan to withdraw her troops from the positions they had captured in Manchuria by November 16th, at which date the Council would reassemble in Paris.

When, however, this date arrived it was found that not only had Japan not withdrawn her troops, but had, in fact, extended her line and at the moment when the Paris Session of the Council opened fighting was in progress.

The subsequent deliberations of the Council, which was unable to persuade Japan to make any movement towards withdrawal, resulted only in the despatch to Manchuria of a League Commission with very restricted terms of reference.

The Manchurian dispute disclosed many of the weak points in the League machinery, and resulted in considerable loss of prestige to that body, many Powers feeling that the guarantee of security contained in the Covenant had been put to the test and found wanting.[1]

The events of the last months of the year 1931 may be said, then, to have added in no way to the hopes and chances of success of the Disarmament Conference.

[1] For details of the Sino-Japanese Dispute see *Bulletin of International News*, Vol. VIII, Nos. 9, 10 and 11.

CONCLUSION

AND now, having traced the history of Disarmament and Security for the past seven years, it is necessary to look back— and forward; to review what has been achieved in the past; to descry what are the prospects for the future.

In the realm of disarmament there have been two definite achievements, the London Naval Treaty and the Draft Disarmament Convention. By the first of these the three great Ocean Powers were enabled to reach a basis of agreement by which they can materially effect the reduction of their navies. Yet, we are reminded, in the words of the French Memorandum of July 21, 1931, "The success attained was only partial because, after all, in the case of two of the participants in the London Conference, it proved impossible to leave out of account conditions growing out of differences in geographical situation, with the resulting consequences in the matter of security."

The very fact that the Draft Disarmament Convention exists is in itself a great step forward. It is at least a basis of discussion, if not a concrete foundation on which to build, at least a blue-print, capable of alteration and amendment. It is deeply to be regretted, however, that its adoption was only reached at the expense of German goodwill and that its acceptance by France, who, it must be confessed, holds the key to the situation, was only secured on condition of the perpetuation of the unequal status of Germany and of additional security.

So it is once more made evident that security dominates the picture. What has been done in this field ? On paper the accumulation of instruments of security is formidable. Since the Locarno Treaties of 1925 there have been framed the Kellogg Pact, the General Act for the Pacific Settlement of International Disputes, the Convention for Financial Assistance, the General Convention to Improve the Means of Preventing War, and in addition a large number of bilateral treaties of arbitration, conciliation and judicial settlement, a variety of model treaties adopted by the Assembly of 1928 and numerous adherences to the Optional

Clause of the Statute of the Permanent Court of International Justice.

But the mere multiplication of treaties and conventions means nothing, just as in the final analysis mere disarmament means nothing. What is the effect of these agreements? Have they succeeded in allaying fear? Do they create that illusory degree of security necessary not only for disarmament but for that change of heart which alone can make a reduction of armaments worth while? Do they, for example, satisfy the needs of France?

The answer may be found in that speech of M. Maginot already quoted.

"If the nations . . . agree to achieve a form of mutual assistance represented by a coalition of their united strength against all aggressors, we should be the first to accept a reduction of our military forces, nay, more, to reduce them still further. But if this indispensable guarantee is not offered . . . then we have reached the extreme limit of disarmament."

From this, and other official utterances of French statesmen,[1] we are led to believe that nothing short of the revival of the security provisions of the Geneva Protocol will satisfy France, and it must be considered before the coming Conference whether or not this is too great a price to pay.

Viewed then in this light the chances of success for the Disarmament Conference seem slender indeed, but the picture conjured up in the event of its failure is horrific. The policy of concession may be said to have been the evil spirit of the Preparatory Commission, yet if France and Germany do not come imbued with it to the Conference in February 1932 that body will be sterile from the start and the worst prognostications fulfilled.

In reality it is now the entire international situation that must be altered. The spirit of confidence, lacking so much in every sphere of modern life, whether political, financial or

[1] The French Memorandum definitely states that the Protocol contained the necessary solution to the problem, and M. Briand in his speech before the Assembly on September 11th advocated the same principle. France has never ceased to mourn openly the decease of the Protocol, nor to work ardently for its resurrection.

economic, must be restored. This way alone lies economic reconstruction, this way alone lies European security. The alternative is chaos, and chaos more complete and devastating than ever existed during the Great War.

For fundamentally the problem is not a political nor a technical but a psychological one, and it is this—Can the nations of the world renounce war with their minds as well as with their lips and pens, subconsciously as well as consciously? If this is possible, then the rest will "follow as the night the day," but if not, then we are all merely "taking an unconscionably long time dying." Is it impossible? Is human nature so bankrupt of ingenuity that in its most critical hour, its moment of darkest dilemma, it cannot devise some new ethic, some better moral code than that under which we live to-day and which has proved so signal a failure?

Upon the issue of the Conference of 1932 hangs more than the solution of the technical and political problem of disarmament. but also the ultimate future of modern civilization. No State can lightly accept the responsibility for its failure.

NATIONAL ATTITUDES TOWARDS DISARMAMENT

THE discussions and work of the Preparatory Disarmament Commission and the reactions of different Governments towards such proposals as the Briand Memorandum of 1930 have made it possible to crystallize into a few words the various national attitudes towards disarmament. It would seem that a brief summary of their attitudes would make a fitting epilogue to a study of the subject.

GREAT BRITAIN

Primarily Great Britain is concerned with naval disarmament, her interest in the reduction of land armaments being somewhat more academic. For this reason she, with the United States and Japan, have gone further in their respective contributions to disarmament than any of the other Powers. The Washington and London Agreements have done much to limit and reduce the three greatest navies in the world and to remove the growing rivalries which existed between the Powers concerned.

By reason of these agreements and because of the reduction in land armaments which Great Britain's geographical position has enabled her to make, Mr. Ramsay MacDonald was able to inform the House of Commons on June 29, 1931 that "an examination of the figures of the personnel of other countries will show that they have increased in much the same proportion as ours have decreased." After quoting the cost of British armaments in 1914, 1924 and 1930, and comparing them with the cost of armaments in the United States, France, Italy, Japan and Germany, the Prime Minister gave the House the following figures:

"In 1914 the naval personnel of the United Kingdom totalled 151,000. In 1924 the figure was 99,453. In 1931 it was 93,630, a reduction of 57,370 since 1914, and of 5,823 since 1924. Turning to the army, in 1914 our strength was 186,420, exclusive of forces maintained at the expense of India and of Colonial Governments. The exclusion still holds good. In 1924 it was 161,600, and in 1931, 148,800. There has, therefore, been a decrease of 37,600 since 1914, and of 12,800 since 1924."

This debate of June 29th more than anything else illustrates the true attitude of Great Britain towards disarmament. All three Parties were substantially in agreement with the Prime Minister's thesis that this country must honour the pledges given in her name to the world under Article VIII of the Covenant and to Germany by the preamble of Part V of the Treaty of Versailles, in the Reply of the Allied and Associated Powers to the German Peace Commission dated June 16, 1919, and in the final Protocol of the Locarno Conference. "This country," said Mr. MacDonald, "has been swift, patient and persistent in carrying out what it believed to be its obligations."

Equally unanimous was the consensus of opinion in the Prime Minister's view that though Great Britain had given an example, the limit of unilateral disarmament had been reached. "The reduction must be all round. We have gone pretty near to the limit of example."

In the matter of security the policy of Great Britain is easily defined. It is based upon the Chamberlain formula of "Special agreements to meet special needs." British policy is loyally to fulfil its obligations assumed under the Covenant of the League, but not to add to these obligations either by their elaboration or by adhering to any general agreement for the guarantee of security such as the Treaty of Mutual Assistance or the Geneva Protocol.

The United States of America

The United States occupies a somewhat unique position with regard to disarmament. She is under no international obligation to disarm, and yet it was on her initiative that the first two post-war Disarmament Conferences—the Washington Conference of 1921–22 and the Geneva Conference of 1927—were summoned.

There has always existed in America, long before the Great War, a very real and genuine desire for disarmament. This feeling became intensified after the War and was fortified by a growing nationalism that cried out for naval parity with England. Was this parity to be achieved by building up to England's strength or by mutual reduction? For the time it seemed as if the first course was to be followed and that a second armaments race would be initiated. Thanks to a display of conciliation and real statesmanship on both sides of the Atlantic, such a misfortune was avoided and the Washington and London Naval Agreements of 1922 and 1930 obviated to a very great extent the danger of further rivalry.

America has therefore achieved her own immediate aim and can afford to approach the problem of European disarmament with a refreshingly impartial outlook. The approach is, however, guided and influenced by one very important factor. The United States is the great creditor nation of the world. Debts and reparations have repeatedly been said to be at the root of the present state of world-wide depression. Is the United States willing to extend for an indefinite period the offer contained in Mr. Hoover's historic proposal of June 1931? Here lies the strong and intimate connection between War Debts and Armaments.

The United States is unwilling to consider any scaling down or post-ponement of the inter-Allied War Debts which might release large sums of money in Europe for additional armaments. It is, however, conceivable, and has even been mooted, that the American Delegation might come to the Disarmament Conference with some such proposal as this. "Let the debtor nations reduce their armaments budgets by 25 per cent. and the United States will consent to cut their debt payments by 50 per cent."[1] There is little doubt that such an offer would be a powerful influence in certain quarters which might be untouched by other arguments.

The most cogent force which drives the United States itself towards disarmament is that of economic pressure. The deficit for the fiscal year closing on June 30, 1931 was $903,000,000 (£180,600,000 at par exchange) as compared with a surplus of $184,000,000 (£36,800,000) for the year ending June 30, 1930. The first quarter of the fiscal year 1931–32 closed on September 30, 1931, with a deficit of $380,495,000 (£76,099,000), foreshadowing a deficit for the year of approximately $1,500,000,000 (£300,000,000).

To bridge this enormous gap in the national budget, the most drastic economies are proposed, including a "cut to the bone," amounting to over £12,000,000 in naval expenditure. Amongst the proposals for effecting this curtailment are the laying-up of a fifth of the United States Navy; the reducing of personnel by from 4,000 to 5,000 and the closing of a number of naval stations.

It is very probable that such initiative on the part of the United States would have a most salutary effect on the Conference.

FRANCE

In speaking on June 29th on the position of France with regard to disarmament, the Prime Minister of Great Britain requested the House of Commons to use its imagination. This is really unnecessary. A mere recapitulation of the facts of history is sufficient to explain the French mentality.

Three times within a hundred years, and twice within living memory, France has been invaded and bled white, each time by the same Power. As a result of this repeated experience France has become obsessed with a sense of insecurity. The most illuminating example of the power of this obsession is the Treaty of Versailles, whereby France sought at last to obtain her security against Germany. For a variety of reasons, some of which have already been summarized in this book, the provisions of the Treaty have in the course of years undergone modification. France has therefore been forced to fall back to a great extent upon her own resources to guarantee her security. In the summer of 1931 she had reached a position, politically, militarily and financially, in which she could justly be said to dominate Europe. She had at last achieved national security by dint of her own efforts and was unwilling to abandon this possession of power except on her own terms.

The national attitude is clearly set out in the French Government's

---

[1] See *La République*, October 3, 1931. The project was also being discussed as early as the winter of 1930, when the author was in the United States.

Memorandum published on July 21, 1931. It is based upon four fundamental principles:

1. No action can be taken towards disarmament save with the general idea of common action.
2. The progress of disarmament must be correlated with that of security.
3. Respect for the disarmament obligations imposed by Treaty on certain States is the very basis of all work for disarmament.
4. It does not follow from this necessary respect for Treaties that one should a priori adopt the methods and statistics used in the Treaties for the purpose of securing disarmament.

In effect these conditions mean that France will only disarm if the perpetuation of the present state of German armaments is recognized and if some kind of general guarantee of security is accepted similar in nature to the Geneva Protocol.

The principal line of disarmament adopted by France has been the reduction of the period of compulsory service with the colours. In 1923 this period was reduced from three years to eighteen months, and later in 1928 to twelve months.

On the other hand, the cost of the French army has, during the last six years (i.e. since 1924), increased by over £20,000,000, and the cost of the navy by £10,000,000. This additional expenditure may partially be accounted for by the growing rivalry of Italy. Strategically speaking, France regards Italy as a potential ally of Germany in the event of war, and she must therefore maintain a fleet and army equal to the combined forces of these two States.

There is also a tendency amongst even the highest French political and military opinion to advance the dangerous and unfortunate argument that French armaments are the last bulwark against Bolshevism. As has often been demonstrated by leading citizens of the Soviet Union, the greatest factor in favour of Bolshevism would be a universal financial breakdown, and one of the causes most calculated to bring such a disaster about is precisely the existing burden of armaments.

Of all States participating in the Disarmament Conference France is in the position to make the greatest contribution to its success or failure.

GERMANY

To Germany disarmament is presented in a different aspect from that in which it appears to the other Powers. Alone among them Germany stands disarmed and, militarily speaking, helpless, her volunteer army of 100,000 men without reserves, without heavy artillery, tanks or military aircraft; her navy, strictly limited in number, category and tonnage, without submarines. To Germany the question of disarmament is not theoretical but practical; disarmed herself, she is eager to see other nations follow suit.

Ever since Germany became a Member of the League of Nations in 1926 her representatives, both in the Assembly, the Council and the Preparatory Commission, have urged on the other Powers the necessity of honouring their pledges given to Germany in the Treaty of Versailles and subsequently. Disarmament was the keystone upon which Herr Stresemann based his policy of fulfilment and only in the belief that disarmament could be best brought about by this means was able to bring Germany into the League.

The prevailing influence in the German attitude towards disarmament is that of inferiority, hence as a natural corollary comes the demand for equality. Either let the ex-Allied Powers disarm to Germany's level, or if they are unwilling to do this let Germany be allowed to re-arm to a certain point to which the ex-Allies agree to reduce. This briefly is the German argument, and in either case the stigma of inequality would be removed.

This attitude explains the deep disappointment and resentment felt in Germany at the adoption of the Draft Disarmament Convention of 1930. In this document Germany saw the perpetuation of the *status quo* in armaments established in the Treaty of Versailles, and a reaffirmation of the doctrine of one law for the victor and another for the vanquished. Such being the case she had no choice but to reject the Draft Convention.

It is to this doctrine of equality that France has shown herself to be so implacably opposed, and has let it be known that one of her primary conditions of disarmament is the respecting of treaty obligations by Germany. In other quarters, however, there has been an increase of sympathy for the German thesis especially in regard to equality of method in disarmament, and this is well illustrated by the fact that the Conference of the International Federation of League of Nations Societies held at Budapest in July 1931 adopted a resolution declaring it to be "indispensable that the League of Nations should officially recognize the principle of equality in disarmament between the 'vanquished' and the 'victorious' Powers and that the 1932 Conference must begin to effect such equality."

They considered, however, that such equality should be effected not by increasing armaments already reduced under the Treaties, "but by the proportionate reduction of those of other States." In addition they recorded their opinion that the principle of limitation and reduction of armaments should be the same for all States, and that consequently each State should be bound to limit the amount budgeted for its army, navy and air force, and that the prohibition of certain material, naval, land or air, enjoined in the Treaties, should apply to all States signatory to the Convention.

It is of the greatest importance that some compromise be reached before the Conference between the present intransigencies of Germany and France. For if some satisfaction is not given to the claims of Germany, she must leave the Conference and may leave the League, an action which would be both deplorable and disastrous to that institution, since in all probability she would not go alone.

On the other hand, Germany has so strong a case that it may easily be spoiled by over-statement (a tendency too strong in German diplomacy) and she would be well advised to come to the Conference with constructive counter-proposals to the Draft Convention rather than adopt the attitude of an early Christian martyr.

ITALY

The attitude of Italy towards disarmament is simplicity itself and can be defined very briefly. It is governed by a desire for parity with France, and Italy is prepared to reduce her armed forces to any point to which her neighbour may make similar reduction. Meantime parity must be achieved, disarmament or no disarmament, and in deference to this Italian naval expenditure has been increased by £7,000,000 since 1924, and in the last six years the cost of the Italian army has risen by over £15,000,000.

Evidence, however, that Italy is genuinely interested in disarmament is provided by the Italian proposal for an Arms Truce adopted by the Twelfth Assembly, a very real contribution towards the success of the Disarmament Conference.

THE U.S.S.R.

And what of the Soviet Union? Here lies the great enigma of Europe and Asia, and upon her attitude towards disarmament more depends than on that of any other State, save France. For without the adherence of the U.S.S.R. any Convention adopted by the Disarmament Conference will be useless, since none of the Border States in Europe or Asia can disarm without corresponding action by their powerful and mysterious neighbour.

The size and cost of the Soviet armed forces—they are costing more than two and a half times as much as in 1924—are one of the arguments put forward by France in favour of her maintenance of a large army. In the course of the House of Commons debate on June 29th, Mr. Winston Churchill accepted this view and went so far as to say that it was not in the interests of Europe that the French army—the last bulwark against bolshevism—should be seriously weakened, or that we should press "unreasonably" for its reduction.

It is true that in the relations between the U.S.S.R. and the rest of the world neither side has given much grounds for the establishment of confidence and the feeling of security. The Union professes continued fear of an attack being made on her by the Capitalist Powers and the record of the Menshevik Trials of 1930 is eloquent of the propaganda put out to this effect. On the other hand, the European Border States are frequently thrown into frenzies of alarm by the movement of Soviet Divisions on their Eastern Frontiers.

This is not an atmosphere congenial to disarmament, and yet we are forced to admit, and M. Litvinoff has never allowed the world to forget, that the only plan for world disarmament on a bolder scale was submitted to the Preparatory Commission by the Soviet Delegation and rejected. The Soviet Union has in its turn rejected the Commission's Draft Convention with scorn and mockery, and it is probable that her delegates will come to the Conference with an elaboration of her own plan. What is required from her, however, is an undertaking for political rather than technical disarmament, and this is exactly the point on which the Moscow Disarmament Conference of 1922 broke down. For propaganda is the moral sustenance of the Union, and its abandonment, even nominally, would mean self-confessed failure.

TEXT OF DRAFT DISARMAMENT CONVENTION

Article 1

THE High Contracting Parties agree to limit and, so far as possible, to reduce their respective armaments as provided in the present Convention.

PART I—PERSONNEL

CHAPTER A—EFFECTIVES

Article 2

The average daily effectives in the land, sea and air armed forces and formations organized on a military basis of each of the High Contracting Parties shall not exceed, in each of the categories of effectives defined in the tables annexed to this Chapter, the figure laid down for such party in the corresponding column of the said tables.[1]

Article 3

The average daily effectives are reckoned by dividing the total number of days' duty performed in each year by the number of days in such year.

Article 4

By formations organized on a military basis shall be understood police forces of all kinds, gendarmerie, Customs officials, forest guards, which, whatever their legal purpose, are, in time of peace, by reason of their staff of officers, establishment, training, armament, equipment, capable of being employed for military purposes without measures of mobilization, as well as any other organization complying with the above condition.

By mobilization, within the meaning of the present article, shall be understood all the measures for the purpose of providing the whole or part of the various corps, services and units with the personnel and material required to pass from a peace-time footing to a war-time footing.

CHAPTER B—PERIOD OF SERVICE

Article 5

The provisions of this Chapter apply only to effectives recruited by conscription.

---

[1] The blank tables are not printed throughout.

Article 6

For each of the High Contracting Parties concerned, the maximum total periods of service to which the effectives recruited by conscription are liable in the land, sea or air armed forces or formations organized on a military basis respectively shall not exceed the figures laid down for such party in the table annexed to this Chapter.

Article 7

For each man, the total period of service is the total number of days comprised in the different periods of service which he is liable under the national law to perform.

Article 8

As an exception, each of the High Contracting Parties concerned may exceed the limits which he has accepted by the table annexed to this Chapter in so far as, owing to a falling-off in the number of births, such an increase may be necessary to enable the maximum total number of effectives fixed in his case by the tables annexed to Chapter A of this part to be attained.

It is understood that any High Contracting Party which avails itself of this option will immediately notify the measures taken and the reasons justifying them to the other High Contracting Parties and to the Permanent Disarmament Commission referred to in Part VI of the present Convention.

Article 9

In any case, the total period of service shall not exceed . . . months.

PART II—MATERIAL

CHAPTER A—LAND ARMAMENTS

Article 10

(Provisional text subject to the drafting of the Annex)

The annual expenditure of each High Contracting Party on the upkeep, purchase and manufacture of war material for land armaments shall be limited to the figures laid down for such Party, and in accordance with the conditions prescribed, in the annex . . . to this Article.

CHAPTER B—NAVAL ARMAMENTS

Article 11

Throughout the duration of the present Convention, the global tonnage of the vessels of war of each of the High Contracting Parties, other than the vessels exempt from limitation under Annex I to this Chapter and the special vessels enumerated in Annex II, shall not exceed the figure laid down for such Party in Table I annexed to this Chapter.

Article 12

Table II annexed to this Chapter shows, by tonnage per category, the way in which each High Contracting Party intends to distribute during the period of application of the present Convention the global tonnage which is limited in the case of such Party to the figure laid down in Table I.

Article 13

Within the limits of the global tonnage fixed for such Party in Table 1, and failing any stricter conditions resulting from special conventions to which it is or may become a party, each of the High Contracting Parties may modify the distribution shown for it in Table II, subject to the following conditions:

(1) The tonnages by category shown for each High Contracting Party in Table II shall in no case be the object of increase beyond the figures shown for it in Table III annexed to this Chapter.

(2) Before the laying-down of the ship or ships for the construction of which the transferred tonnage has been assigned, due notice must be given to all the other High Contracting Parties and the Secretary-General and the Permanent Disarmament Commission of the amount of tonnage transferred, the length of such notice being that laid down for each of the High Contracting Parties in Table III.

Article 14

No capital ship shall exceed 35,000 tons (35,560 metric tons) standard displacement or carry a gun exceeding 16 inches (406 mm.) in calibre.

Article 15

No aircraft carrier shall exceed 27,000 tons (27,432 metric tons) standard displacement or carry a gun with a calibre in excess of 8 inches (203 mm.).

No aircraft carrier of 10,000 tons (10,160 metric tons) or less standard displacement shall carry a gun exceeding 6·1 inches (155 mm.) in calibre.

If the armament carried includes guns exceeding 6·1 inches (155 mm.) in calibre, the total number of guns carried, except anti-aircraft guns and guns not exceeding 5·1 inches (130 mm.), shall not exceed ten. If, alternatively, the armament contains no guns exceeding 6·1 inches (155 mm.) in calibre, the number of guns is not limited. In either case, the number of anti-aircraft guns and of guns not exceeding 5·1 inches (130 mm.) in calibre, is not limited.

Article 16

No submarine shall exceed 2,000 tons (2,032 metric tons) standard displacement or carry a gun exceeding 5·1 inches (130 mm.) in calibre.

Article 17

No vessel of war exceeding the limitations as to displacement or armament prescribed by the present Convention shall be acquired by, or constructed by, for or within the jurisdiction of any of the High Contracting Parties.

Article 18

In regard to the replacement of the vessels of war limited by the present Convention, the High Contracting Parties will comply with the rules set out in Annex IV to this Chapter.

Article 19

No preparation shall be made in merchant ships in time of peace for the installation of warlike armaments for the purpose of converting such ships into vessels of war, other than the necessary stiffening of decks for the mounting of guns not exceeding 6·1 inches (155 mm.) in calibre.

Article 20

In the event of a High Contracting Party's being engaged in war, such Party shall not use as a vessel of war any vessel of war which may be under construction within its jurisdiction for any other Power, or which may have been constructed within its jurisdiction for another Power and not delivered.

Article 21

Each of the High Contracting Parties undertakes not to dispose, by gift, sale, or any mode of transfer, of any vessel of war in such a manner that such vessel may become a vessel of war in the navy of any foreign Power.

Article 22

Any vessels of war which have to be disposed of as being surplus to the tonnage figures allowed by the present Convention shall be disposed of in accordance with the rules set out in Annex V to this Chapter.

Article 23

Existing ships of various types, which, prior to April 1, 1930, have been used as stationary training establishments or hulks, may be retained in a non-seagoing condition.

Article 24

(Provisional text, subject to the drafting of the Annex)

The annual expenditure of each High Contracting Party on the upkeep, purchase and manufacture of war material for naval armaments shall be limited to the figures laid down for such Party, and in accordance with the conditions prescribed, in Annex . . .

CHAPTER C—AIR ARMAMENTS

Article 25

The number and total horse-power of the aeroplanes, capable of use in war, in commission and in immediate reserve in the land, sea and air armed forces of each of the High Contracting Parties shall not exceed the figures laid down for such Party in the corresponding columns of Table I annexed to this Chapter.

The number and total horse-power of the aeroplanes, capable of use in war, in commission and in immediate reserve in the land, sea and air formations organized on a military basis of each of the High Contracting Parties shall not exceed the figures laid down for such Party in the corresponding columns of Table II annexed to this Chapter.

Article 26

The number, total horse-power and total volume of dirigibles, capable of use in war, in commission in the land, sea and air armed forces of each of the High Contracting Parties shall not exceed the figures laid down for such Party in the corresponding columns of Table III annexed to this Chapter.

The number, total horse-power and total volume of dirigibles capable of use in war, in commission in the land, sea and air formations organized on a military basis of each of the High Contracting Parties shall not exceed the figures laid down for such Party in the corresponding columns of Table IV annexed to this Chapter.

Article 27

Horse-power shall be measured according to the following rules . . .

The volume of dirigibles shall be expressed in cubic metres.

Article 28

1. The High Contracting Parties shall refrain from prescribing the embodiment of military features in the construction of civil aviation material, so that this material may be constructed for purely civil purposes, more particularly with a view to providing the greatest possible measure of security and the most economic return. No preparations shall be made in civil aircraft in time of peace for the installation of warlike armaments for the purpose of converting such aircraft into military aircraft.

2. The High Contracting Parties undertake not to require civil aviation enterprises to employ personnel specially trained for military purposes. They undertake to authorize only as a provisional and temporary measure the seconding of personnel to, and the employment of military aviation material in, civil aviation undertakings. Any such personnel or military material which may thus be employed in civil aviation of whatever nature shall be included in the limitation applicable to the High Contracting Party concerned in virtue of Part I, or Articles 25 and 26, of the present Convention, as the case may be.

3. The High Contracting Parties undertake not to subsidize, directly or indirectly, air lines principally established for military purposes instead of being established for economic, administrative or social purposes.

4. The High Contracting Parties undertake to encourage as far as possible the conclusion of economic agreements between civil aviation undertakings in the different countries and to confer together to this end.

PART III—BUDGETARY EXPENDITURE

Article 29

(Provisional text subject to the drafting of the Annex)

The total annual expenditure of each of the High Contracting Parties on his land, sea and air forces and formations organized on a military basis shall be limited to the figure laid down for such Party and in accordance with the conditions prescribed in the Annex. . . .

PART IV—EXCHANGE OF INFORMATION

Article 30

For each category of effectives defined in the model tables annexed to this Article, the exchange of information each year shall apply to the average daily number of effectives reached during the preceding year in the land, sea and air armed forces and formations organized on a military basis of each of the High Contracting Parties.

For this purpose, each of the High Contracting Parties will forward to the Secretary-General of the League of Nations, within. . . . . months after the end of each year, the necessary information to enable the said tables to be drawn up in the case of such Party. Each Party shall attach to this statement an explanatory note showing the elements on which the figures supplied are based, and stating, in particular, for each sort of effectives (recruits, militiamen, reservists, territorials, etc.) the number of these effectives and the number of days' service they have performed.

The said tables shall be drawn up and published with the explanatory note referred to above by the Secretary-General not later than . . . . in each year.

Article 31

If any youths have compulsorily received, during any year, preparatory military training within the jurisdiction of any High Contracting Party, such Party shall communicate to the Secretary-General of the League of Nations, within . . . . . . x months after the end of each year, the number of youths who have received such instruction.

The above information shall be published by the Secretary-General not later than. . . . . in each year.

Article 32

The High Contracting Parties concerned shall forward to the Secretary-General of the League of Nations at the end of each year the following information as to the provisions of their law relating to the effectives recruited by conscription in their land, sea and air forces and formations organized on a military basis respectively;

(1) The total number of days comprised in the first period of service;
(2) The total duration in days of the ensuing periods.

The above information shall be published by the Secretary-General not later than............in each year.

Article 33

Each of the High Contracting Parties shall, within............months from the end of each budgetary year, communicate to the Secretary-General of the League of Nations a statement drawn up in accordance with a standard model, showing by categories of materials the total actual expenditure in the course of the said year on the upkeep, purchase and manufacture of war materials of the land and sea armed forces and formations organized on a military basis of such Party.

The information contained in this statement shall be published by the Secretary-General not later than............in each year.

Article 34

Within one month after the date of laying down and the date of completion respectively of each vessel of war, other than the vessels exempt from limitation under Annex I to Chapter B of Part II, laid down or completed by or for them or within their jurisdiction after the coming into force of the present Convention, the High Contracting Parties shall communicate to the Secretary-General of the League of Nations the information detailed below:

(a) The date of laying down the keel and the following particulars:
Classification of the vessel and for whom built (if not for the High Contracting Party);
Standard displacement in tons and metric tons;
Principal dimensions—namely, length of water-line, extreme beam at or below water-line;
Mean draught at standard displacement;
Calibre of the largest gun.
(b) The date of completion, together with the foregoing particulars relating to the vessel at that date.

The above information shall be immediately communicated by the Secretary-General to all the High Contracting Parties and shall be published by the Secretary-General not later than............ in each year.

Article 35

Each of the High Contracting Parties shall communicate to the Secretariat of the League of Nations the name and the tonnage of any vessel constructed in accordance with Article 19. (Chapter II.) With regard to existing vessels of this type, this communication shall be made within two months after ratification of the present Convention. With regard to vessels to be constructed, the communication shall be made on the date of completion.

Article 36

For each of the categories of aircraft defined in the model tables annexed to this Article, the exchange of information shall apply to the maximum figures attained in each year in respect of the number and total horse-power, and for dirigibles the total volume, by the aircraft referred to in Articles 25 and 26 of the present Convention.

For this purpose, each of the High Contracting Parties will forward to the Secretary-General of the League of Nations within............ months after the end of each year the necessary information to enable the said tables to be drawn up in the case of such Party.

The tables referred to in the preceding paragraph shall be drawn up and published by the Secretary-General not later than............in each year.

Article 37

In order to ensure publicity as regards civil aviation, each of the High Contracting Parties shall indicate within x months after the end of each year to the Secretary-General of the League of Nations the number and total horse-power of civil aeroplanes and dirigibles registered within the jurisdiction of such Party. Each Party shall also indicate the amounts expended on civil aviation by the Government and by local authorities.

The above information shall be published by the Secretary-General not later than............in each year.

Article 38

Each of the High Contracting Parties shall communicate to the Secretary-General of the League of Nations within............months of the end of each budgetary year a statement drawn up in accordance with the standard model annexed to this Article showing the total amounts actually expended in the course of the said year on the land, sea and air armaments of such Party.

The information supplied in this statement shall be published by the Secretary-General not later than............in each year.

PART V—CHEMICAL ARMS

Article 39

The High Contracting Parties undertake, subject to reciprocity, to abstain from the use in war of asphyxiating, poisonous or similar gases, and of all analogous liquids, substances or processes.

They undertake unreservedly to abstain from the use of all bacteriological methods of warfare.

PART VI—MISCELLANEOUS PROVISIONS

CHAPTER A—PERMANENT DISARMAMENT COMMISSION

Article 40

There shall be set up at the seat of the League of Nations a Permanent Disarmament Commission with the duty of following the execution of the present Convention. It shall consist of x (figure to be fixed by the Conference) members appointed respectively by the Governments of ....(list to be drawn up by the Conference).

Members of the Commission shall not represent their Governments. They shall be appointed for x years, but shall be re-eligible. During their term of office, they may be replaced only on death or in the case of voluntary resignation or serious and permanent illness.

They may be assisted by technical experts.

Article 41

The Commission shall meet for the first time, on being summoned by the Secretary-General of the League of Nations, within three months from the entry into force of the present Convention, to elect a provisional President and Vice-President and to draw up its Rules of Procedure.

Thereafter it shall meet annually in ordinary session on the date fixed in its Rules of Procedure.

It may also, if summoned by its President, meet in extraordinary session in the cases provided for in the present Convention and whenever an application to that effect is made by a High Contracting Party.

Article 42

The Commission shall have full power to lay down its own Rules of Procedure on the basis of the provisions of the present Convention.

Article 43

The Commission may only transact business if at least two-thirds of its members are present.

Article 44

Any High Contracting Party not having a member of its nationality on the Commission shall be entitled to send a member appointed for the purpose to sit at any meetings of the Commission during which a question specially affecting the interests of that Party is considered.

Article 45

Each member of the Commission shall have only one vote.

All decisions of the Commission shall be taken by a majority of the votes of the members present at the meeting.

In the cases provided for in Articles 50 and 52 the votes of members appointed by the Parties concerned in the discussion shall not be counted in determining the majority.

A minority report may be drawn up.

Article 46

Each member of the Commission shall be entitled on his own responsibility to have any person heard or consulted who is in a position to throw any light on the question which is being examined by the Commission.

Article 47

Each member of the Commission shall be entitled to require that, in any report by the Commission, account shall be taken of the opinions or suggestions put forward by him, if necessary in the form of a separate report.

Article 48

All reports by the Commission shall, under conditions specified in each case in the present Convention, or in the Rules of Procedure of the Commission, be communicated to all the High Contracting Parties and to the Council of the League of Nations, and shall be published.

Article 49

The Permanent Disarmament Commission shall receive all the information supplied by the High Contracting Parties to the Secretary-General of the League in pursuance of their international obligations in this regard.

Each year, the Commission shall make at least one report on the information submitted to it and on any other information that may reach it from a responsible source and that it may consider worth attention, showing the situation as regards the fulfilment of the present Convention.

This report shall be communicated forthwith to all the High Contracting Parties and to the Council of the League and shall be published on the date fixed in the Rules of Procedure of the Commission.

CHAPTER B—DEROGATIONS

Article 50

If, during the term of the present Convention, a change of circumstances constitutes, in the opinion of any High Contracting Party, a menace to its national security, such High Contracting Party may suspend temporarily, in so far as concerns itself, any provision or provisions of the present Convention, other than those expressly designed to apply in the event of war, provided:

(a) That such Contracting Party shall immediately notify the other Contracting Parties and at the same time the Permanent Disarmament Commission, through the Secretary-General of the League of Nations, of such temporary suspension, and of the extent thereof.

(*b*) That simultaneously with the said notification, the Contracting Party shall communicate to the other Contracting Parties, and at the same time, to the Permanent Disarmament Commission through the Secretary-General, a full explanation of the change of circumstances referred to above.

Thereupon the other High Contracting Parties shall promptly advise as to the situation thus presented.

When the reasons for such temporary suspension have ceased to exist, the said High Contracting Party shall reduce its armaments to the level agreed upon in the Convention, and shall make immediate notification to the other Contracting Parties.

CHAPTER C—PROCEDURE REGARDING COMPLAINTS

Article 51

The High Contracting Parties recognize that any violation of the provisions of the present Convention is a matter of concern to all the Parties.

Article 52

If, during the term of the present Convention, a High Contracting Party is of opinion that another Party to the Convention is maintaining armaments in excess of the figures agreed upon or is in any way violating or endeavouring to violate the provisions of the present Convention, such Party may lay the matter, through the Secretary-General of the League of Nations, before the Permanent Disarmament Commission.

The Commission, after hearing a representative of the High Contracting Party whose action is questioned, should such Party so desire, and the representative of any other Party which may be specially concerned in the matter and which asks to be heard, shall as soon as possible, present a report thereon to the High Contracting Parties and to the Council of the League. The report and any proceedings thereon shall be published as soon as possible.

The High Contracting Parties shall promptly advise as to the conclusions of the report.

If the High Contracting Parties directly concerned are Members of the League of Nations, the Council shall exercise the rights devolving upon it in such circumstances in virtue of the Covenant with a view to ensuring the observance of the present Convention and to safeguarding the peace of nations.

CHAPTER D—FINAL PROVISIONS

Article 53

The present Convention shall not affect the provisions of previous treaties under which certain of the High Contracting Parties have agreed to limit their land, sea or air armaments, and have thus fixed in relation to one another their respective rights and obligations in this connection.

The following High Contracting Parties . . . signatory to the said treaties declare that the limits fixed for their armaments under the present Convention are accepted by them in relation to the obligations referred to in the preceding paragraph, the maintenance of such provisions being for them an essential condition for the observance of the present Convention.

Article 54

If a dispute arises between two or more of the High Contracting Parties concerning the interpretation or application of the provisions of the present Convention, and cannot be settled either directly between the parties or by some other method of friendly settlement, the parties will, at the request of any one of them, submit such dispute to the decision of the Permanent Court of International Justice or to an arbitral tribunal chosen by them.

Article 55

The present Convention shall be ratified by the High Contracting Parties in accordance with their respective constitutional methods. The instruments of ratification shall be deposited with the Secretary-General of the League of Nations.

The present Convention shall come into force, for each Party whose instrument of ratification has been deposited, as soon as the instruments of ratification have been deposited by . . . (list to be drawn up by the Conference).

(Should the present Convention not have come into force in accordance with the preceding paragraph by . . . . the High Contracting Parties shall be invited by the Secretary-General of the League of Nations to meet and consider the possibility of putting it into force. They undertake to participate in this consultation, which shall take place before . . . .)

Article 56

Each of the High Contracting Parties will take the necessary measures for carrying the provisions of the present Convention into effect as soon as it has come into force for such Party.

Article 57

Subject to the provisions of Articles 58 and 59, the present Convention shall remain in force for . . . . years. It shall remain in force after the expiration of that period except in so far as it may be amended, superseded or denounced under the conditions specified in the following Articles.

Article 58

Before the end of the period of x years provided for in the preceding Article, and not less than y years after its entry into force, the present Convention shall be re-examined by the High Contracting Parties meeting in Conference.   The date of this meeting shall be fixed by the Council of the League of Nations, after taking cognizance of the opinion of the Permanent Disarmament Commission and of the intentions of the High Contracting Parties non-members of the League of Nations.

The above-mentioned Conference may, if necessary, revise the present Convention and establish fresh provisions in substitution therefor, fixing their period of duration and laying down general rules regarding their examination and subsequent revision, if the latter is required.

Article 59

Before the end of the period of y years provided for in the preceding Article, but not less than z years after the entry into force of the present Convention, the procedure for examination and revision laid down in that Article may also be carried out at the request of a High Contracting Party, with the concurrence of the Permanent Disarmament Commission, if the conditions under which the engagements stipulated in the Convention were contracted have undergone, as the result of technical transformations or special circumstances, changes justifying a fresh examination and, if necessary, the revision of such engagements.

Article 60

In the course of a conference held in the circumstances provided for in the two preceding Articles, any High Contracting Party shall be entitled to notify its intention to denounce the present Convention.

Such denunciation shall take effect two years after its date, but in no case before the expiration of the period of x years mentioned in Article 57.

INDEX